FIFTH EDITION

W9-AHF-268

The Bedford
RESEARCHER

Mike Palmquist

Colorado State University

Bedford/St. Martin's   Boston ◆ New York

For Bedford/St. Martin's

Vice President, Editorial, Macmillan Higher Education Humanities: Edwin Hill
Editorial Director for English and Music: Karen S. Henry
Publisher for Composition and Business and Technical Writing
and Developmental Writing: Leasa Burton
Executive Editor: Molly Parke
Developmental Editors: Michelle McSweeney, Sarah Macomber
Editorial Assistant: Rachel Childs
Production Editor: Laura Clark, Kendra LeFleur
Production Supervisor: Steve Cestaro
Marketing Manager: Emily Rowin
Copy Editor: Steve Patterson
Indexer: Leoni McVey
Director of Rights and Permissions: Hilary Newman
Senior Art Director: Anna Palchik
Text Design: Claire Seng-Niemoeller
Cover Design: Billy Boardman
Composition: Jouve
Printing and Binding: RR Donnelley and Sons

Manufactured in China.
9   8   7   6   5
f   e   d

For information, write: Bedford/St. Martin's, 75 Arlington Street, Boston, MA 02116
(617-399-4000)

ISBN: 978-1-4576-7454-9

Preface for Instructors

When I wrote the first edition of *The Bedford Researcher*, I focused on both enduring challenges facing writers who work with information and a new set of challenges brought about by what was then a relatively recent revolution in information technology. Those new challenges included the explosive growth in the amount of information available to writers, the rapidly expanding variety of media and genres used by writers to share their work, the critical importance of evaluating sources that—at first glance—appear to be "just like" the sources in a library, and the demands of managing information effectively and efficiently.

In the fifteen years that have passed since I reflected on those challenges, much has changed. Google has become far more than a search engine. Handheld devices, among them iPhones and iPads, Galaxy Notes and Windows Phones, Nooks and Kindles and the latest smartwatches, have created a world in which information is available at the swipe of a finger or the sound of your voice. And librarians have become far more concerned with maintaining digital access to journals and databases than with expanding their collections of print materials.

Today, writers live and work in a complex and rapidly evolving information ecology. They connect via wire, wifi, and cellular networks. They keep in touch with each other through social media. And they wonder where the boundary lies between the personal and the public. As they work with information, however, they find that not everything has changed. As was the case in the mid-twentieth century—and, for that matter, in the centuries that preceded it—writers must still consider their purpose and the needs and interests of their readers; they must still make choices about genres and design; they are still shaped by the social, cultural, and historical contexts in which they work; and they must still grapple with limitations and take advantage of opportunities they encounter as they work on their research writing projects.

Meeting these new challenges while maintaining a focus on the fundamental relationships among writers, readers, genres, and contexts can tax even the most experienced writers. Our students, then, face a doubly difficult task: learning the core principles of research writing and mastering the technological context that has vastly complicated the rhetorical situations in which they find themselves. As I've reflected on the challenges facing our students, I've become convinced that students can be most successful if we help them understand research writing both conceptually and practically, combining a rhetorical framework with the accessible guidance students need to help them navigate the world of academic research writing.

In this edition, I've worked to improve *The Bedford Researcher*, both as a classroom text and a resource for student researchers. I've strengthened the notion that academic research is an act of "joining a conversation." I've expanded my treatment of researching in various disciplinary contexts, and I've added new coverage of writers' roles. I've also added new activities for students working in groups, and I've streamlined some of the content and features from the previous edition, such as *What's My Purpose?* and *Information Literacy* sections, so that they are more smoothly integrated into the text.

Features

The Bedford Researcher is based on the premise that the decisions good research writers make are shaped primarily by rhetorical concerns—the writer's purposes and interests; the readers' needs, interests, values, and beliefs; the setting in which a document is written and read; and the requirements and limitations associated with an assignment. To illustrate this premise, the book presents research writing as a process of choosing, learning about, and contributing to a conversation among readers and writers.

Complete Coverage of the Research Writing Process As in the previous editions, the text is divided into five parts. The first four parts correspond to the stages of an idealized research writing process, although the book stresses the recursive nature of research writing. The fifth part focuses on documentation systems. Part 1, Joining the Conversation, introduces the concept of research writing as a social act. It helps students understand that research writing involves exploring conversations among writers and readers, narrowing their focus to a single conversation, and developing a research question to guide their inquiry within that conversation. Part 2, Working with Sources, establishes the importance of reading critically, evaluating sources, managing information, taking notes, and avoiding plagiarism. Part 3, Collecting Information, helps students search for information using digital resources, print resources, and field research methods. Part 4, Creating Your Document, guides students as they develop their thesis, organize their information and ideas, frame their argument, develop an outline, draft their document, integrate source material, revise and edit their drafts, and design their document. Finally, Part 5, Documenting Sources, provides comprehensive and up-to-date chapters on MLA, APA, *Chicago*, and CSE styles.

Engaging and Useful Apparatus The book is designed so that students can find information easily and work competently through each stage of their projects. Each chapter is structured around a set of *Key Questions* that enables students to find information quickly and ends with *Quick Reference* boxes to stress the chapter's main points. Throughout the book, *My Research Project* activities, in-depth tutorials, and numerous illustrations and tables teach students how to keep their projects on track.

The design employs clear and accessible illustrations, annotations, checklists, activities, and documentation guidelines—the parts of the text students will return to as they write.

A Conversational, Student Friendly Tone I've written *The Bedford Researcher* in an accessible, easy-to-follow style that treats students with respect. I want students to gain confidence in their ability to write well, conduct research effectively, and think critically. Clear, relevant examples address students' questions about research writing by concretely illustrating writing, research, and critical reading strategies.

Detailed Case Studies of Real Student Researchers   The work of seven featured writers, real students who undertook a variety of research writing projects in a variety of disciplinary contexts, is featured in the text. Their work—in the form of traditional research essays, Web sites, and multimodal essays—provides accessible models for your students as they conduct their own research and draft their own documents.

A Cross-Curricular, Multimodal Companion   Because students need a research text suitable for a variety of academic purposes, *The Bedford Researcher* and its companion Web site feature examples and models that span disciplines as well as contexts, providing research writing help for composition courses and beyond. Guidelines for writing papers and detailed citation models are provided for a multitude of source types in MLA style, APA style, *Chicago* style, and CSE style. In addition, Chapter 16, Designing Documents, and Chapter 18, Presenting Your Work, include detailed discussions, examples, and checklists that will help students draft, design, and share a wide range of genres, from traditional essays to multimodal essays, Web sites, and oral, multimedia, and poster presentations.

Help with Analyzing and Developing Arguments   Extensive coverage of argument, both as a writing strategy and as a framework for reading sources critically and actively, is included in Part 4, Creating Your Document. Here students will learn how to establish a position on an issue, how to develop a line of argument, and how to support an argument with reasons and evidence. They will also learn to spot logical fallacies and avoid them in their own writing.

Extensive and Up-to-Date Coverage of Digital Sources and Tools   The text offers relevant, hands-on advice for searching for and evaluating audio, video, and other digital sources; searching for e-books; saving and organizing sources with personal and social bookmarking sites and Web capture tools; integrating images, audio, and video into multimodal documents and multimedia presentations; and revising and editing with digital tools.

New to This Edition

This edition of *The Bedford Researcher* features the following updates:

An Introduction to Academic Research That Builds on Student Knowledge and Experience   The opening chapters now give students more practical advice on how to join an academic conversation. New content, visual diagrams, and student examples all help beginning researchers conduct meaningful inquiry. Later chapters also include improved guidance for students, including a new explanation of the important differences among popular, scholarly, and professional sources; a new section on addressing opposing arguments; and expanded coverage of avoiding plagiarism.

Deeper Coverage of Disciplinary Context   Additional context-specific material, including more discipline-specific examples from the popular featured writers throughout the research process, illustrate the ways in which research questions, methods of inquiry, and writing conventions vary among disciplines.

New Coverage of Writers' Roles—such as reporter, interpreter, advocate, and problem-solver—show students how to structure their research and writing around a useful framework. Also included is a new section on how to develop a portfolio using appropriate materials and publishing tools.

An Improved Classroom Resource   New *Working Together* boxes throughout the text encourage in-class discussion and facilitate group research and writing activities. The revising and editing chapter now includes expanded peer-review guidelines for students.

Get the Most out of Your Course with *The Bedford Researcher*

Bedford/St. Martin's offers resources and format choices that help you and your students get even more out of your book and course. To learn more about or to order any of the following products, contact your Bedford/St. Martin's sales representative, email sales support (**sales_support@bfwpub.com**), or visit the Web site at **macmillanhighered.com/bedfordresearcher/catalog**.

LaunchPad Solo for *The Bedford Researcher:* Where Students Learn

LaunchPad Solo provides engaging content and new ways to get the most out of your course. Get **unique, book-specific materials** in a fully customizable course space; then assign and mix our resources with yours.

- **Curated Content**—including readings, videos, tutorials, and more—is **easy to adapt and assign** by adding your own materials and mixing them with our high-quality multimedia content and ready-made assessment options, such as **LearningCurve** adaptive quizzing. Downloadable *My Research Project* activities help students at each point during the research writing process, while featured student writers offer examples of text and multimodal research projects.
- LaunchPad Solo also provides access to a **gradebook** that provides a clear window on the performance of your whole class, individual students, and even individual assignments.

- A **streamlined interface** helps students focus on what's due, and social commenting tools let them **engage**, make connections, and learn from each other.

To get the most out of your course, order LaunchPad Solo for *The Bedford Researcher* packaged with the print book **at no additional charge**. (LaunchPad Solo for *The Bedford Researcher* can also be purchased on its own.) An activation code is required. To order LaunchPad Solo for *The Bedford Researcher* with the print book, use ISBN 978-1-319-01912-9.

Choose from Alternative Formats of *The Bedford Researcher*

Bedford/St. Martin's offers a range of affordable formats, allowing students to choose the one that works best for them. For details, visit **macmillanhighered.com/bedfordresearcher/formats**.

- **Bedford e-Book to Go** A portable, downloadable e-book is available at about half the price of the print book. To order the *Bedford e-Book to Go*, use ISBN 978-1-4576-9475-2.

- **Other popular e-book formats** For details, visit **macmillanhighered.com/ebooks**.

Package with Another Bedford/St. Martin's Title and Save

Get the most value for your students by packaging *The Bedford Researcher* with a Bedford/St. Martin's handbook or any other Bedford/St. Martin's title for a significant discount. To order, please request a package ISBN from your sales representative or email sales support (**sales_support@bfwpub.com**).

Select Value Packages

Add value to your text by packaging one of the following resources with *The Bedford Researcher*. To learn more about package options for any of the following products, contact your Bedford/St. Martin's sales representative or visit **macmillanhighered.com/bedfordresearcher/catalog**.

LearningCurve for Readers and Writers, Bedford/St. Martin's adaptive quizzing program, quickly learns what students already know and helps them practice what they don't yet understand. Game-like quizzing motivates students to engage with their course, and reporting tools help teachers discern their students' needs. *LearningCurve for Readers and Writers* can be packaged with *The Bedford Researcher* at a significant discount. An activation code is required. To order *LearningCurve* packaged with the print book, contact your sales representative for a package ISBN. For details, visit **learningcurveworks.com**.

i-series This popular series presents multimedia tutorials in a flexible format — because there are things you can't do in a book.

- **ix visualizing composition 2.0** helps students put into practice key rhetorical and visual concepts. To order *ix visualizing composition* packaged with the print book, contact your sales representative for a package ISBN.

- **i-claim: visualizing argument** offers a new way to see argument—with 6 multimedia tutorials, an illustrated glossary, and a wide array of multimedia arguments. To order *i-claim: visualizing argument* packaged with the print book, contact your sales representative for a package ISBN.

Portfolio Keeping, **Third Edition, by Nedra Reynolds and Elizabeth Davis** provides all the information students need to use the portfolio method successfully in a writing course. *Portfolio Teaching,* a companion guide for instructors, provides the practical information instructors and writing program administrators need to use the portfolio method successfully in a writing course. To order *Portfolio Keeping* packaged with the print book, contact your sales representative for a package ISBN.

Make Learning Fun with *Re:Writing 3*

bedfordstmartins.com/rewriting

New open online resources with videos and interactive elements engage students in new ways of writing. You'll find tutorials about using common digital writing tools, an interactive peer review game, Extreme Paragraph Makeover, and more—all for free and for fun. Visit **bedfordstmartins.com/rewriting**.

Instructor Resources

bedfordresearcher.com

You have a lot to do in your course. Bedford/St. Martin's wants to make it easy for you to find the support you need—and to get it quickly.

Teaching with **The Bedford Researcher** is available as a PDF that can be downloaded from the Bedford/St. Martin's online catalog at the URL above. In addition to chapter overviews and teaching tips, the instructor's manual includes sample syllabi, correlations to the Council of Writing Program Administrators' Outcomes Statement, and classroom activities.

Teaching Central offers the entire list of Bedford/St. Martin's print and online professional resources in one place. You'll find landmark reference works, sourcebooks on pedagogical issues, award-winning collections, and practical advice for the classroom—all free for instructors. Visit **macmillanhighered .com/teachingcentral**.

Bits collects creative ideas for teaching a range of composition topics in an easily searchable blog format. A community of teachers—leading scholars, authors, and editors—discuss revision, research, grammar and style, technology, peer review, and much more. Take, use, adapt, and pass the ideas around. Then, come back to the site to comment or share your own suggestion. Visit **bedfordbits.com**.

Acknowledgments

With each edition of *The Bedford Researcher*, I have offered my thanks to my family—my wife, Jessica; my daughter, Ellen; and my son, Reid. I do so again, knowing how much easier it has been to write with their support, their patience, and their willingness to share their reactions to my ideas. I remain deeply grateful for the guidance and support I received from David Kaufer, Chris Neuwirth, and Richard Young, who helped me, in graduate school and in the many years since, to think critically and carefully about the relationships among rhetoric, pedagogy, and technology. I offer my thanks as well to my colleagues Sue Doe, Will Hochman, Lynda Haas, and Nick Carbone for their willingness to share ideas and offer support as I worked on this book. I am also grateful to Liz Jackson, for her thoughtful and thorough revision of the instructor's manual.

I have benefited immensely from the thoughtful advice and suggestions for improvement from the many colleagues who took the time to review this book: Clinton Atchley, Henderson State University; Andrea Bewick, Napa Valley College; Bill Condon, Washington State University; Anne Corbitt, Kennesaw State University; Michael Delahoyde, Washington State University; Aaron DiFranco, Napa Valley College; Mark Gardner, Kennesaw State University; Dawn Haggerty, Herzing University–Kenosha Campus; Christine Heilman, Georgia Gwinnett College; Michael Hricik, Westmoreland County Community College; Greg Kemble, Yuba College; Gary Leising, Utica College; Sally Levan, Gannon University; Emmett Lombard, Gannon University; Angela Megaw, Gainesville State College; Kathleen Mollick, Tarleton State University; Bryan Moore, Arkansas State University; John Michael Mutschelknaus, St. Mary's University of Minnesota, Rochester Center; Caroline Nobile, Edinboro University of Pennsylvania; Colleen Reilly, University of North Carolina–Wilmington; John Repp, Edinboro University of Pennsylvania; Jeffrey D. Simmons, Syracuse University; Jennifer Stewart, Indiana University–Purdue University Fort Wayne; Carol Warren, Georgia Perimeter College; Cheryl Windham, Jones County Junior College; Susan Wright, Montclair State University; and three anonymous reviewers. Their reactions, observations, and good ideas led to many of the improvements in this edition.

I have once again been fortunate to work with a dedicated and professional group of editors at Bedford/St. Martin's. My development editors, Sarah Macomber and Michelle McSweeney, offered timely advice, excellent editorial feedback, and all the support a writer could ask for as I worked on this edition. I offer my thanks to Laura Clark and Kendra LeFleur, who directed the production of the book, and Steve Patterson, who copyedited the manuscript. I am grateful, once again, for the extraordinary design work of Claire Seng-Niemoeller. I am indebted as well to Editorial Director Karen Henry for her good advice and able leadership of the editorial team. And I am grateful for the hard work and good ideas of editorial assistant Rachel Childs. I am grateful as well to Denise Wydra and Leasa Burton for their support of *The Bedford Researcher* and for their thoughtful suggestions about the directions this new edition might take.

Finally, I offer my thanks to the seven student writers who shared their work, their time, and their insights into their research writing processes with the readers of this book: Alexis Alvarez, Nicholas Brothers, Elizabeth Leontiev, Lauren Mack, Cori Schmidtbauer, Brandon Tate, and Josh Woelfle. As I worked on this edition, their work served as a constant reminder that research writing is a process of continuous discovery and reflection.

Mike Palmquist
Colorado State University

Introduction for Writers

You live in the information age. You surf the Web, text your friends, download music and videos, use email, send instant messages, carry a mobile phone, watch television, read magazines and newspapers, listen to podcasts, view advertisements, attend public events, and meet and talk with others. Understanding how to work with information is among the most important writing skills you can have. In fact, most of the writing that you'll do in your lifetime — in college courses or for a career or community project — requires this skill. Take as examples the following types of documents — all of which require a writer to use information from sources:

- college research essays
- informative Web sites
- feature articles in a newspaper or magazine
- product brochures or promotional literature
- market research analysis to help start a new business or launch a new product
- proposals to a school board or community group
- PowerPoint presentations for business meetings
- letters of complaint about a product or service
- restaurant reviews or travel guides

Because such a wide range of documents relies heavily on a writer's ability to work with information, *The Bedford Researcher* is not so much about research papers as about research writing. What I hope you'll take from this text is a way of thinking about how to conduct research and write a document based on the sources of information you find.

The primary goals of *The Bedford Researcher* are to help you learn how to:

- choose and learn about a topic
- read critically, evaluate, and take notes
- develop a research question, thesis statement, and line of argument
- collect and manage information
- develop, write, revise, and design an effective document
- document sources of information

Meeting these goals requires thinking about research writing in a new way. Research writing is more than simply searching for and reporting information; it is a process of inquiry — of asking and responding to key questions. Instead of thinking of research writing as an isolated activity, think of it as a social act—a conversation in which writers and readers exchange information and ideas about a topic.

The research writing process you'll follow in this book consists of five main activities, which correspond to the five parts of this book:

Part 1: Joining the Conversation ❯ Chapters 1, 2, and 3 focus on getting started, exploring and narrowing your topic, and developing your research question and proposal.

Part 2: Working with Sources ❯ Chapters 4 through 8 address reading critically, evaluating sources, managing information, taking notes, and avoiding plagiarism.

Part 3: Collecting Information ❯ Chapters 9 through 11 discuss searching for information with digital resources, print resources, and field research methods.

Part 4: Creating Your Document ❯ Chapters 12 through 18 focus on developing your thesis statement and line of argument; organizing and drafting your document; integrating sources; writing with style; and revising, editing, and designing your document.

Part 5: Documenting Sources ❯ Chapters 19 through 23 discuss the reasons for documenting sources and provide detailed guidance on four of the most commonly used documentation systems—MLA, APA, *Chicago*, and CSE.

As you read about these activities and carry them out in your own research project, keep in mind that they reflect a typical writing process—not a step-by-step recipe. Also keep in mind that the writing process seldom follows a straight line from choosing a topic to producing a polished document; most writers move back and forth among writing processes, rethinking their steps and revising their ideas as they work on their writing projects. Whatever your process turns out to be, remember that the order you follow is far less important than adapting these processes to the needs of your particular project.

Support Throughout Your Research Writing Process

The Bedford Researcher offers a wealth of support—in the book and on the companion Web site—to help you complete a research project.

In the Text

The textbook you are holding provides step-by-step guidance for writing research documents. It includes clear descriptions of research writing strategies, examples, activities, documentation guidelines, and model citations.

Color-coded Tabs help you find information quickly.

Key Questions begin each chapter and enable you to match your research writing needs to the material in the chapter.

Checklists offer at-a-glance views of a specific research or writing process. They can help you make sure that you've completed the process thoroughly and thoughtfully.

What's My Purpose? **Sections** help you consider—and reconsider—your purpose at every stage of the research writing process. Whether you are writing to inform or trying to persuade your readers to take action on an issue, the questions and guidance in the *What's My Purpose?* boxes help keep your project focused and manageable.

Framing My Argument **Sections** help you construct your argument one step at a time and use evidence skillfully. They show how your argument is developed over the course of the entire research writing process, not just at the moment you compose your thesis statement.

Information Literacy **Sections** offer suggestions and identify opportunities as you find, evaluate, and integrate information from print, digital, and field sources. They address important, but lesser-known, facts about research and provide tips for using advanced resources.

Annotated Examples make it easier for you to learn from the many illustrations and screen shots throughout the text. Annotations point out the features and processes at work in a document or tool to help you get the most out of the resources at hand.

My Research Project **Activities** connect what's in the text with your own research writing. They show you how to put the text's practical advice to work and learn more about your own writing process.

Tutorials in the book provide you with extra help for important research writing issues, such as developing a research question, evaluating Web sites, and integrating quotations. They break each process down into steps and use examples to demonstrate a research writer's approach.

Quick Reference **Boxes** at the end of every chapter give you a brief overview of steps to take before you move on.

Cross-references to LaunchPad Solo for *The Bedford Researcher* help you extend your knowledge online at **bedfordresearcher.com**.

Contents

(III) Collecting Information   141

9   Searching for Information with Digital Resources   143

IV   Creating Your Document   199

The Bedford Researcher

I	**Joining the Conversation**
II	Working with Sources
III	Collecting Information
IV	Creating Your Document
V	Documenting Sources

PART I

Joining the Conversation

Working on a research writing project is similar to joining a conversation. Before you contribute to the conversation, listen carefully to what others are saying. By reading widely, talking with knowledgeable people, and making firsthand observations, you can gain the knowledge you need to add your voice to the discussion.

In Part I you'll read about how to get started, how to choose an appropriate topic, how to explore and refine your topic, and how to develop a clearly stated research question and research proposal.

Part I
Joining the Conversation

1 **Getting Started**
2 Exploring and Focusing
3 Developing Your Research
Question and Proposal

1

Getting Started

Getting started can be the hardest part of a research writing project. You'll likely find yourself staring at a blank computer screen or twirling a pen in your fingers as you ask, "Is this project really necessary?" or "What in the world should I write about?"

This chapter helps you get started. It explains how you can use your experiences in spoken and online conversations to gain confidence as a writer. It provides an overview of research writing processes and project management strategies. And it discusses how to select, reflect on, and take a position on an appropriate topic.

1a

How can I research and write with confidence?

Even writers who are new to research writing can approach it confidently. That confidence is founded on the recognition that research writing is similar to something you already do well: engage in conversations with people who share your interests in a subject. Your confidence will increase as you learn about the processes involved in research writing and the situations in which it takes place. It will grow as you gain an understanding of the role technology plays in writing of all kinds. And it will become even stronger as you take ownership of your research writing projects.

Think of Writing as a Form of Conversation

Throughout this book, writing is treated as an activity similar to engaging in conversation. As a writer, the conversations you might join will vary widely, from discussions of popular and political issues to conversations about your profession or discipline to exchanges about historical and cultural issues. As you engage in these conversations, you'll create documents that move a conversation forward, using designs that reflect your purposes and those of your readers. By thinking of writing as conversation, you'll be able to use your already extensive understanding of how conversations work to become a confident, effective writer.

Reflect on Your Experience in Conversations   Think about the last time you were at a party, reception, or some other public gathering. When you arrived, you probably walked around, said hello to friends, and listened in on several conversations. Before long, you probably joined a group that was talking about something you found interesting.

If you're like most people, you didn't jump right into the conversation. Instead, you listened for a few minutes and thought about what was being said. Perhaps you learned something new. Eventually, you added your voice to the conversation, other members of the group picked up on what you said, and the conversation moved along.

You can use your understanding of how conversations work to become a better writer. By thinking of writing as a conversation, you'll realize that good writing involves more than simply stating what you know. You'll see writing, instead, as a process of joining, reflecting on, and contributing to a conversation about a topic or issue.

Thinking of writing as a form of conversation allows you to build on skills you already possess. In addition, because written conversations take place over much longer periods of time than spoken conversations do, you can use your conversational skills to far greater advantage. You can thoroughly consider your purposes and analyze your readers' needs, interests, knowledge, experiences, values, and beliefs. And you can explore the contexts—physical, social, and cultural—that will shape how your document is written and read.

Use Your Understanding of Conversations to Write Confidently   Much like a spoken conversation, a written conversation involves an exchange of information, ideas, and arguments among readers and writers. Instead of spoken words, however, the people engaged in the conversation communicate through written documents. Just as most people listen to what's being said before contributing to a conversation, most writers begin the process of writing about a topic by reading.

After they've read about a topic, most writers reflect on what they've learned and search for something new to offer to the other members of the conversation. Then they contribute to the conversation by writing their own document. In turn, that document will be read by other participants in the conversation. If these participants are interested, concerned, or even offended by what another writer has added to the conversation, they might write their own documents in

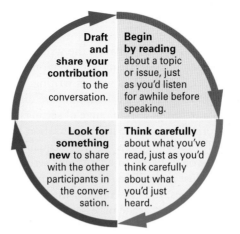

FIGURE 1.1 Thinking of writing as a form of conversation

response. In this sense, a conversation among writers and readers becomes a circular process in which the information, ideas, and arguments shared through documents lead to the creation of new documents.

My Research Project

Create a Research Log

Create your research log now so you'll be prepared to face the challenges of planning and carrying out your project. A research log can take many forms.

- a notebook
- a word processing file or a folder on a laptop or desktop computer
- a folder or binder
- a set of note cards
- notes taken on a smartphone or a tablet
- a voice recorder

Although it might seem like extra work now, creating a research log as you begin your project will save time in the long run. You can also use Web resources to make progress on your research writing project, keep track of sources, and decide how to use sources to develop and present your argument.

bedfordresearcher.com
My Research Project Activities > Create a Research Log

Use Your Experiences with Technology to Improve Your Writing Interestingly, if you ask people who spend significant amounts of time online whether they do much writing, they'll often say they don't. They don't think of creating text messages, email messages, or status updates as writing. Yet it is. And the writing you've done in these settings can help prepare you for the writing you'll be asked to do in class or at a job.

Of course, there are differences between the writing you do online and the writing you do in an academic essay. Using abbreviations such as OMG or LOL in an essay might go over just about as well as writing "In summary, the available evidence suggests" in a text message. Despite these differences, you can build on your experiences as a writer in a wide range of settings. Just as you will adapt your tone or level of formality in a spoken conversation to the people involved in the conversation—for example, treating new acquaintances differently than you treat old friends—you're likely to adapt your writing to the situation in which you find yourself. Just as you'll tailor your comments to friends when you write on their Facebook pages, you can consider the interests and experiences of the people who will read your next academic essay. And just as you've learned to be critical—even suspicious—of what you read online, you can apply the same caution to your reading of the sources you encounter as you work on assignments.

My Research Project
Find a Written Conversation

We're surrounded by written conversations. Some focus on politics, others on sports, and still others on issues in an academic discipline. You'll find contributions to conversations on the front page of newspapers, on Web sites such as CNN.com and Foxnews.com, in academic and professional journals, and in the blogs at Tumblr or Blogger.com. Spend some time locating a conversation about a topic that interests you. Use the following prompts to find the conversation.

1. **List a topic that interests you.** Because you'll be searching for sources, jot down a list of search terms, or keywords (p. 144), that you can use to locate sources on the topic.

2. **Choose a newspaper or magazine or search for sources.** Browse the newspaper or magazine or search for sources on a Web search site (p. 34), a library database (p. 34), or a library catalog (p. 32) using the keywords you jotted down about your topic.

3. **Identify sources that seem to address the topic.** Skim each source (p. 36) to get a sense of how it addresses your topic.

4. **Decide whether the sources are engaged in the same conversation.** Ask whether the sources are addressing the same topic. If they are, list the ways in which they are "talking" to one another about the topic. Identify any agreements, disagreements, or differences in their approach to the topic.

5. **Reflect on the conversation.** Ask whether the sources you've identified tell you enough to understand the conversation. Consider whether you might need to locate more sources to give you a fuller picture of the conversation.

bedfordresearcher.com
My Research Project Activities > Find a Written Conversation

Understand the Rhetorical Nature of Writing Situations (?) WHAT'S MY PURPOSE?

Your confidence as a writer will grow as you gain an understanding of the situations in which writing takes place. A writing situation is another name for *rhetorical situation*, a concept that has been studied for thousands of years. The ancient Greeks, and in particular Plato, Socrates, and Aristotle, contributed in important ways to our understanding of rhetorical situation. So did rhetoricians in China, Japan, India, Africa, Rome, and the Arab world, to name only a few. Viewing writing as a rhetorical act helps us understand how writers or speakers pursue their purposes, consider the needs and interests of their audiences, adapt to the conditions in which they address their audiences, and present, organize, or design their documents or speeches.

This book is based strongly on a rhetorical approach to writing. Throughout the book, you'll find discussions of how you might pursue your purposes and take on various roles; how readers' reactions are affected by their needs, interests, knowledge, experience, values, and beliefs; and how contexts shape how documents are written and read. You'll also find discussions of not only the opportunities you can take advantage of as you create your contribution to a conversation but also the limitations that will reduce your choices about how to craft your document. Writing situations—the phrase we'll use in this book to refer to rhetorical situations—are shaped by these and other important factors, including the sources you use and the type of document you decide to write.

As you read this book, look for What's My Purpose? sections like this one. They will help you consider and reconsider your purpose throughout your research writing process.

Writers Have Purposes and Biases   As is the case with spoken conversations, writers join written conversations for particular purposes. Some writers seek to inform their readers, for example, while others attempt to convince or persuade their readers. As they pursue their purposes, they are influenced by their needs, interests, knowledge, experiences, values, and beliefs. For example, a person who suffers from asthma might need to ensure that plans to build a coal-powered electrical generating plant near his neighborhood will take health concerns into account. Another person with a strong interest in the use of clean coal technologies might want to support proposed legislation on reducing power-plant emissions. Still others, such as those employed by the power industry, might be concerned about how proposed legislation on power-plant emissions might affect their employment.

Writers often have more than one purpose for writing a document. Writers of academic essays, for instance, might complete their essays not only to earn a grade and pass the course but also to learn about a particular topic or improve their composition skills. Similarly, writers of newspaper and magazine articles usually write because an editor has given them an assignment. But they often find themselves interested in their subjects and end up writing as much for themselves as for their readers.

Writers also enter a conversation with a set of experiences, attitudes, and beliefs that bias their understanding of the conversation. These biases shape writers' interpretation of what they read, influencing their initial understanding of the information, ideas, and arguments they encounter as they learn about a conversation. Biases are often characterized as negative. Sometimes they are, particularly when they are based on limited experiences, incomplete understanding, or a lack of openness to new information and ideas. In general, however, biases are better understood as the reasonable influence of knowledge and experience on writers' reactions to and attempts to make sense of a conversation.

Readers Have Purposes and Biases   Just as writers have purposes and biases, so do readers. Among other purposes, readers often want to learn about a subject, assess or evaluate ideas and arguments, or understand opposing perspectives. And like writers, readers are strongly affected by their own needs, interests, knowledge, experiences, values, and beliefs.

As you craft your contribution to a written conversation, ask who your readers are likely to be. Then reflect on their values and beliefs, determine what they are likely to know about your subject, and take into account their likely experiences—if any—with the subject. Ask what your readers need to know about a subject and what they might be interested in knowing. Most important, ask why readers might want to read your document—and what might cause them to stop reading. In short, attempt to understand and connect with your readers.

Writers Adopt Roles to Achieve Their Goals and Address Their Readers   A role is a way of relating to your readers. The roles you take on will reflect your purpose, your understanding of your readers, and the type of document—or genre—that you plan to write. Your purpose has perhaps the largest influence on your role. In general, writers seek to accomplish one of three goals: to help readers learn something new, to change their attitudes or beliefs, or to get them to agree to take action of some kind. Table 1.1 presents some of the roles writers might choose to achieve their goals and address the expectations of their readers.

These roles are not mutually exclusive. For example, a writer might create a Web site to inform readers about the potential benefits of wind power. Later, that writer might decide to advocate its use, suggesting strategies for increasing our reliance on wind power.

Writing Builds on the Work of Others   One of the most important ways in which writing situations resemble spoken conversations is their reliance on taking turns. In spoken conversations—at least in those that are productive—people take turns sharing their ideas. To move the conversation forward, speakers build on what has been said, often referring to specific ideas or arguments and identifying the speakers who raised them. Comments such as "As Ellen said . . ." and "Reid made a good point earlier when he pointed out that . . ." are frequently made in spoken conversations. They show respect for the contributions made by others and help speakers align themselves with or distance themselves from other members of the conversation.

TABLE 1.1 WRITING ROLES

Role	Actions	Goals
Advocate	Argue about an issue	To convince, persuade, or mediate a dispute among readers
Reporter	Present information on an issue without adopting an argumentative position	To inform readers
Observer	Consider a topic by sharing what is learned through the process of reflecting on it	To share reflections on an individual, event, object, idea, or issue
Interpreter	Apply an interpretive framework to a subject and seek answers to an analytical question	To analyze and explain the significance of an idea, event, or issue
Evaluator	Make judgments about an individual, event, object, or idea	To assess how well something meets a given set of criteria
Problem Solver	Identify and define a problem; discuss the effects of a problem; assess solutions to a problem; offer a solution to a problem	To make progress on developing a solution to a problem
Inquirer	Conduct research and other forms of inquiry; report results	To share new knowledge with readers
Entertainer	Although seldom a primary goal of academic or professional writing, research writers often write articles in an entertaining way in an attempt to maintain their readers' interest.	To amuse or divert readers

Written conversations also build on earlier contributions. Writers refer to the work of other authors to support their arguments, provide a context for their own contributions, or differentiate their ideas from those advanced by other authors. For example, an opinion columnist might show how her ideas differ from those offered by other members of the conversation by quoting a statement made by another columnist. Later in the same column, she might use a statement made by yet another author to support her argument.

Writers also use sources to introduce new ideas, information, and arguments to a conversation. A blogger concerned with challenges associated with new government health care programs, for example, might share information from a congressional hearing. Similarly, a reporter might conduct research on new developments in the health care industry trends and use what she learns to inform readers about the implications of those developments. When writers use sources in this way, they provide citations to indicate that the information is provided by other authors and to help readers locate the sources should they wish to review them.

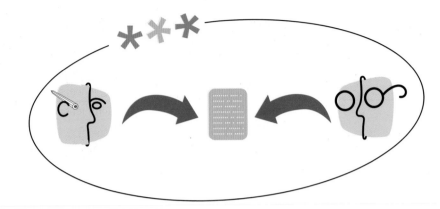

FIGURE 1.2 The Writing Situation

Even when writers do not refer directly to other sources, the work of other writers is likely to influence their thinking about a subject. As you compose your contribution to a conversation, be aware that what you've read, heard, seen, and experienced will shape your thinking about the subject — and by doing so, these sources will affect the information, ideas, and arguments in your document.

Contexts Shape Writing Situations   Writing seldom occurs in a vacuum. If you are writing a document for a single reader, for example, the social relationship you have with your reader and the experiences you share will influence your decision about what type of document to create, what you include in your document, how you express your ideas, and how you design your document. If you are writing a document for multiple readers — as might be the case if you are sharing your ideas through a blog or a social networking site, writing for publication in a newspaper or magazine, creating a progress report at work, or publishing a journal article in a particular academic or professional discipline — your writing will be shaped by technological, professional, and disciplinary contexts.

Social contexts   refer to the relationships between writers and readers. Are they friends? Colleagues? Co-workers? Supervisor and employee? Instructor and student? Online acquaintances? Complete strangers? Whatever the social dynamic, it will influence the way the writer approaches the writing situation.

Cultural and historical contexts   refer to a larger set of similarities and differences among readers. The attack on the World Trade Center on September 11, 2001, is one example of a historical event that has strongly affected — and continues to affect — the people of the United States, influencing much of what has been written not only in newspaper and magazine articles, but also on Web sites, in professional journals, and in political blogs. Similarly, widely shared cultural values — such as a belief in the importance of personal freedom — can shape writers' and readers' willingness to accept arguments that run counter to those values.

Disciplinary and professional contexts   refer to the shared experiences of members of particular disciplines, such as chemistry or sociology. As disciplines develop over time, members of a discipline develop consensus about the kinds of documents, such as journal articles or grant proposals, that are best used to share information, ideas, and arguments. Agreements also develop about how to document sources of information, how to report new findings, and how to offer criticism of previous work in the field.

Physical and technological contexts   refer to the conditions shaping the writing and reading of a document. If you know that your readers will give your document undivided attention over a lengthy period of time (as might be the case with a report written for a class), you're likely to choose a type of document that allows you to present your position in enough detail to get your point across—such as an academic essay or a journal article. If, on the other hand, you know that your readers will devote limited time to your document or will be reading it in a noisy room (perhaps on a commuter train or in an airport terminal), you might write a document that can be read quickly, such as a magazine article or blog post. Similarly, if you know that your document will be read on a tablet or phone screen, you might make different design choices than if you know it will be read in print or on a large computer monitor.

Writing Situations Influence Genre Choices and Design Decisions   As you work on your research writing project, you can draw on two powerful tools: genre and design. Genre (types of documents) and design (the appearance of those documents) are closely related. In fact, the characteristic design of a particular type of document—for example, the use of columns, headings, and photographs in a newspaper article—can help you distinguish one type of document from another.

Writers make choices about genre and the design of their documents largely in response to physical, social, and disciplinary contexts. They recognize that they are more likely to accomplish their purposes if they create documents that meet their readers' expectations, that are designed to help readers understand ideas and information, and that present their arguments clearly and effectively.

Genre   refers to general categories of documents. Opinion columns, academic essays, scholarly articles, and blogs are all genres. So are personal journals, thank-you letters, and posts on social networking sites. Typically, genres develop to help writers accomplish a general purpose. Informative essays, for example, help writers demonstrate their knowledge to an instructor, while informative articles in newspapers, magazines, and newsletters help writers share information and ideas with their readers. Opinion columns and letters to the editor, in contrast, are often used by writers to advance arguments.

In most cases, genres are social inventions, shaped by the social, cultural, and disciplinary contexts from which they emerge. When writers and readers form a community—such as an academic discipline, a professional association, or a group that shares an interest in a particular topic or activity—they begin to develop characteristic ways of communicating with one another. As the needs and interests of a community change, genres will evolve to reflect those needs and interests. In some cases, a genre will change. Academic essays, for example, might begin to make greater use of color and illustrations. In other cases, a single genre, such as Web sites, might evolve into several more specialized genres, such as blogs, social networking sites, and news sites.

Design   —or more specifically, document design—involves the use of visual elements such as fonts, colors, page layout, and illustrations to enhance the effectiveness of written documents. A well-designed chart, for example, can be far more effective at conveying complex information to a reader than even the most clearly written paragraph can. Similarly, the emotional impact of a well-chosen illustration, such as a photograph of a starving child or a video clip of aid workers rushing to help victims of a natural disaster, can do far more than words alone to persuade a reader to take action. Throughout this book, you'll find design treated as a central writing strategy, and you'll find numerous examples of the design characteristics of the genres discussed in each chapter. You'll also find in-depth discussions of design in Chapters 18, 19, and 21.

One of the most important influences on writers' decisions about genre and design is the discipline for which they are writing. In general, writers in most academic disciplines will rely heavily on scholarly journals to share their work. Writers in the sciences are more likely to report major findings in conference proceedings, however, than are writers in the humanities and social sciences. In turn, writers in the humanities and social sciences are more likely than those in the sciences to share important new work through edited collections and scholarly monographs. Similarly, the choice of citation system is strongly influenced by disciplinary context. Publications in the humanities are likely to use the Modern Language Association (MLA) and *Chicago Manual of Style* systems, while writers in the sciences are more likely to use the system developed by the Council of Science Editors. Design choices—such as the use of tables, charts, graphs, photographs, and other illustrations—are also strongly influenced by discipline. To learn more about the design conventions in your discipline, locate recent publications and look for shared design elements.

Writing Situations Present Limitations and Opportunities   Each writing situation presents a writer with limitations and opportunities. You might be required to use a particular documentation system or expected to produce a document of a specific length. You might also find yourself presented with opportunities, such as access to useful databases or experts on your topic. Recognizing the limitations and opportunities associated with your writing situation can help you work more effectively, efficiently, and confidently.

Understand and Manage Your Research Writing Processes

Research writing involves learning about a topic, taking a position on that topic, and sharing your position with your readers. Understanding how to carry out and manage the processes involved in research writing will help you write with confidence.

WORKING TOGETHER

Analyze a Writing Situation

Work together with your classmates to analyze a writing situation. Generate a list of documents that members of the group have written recently. Then choose one and analyze its writing situation. To conduct your analysis, respond to the following prompts.

1 **What was written?** Describe the document in enough detail to allow other members of the class to understand its main point. Identify the genre and describe its design features.

2 **What were the writer's purposes?** List the purpose or purposes that drove the writer's work on the document. Why did he or she write it? What did he or she hope to gain by writing it? How was the writer's purpose shaped by his or her needs, interests, knowledge, experiences, values, and beliefs?

3 **Who were the intended readers?** Describe the people who might have been expected to read the document, and list their purpose or purposes for reading it. How would their reading of the document have been shaped by their needs, interests, knowledge, experiences, values, and beliefs?

4 **What sources were used in the document?** Identify the sources of information, ideas, and arguments used in the document. Indicate how the sources were used (for example, to support a point or to differentiate the writer's ideas from those of another author).

5 **What contexts shaped the writing and reading of the document?** Identify the physical, technological, social, cultural, and disciplinary contexts that shaped the writer's work on the document and the readers' reading of it.

6 **What limitations and opportunities affected the writing of this document?** Reflect on the potential requirements the writer might have faced. Think about the likely limitations and opportunities that might have shaped the writer's decisions.

View Research Writing Processes as Flexible and Overlapping   Writing processes are best understood as a set of related activities that writers engage in over the course of a writing project. It is rare to see writers carrying out these activities in precisely the same way. In fact, few writers use exactly the same process each time they work on a project. Instead, they assess their writing situation and adapt their writing and research processes to fit that situation.

The discussions of "the research writing process" in this book, as a result, are not intended to provide a one-size-fits-all recipe for success. As a writer, you'll be the best judge of which processes are most appropriate for a given writing project. To make that judgment, however, requires a thorough understanding of your options. Figure 1.3 illustrates the processes that writers typically engage in as they work on research writing projects.

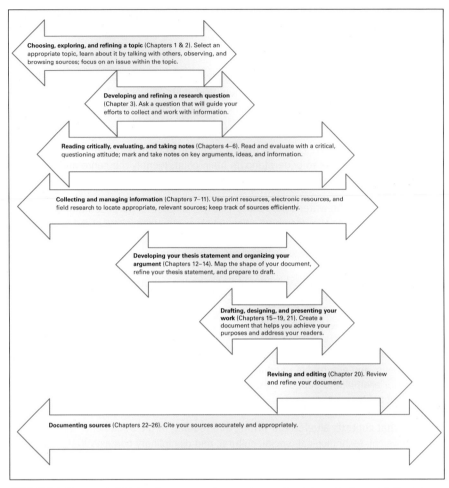

Choosing, exploring, and refining a topic (Chapters 1 & 2). Select an appropriate topic, learn about it by talking with others, observing, and browsing sources; focus on an issue within the topic.

Developing and refining a research question (Chapter 3). Ask a question that will guide your efforts to collect and work with information.

Reading critically, evaluating, and taking notes (Chapters 4–6). Read and evaluate with a critical, questioning attitude; mark and take notes on key arguments, ideas, and information.

Collecting and managing information (Chapters 7–11). Use print resources, electronic resources, and field research to locate appropriate, relevant sources; keep track of sources efficiently.

Developing your thesis statement and organizing your argument (Chapters 12–14). Map the shape of your document, refine your thesis statement, and prepare to draft.

Drafting, designing, and presenting your work (Chapters 15–19, 21). Create a document that helps you achieve your purposes and address your readers.

Revising and editing (Chapter 20). Review and refine your document.

Documenting sources (Chapters 22–26). Cite your sources accurately and appropriately.

FIGURE 1.3 Research Writing Processes. As you learn about your topic and reflect on your progress, you'll move back and forth among these processes.

Understand How to Manage Your Research Writing Project   Understanding how to manage a research writing project can also help you write with confidence. Project management strategies include setting aside time to work on the project, deciding when and in which order you should carry out various research writing processes, deciding how to manage the information you collect (see Chapter 7), and monitoring your progress on the project.

Time management is particularly important to the success of a project. If you don't schedule your time well, for example, you might spend far too much time collecting information and far too little working with it. As you begin thinking about your research writing project, consider creating a project timeline. A timeline can help you identify important milestones in your project and determine when you need to reach them.

My Research Project
Create a Project Timeline

In your research log, start a project timeline like the one shown here. The steps in your process might be different, of course, but many research writing projects follow this general process. As you create your timeline, keep in mind any specific requirements of your assignment, such as handing in a first draft, revised drafts, and so on.

PROJECT TIMELINE		
Activity	Start Date	Completion Date
Select your topic		
Explore your topic		
Refine your topic		
Develop your research question		
Read and evaluate information		
Begin to take a position		
Take notes		
Plan your search for information		
Collect information		
Organize your information		
Draw conclusions about your topic		
Develop your thesis statement		
Identify reasons and evidence		
Organize your document		
Write the first draft of your document		
Review and revise your first draft		
Write and revise additional drafts		
Edit your draft		
Design your document		
Finalize in-text and end-of-text citations		
Publish and submit your document		

bedfordresearcher.com
My Research Project Activities > Create a Project Timeline

Be Aware of New Technological Opportunities　ⓘ **INFORMATION LITERACY**　Experienced writers know that the tools we use to write affect not only how we write, but also how we access information, reach our readers, and design our documents. It's become a cliché to say "there's an app for that." For research writers, however, it's a factual statement. The number of apps, software programs, devices, and services that are relevant to research writing grows at a steady pace, offering new ways of accessing information, composing documents, and designing and distributing our work. These new writing resources are likely to have an effect on how and what you write. Throughout this book, you'll find discussions of how new resources might help you accomplish your goals as a writer—and where you might turn to find the newest developments in writing technologies. You can identify them by the Information Literacy icon. ▪

Take Ownership of Your Project　Confident research writers have a strong personal investment in their research writing project. Sometimes this investment comes naturally. You might be interested in your topic, committed to achieving your purposes as a writer, intrigued by the demands of writing for a particular audience, or looking forward to the challenges of writing a new type of document, such as a Web site or a magazine article. At times, however, you need to create a sense of personal investment by looking for connections between your interests and your writing project. This can be a challenge, particularly when you've been assigned a project that wouldn't normally interest you.

The key to investing yourself in a project you wouldn't normally care about is taking ownership of the project. To take ownership, ask yourself how your project might help you pursue your personal, professional, or academic interests. Think about how the project might help you meet new people or learn new writing or research strategies. Or look for unique challenges associated with a project, such as learning how to develop arguments or use document design techniques more effectively. Your goal is to feel that you have a stake in your research writing project by finding something that appeals to your interests and helps you grow as a researcher and writer.

1b

How can I approach an assignment?

Research writers in academic and professional settings usually work in response to an assignment. You might be given general guidelines, such as "choose a topic in your major"; you might be asked to choose a topic within a general subject area, such as race relations; or you might be given complete freedom in your choice of topic. To get started on an assignment, consider your writing situation, generate ideas about potential topics, and choose the most promising topic.

FEATURED WRITERS

Discussions throughout this book are illustrated by seven featured writers—real students who crafted a variety of research projects, including traditional essays, a multimodal essay, and a Web site. You can learn from these real-life examples as you plan and conduct your own research, and draft and revise your own document.

Alexis Alvarez • Writing about the Impact of Competitive Sports on Adolescent Girls
Alexis wrote an informative research essay about the effects competitive sports can have on adolescent girls. She explored the general topic of competitive sports and women before refining her topic to the use of steroids by female teenaged athletes. You can read her essay on p. 388.

Nicholas Brothers • Writing about Private Military Corporations and the War on Terror
Nicholas wrote a research essay that analyzed and argued against the growing importance of private military corporations in U.S. wars. He supported his analysis and argument with published sources and interviews. You can read his essay on p. 417.

Elizabeth Leontiev • Writing about the Impact of the U.S. War on Drugs on Coca Farmers in South America
Elizabeth wrote an argumentative research essay for her composition course. She explored the general topic of the war on drugs and then joined a conversation about the effects of U.S. efforts to eradicate coca farming in South America. You can read her research essay on p. 363.

Lauren Mack • Writing a Multimodal Essay about Saving Coral Reefs
Lauren Mack wrote a multimodal essay—an essay created in PowerPoint that used text, images, audio, and video to convey an argument—about the importance of saving coral reefs. You can read her multimodal essay at **bedfordresearcher.com**.

Cori Schmidtbauer • Writing about Portia's Unconventional Role in *The Merchant of Venice*
Cori wrote an analytic research essay that addressed whether Portia fits the ideal of the Renaissance woman. She used sources from literary theorists to debate whether Shakespeare's play was ahead of its time. You can read her essay at **bedfordresearcher.com**.

Brandon Tate • Creating a Web Site about Hydraulic Fracturing
Brandon created a Web site about hydraulic fracturing, a process used during drilling for gas or oil to release hydrocarbons from rock formations. Widely known as fracking, its use had become an important topic of discussion in his community. You can view his Web site at **bedfordresearcher.com**.

Josh Woelfle • Writing a Scientific Essay about Cancer Research
Josh, who was enrolled in a life-sciences seminar, wrote an informative essay exploring promising new treatments for cancer. You can read his essay on p. 441.

Consider Your Writing Situation

Your assignment will provide important clues about what your instructor and your other readers will expect. To uncover those clues, ask yourself the following questions about your research writing situation.

Who are my readers and why would they read my document?   Your assignment might identify your readers, or audience, for you. If you are writing a research project for a class, one of your most important readers will be your instructor. You are also likely to have additional readers, such as your classmates, people who have a professional or personal interest in your topic, or if your project will be published in print or online, the readers of a particular newspaper, magazine, or Web site. If you are writing in a business or professional setting, your readers might include supervisors, customers, or other people associated with the organization. In some cases, you might be asked to define your own audience. As you consider possible topics, ask yourself which subjects these readers would be most interested in learning about. Featured writer Cori Schmidtbauer, for example, would probably not have written about the work of William Shakespeare if her target audience had been the readers of a magazine such as *PC World* or *Street Rod*.

What will influence me and what will influence my readers?   Research writers aren't mindless robots who churn through sources and create documents without emotion or conviction — or at least they shouldn't be. Your topic should interest you. An appropriate topic will keep you motivated as you carry out the work needed to complete your research project successfully. Your project should also be your own, even if it's been assigned to you. One of the most important things you can do as a research writer is to make a personal connection with the topic. To make that connection, look for topics that can help you pursue your personal, professional, and academic interests.

Readers are influenced by their interest in a particular topic, their knowledge of the topic, and their values and beliefs. If your readers have no interest in your topic, know little about it, or are offended by it, you aren't likely to meet with much success.

What type of document am I writing?   Assignments often specify the type of document — or genre — you will be writing. You might be asked to write essays, reports, Web sites, articles, opinion columns, letters to the editor, multimedia presentations, brochures, or any of a number of other genres. The genre that is assigned will have an impact on the kinds of topics you choose. For example, consider the differences among the topics addressed in articles in news magazines such as *Time* and *Newsweek*, the topics addressed in scholarly journals in biology, and the topics addressed on Web sites published by the U.S. Department of Education. Genre will also affect your decisions about the design of your document. To better understand the relationships among genre, design, and topic, review the research essay written by featured writer Alexis Alvarez, the

Web site developed by featured writer Brandon Tate, and the multimodal essay written by featured writer Lauren Mack. As you reflect on potential topics for your research writing project, keep in mind the type of document specified in your assignment.

What contexts will affect my work on the document? Assignments often give important clues about the contexts — or settings — in which a document will be read. Contexts range from the immediate shared experiences of readers and writers, to shared cultures, histories, and disciplines, to the physical settings in which documents are written and read (p. 10).

For students, one of the most important social and cultural contexts shaping their written work is academic life itself, that complex mix of instructors, fellow students, classes, tests, labs, and writing assignments that you negotiate on a daily basis. As you analyze an assignment, ask whether it will require you to consider particular disciplinary contexts, whether you'll be asked to consider your class as a community, whether you'll be asked to address readers outside of your class setting, and what physical settings might be involved in the writing and reading of your document.

What role will I adopt toward my readers? A role is a way of relating to your readers. The roles you take on will reflect your purpose, your understanding of your readers, and the type of document you plan to write. As you consider which topics might interest you, think about how you plan to relate to your readers. Some topics will be more appropriate for an assignment that asks you to interpret an object, event, or process for your readers, while others will be more appropriate for assignments that ask you to inform or persuade or solve problems. For a list and explanation of the roles you might adopt, see Table 1.1 on page 9.

What will affect my ability to work on this project? The requirements of your assignment, the limitations you will face as you work, and the opportunities you can capitalize upon will affect your ability to work on your research project.

Requirements and limitations If you are writing your research project for a class, examine the requirements of your assignment.

- the type of document — or genre
- the required length or page count
- the project due date
- the number and type of sources you can use (digital, print, and field)
- any suggested or required resources, such as a library catalog or database
- specific requirements about the organization and structure of your document (title page, introduction, body, conclusion, works cited list, and so on)
- expected documentation format (such as MLA, APA, *Chicago*, or CSE)

- any intermediate reports or activities due before you turn in the final project document (such as thesis statements, notes, outlines, and rough drafts)

You might also face limitations, such as lack of access to information or lack of time to work.

Determining your requirements and limitations will help you weigh the potential drawbacks of a topic. You might find that you need to narrow the scope of your topic significantly given your time and page limit.

Opportunities   Sometimes writers get so wrapped up in the requirements and limitations of the assignment that they overlook their opportunities. As you think about your topic, ask yourself whether you can take advantage of opportunities such as:

- access to a specialized or particularly good library
- personal experience with and knowledge about a topic
- access to people who are experts on a topic

For example, Alexis Alvarez thought about her personal experiences and those of her friends before deciding to focus on the impact of competitive sports programs on adolescent girls.

Generate Ideas about Potential Topics

You can use prewriting activities such as brainstorming, freewriting, looping, clustering, and sentence starters (writing prompts in which you fill in the blanks) to generate ideas about potential topics.

Brainstorm   Brainstorming involves listing ideas as they occur to you. This list should not consist of complete sentences—instead, simply jot down the ideas that come into your head as you think of them. Brainstorming is most successful when you avoid censoring yourself. Although you'll end up using only a few of the ideas you generate during brainstorming, don't worry until later about weeding out the useful ideas from the less promising ones.

Brainstorming sessions are usually conducted in response to a specific question. Featured writer Lauren Mack generated the following list in response to the question, "What interests me personally about this project?"

I already know a lot about marine biology from my courses, and I learned a lot about the fragility of sea life from my dive trip to the Florida Keys last spring.

I'd like to do more research and learn about ways marine life can be protected.

Some of my connections from my internship at the New England Aquarium would be great resources for my research.

The documentary film about the ocean that I worked on last summer also sparked my interest in the topic and would also provide good background information.

TUTORIAL

How do I analyze the audience for a research writing assignment?

Learn about your readers by looking for clues about their needs, interests, and expectations.

COMP 150: College Composition Portfolio 3: Engaging in a Public Issue

Due Date: May 2nd at the beginning of class

1 Analyze the assignment's purpose for clues about your audience.

2 Look for terms such as *reader* and *audience*. Then examine the text near those terms for clues about your readers' expectations.

3 Identify clues about the assignment's genre; look for terms such as *essay*, *report*, *argument*, *article*, or *Web site*.

In this essay, you will write a public response — an article or essay directed to a specific publication — for readers who are interested in the issue you analyzed in your last portfolio. To accomplish this goal, you will: (a) assess the writing situation surrounding the issue; (b) collect information from a variety of sources, including written texts, personal experience, and, if appropriate, field research; (c) evaluate your sources to choose those that best support your argument; and (d) make a sufficiently narrow argumentative claim and support that claim with sound reasoning and evidence.

You should address your article or essay to readers of a publication that has published work about your issue. You will need to analyze the publication, its readers (specifically, their needs, interests, knowledge, experiences, values, and beliefs), and the writing situation that has shaped discourse about this issue. In general, your audience is likely to expect you to thoroughly explain the points you are making and to support your argument using appropriate forms of evidence. In addition, it is likely that your audience will expect you to use a reasonable tone, to respect your readers and sources, and to avoid slang. Your readers are also likely to expect you to acknowledge and cite your sources in a manner consistent with other sources published by your target publication.

My Research Project

Generate Ideas by Brainstorming

In your research log, brainstorm responses to the following questions.

- What do I want to accomplish with this project?
- What interests me personally about this project?
- What interests me academically about this project?
- Who are my readers?
- What topics do my readers need to read about?
- What topics would my readers like to read about?

bedfordstmartins.com
My Research Project Acitivities > Generate Ideas by Brainstorming

Freewrite   When freewriting, you write full sentences quickly, without stopping and—most important—without editing what you write. You might want to start with one of the ideas you generated in your brainstorming activity, or you can begin your freewriting session with a phrase such as "I am interested in my topic because. . . ." After brainstorming about the general topic of protecting marine life, Lauren focused her freewriting on her readers' purposes and interests. The following is an excerpt from Lauren's freewriting.

> Everyone loves the ocean and has a general understanding of its significance to our global environment. My readers probably want to know about the challenges facing the health of our oceans and what can be done to protect them. They may want to know whether the problems are natural or caused by humans. They may also want to know what could happen if we don't take action. And they may want to know what they can do as individuals to make a difference.

Lauren did not edit her work or worry about spelling, grammar, or style.

My Research Project

Generate Ideas by Freewriting

In your research log, freewrite in response to one of the following prompts, replacing the blanks with the ideas for topics that you generated during your brainstorming session. Before you begin, set a goal of a certain number of minutes or a set amount of pages you will write.

- Writing about ____ will help me accomplish the following purposes. . . .
- I am personally interested in ____ because. . . .
- I am academically interested in ____ because. . . .
- My readers need or would like to know about ____ because. . . .

bedfordresearcher.com
My Research Project Activities > Generate Ideas by Freewriting

Some writers set a timer and freewrite for five, ten, or fifteen minutes; others set a goal of a certain number of pages and keep writing until they have met that goal. (Hint: If you find it difficult to write without editing, try blindwriting—freewriting on a computer with the monitor turned off.)

Use Looping   Looping is an alternative form of freewriting. During a looping session, you write for a set amount of time (say five minutes) and then read what you've written. As you read, identify one key idea in what you've written and then write for five minutes with the new key idea as your starting point. Lauren, for example, wrote in response to a sentence she had generated during freewriting, "And they may want to know what they can do as individuals to make a difference."

> My readers will be both my marine biology professor, who probably knows a lot about the causes and cures of damage to marine life, and my fellow students, who know the basic stuff that I know, such as the fact that both climate change and human pollution are affecting ocean life. But readers will want some specific information about steps we can take to decrease damage to the ocean. They'll need to see it as relevant to their own lives, even if they don't have the passion for sea life that I have.

My Research Project

Generate Ideas by Looping

In your research log, select a response from your freewriting activity and carry out the following looping exercise.

1. Paste the response at the top of your word processing file or write it at the top of a page in your notebook. Then freewrite for five minutes about the response.

2. Identify the best idea in this freewriting.

3. Freewrite for five more minutes about the idea you've identified.

Repeat the process until you've refined your idea into a potential topic.

bedfordresearcher.com
My Research Project Activities > Generate Ideas by Looping

Use Clustering   Clustering involves presenting your ideas about a potential topic in graphical form. Clustering can help you gain a different perspective on a topic by helping you map out the relationships among your ideas. It can also help you generate new ideas. Featured writer Nicholas Brothers used clustering to map out his ideas and further refine his topic (see Figure 1.4).

When you have completed your brainstorming, freewriting, looping, and clustering activities, review what you've written. You'll most likely find that these prewriting techniques have generated a useful list of ideas for a topic.

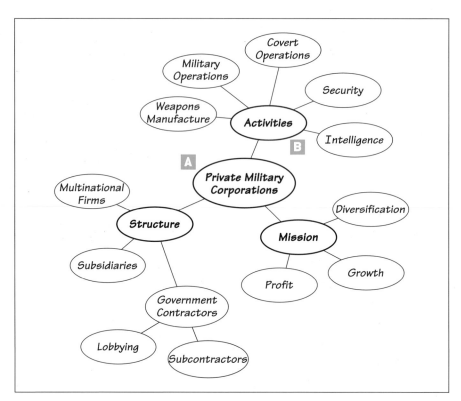

FIGURE 1.4 A Cluster of Ideas Created by Nicholas Brothers

A   Nicholas listed a central idea and three key areas to explore.

B   Key areas are also linked to related ideas.

My Research Project

Generate Ideas by Clustering

In your research log, generate additional ideas about your potential topic by using a clustering exercise.

1. In the middle of a sheet of paper, or in the center of a digital document (word processing file or graphics file), write your potential topic.

2. Identify ideas that are related to your central topic and list them near it. Think about the importance and relevance of each related idea, and draw lines and circles to show the relationships among your ideas.

3. Write additional ideas related to the ideas in Step 2. In turn, draw lines and circles to show their relationships to the other ideas in your cluster.

4. Repeat the process until you've created a cluster of ideas that represents your current understanding of the topic you are considering.

bedfordresearcher.com
My Research Project Activities > Generate Ideas by Clustering

Use Sentence Starters   Sentence starters help you generate ideas by "filling in the blanks" in each sentence. The following sentence starter was used by featured writer Josh Woelfle to generate ideas about his writing assignment.

Sentence Starter: Although we know that ____, we also know that ____.

Although we know that conventional cancer treatments such as chemotherapy and radiation have significantly reduced deaths from cancer, we also know that they can bring with them a great deal of pain and have important and often painful side-effects.

There are nearly as many sentence starters as there are ideas about how to structure a sentence. You can make up your own or you can try some of the following.

Exploring Interests

I would like to understand [how / why / whether] ____ happened.

I want to know more about ____.

I am interested in ____ because ____.

Explaining

There are three reasons this is [true / not true / relevant / important / essential]. First, ____. Second, ____. Third, ____.

We can [change / improve / fix] this by ____.

To accomplish ____, we must ____.

People do this because ____.

We were trying to ____, but we ended up ____.

Interpreting and Analyzing

This means that ____.

If we were starting over, we would ____.

It has always been the case that ____.

Understanding Causes and Effects

When I was ____, I decided ____. That decision has ____.

When I was ____, I believed ____. But now I believe ____.

The root cause of this problem is ____.

This happened because ____.

Predicting

When this happens, ____.

We would prefer that ____ were true, but we must recognize that ____.

Too often, we ____.

If we ____, then ____.

Stating Beliefs

I believe _____.

We have to _____.

I want to _____.

Exploring Possibilities

If this is [true / happening / important], then _____.

Sometimes, _____.

We could _____.

How can we _____?

Evaluating

The most important aspect of _____ is _____.

This is better because _____.

Comparing and Contrasting

Like _____, _____.

Unlike _____, _____.

I know _____, but I don't know _____.

My Research Project

Generate Ideas with Sentence Starters

In your research log, generate ideas about your potential topic by using sentence starters.

1. Choose a category, such as "exploring possibilities," that is appropriate for your assignment.

2. Choose one of the sentence starters in the category.

3. Use the sentence starter as the basis for freewriting.

4. Repeat the process with one or two other sentence starters

5. Identify useful ideas. If necessary, try some other sentence starters.

bedfordresearcher.com
My Research Project Activities > Generate Ideas with Sentence Starters

Choose an Appropriate Topic [FRAMING MY ARGUMENT]

In the most general sense, your topic is what you will research and write about — it is the foundation on which your research writing project is built. An appropriate topic, however, is much more than a simple subject heading in an almanac or encyclopedia. It is a subject of debate, discussion, and discovery. As you prepare to choose a topic, consider writing situation, the time and effort you'll put into your research writing project, and the characteristics of appropriate topics.

Look for Framing My Argument sections like this one throughout this book. They provide advice on developing sound arguments and using appropriate evidence.

Reflect on Your Writing Situation   After you've spent time thinking and generating ideas about potential topics for your research project, review the topics you've identified and see whether you're ready to choose a topic. As you carry out your review, think carefully about the level of interest you and your readers might have in the topic, the number of readers who will be interested in the topic, and the appropriateness of the topic for your assignment.

In most cases, your first concern should be your personal interest in the topic. Once you've found a topic that you think will sustain your interest, consider the needs and interests of your readers. In some cases, you might also consider the number of readers who will be interested in the topic. Some topics, such as government use of private military corporations, which is addressed by Nicholas Brothers, will appeal to a large number of readers. For Nicholas, those readers included people with friends or family serving overseas and individuals who are concerned about the growth of government spending. Other topics, such as the unconventional role of Portia in William Shakespeare's *The Merchant of Venice*, which was addressed by Cori Schmidtbauer, will appeal to a smaller group of readers — in this case, literary scholars or devoted fans of Shakespeare's dramas. Despite differences in the number of readers likely to be interested in these two topics, however, Nicholas and Cori found their topics personally intriguing and each proved to be the starting point for a successful research project.

Think of Your Topic as a Conversation You'd Like to Join   Thinking of your topic as a topic of conversation is critical to your success as a research writer. Research writing goes beyond merely locating and reporting information. Instead, it is an ongoing process of inquiry in which you must consider your purposes, your readers, and the conventions associated with the type of document you plan to write. Ultimately, research writing is about taking and sharing a position on your topic. In some cases, this will involve sharing your understanding or evaluation of a topic with your readers. In other cases, it will involve attempting to convince them to accept your argument about a topic. In still other cases, it will involve sharing your interpretation or analysis of a topic with your readers. Sharing your position — and the information, ideas, and arguments you draw on to support it — allows you to contribute to and advance a conversation about your topic.

Look for a Topic Appropriate to Your Writing Situation   As you reflect on the list of potential topics you've generated, keep in mind the characteristics of topics that are well-suited to research writing projects. In general, appropriate topics share the following qualities.

- **Relevance.** A good topic will be relevant to your personal life, your academic discipline or profession, or the assignment you have been given. A great topic will be relevant to all of these.

- **Specificity.** A good topic will be broad enough to interest you and your readers, yet narrow enough to address within the length and time limitations of your assignment. If you begin with a broad topic, such as "food," you'll want to narrow it eventually to something more manageable, such as "organic food in fast-food restaurants."

- **Current Interest.** Without exception, good topics are the subject of debate or discussion. A topic need not be controversial—it might simply be something readers want to learn about—but many topics certainly are, and generally the more controversial a topic the easier it will be to find sources that are relevant to your research writing project.

- **Accessible.** Keep in mind that you need to be able to locate sources on your topic. If you choose a topic that is too cutting edge, technical, arcane, or obscure, you may have trouble doing your research within the parameters of the assignment.

Be Flexible   As you consider your choice of topic, remember that your decision is subject to change. It's a starting point, not a final destination. As you explore your topic, you'll begin to focus on a specific issue—a point of disagreement, uncertainty, concern, or curiosity—that is being discussed by a community of readers and writers. As you learn about your topic, you might find that related topics are more appealing or more appropriate. You might even find that you need to rethink your choice completely.

> **QUICK REFERENCE**

Getting Started

☑ Build confidence by thinking of writing as a form of conversation. (p. 4)

☑ Create a research log to manage information and ideas as you work. (p. 5)

☑ Increase confidence by understanding the rhetorical nature of writing situations. (p. 7)

☑ Learn about the role of genre and design in research writing. (p. 11)

☑ Gain confidence about research writing by becoming acquainted with research writing processes. (p. 12)

☑ Develop a project timeline to help manage your time. (p. 15)

☑ Begin working with your assignment by reflecting on your research writing situation. (p. 18)

☑ Generate ideas about appropriate topics by brainstorming, freewriting, looping, clustering, and using sentence starters. (p. 20)

☑ Choose a promising and appropriate topic. (p. 26)

Part I
Joining the Conversation

1	Getting Started
2	**Exploring and Focusing**
3	Developing Your Research Question and Proposal

2

Exploring and Focusing

> **Key Questions**
>

Exploring involves gaining a general understanding of the issues—points of disagreement, uncertainty, concern, or curiosity—within a topic. Focusing on a single issue lays the groundwork for developing the research question that will frame your thinking about that issue and guides your efforts to gain a comprehensive understanding of it.

2a

How can I explore my topic?

The previous chapter discusses the similarities between spoken and written conversations. At this early stage in your research writing process, as you begin to explore your topic, it's easy to see the similarities between spoken and written conversations. Essentially, as you explore your topic you'll find yourself listening in on conversations about several issues so that you can choose the one that intrigues you most.

Step 1: Create a Plan to Explore Your Topic   ❓ WHAT'S MY PURPOSE?

Before you start exploring your topic, create an informal research plan. Your plan should reflect your purpose for working on the project and provide directions for locating, collecting, and managing information. The most common elements of a research plan include:

- a list of people with whom you can discuss your topic, including people who know a great deal about or have been involved with the topic and people, such as librarians, who can help you locate information about your topic
- a list of questions to ask people who can help you explore your topic
- a list of settings you might observe to learn more about your topic
- a list of resources to search and browse, such as library catalogs, databases, Web search sites, and Web directories
- a system for keeping track of the information you collect

After you create your plan, use it to guide your work and to remind yourself of steps you might overlook. A note such as "talk to Professor Chapman about recent clinical studies" can come in handy if you've become so busy searching the Web or your library's catalog that you forget about your other plans for exploring your topic. After you've drafted your plan, share it with your instructor, your supervisor, or a librarian, who might suggest additional resources, shortcuts, and alternative strategies. Take notes on the feedback you receive and, if necessary, revise your plan.

My Research Project
Create a Plan to Explore Your Topic

In your research log, answer the following questions.

- Who can help me learn more about my topic?
- What questions should I ask people on my list?
- What settings can I observe to learn more about my topic?
- What resources can I search or browse to learn more about my topic?
- How can I keep track of information I collect as I explore my topic?

Using your responses, write your plan as a series of steps and ask your instructor, your supervisor, or a librarian to review it.

bedfordresearcher.com
My Research Project Activities > Create a Plan to Explore Your Topic

Step 2: Discuss Your Topic with Others

Talking about your topic with people who know about it or have been affected by it can provide you with insights that are not available through other sources. An instructor, a supervisor, or a librarian can also help you identify additional resources.

Featured writer Alexis Alvarez explored her topic—women and competitive sports—in part by talking with family members and friends who had competed in organized sports. These discussions helped Alexis better see the many different issues she could pursue within her topic.

You can also explore a topic by conducting formal interviews (p. 183) or by writing letters and email messages (p. 197). If you are uncertain about how to find people you can interview about your topic, you might start by visiting a Web discussion forum, message board, or blog devoted to discussion of serious issues. (For an example, visit the *New York Times* political blog, The Caucus, at **thecaucus.blogs.nytimes.com**.)

Step 3: Conduct Preliminary Observations

Observation is a powerful tool, especially when you are just getting started on a research project. Like discussing your topic with others, observing can provide you with valuable information that isn't available from other sources.

Featured Writer Alexis Alvarez used observation to help explore her topic, the effects of competitive sports on adolescent girls. Alvarez observed friends and relatives who are competitive athletes, which provided her with a different perspective than she could have gained through other information-gathering techniques.

Step 4: Identify Useful Types of Sources

Depending on your topic, some types of sources will be more useful than others. For example, if you are interested in a topic such as featured writer Brandon Tate's (hydraulic fracturing) and want to learn about the latest developments in the debate about its use, you might focus on government and industry Web sites, trade and professional journals, newspapers, magazines, and blogs. If you are interested in a topic such as Shakespearean drama, as featured writer Cori Schmidtbauer was, you would focus on books and articles in scholarly journals. Note the following characteristics of sources you might collect and review.

- **Books** undergo a lengthy editorial process before they are published, and librarians evaluate them before adding them to a library collection.

- **Articles in scholarly journals** also undergo a lengthy editorial process before they are published. Most are reviewed—evaluated for accuracy, complete-ness, and methodological soundness—by experts in the field before they are accepted for publication. You can usually recognize a scholarly journal by its listing of an editorial board, the use of works cited lists and in-text citation in articles found in the journal, and the presence of the words *peer reviewed*, *blind reviewed*, or *refereed*.

- **Articles in trade and other professional journals** do not always go through a strict review process. You can find out whether articles are reviewed by looking at the submission policies printed in the journal.

- **Articles in magazines and newspapers** are usually reviewed only by the edi-tors of the publication. Editorials typically represent an editor's or editorial board's opinion on an issue and are not subject to review. Similarly, opinion columns and letters to the editor seldom go through a review process.

- **Web sites,** unlike sources found in a library, do not go through a review process. They are created by organizations, corporations, educational and government institutions, and individuals. Their purposes vary widely, as do their quality and reliability.

- **Blogs** are a specialized type of Web site that allows individuals and groups to post entries on a topic or an issue.

- **Media sites,** such as YouTube (**youtube.com**), provide access to video, music and audio, and various forms of animations.

- **Theses and dissertations** are final projects for students in graduate programs. Theses and dissertations vary in quality and reliability, although they have been reviewed and approved by committees of professors.

- **Other sources** include maps, videotapes, audiotapes, and multimedia items such as CD-ROMs and DVDs. These can be found in many library collections.

Step 5: Find Sources

After you've talked with others about your topic and observed relevant settings, take advantage of the work other writers have done on the topic by finding and reviewing sources.

Search Your Library's Catalog   Library catalogs allow you to search for sources by keyword, title, and author. Before you begin your search, generate a list of words and phrases associated with your topic. If you already know the names of authors or the titles of books or periodicals related to your topic, search for them. At this point, however, you'll usually conduct a keyword search on your topic. For more about searching library catalogs, see p. 154.

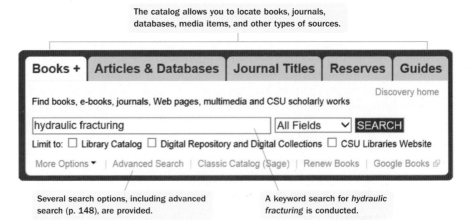

The catalog allows you to locate books, journals, databases, media items, and other types of sources.

| Books + | Articles & Databases | Journal Titles | Reserves | Guides |

Find books, e-books, journals, Web pages, multimedia and CSU scholarly works

Discovery home

hydraulic fracturing   All Fields ⌄   SEARCH

Limit to: ☐ Library Catalog ☐ Digital Repository and Digital Collections ☐ CSU Libraries Website

More Options ▾ | Advanced Search | Classic Catalog (Sage) | Renew Books | Google Books ⎘

Several search options, including advanced search (p. 148), are provided.

A keyword search for *hydraulic fracturing* is conducted.

FIGURE 2.1 Library Catalog Search Page [Courtesy of Morgan Library, Colorado State University.]

WORKING TOGETHER

Plan Your Search for Sources

Before you visit the library, search a database, or browse the Web, sit down with a group of classmates to generate ideas for a search. To carry out this activity, follow these steps.

1 Explain your subject and discuss your purpose for informing readers. If your readers go beyond the instructor and your classmates, describe your readers and their needs, interests, knowledge, experiences, values, and beliefs. Talk briefly about specific ideas you have for gathering information on your subject.

2 Once you've explained your subject, the other members of your group should brainstorm ideas about useful resources for locating sources, such as the library catalog, specific databases, useful Web sites and directories, and relevant field research methods.

3 For each resource that has been identified, the group should brainstorm suggestions for using it effectively. For example, the group might generate a list of specific keywords and phrases to use in your search, create a list of good candidates for an interview and useful interview questions, and make suggestions about what to look for in an observation.

4 At the end of the discussion, ask any questions you have about the resources and search strategies your classmates have suggested.

5 If you are working face-to-face, take notes on the discussion. If you are using a chat or instant-messaging program, record a transcript of the session. The goal of the session should be to generate as many useful search resources and strategies as possible. Don't rule out any ideas, no matter how trivial or ridiculous they might seem at first. When the exchange is completed, turn to the next writer and repeat the process.

My Research Project

Record Your Search Results

As you explore your topic, record your searches.

1. Identify the library catalogs, databases, and Web sites you search.

2. List the words and phrases you use in your searches.

3. Note the quality and quantity of results produced by each search.

4. Recording search results will allow you to conduct these searches again or conduct the same searches on different search sites or databases.

bedfordresearcher.com
My Research Project Activities > Record Your Search Results

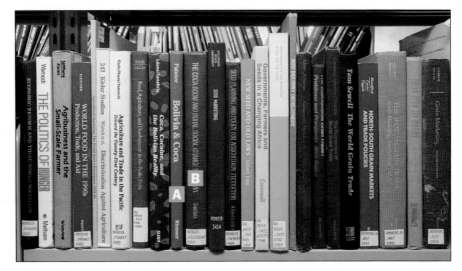

FIGURE 2.2 Browsing the Shelves in a Library [Courtesy of Morgan Library, Colorado State University.]

A If you located the book *Bolivia & Coca* . . .

B . . . browse the shelves to find related works such as *The Coca Boom and Rural Social Change in Bolivia*.

C Locate related sources by reading a book's works cited list, footnotes, endnotes, or in-text citations.

Browse Your Library's Shelves   Once you've located a relevant book or periodical through your library's catalog, you can usually find other sources about your topic on the same or nearby shelves (see Figure 2.2). Scan the titles of those works to locate additional sources you might not have found in your catalog search.

Browse Newsstands and Bookstores   If your topic is a current one, browse at a newsstand for specialty newspapers and magazines to which your library doesn't subscribe. If your topic has a broad, popular appeal, you might look at the books in a large bookstore or on a bookseller's online store or Web site.

Search Databases   ℹ️ **INFORMATION LITERACY**   Databases organize information as records (or entries) on a particular topic. Most databases provide publication information about articles in journals, magazines, and newspapers. You can search databases in much the same way that you can search a library catalog (see Figure 2.3). If you have difficulty locating databases or aren't sure which databases are appropriate for your topic, ask a reference librarian for assistance. To learn more about searching databases, see p. 158. ■

Search the Web   Web searches allow you to locate quickly a great deal of information about your topic—although not all of it will be as reliable as the sources you locate through a library catalog or database. To start searching the Web, visit one of the leading search sites (see Figure 2.4), such as Ask (**ask.com**), Bing (**bing.com**), Google (**google.com**), or Yahoo! (**yahoo.com**).

Brandon searched for *hydraulic fracturing.*

Brandon limited his search to full-text sources.

Brandon set a date range to locate only recent sources.

FIGURE 2.3 Brandon Tate's Initial Search in the Academic Search Premier Database [Courtesy of EBSCO.]

Google   hydraulic fracturing site:gov

About 82,900 results (0.23 seconds)

Brandon restricted his search for *hydraulic fracturing* to government sites (p. 166).

FIGURE 2.4 Brandon Tate's Initial Search on Google

Browse Electronic Mailing Lists, Web Discussion Forums, Message Boards, Twitter Feeds, Blogs, and Wikis   These resources can be excellent sources of information, but they can also contain some outrageous misinformation. Because

My Research Project

Manage Sources in Your Research Log

A critical aspect of working with sources is deciding how to manage them so that you can easily locate information when you need it. You can choose from several options.

- Saving, downloading, or emailing sources
- Adding sources to cloud-based services such as DropBox, iCloud, or SkyDrive
- Organizing your sources with Web-based tools, such as Google Drive or Delicious
- Printing sources and saving them in a notebook or folder

These and related strategies are discussed in Chapter 7.

bedfordresearcher.com
My Research Project Activities > Manage Sources in Your Research Log

most of these resources are unmoderated—that is, anything sent to them is published—you'll find everything from expert opinions to the musings of folks who know little or nothing about your topic. When read with a bit of skepticism, however, the messages can help you identify issues within your topic. For more on these online resources, see Chapters 5 and 9.

Step 6: Review, Mark, and Annotate Sources

As you explore a topic, you'll read quickly and widely by skimming sources and recording your reactions to them. Later, after you've identified sources that you want to examine more closely, you'll read some of these sources critically (p. 68). At this point in your research process, skimming—reading just enough to get a general idea of what a document is about—enables you to gather information quickly from written sources. Figures 2.5 and 2.6 illustrate strategies for skimming brief print documents and Web pages. Key strategies include identifying the type of document—or genre—you are skimming; scanning titles, headings and subheadings, and figure captions; reading the first and last sentences of paragraphs; scanning menus and other navigation aids; and looking for information

Check the title for clues about content.

Skim opening paragraphs for the purpose and scope of the document.

Check headings and subheadings to learn about content and organization.

Skim captions of photos and figures, which often highlight important information, ideas, and arguments.

Read the first and last sentences of paragraphs to find key information.

FIGURE 2.5 Skimming a Print Document [Courtesy of the U.S. Geological Survey.]

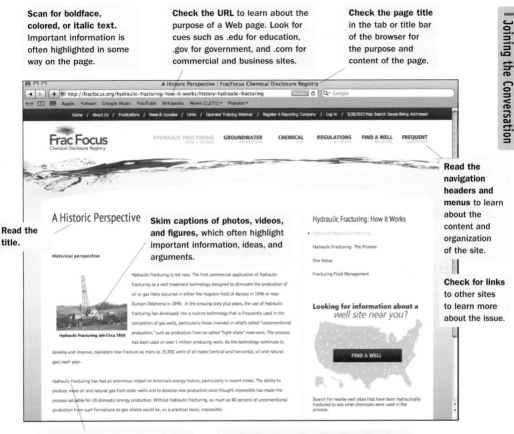

Scan for boldface, colored, or italic text. Important information is often highlighted in some way on the page.

Check the URL to learn about the purpose of a Web page. Look for cues such as .edu for education, .gov for government, and .com for commercial and business sites.

Check the page title in the tab or title bar of the browser for the purpose and content of the page.

Read the navigation headers and menus to learn about the content and organization of the site.

Read the title.

Skim captions of photos, videos, and figures, which often highlight important information, ideas, and arguments.

Check for links to other sites to learn more about the issue.

Read the first and last sentences of paragraphs to find key information.

Check for information about the author to learn about the author's background, interests, and purposes for writing the document.

FIGURE 2.6 Skimming a Web Page [Screen image courtesy of FracFocus.]

about authors and publishers. If you are reading a longer document, such as a book or report, consider these additional strategies.

- **Check the table of contents,** if one is provided. It will give you a useful overview of the document's content and organization.

- **Check the index,** if one is provided, to learn more about the content of the document.

- **Check the glossary,** if one is provided. The terms that are defined can provide clues about the focus of the document.

- **Check the works cited list,** if one is provided, to learn about the types of evidence used in the document.

- **Check for pull quotes** (quotations or brief passages pulled out of the text and set in larger type elsewhere on the page), which often call attention to important information, ideas, and arguments in a document.

- **Check for information about the author** to learn about the writer's background, interests, and purposes for writing the document.

  As you skim your sources, do the following.

- Mark them by highlighting or underlining important passages so that you'll be able to locate key passages easily later in your research writing process (see Figure 2.7).

- Annotate them by briefly recording in the margins or in digital comments your initial reactions to a source.

- Take brief notes in your research log. For example, you might note similarities or differences among your sources, such as different proposals for solving a problem or different interpretations of an issue. These notes allow you to start to pull together the information, ideas, and arguments that several of your sources touch on.

Learn more about annotating, marking, and taking notes on sources in Chapters 4 and 6.

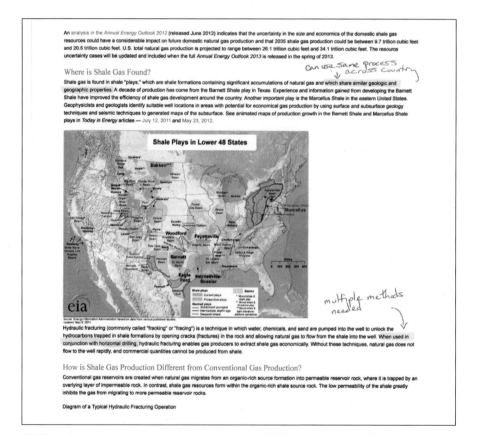

FIGURE 2.7 Brandon Tate's Annotations and Highlighting on a Printout of a Page from an Online Magazine [U.S. Department of Energy.]

My Research Project

Explore Your Topic

As you work through the strategies discussed in this chapter, use the following activity to keep track of your topic exploration in your research log.

1. What is my topic?

2. Have I discussed my topic with others? If so, what have I learned? If not, who are likely candidates for interviews—such as librarians, instructors, and people involved with or affected by my topic—and what questions should I ask them?

3. Are there any preliminary observations I should conduct? Have I done so? If so, what have I learned?

4. Have I identified types of sources that are appropriate for my project? What kind of sources are they?

5. Have I found and reviewed sources? Have I searched the library catalog and browsed the shelves? Have I searched databases and the Web? Have I skimmed, marked, annotated, and taken brief notes on the sources I've found? If so, what have I learned about my topic?

bedfordresearcher.com
My Research Project Activities > Explore Your Topic

2b

How can I focus on an issue?

Once you've explored your topic, your most important goal is to focus on a specific issue. Issues are points of disagreement, uncertainty, concern, or curiosity that are being discussed by communities of readers and writers.

As she explored the general topic of protecting marine life, Lauren Mack read sources, viewed films and videos, talked with her professor and other specialists about her topic, and kept a running list of ideas and information that interested her. Lauren started to make connections among the wide range of information, ideas, and arguments she encountered, and she was ultimately able to focus on the single issue that interested her most: the problems facing coral reefs.

Moving from your topic to a single issue about that topic involves identifying conversations about issues in your topic, assessing your interest in the issues, and asking whether writing about this issue will allow you to achieve your purposes as a writer.

Step 1: Identify Conversations about Issues in Your Topic

Identifying conversations about issues in your topic is the first step in determining which issue is most appropriate for your research project. As you work through this process, look for patterns in the information, ideas, and arguments you encounter in your sources.

Find Central Concepts Repeated in Your Sources   When several sources refer to the same idea, you can assume that this information is central to the topic. For instance, as Alexis Alvarez looked at articles and Web sites about the impact of competitive athletics on adolescent girls, she found repeated references to self-esteem, confidence, and performance-enhancing drugs. Noticing this repetition enabled Alexis to identify some of the important conversations about her topic.

Find Broad Themes Discussed in Your Sources   Sources that discuss the same general theme are most likely involved in the same conversation. Featured writer Elizabeth Leontiev found that some of the sources she explored focused on the history of the U.S. war on drugs, some focused on its cost, others focused on its effectiveness, and still others focused on the impact of the war on drugs both in Central and South America. By noting these broad themes, Elizabeth was able to identify some of the key conversations taking place about her topic.

Find Disagreements among Your Sources   Some sources will explicitly indicate that they disagree with arguments, ideas, or information in other sources. For example, Brandon Tate found that some sources reported on the economic value of fracking, while others argued that fracking posed unacceptable risks to drinking water supplies and local air quality. Looking for such explicit statements of disagreement helped Brandon identify a group of sources that were engaged in conversation with one another.

Find Recurring Voices in Your Sources   As you read sources, you might find that some authors write frequently about your topic or that some authors are referred to frequently by other writers. These authors might have significant experience or expertise related to the topic, or they might represent particular perspectives on the topic. Stay alert for these recurring voices.

Step 2: Assess Your Interest in the Issues

Once you've identified issues that are being discussed in your sources, you are ready to assess the importance and relevance of those issues. Determine your personal interest in each issue by asking what interests you most about each one. Identifying personal connections between your sources and your own interests will help you focus on an issue that will sustain your interest throughout the course of your research project.

Alexis Alvarez, for example, drew on her personal experiences and her knowledge of the experiences of friends and family as she considered issues related to the topic of women and competitive sports. She had been surprised to learn about the use of performance-enhancing drugs among young athletes. She found herself wondering whether any of her friends or her sister's teammates might know of athletes who had used steroids. As she thought more about the topic, she found herself returning to the issue of performance-enhancing drugs.

TUTORIAL

How can I identify conversations in my sources?

You can identify conversations taking place in your sources by looking for patterns. Creating a four-column table like the one below can help you sort things out. In this example, Elizabeth Leontiev notes that three of her sources talk about the effectiveness of the U.S. war on drugs. She used this conversation as the basis for her research on the impact of U.S. drug policy on South American coca farmers.

1 Record the source. Here, Elizabeth uses the authors' last names.

2 Record concepts that are repeated in your sources.

3 Record other broad themes that you've noticed in your sources.

4 Note points on which the sources disagree.

5 Note the sources that these sources are citing. (You might use them later.)

Source	Gordon	Forero	Logan
Repeated Concepts	"zero cocaine, not zero coca"	"zero cocaine, not zero coca"	
Broad Themes	Overall effectiveness of U.S. war on drugs	Overall effectiveness of U.S. war on drugs	U.S. interference in affairs of other countries
Disagreements	U.S. policy of coca extermination—argues it has failed	U.S. policy of coca extermination—focuses on political issues	U.S. policy of coca extermination—argues policy is likely to change
Key Voices	Forero, Chipana, Morales	Morales	Morales, Reinicke

Step 3: Choose an Issue   [FRAMING MY ARGUMENT]

After you've assessed the issues you've found during your exploration of your topic, select the strongest candidate and the one that interests you most. Think, too, about the level of interest your readers might have in the issue and whether writing about it will help you achieve your purposes as a writer.

Evaluate each issue by asking yourself the following questions. As you do so, you can follow Alexis Alvarez's responses to the questions.

Will selecting this issue help me achieve my purposes as a writer? Review your purpose and examine how each of the issues you have identified will help you best accomplish it.	As she reviewed her assignment, Alexis considered three issues she had identified as she explored her topic: parent-child relationships, the impact of competitive sports on social development, and the use of performance-enhancing drugs (PEDs) by younger athletes. She found herself drawn to the use of PEDs because her strong reaction to it suggested she might want to investigate and make an argument about it.
Will my readers want or need to read about this issue? Ask yourself which issue your readers would be most interested in or would most need to know about.	Her instructor had asked her to consider either her classmates or members of her home community as the audience for her essay. In part because she was surprised by the early age at which some athletes began using PEDs, Alexis thought that many of her readers would be as well. Even if they didn't need to know about it, she thought, they'd probably be as interested and surprised as she was.
Is this issue appropriate for my project's context? Consider the social and disciplinary contexts in which you are writing. If you are writing for a science class, for example, ask whether the issue will meet the expectations of your instructor and other readers.	Alexis felt that the issue was both significant and relevant enough to meet the needs of her assignment. She felt that the sources she had read so far— some published in scholarly journals and others on the Centers for Disease Control Web site—would be appropriate for her course context.
Is this issue appropriate for the type of document I plan to write? Some issues that are well suited for editorials and opinion columns in your school newspaper, for example, might not be suitable for an academic or a professional paper.	Alexis's assignment required her to use a range of sources, including scholarly books and articles. As she explored her topic, she had found newspaper articles, books, scholarly journal articles, and government Web sites that addressed the use of PEDs in competitive youth soccer. To confirm that she was on the right track, Alexis checked in with her instructor, who agreed that the issue would be appropriate for her assignment.

Is this issue compatible with my requirements and limitations? Determine whether you can address an issue reasonably, given your assignment due date.	Based on her initial explorations, Alexis felt that she could work within the length limitations of her assignment and meet the assignment due date. Alexis's early research also showed her that she could meet the requirement to use a range of sources, including scholarly books and articles.
What opportunities do I have if I choose this issue? Identify any special resources that might be available to you, such as access to a special collection in a library, experts on an issue, or individuals who have been affected by it.	Alexis decided that, in addition to the sources she had been able to find in her library and on the Web, she could gain a first-hand perspective on the issue by talking with her sister and friends who played competitive sports.

Table 2.1 shows the topics explored by the featured writers and the issues they addressed.

TABLE 2.1 THE PROGRESSION FROM TOPIC TO CONVERSATION

Featured Writer	Topic	Issue
Alexis Alvarez	Women and competitive sports	Steroid use among adolescent girls involved in competitive sports
Nicholas Brothers	Private military corporations	Use of private military corporations to support the U.S. war on terror
Elizabeth Leontiev	The war on drugs	Impact of U.S. war on drugs on South American coca farmers
Lauren Mack	Protecting marine life	The problems facing coral reefs
Cori Schmidtbauer	William Shakespeare's dramas	Portia's unconventional role in *The Merchant of Venice*
Brandon Tate	Hydraulic fracturing ("fracking")	Impact of fracking on the environment and the economy
Josh Woelfle	A cure for cancer	Promising new treatments for cancer

My Research Project

Choose an Issue within Your Topic

In your research log, complete the following activity to focus your topic on a single issue.

1. What are the three most important issues I have identified so far?

2. Of these issues, which one will best help me sustain my interest in this project?

3. Which one will best help me achieve my purposes as a writer?

4. Which one will best address my readers' needs, interests, knowledge, experiences, values, and beliefs?

5. Which one is best suited to my context (social, cultural, historical, disciplinary, physical)?

6. Which one is most appropriate for the type of document I plan to write?

7. Which one best fits the requirements of my assignment?

8. Which one has the fewest limitations?

9. Which one allows me to best take advantage of opportunities?

10. Based on these answers, the issue I want to choose is:

bedfordresearcher.com
My Research Project Activities > Choose an Issue within Your Topic

> **QUICK REFERENCE**

Exploring and Focusing

☑ Get organized by creating a plan to explore your topic. (p. 30)

☑ Discuss your topic with people who know about or have been affected by it. (p. 30)

☑ Conduct preliminary observations. (p. 31)

☑ Identify useful types of sources. (p. 31)

☑ Begin finding and managing written sources. (p. 32)

☑ Review and record you initial reactions to your sources by skimming, marking, and annotating. (p. 36)

☑ Identify conversations about issues related to your topic. (p. 39)

☑ Assess your interest in the issues. (p. 40)

☑ Choose an issue. (p. 42)

3

Developing Your Research Question and Proposal

Your research question provides the foundation for developing your position—the main point you will make about your issue. It also guides your efforts to develop a research proposal, create a search plan, and collect information.

3a

How can I develop my research question?

A research question directs your efforts to collect, critically read, evaluate, and take notes on your sources. Most research questions are narrowly focused, allowing writers to collect information in time to meet deadlines. Research questions are also subject to revision as writers learn more about an issue. It's best, at this early stage in your project, to think of your research question as a flexible guide.

Developing your research question involves reflecting on your issue and disciplinary context, focusing on your role, focusing on an aspect of your issue, and refining your question.

Step 1: Reflect on Your Issue and Disciplinary Context   ❓ WHAT'S MY PURPOSE?

As you've explored your topic and focused on your issue, you've learned more about the conversation you've decided to join. The sources you've read have helped you gain an understanding of some of the most important information, ideas, and arguments shaping the conversation. You might also have had the opportunity to talk with others about your issue and perhaps even to conduct observations. If you're like most research writers, your initial thoughts about your topic and issue have changed as you've carried out your investigations.

As you begin generating ideas for a research question, ask whether what you've learned about the issue has changed your understanding of your writing situation. Then ask yourself what you'd like to learn next. As you ask these questions, consider how disciplinary or professional contexts might shape the questions you can ask. If you are writing a research report for a biology class, for example, your understanding of the kinds of questions biologists typically ask about issues will come into play. That's true for virtually every discipline and profession, each of which has areas that are of interest to its members and each of which has particular ways of asking questions about those areas of interest (see Table 3.1).

TABLE 3.1 DISCIPLINARY QUESTIONS

Discipline	Types of Questions	Examples
Humanities	Interpretive questions about literature, music, philosophy, rhetoric, and the arts	How did the acceptance of Manet's painting style open the door for Impressionism? What similarities does Toni Morrison's character Amy Denver in *Beloved* share with Twain's character Huck Finn?
Social Sciences	Questions about factors that affect human behavior	What is the significance of social networking sites such as Facebook in modern-day protest movements? What factors contribute to a person becoming a mass murderer?
Sciences	"How" and "why" questions about the natural world, including both the environment and living beings	How can we combat the obesity epidemic among school-age children? What are the preventable causes of global warming?
History	"How" and "why" questions about past events	What role did evangelicalism play in the American conservative movement of the twentieth century? Why did fascism ultimately fail in Italy in the 1940s?

Similarly, your understanding of the kinds of genres typically used to communicate within the discipline or profession—such as articles, presentations, and essays—will shape your work on your research question. Some genres, such as books and longer reports, are well suited to broader questions. Others, because of their comparative brevity (think of poster sessions, conference presentations, reports, and essays), are better suited to highly focused research questions.

Step 2: Focus on Your Role   [FRAMING MY ARGUMENT]

Your role as a writer—the manner in which you'll relate to your readers—will have a profound impact on your decisions about your research question. Writers who inform their readers, for example, develop strikingly different questions than those who seek to persuade them to take action. Had featured writer Brandon Tate decided to inform his readers about the impact of hydraulic fracturing on air and water quality, for example, he might have pursued questions such as the following.

> What are the effects of fracking on local air and water quality?
>
> How have opponents of fracking characterized its impact on air and water quality?
>
> What have recent scientific research studies indicated about the impact of fracking on air and water quality?

In contrast, had Brandon adopted the role of advocate, his research questions might have resembled the following.

> In light of recent findings about the impact of fracking on air and water quality, should Coloradoans enact legislation to ban fracking?
>
> Given scientific evidence that fracking has a negative effect on air and water quality, should the government establish regulations that might reduce or eliminate those effects?
>
> Given scientific evidence that fracking has a negative effect on air and water quality, what steps should Coloradoans take to mitigate its effects?

The roles writers can adopt vary widely (p. 9). Table 3.2 provides a list of some of the most important roles you might adopt and offers examples of the kinds of questions writers adopting a particular role might ask. These questions serve as sentence starters that you can use to generate potential research questions (p. 25).

Step 3: Focus on an Aspect of Your Issue

You can begin to generate potential research questions by using freewriting (p. 22), looping (p. 23), the sentence starters found in Table 3.2 (p. 48), and the question matrix found in the My Research Project activity on p. 50. As you

TABLE 3.2 THE RELATIONSHIP AMONG ROLES AND RESEARCH QUESTIONS

Purpose	Role	General Questions
To Inform	Reporter	What is known—and not known—about _____?
		How might we define _____?
To Create and Share New Knowledge	Inquirer	What causes _____?
		What are the effects of _____?
		What can [cure / repair / prevent] _____?
To Reflect	Observer	What are the implications of _____?
		How can we learn from the example of an individual or group?
		What can we gain from thinking about an idea, a work of art, a work of literature, or a performance?
To Evaluate	Evaluator	What conclusions—merited or not—have writers and readers already made about _____?
		What assumptions are shaping current thinking about _____?
		What are the best choices available for addressing _____?
		What are the relative strengths and weaknesses of _____?
To Analyze	Interpreter	What has occurred in the past that is relevant to _____?
		What causes _____?
		What are the effects of _____?
		Does the data suggest that _____ [is / is the result of] a trend?
		What is likely to happen [to / as a result of] _____?
		In what ways is _____ similar to _____?
		In what ways does _____ differ from _____?
To Solve Problems	Problem Solver	Why is _____ a problem?
		What is the best solution to _____?
		Why should we adopt _____ as a solution to _____?
To Convince (Change Readers' Beliefs or Attitudes), **Persuade** (Cause Readers to Take Action), **or Mediate** (Seek to Establish Common Ground among Readers)	Advocate	What are the origins of this argument?
		What is the status of this argument?
		Who has made the best arguments about _____?
		What do the writers and readers involved in conversation about _____ want to [see happen / avoid happening]?
		What should be done about _____?
		How should _____ be accomplished?
		How can we find common ground about _____?

TUTORIAL

How do I generate research questions consistent with my role?

Each role listed in Table 3.2 is associated with sentence starters you can use to generate potential research questions. Once you've identified your purpose and chosen the role you'll adopt as you work with your readers, you can use these sentence starters to generate potential research questions.

Adopting the role of interpreter, for example, featured writer Lauren Mack might have generated the following research questions about her issue, the problems facing coral reefs.

Interpreter

What has occurred in the past that is relevant to _____?
- the potential extinction of many forms of coral?
- efforts by state and local governments to preserve coral reefs?

What causes _____?
- individuals to act in ways that contribute to the demise of coral reefs?
- nonprofit organizations to work to preserve coral reefs?
- government agencies to adopt regulations that might lead to the demise of coral reefs?

What are the effects of _____?
- damaging or destroying coral reefs?
- commercial activity on coral reefs?
- overfishing on coral reefs?

Does the data suggest that _____ [is / is the result of] a trend?
- the die-off of coral reefs?
- individual action to preserve coral reefs?

What is likely to happen [to / as a result of] _____?
- the communities that rely on coral reefs for commercial benefits?
- aquatic species that rely on the ecosystem provided by coral reefs?

In what ways is _____ similar to _____?
- damage to coral reefs similar to the systematic killing of the plains bison in the 1800s?

In what ways does _____ differ from _____?
- the commercial exploitation of coral reefs differ from past exploitation of old growth forests?

generate potential questions, consider both your role and general areas of focus within the issue you've decided to address. The following areas often lead to useful lines of inquiry.

- **Information.** What is known — and not known — about an issue?

- **History.** What has occurred in the past that is relevant to an issue?

- **Assumptions.** What conclusions — merited or not — have writers and readers already made about an issue?

- **Goals.** What do the writers and readers involved in conversation about this issue want to see happen (or not happen)?

- **Outcomes.** What has happened so far? What is likely to happen?

- **Policies.** What are the best procedures for carrying out actions? For making decisions?

With your issue and role in mind, you can generate questions using one or more of these areas as a starting point. In addition, you can narrow the focus of your questions by exploring the intersections between these areas and specific thinking processes, such as examining trends, similarities and differences, and cause/effect relationships.

Step 4: Choose and Focus Your Research Question

Review your potential research questions and select a question that interests you and is appropriate for your research writing situation. You should be confident that you will be able to respond to the question in a substantive and useful way. You should also be confident that your response will be neither too simplistic nor too ambitious to address in an essay. Questions that can be answered with an unelaborated "yes" or "no" response, for example, are not generally pursued in a research writing project. It is also the case, however, that many initial research questions are far too broad to serve as the basis for a focused research project.

My Research Project

Generate a Matrix of Research Questions

Use the table on p. 51 to generate potential research questions. You need not complete every cell in the table and you can create more than one question in each cell. To complete the activity, choose a column, such as "Information," and then generate questions to focus on, for example, defining what is known about the issue, tracing causes and effects, charting trends, and so on.

To generate questions, use freewriting or the sentence starters found on pp. 25–26.

bedfordresearcher.com
My Research Project Activities > Generate a Matrix of Research Questions

	Definition (Describe specific aspects of the issue.)	Causes and Effects (Ask what leads to a specific result.)	Trends (Ask about sequences of events.)	Relationships (Examine connections between aspects of an issue.)	Similarities and Differences (Compare and contrast.)	Strengths and Weaknesses (Assess relative merits.)
Information: What is known—and not known—about an issue?						
History: What has occurred in the past that is relevant to an issue?						
Assumptions: What conclusions— merited or not—have writers and readers already made about an issue?						
Goals: What should happen (or not happen)?						
Outcomes: What has happened so far? What is likely to happen?						
Policies: What are the best procedures for carrying out actions? For making decisions?						

In general, a research question that is too broad will lead to answers requiring far more space to answer than most writing assignments allow, while a question that is too narrow will lead to answers that are so specific that they will fail to interest most readers. In both cases, the document that emerges will usually lack depth and fail to make a useful contribution to the conversation.

Too Broad:

How did real estate development on the East Coast of the United States affect the environment during the twentieth century?

Too Narrow:

In what ways has source-point pollution of the Minnesota River affected the profit margins of women-owned metal fabrication companies in the Mankato area?

Balanced Focus:

How can we best address drinking-water problems caused by the dumping of polluted lake water into Florida rivers and estuaries?

Too Broad:

How does public education vary among industrialized nations?

Too Narrow:

Do first-grade teachers prefer Expo or Quill dry-erase markers?

Balanced Focus:

How can the use of tablets improve reading fluency among U.S. fourth-grade students?

Consider how specific question words can help you create a focused research question. If you are interested in conducting an analysis, for example, you might use the words *what, why, when, where, who,* and *how.* If you are interested in informing readers about the goals or outcomes associated with a particular issue, you might use the words *would* or *could.* If the conversation focuses on determining an appropriate course of action, as might be the case if you were adopting the role of an advocate, generate questions using the word *should.* Take a look at the differences in the following questions.

- **What** are the benefits of hydraulic fracturing?

- **Would** it be feasible to require oil and gas producers to reduce or eliminate the use of chemicals during hydraulic fracturing?

- **Should** the federal government pursue legislation to reduce the environmental and health impacts of hydraulic fracturing?

Each question would lead to differences in how to search for sources of information, which sources to use in a project document, what role to adopt as a writer, and how to organize and draft the document.

WORKING TOGETHER

Craft Focused Research Questions

Working with a small group of writers, use question words to focus potential research questions. To prepare for the activity, review your list of potential research questions and identify two or three that interest you most. Then carry out the following activities.

1 Taking turns with other members of the group, **share a research question** and ask the other members of the group to brainstorm variations on the question that use the question words *who, what, where, when, how, why, would, could,* and *should.* Take notes on the variations.

2 After you have each shared your best research questions, **review your notes.** Highlight the variations on the questions that will help you best accomplish your purpose and address the needs and interests of your readers.

3 Taking turns, **share your conclusions** with the group. Ask for reactions and additional suggestions. Take notes.

4 After the activity, **review your notes** and determine whether you should revise your research question.

Step 5: Refine Your Research Question

Choose the research question that emerged from the research project activity *Craft Focused Research Questions.* Refine your question by referring to shared assumptions and existing conditions, narrowing its scope, and conducting preliminary searches.

Refer to Shared Assumptions and Existing Conditions   You can refine your research question by using qualifying words and phrases to narrow its scope, by calling attention to assumptions that have been made by the community of writers and readers who are addressing your issue, or by referring to existing conditions relevant to your issue. Note the difference between the following three versions of featured writer Alexis Alvarez's research question.

Original Question:

What should be done about steroid use by adolescent girls involved in competitive sports?

Alternative 1:

Even though we know that widespread drug testing of all athletes, younger and older, is impossible, what should be done about steroid use by adolescent girls involved in competitive sports?

Alternative 2:

Given the lack of knowledge among athletes and their parents about the health consequences of steroid use, what should be done about steroid use by adolescent girls involved in competitive sports?

As you refine your research question, you might use conditional words and phrases such as the following.

Mix . . .	and Match
Although	we know that . . .
Because	it is uncertain . . .
Even though	it is clear that . . .
Given that	studies indicate . . .
In light of	recent events . . .
Now that	it has been shown . . .
Since	the lack of . . .
While	we cannot . . .

Narrow the Scope of Your Research Question   Early research questions typically suffer from lack of focus. You can narrow the scope of your question by looking for vague words and phrases and replacing them with more specific words or phrases. The process of moving from a broad research question to one that might be addressed effectively in a research essay might produce the following sequence.

Original Research Question:

What is behind the increased popularity of women's sports?

Refined:

What has led to the increased popularity of women's sports in colleges and universities?

Further Refined:

How has Title IX increased opportunities for women athletes in American colleges and universities?

In this example, the writer has narrowed the scope of the research question in two ways. First, the writer has shifted its focus from women's sports in general to women's sports in American colleges and universities. Second, the writer has moved from a general focus on increased popularity of women's sports to a more specific focus on opportunities brought about by Title IX, federal legislation that mandated equal opportunities for women athletes. Table 3.3 shows the featured writers' progress from a general topic to a focused issue to a refined research question.

Conduct Preliminary Searches   One of the best ways to test your research question is to conduct some preliminary searches in a library catalog or database or on the Web. If you locate a vast amount of information in your searches, you might need to revise your question so that it focuses on a more manageable

TUTORIAL

How do I refine my research question?

The first draft of your research question might be too broad, which can make it difficult for you to focus your research efforts. Refine your initial research question so that you can collect information efficiently.

In this example, Brandon Tate refines his research question about the impact of hydraulic fracturing on local air and water quality. He used his research question as he collected and worked with sources, and later, he developed his thesis statement to answer his question.

Preliminary Research Question:
What should we do about hydraulic fracturing?

1 Refer to shared assumptions and existing conditions by using phrases such as *although it is clear that . . .*, *because we cannot . . .*, and *given that studies have shown. . . .*

Given the national commitment to reducing our reliance on foreign oil, what should we do about hydraulic fracturing?

2 Identify vague words and phrases, such as *what should we do about*, and replace them with more specific language.

Given the national commitment to reducing our reliance on foreign oil, what steps can U.S. citizens take to ensure that environmental concerns play an important role in the regulation of hydraulic fracturing?

3 Using these specific terms, conduct preliminary searches in your library catalog, databases, and on the Web. If you get too many results, narrow your focus even further. (Here, Brandon narrows his target audience from U.S. citizens to Colorado citizens and focuses on passing a statewide referendum.)

Given the national commitment to reducing our reliance on foreign oil, what steps can Colorado citizens take to pass a statewide referendum regulating hydraulic fracturing?

aspect of the issue. In contrast, if you find almost nothing in your search, you might need to expand the scope of your research question.

TABLE 3.3 THE FEATURED WRITERS' RESEARCH QUESTIONS

Featured Writer	Topic	Issue	Initial Research Question	Final Research Question
Alexis Alvarez	Women and competitive sports	Steroid use among adolescent girls involved in competitive sports	What are the effects of competitive sports on adolescent girls?	What should be done about steroid use by adolescent girls involved in competitive sports?
Nicholas Brothers	Private military corporations	Use of private military corporations to support the U.S. war on terror	How important have private military corporations become for the U.S. military?	What roles do private military corporations play in the U.S. military's war on terror?
Elizabeth Leontiev	The war on drugs	Impact of U.S. war on drugs on South American coca farmers	What are the effects of the U.S. war on drugs on South America?	How can we reduce the economic impact of the war on drugs on South American coca farmers?
Lauren Mack	Protecting marine life	The problems facing coral reefs	What are the threats to coral reefs?	Why are coral reefs important, and what can be done to protect them from destruction?
Cori Schmidtbauer	William Shakespeare's dramas	Portia's unconventional role in *The Merchant of Venice*	How are women portrayed in Shakespeare's plays?	How does Portia's character in *The Merchant of Venice* fit the ideal of an Elizabethan woman?
Brandon Tate	Hydraulic fracturing	Impact of fracking on local air and water quality	What do readers need to know to form an educated opinion about hydraulic fracturing?	What do individuals need to know to develop an informed opinion about the controversial issue of hydraulic fracturing?

Josh Woelfle	A cure for cancer	Promising new treatments for cancer	What new treatment options are available for cancer patients?	What makes new cancer treatments potentially superior to traditional treatments such as chemotherapy and radiation?

3b

How can I create a research proposal?

A research proposal—sometimes called a prospectus—is a formal presentation of your plan for your research writing project. A proposal helps you pull together the planning you've done on your project, identify areas where you need additional planning, and assess the progress you've made so far.

Unlike a research plan (p. 30), which is designed primarily to help *you* decide how to collect information, a research proposal is addressed to someone else, usually an instructor, a supervisor, or a funding agency. Although the specific format for research proposals can vary widely across disciplines, a research proposal typically includes the following parts.

- A title page
- An introduction that identifies your topic, issue, and/or research question
- A review of literature
- An explanation of how you will collect information
- A project timeline
- A working bibliography

In addition to these core elements, you can also provide an abstract or executive summary, offer an overview of key challenges, and include a funding request. You can read about how to develop each of these core and optional elements below.

Identify Your Topic, Issue, and Research Question

A title page and introduction offer your readers an overview of the topic and issue you'll address in your project document. Your title page should include the working title of your research writing project, your name and contact information, and the date. Your introduction should identify the topic you've chosen and the issue you've decided to address; state your research question and, if you have created one, your position on the issue (p. 70); describe your purpose; and identify and describe your readers. It should also identify the type of document you'll create and explain how your choice of genre reflects your purpose, your understanding of your readers, and the contexts that will shape your work on your research project.

Provide a Review of Literature

A review of literature presents an overview of the key information, ideas, and arguments in the sources you've collected so far. You should identify the most useful sources you found during your exploration of your topic and explain why you found them useful. Keep in mind, however, that a review of literature goes beyond the simple list of sources that are typically found in a working bibliography by offering a discussion of important approaches to your issue. That is, a review of literature focuses not so much on individual sources as on groups of sources and the shared ideas or positions taken by groups of sources. Focusing on general approaches to an issue, as opposed to the individual positions adopted in particular sources, can help you understand the major ideas that are being considered in the conversation you are planning to join. By understanding existing approaches to an issue, you can determine whether you agree with any of those approaches or whether you want to introduce a completely new approach. In turn, this will help you develop your own individual position on the issue.

For an example that illustrates how key approaches to an issue can be discussed, see featured writer Nicholas Brothers's review of literature on p. 61.

Explain How You'll Collect Information

Your research proposal should help your reader understand how you will collect information. Your plan should identify:

- the types of sources you intend to collect (such as books, journal articles, or opinion columns). Read about types of sources on p. 32.
- the types of search tools (such as library catalogs, databases, and Web search sites) and research methods (such as browsing library shelves, consulting librarians, or conducting surveys) you want to use. You can learn about search tools in Chapter 9, library research in Chapter 10, and field research in Chapter 11.
- the types of strategies (such as simple and advanced database searches or field research) that you intend to use in your searches (pp. 146-54).
- the schedule you will follow as you carry out your searches (p. 59).

i **INFORMATION LITERACY** Your research question will influence your decisions about how you will collect information. For example, you can use your research question—and, if you've developed one, your position on your issue (p. 70)—to help identify keywords and phrases that might be used in database, catalog, and Web searches. ▪

Develop a Project Timeline

A project timeline will give your reader an indication of the range of days, weeks, or months over which you will be completing your research and writing your document. Your timeline can range from a general description of the number of days or weeks you'll devote to your project to a detailed list of key project activities and the amount of time devoted to completing them. If you are working on a group project, a project timeline can be especially useful, since it will require discussion of individual responsibilities for completing tasks and deadlines for completing them.

Compile a Working or Annotated Bibliography

A working bibliography lists the sources you've collected so far. Sometimes you will be asked to create an annotated bibliography, which contains a brief description of each source. Your working or annotated bibliography should conform to the documentation system (such as MLA, APA, *Chicago*, or CSE) specified by your instructor, supervisor, or funding agency. For more information on bibliographies, see p. 119.

Clarify and Elaborate on Your Core Proposal

Depending on your purpose, your reader, and the scope of your research writing project, you can choose to include several optional elements.

- **An abstract or executive summary** provides a brief summary—usually fifty to two hundred words—of your project. It should allow your reader to gain a general understanding of your project and your plans for completing it. Writers who wish to provide additional information, such as explanations of their personal interest in an issue, can provide an introduction, as Nicholas Brothers does in his research proposal (p. 60).

- **An overview of key challenges** allows you to share your thoughts about potential problems you'll need to address as you work on your project. This section of your research proposal might discuss difficulties you're likely to encounter, such as locating or collecting specific types of sources, gaining enough knowledge about an issue to develop a credible position, or finding enough respondents for a survey. It also provides an opportunity for your instructor, supervisor, or potential funder to respond by suggesting strategies for meeting specific challenges.

- **A funding request and rationale** provides a budget that identifies costs for key project activities, such as conducting your search, reviewing the sources you collect, writing and designing the document, and publishing or distributing the document.

Writing a formal research proposal allows you to reflect on the work you've done so far and get feedback on your plans to carry out your project. Perhaps more important, it requires you to make decisions about the best strategies for completing your project.

Brothers 1

Nicholas Brothers

English 108: College Writing and Research

Dawn Terrick

September 17, 2013

Research Proposal: Private Military

Corporations and the War on Terror

Introduction: For my research project, I would like to explore the world of the modern private military corporation (PMC). Mercenaries have been used throughout history by countries all over the world. With few exceptions, they have suffered a poor reputation; seen as unprofessional and unreliable, they went unused by many first-world nations in the age of standing professional armies. Yet, in recent years, PMCs have morphed into corporate entities and gained new respect. But is this respect deserved? Throughout the Afghanistan and Iraq conflicts, the United States' use of private military corporations has increased to what I consider startling levels.

While I will strive to be as objective as possible when conducting my research, my prior personal interest in this issue has always put me at odds with the supporters of PMCs. Fundamentally, I believe that overreliance on contractors is a danger to national and international security. However, it is entirely possible that, with further study, I will gain a new appreciation for PMCs and their personnel.

> Position statement is clear and concise.

My purpose is ultimately to build an argument about the United States' continued use of PMCs. To present my position on the issue, I will need to inform my readers about the history of PMCs and analyze the corporations' evolving role in our country's military engagements. My readers are my class peers (from many different backgrounds and studying different subjects) and my instructor. Although there is a wide range of scholarship and reportage on this topic, I believe the general public remains unaware of the pervasiveness of these corporations. It's my hope that upon reading my paper, the layperson will have a better understanding of how and why PMCs are involved in the wars in Iraq and Afghanistan. I will be creating an academic essay and a brief presentation to convey my research and argument to my readers. The print format of the essay will allow readers to follow my logic at their own pace and reread sections of the essay as needed, and it will also provide them an easy way to look up the sources I use if they want to explore the topic further — which I hope they will. The presentation will allow me to explain a complicated issue in a more conversational format and answer any questions.

> Discussion of purpose addresses the writer's intent and the readers' needs.

Brothers 2

I plan to begin my paper with background information — mostly recent history unless I find something compelling from the distant past that I feel readers must know to better understand the present. I would like to explore the practical and moral costs of using PMCs. In doing so, I will likely focus on specific companies and incidents during the "War on Terror" years.

Research Question: What roles do private military corporations play in the U.S. military's war on terror?

> The research question is open-ended but focuses on a specific time and place.

Review of Literature: The book that originally piqued my interest in this topic was Jeremy Scahill's *Blackwater: The Rise of the World's Most Powerful Mercenary Army*, which depicts PMCs as very dangerous entities. Articles I've come across in publications such as *Salon.com* and *Mother Jones* also strongly criticize PMCs. On the complete opposite end of the spectrum are the corporate Web sites of the PMCs, which of course paint their contractors in only the most positive light. I found a more evenhanded approach to the topic in P. W. Singer's *Corporate Warriors: The Rise of the Privatized Military Industry*, which provides a solid overview of the history of PMCs and explains their structure and functions.

> The literature review helps Nicholas think about his sources' different positions.

Search Plan and Relevant Sources: I will need to continue to seek out a range of perspectives on PMCs as I develop my own argument. I plan to conduct some field research by interviewing people who have firsthand experience with or expertise on PMCs. My brother, Michael Brothers, is in the military and might agree to an interview, and I plan to look at the research interests of the political science professors at Missouri Western to see if anyone might be able to provide me with insight on the wars from an academic perspective.

I have already located three books on the subject through the library's catalog, and by reading through the citations and sources used by the authors of these books, I have identified several other books that I might explore. In addition, I have used simple keyword and advanced searches on EBSCOhost, LexisNexis, and *NYTimes.com* to find several magazine, newspaper, and scholarly journal articles that provide contrasting viewpoints on the use of PMCs. They range from first-person accounts of PMC operations to academic articles analyzing the history and current use of PMCs.

I'd also like to take a look at some official government reports and read the actual language of some of the laws that surround PMCs. The Department of Defense Web site as well as senators' and representatives' Web sites might be good places to start.

> Nicholas identifies both a general search idea and a specific plan to carry out the search.

Brothers 3

Once my first draft is complete, I might conduct another round of research to help answer any new questions or expand on new supporting points that I've developed.

Project Timeline: I have a little more than one month to complete this project. I already have several solid sources and plan to have my first assignment (the background paper based on what I know so far) completed one week from today. The next week, I'll conduct my interviews and write an interview paper based on my conversations. From there, I will combine the background paper and the interview paper, synthesizing these two drafts along with any new sources I've found. I will receive feedback on my first draft from my classmates and instructor. Then, I'll conduct any additional research needed and revise the draft by the due date of Oct. 20th. After the final draft is submitted, I'll create a reverse outline and summarize my paper's most important points for a brief in-class presentation the following week.

> A general project timeline indicates the time devoted to each stage of the process.

Key Challenges: Finding knowledgeable first-hand sources will be the main problem I will encounter, but I have some candidates in mind in helping me to understand the perceptions of U.S. military personnel, the history of mercenaries, and the political ramifications of their present-day use by the United States. I will contact them soon to inquire about their willingness and availability. I feel that I have already amassed a good deal of research material and plans, but I am wary that my sources so far might be geared toward my inherent bias toward the subject. I would like to make sure I have real opposing views to explore and not just straw men; this is a goal I will continually have to work toward.

> Writing down key challenges helps Nicholas avoid potential problems.

Time is another challenge. I have to conduct field research quickly and synthesize the results of the interview paper with the rest of my research in a short amount of time to create a first draft. I'm also concerned about focusing my topic enough for the paper to make sense — there are a lot of issues related to my topic that are intriguing, from the history of mercenaries to the legal status of PMCs and their lack of culpability for their crimes. Limiting the scope of my project could be difficult given the many aspects of the topic that seem worth addressing.

Working Bibliography

Scahill, Jeremy. *Blackwater: The Rise of the World's Most Powerful Mercenary Army.* 2nd ed. New York: Nation Books, 2007. Print.

This book details the history of the private military corporation formerly known as Blackwater, with a focus on its controversial operations in Iraq and Afghanistan. Scahill is a reporter for *The Nation* and has reported extensively on Blackwater. I will use this book throughout my research project, as Blackwater (now Xe Services) remains one of the most powerful, visible, and divisive PMCs in the world.

Singer, P. W. *Corporate Warriors: The Rise of the Privatized Military Industry.* 2nd ed. Ithaca: Cornell UP, 2008. Print.

This scholarly look at the issue takes a balanced view: Singer is able to see the opportunities that PMCs provide while casting a critical eye at the potentials for abuse. I believe this will be an essential resource due to its balanced viewpoint and thoroughness.

Smith, Eugene B. "The New Condottieri and US Policy: The Privatization of Conflict and Its Implications." *Parameters: US Army War College* 32.4 (2002): 104. *Academic Search Premier.* EBSCO. Web. 11 Feb. 2010.

Written before the invasion of Iraq, this academic article briefly outlines the history of the privatization of warfare and concludes that the United States should employ PMCs due to their track record. At the time of this article's writing, Eugene B. Smith was a lieutenant colonel in the United States Army and served in the United States Central Command area of operations. This article might be useful in understanding the mindset of the military command that has increasingly employed private contractors in the last decade.

The working bibliography summarizes sources and evaluates their usefulness.

My Research Project

Create a Research Proposal

Use the following activity to create a formal research proposal.

1. Provide the working title for your project.

2. Describe your issue.

3. Describe your purpose for working on this project.

4. Describe your readers' needs, interests, knowledge, experiences, values, and beliefs.

5. State your research question.

6. Briefly review key findings about your issue from the sources you found as you explored your topic.

7. Indicate how you'll locate additional information, ideas, and arguments about your issue.

8. Include your project timeline.

9. Include your working bibliography.

10. Discuss the key challenges you face (optional).

11. Identify specific funding requests (optional).

bedfordresearcher.com
My Research Project Activities > Create a Research Proposal

> **QUICK REFERENCE**

Developing Your Research Question and Proposal

☑ Reflect on your issue and disciplinary or professional context. (p. 46)

☑ Consider how your role will shape your research question. (p. 47)

☑ Focus on specific aspects of your issue. (p. 47)

☑ Choose and focus your research question. (p. 50)

☑ Refine your research question. (p. 53)

☑ Develop a research proposal. (p. 57)

The Bedford Researcher

I	Joining the Conversation
II	**Working with Sources**
III	Collecting Information
IV	Creating Your Document
V	Documenting Sources

PART II

Working with Sources

As you work with sources, you'll read critically, evaluate sources, take notes, manage the sources you collect, and guard against unintentional plagiarism. The next five chapters lead you through the process of engaging with the information, ideas, and arguments you will encounter as you work on your research writing project.

Part II
Working with Sources

4	**Reading Critically and Actively**
5	Evaluating Sources
6	Taking Notes
7	Managing Information
8	Avoiding Plagiarism

4

Reading Critically and Actively

> **Key Questions**
>

As you've explored your topic, you've almost certainly read—or, more likely, skimmed—several sources. As you focus your attention on a particular issue, you'll begin to read more carefully, both to learn more about the issue and to understand how you might position your contribution to the issue in light of what others have written. In this chapter, you'll learn how to read sources critically and actively.

4a

How can I read sources critically?

Reading critically means reading with an attitude. It also means reading with your writing situation and research question in mind. Unlike evaluation, which focuses on the suitability of a source for your argument, critical reading is a flexible process that will differ at various points in your research writing process. Through critical reading, you can quickly recognize the questions—points of disagreement, uncertainty, concern, or curiosity—that are under discussion in a written conversation as well as think about how you'll respond to one of these questions.

Read with an Attitude

Reading critically means reading with an attitude. Your attitude will change during your research writing process. As you begin to read your sources critically, your attitude might be one of curiosity. You'll note new information and mark key passages that provide you with insights into the conversation you're joining. You'll adopt a more questioning attitude as you try to determine whether sources fit in your project or are reliable. Later, after you begin to draw conclusions about the conversation, you might take on a more skeptical attitude, becoming more aggressive in challenging arguments made in sources than you were at first.

Regardless of where you are in your research writing process, you should always adopt a critical attitude. Accept nothing at face value; ask questions; look for similarities and differences among the sources you read; examine the implications of what you read for your research project; be on the alert for unusual information; and note relevant sources and information. Most important, be open to ideas and arguments, even if you don't agree with them. Give them a chance to affect how you think about the conversation you've decided to join.

Distinguish between Critical Reading and Evaluating

At first glance, reading critically might seem to be the same as evaluating, which is discussed in detail in the next chapter. Although the two processes are related, they're not identical. Critically reading a source—questioning what it says and thinking about what it means—focuses your attention on making sense of the source. In contrast, evaluation focuses your attention on determining how reliably a source presents its information and how well it meets your needs as a research writer.

 bedfordresearcher.com
LearningCurve > Critical Reading

Approach a Source with Your Writing Situation in Mind **?** **WHAT'S MY PURPOSE?**

One way to get into the habit of reading critically is to approach a source with your writing situation in mind (see Table 4.1). As you read, remember that you are working on your research writing project to make a contribution, to shape

TABLE 4.1 READ A SOURCE WITH YOUR WRITING SITUATION IN MIND

Reflect on . . .	By asking . . .
Your Research Question and Position Statement	Are the information, ideas, and arguments in this source relevant to my research question and position statement?
	Does this source present information, ideas, and arguments that make me reconsider my research question or position statement?
	Does this source provide any new information, ideas, or arguments?
	Does this source offer a new perspective on the conversation?
Your Purpose and Role	Will the information in this source help me accomplish my purpose? Can I use the information in this source as support for points I want to make? Can I use it to illustrate ideas that differ from mine?
	Is the information in this source more useful for my purpose than what I've found in other sources?
	Does the source provide a good model of a convincing argument or an effective presentation of information? Can I learn anything from the presentation of the points and evidence in this source?
Your Readers	Would my readers want to know about the information, ideas, and arguments found in this source?
	Would my readers find the source's information convincing or compelling?
	Would my readers benefit from a review of the argument and evidence presented in this source?
	What are my readers likely to think about the argument and evidence presented in this source? How will they respond to them?
Genre	What type of evidence is usually provided in this type of document?
	How are documents of this type typically organized? Can I find examples of effective organizational strategies in the sources I read?
Design	Does this source provide a useful model for designing my document?
	Will I be expected to provide charts, graphics, photographs, or other types of illustrations? If so, can I learn anything from how illustrations are used in the source?
	Does this source help me understand how I might address the context in which my document will be read?
Requirements and Limitations	If I find useful information in a source, will I be able to follow up on it with additional research? Will I have enough time to follow up on that information?
	How much information can I include in my document? Will my readers be looking for a general overview or a detailed report?

II Working with Sources

your readers' thinking about your issue. Don't hesitate to question the authors who have written before you. You should respect their work, but you shouldn't assume that their conclusions are the last word. Be prepared to challenge their ideas and arguments. If you don't do this, you'll simply repeat the ideas of others instead of advancing your own.

Read Promising Sources More than Once

As you work through your sources, you'll find that many are less relevant to your research project than you'd hoped when you collected them. When you come across one of these sources, move on to the next source. Other sources are worth reading more carefully. When a source offers what appears to be good information, ideas, or arguments, use a three-pass approach.

1. Skim the source to get a general idea of its organization and content (p. 74).
2. Read actively, marking and annotating relevant passages in the text and taking notes on important information, ideas, and arguments (p. 74). Consider the writer's interpretive framework (p. 80), if relevant, and look for similarities and differences among your sources (p. 84).
3. Reread passages that are either particularly promising or difficult to understand (p. 84).

Develop a Position on Your Research Question [FRAMING MY ARGUMENT]

Your research question focuses your attention on your issue, provides the foundation for your search plan, and directs you to specific sources as you collect information. Your research question also provides the basis for developing a position on your issue, which you can also use to guide your critical reading.

The position you develop on your issue serves as an answer to your research question. At this point in your research writing process, your position on your issue is likely to be tentative and incomplete. As you learn more about your issue by reading critically, however, you'll develop and refine your position. Your position, in turn, will provide a foundation for your thesis statement—a formal statement of the main point you want to make about your issue. Figure 4.1 shows the progression from research question to position statement to thesis statement in the context of the research writing process.

As a response to your research question, your position can help you decide whether you agree or disagree with an author—and, thus, whether you want to align yourself with his or her position on the issue. It will also help you judge whether the evidence provided in a source might be of use to you as you develop your argument—either to support your own argument or to illustrate an alternative approach to the issue. As you read critically, always keep your position in mind and test it against the information, ideas, and arguments you encounter in

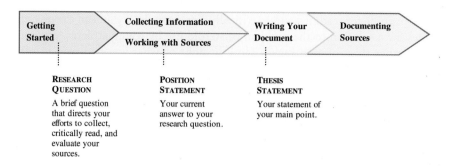

FIGURE 4.1 Moving from a Research Question to a Position Statement to a Thesis Statement

your sources. Remember, however, that your position might change as you learn more about your issue. Be flexible, as a result, and be willing to change your position in response to new and compelling information, ideas, and arguments.

To develop a statement about your position on your issue, brainstorm or freewrite in response to your research question. After reviewing your response, draft a brief statement of your position and use it to guide your critical reading.

Featured Writer Alexis Alvarez's Research Question:

What should be done about steroid use by adolescent girls involved in competitive sports?

Responses:

The typical response to steroid use in sports, such as the Olympics or professional football, seems to be some sort of punishment—losing a medal or being banned from competition for a period of time. But will this work with kids—especially kids who don't seem to have the same level of maturity as older athletes? And what about parents who encourage kids—and most likely provide the funds—to use steroids to get ahead (parents with college scholarship dollars in their eyes, no doubt)? So . . . maybe punishment isn't the answer—or at least it's only part of the answer. It seems from my reading so far that most kids don't understand the negative consequences of using steroids. They only see the potential benefits (making a team, performing at a higher level, getting famous, getting a scholarship, etc.). And parents might not understand those consequences as well. And then some coaches might even get into the act, "helping" kids compete at a higher level, and getting the wins they "need." If kids don't understand the consequences, then education might be useful. And most kids don't like to cheat, so maybe part of the answer is putting more of an emphasis on fair play. And you need to get parents and coaches into some sort of solution too.

Initial Position Statement:

Steroid use by adolescent girls involved in competitive sports might be addressed by educating athletes, parents, and coaches about health consequences and emphasizing fair play.

This statement is too vague to use as a thesis statement, but it would serve as an effective guide for reading sources critically. For example, if you read a source that argues for a solution to the problem of steroid use by young athletes, you could ask whether that solution makes sense in light of what you had read in other sources or whether it is based on a different set of assumptions.

Table 4.2 presents the movement from research question to position statement in the featured writers' projects. Note how each position statement attempts to answer the research question and thus lets readers know what the writer thinks an answer to the research question might be. The development of their position statements marked a significant step for the featured writers in their progress toward writing their final documents. By offering a preliminary answer to their research questions, they began to take ownership of their work: They shifted their focus from learning about the conversations they had decided to join to beginning to develop their contributions to the conversations.

TABLE 4.2 THE FEATURED WRITERS' POSITION STATEMENTS

Featured Writer	Research Question	Position Statement
Alexis Alvarez	What should be done about steroid use by adolescent girls involved in competitive sports?	Steroid use by adolescent girls involved in competitive sports should be addressed by educating athletes, parents, and coaches about health consequences and emphasizing fair play.
Nicholas Brothers	What dangers are associated with U.S. reliance on private military corporations in its war on terror?	The overreliance of the United States on private military corporations is a danger to national and international security.
Elizabeth Leontiev	How can we reduce the economic impact of the war on drugs on South American coca farmers?	The U.S. and South American governments should adopt the "zero cocaine, not zero coca" policy.
Lauren Mack	Why are coral reefs important, and what can be done to protect them from destruction?	Preserving the many benefits of coral reefs—which range from recreational uses, sea life habitats, and potential medical benefits from the species who live in and around them—can be accomplished by working to stop climate change.
Cori Schmidtbauer	How does Portia's character in The Merchant of Venice fit in with Elizabethan ideas of women?	Portia appears to rebel against the expectations of Elizabethan culture.

Featured Writer	Research Question	Position Statement
Brandon Tate	What do individuals need to know to develop informed opinions about the controversial issue of hydraulic fracturing?	Voters should understand the impact of hydraulic fracturing on the environment, the oil and gas industry, and the economy.
Josh Woelfle	What makes new cancer treatments potentially superior to traditional treatments such as chemotherapy and radiation?	In combination with efforts to address multi-drug resistant strains of cancer, enzyme inhibitor-based drugs can combat the disease with far fewer and far less serious side effects.

My Research Project

Draft a Position Statement

In your research log, complete the following activity to draft your position statement.

1. Write your current research question.

2. Brainstorm or freewrite in response to your research question.

3. Select the response that best reflects your current understanding of the conversation you have decided to join. If appropriate, combine responses into one position statement.

4. Write your position statement.

bedfordresearcher.com
My Research Project Activities > Draft a Position Statement

4b

What strategies can I use to read actively?

Once you have thought about your writing situation, drafted your position statement, and decided what to focus on, you're ready to start reading actively. Reading actively means interacting with sources and considering them in light of the conversation you've decided to join. When you read actively, you might do one or more of the following.

- Identify key information, ideas, and arguments by skimming and marking.
- Write questions in the margins.
- Jot down reactions to information, ideas, and arguments.
- Record quotations, paraphrases, and summaries in the form of notes.
- Take notes about how you might use information, ideas, and arguments in your project document.

- Link one part of the source to another visually.
- Identify important passages for later rereading.

As you read sources, use three active-reading strategies: skimming, marking and annotating, and taking notes.

Skim for Organization and Content

Before investing too much time in a source, skim it. Skimming—reading just enough to get a general idea of what a source is about—helps you understand how a source is organized, which can help you more quickly assess its usefulness and relevance. If the source uses a familiar organizational pattern, you'll find it easier to locate key information. You can see examples of what to pay attention to as you skim print documents and Web pages on pages 36–38.

Mark and Annotate Sources

As you read, mark key passages by highlighting or underlining, and make annotations to remind yourself of the importance or potential uses of the information, ideas, and arguments in the passage. Keep your writing situation in mind as you make your annotations. Consider your purpose and role as a writer, and think about your readers' needs, interests, knowledge, experiences, values, and beliefs. Use your annotations to call attention to how you might use the information in each marked or highlighted passage to accomplish your goals as a writer.

Common marking techniques include:

- using a highlighter, a pen, or a pencil to identify key passages in a print source
- attaching notes or flags to printed pages
- highlighting passages in digital texts

You can further engage with your sources by writing brief annotations, or notes, in the margins of print sources and by using commenting tools for digital sources. Many research writers use annotations in combination with marking (see Figure 4.2). If you have highlighted a passage (marking) with which you disagree, as might happen as you read a source with your position in mind, you can write a brief note about why you disagree with the passage (annotating). You might make note of another source you've read that could support your argument, or you might write a reminder about the need to look for information that will help you argue against the passage.

Take Notes

Notes provide a compact, easy-to-review record of the most important information, ideas, and arguments you've found in your sources. Notes can help you keep track of your ideas about significant patterns you've seen in your sources, such as

FIGURE 4.2 Marking and Annotating Sources with Your Argument in Mind [Cato Institute.]

similarities and differences, repeated ideas and arguments, and frequently cited information. Notes can also help you keep track of your thoughts about planning your document. Equally important, careful note taking helps you avoid plagiarism. For these reasons, note taking is one of the most important research writing skills you can draw on as you work on your research writing project.

Notes can include direct quotations, paraphrases, and summaries, as well as your thoughts about your sources as a group and your plans for your document. You can read more about taking notes in Chapter 6. You can read about avoiding plagiarism in Chapter 8.

Source information

Page number

Source: Singer, P. W. *Corporate Warriors: The Rise of the Privatized Military Industry.* Cornell UP, 2008.

Page 157:

The U.S. Defense Science Board estimated that the Department of Defense would save over $6 billion by privatizing and outsourcing in the early 1990s, but these savings have not been demonstrated. One report (RAND) claimed there were no cost savings at all; another (GAO) stated that the estimate was inflated by a minimum of $4.5 billion.

"The recurring pattern is that the military has set a policy of becoming more businesslike. It has not, however, fully examined whether doing so saves money or improves operations."

Paraphrase, written in student's own words

Direct quotation from the source clearly marked with quotation marks

FIGURE 4.3 Notes on a Source

CHECKLIST FOR ACTIVE READING

To read actively, follow these guidelines.

✔ Skim sources to identify key information, ideas, and arguments.

✔ Highlight, underline, add arrows, or draw circles around important passages.

✔ Write questions, jot down reactions, and add reminders in the margins or in digital comments.

✔ Take notes.

4c

What should I pay attention to as I read?

Different research writing projects will require you to pay attention to different things as you read. In general, however, you should pay attention to the following.

- the type of source—or genre—you are reading
- illustrations
- whether the source is a primary or secondary source
- the author's main point
- reasons and evidence offered to support the main point

TUTORIAL

How can I read actively?

Marking and annotating allow you to identify key information, ideas, and arguments; record your reactions to a source; question the source; connect the source to other sources; and note how you might use information, ideas, and arguments.

In this example, featured writer Josh Woelfle marks and annotates a fact sheet from the National Cancer Institute's Web site. Later, he will use information from the fact sheet to shape his argument about the advantages of promising alternative treatments for cancer. [CBS News.]

1 Identify key information, ideas, and arguments.

2 Write questions in the margins.

3 Record your reactions to information, ideas, and arguments in the margins.

4 Note how you might use information, ideas, and arguments in your project document.

5 Link parts of the text visually.

6 Identify important passages for later rereading.

∥ **Wroking with Sources**

- any analytical or interpretive approaches used by the author
- new information (information you haven't read before)
- ideas and information that you find difficult to understand
- ideas and information that are similar to or different from those you have found in other sources

Noting these aspects of a source during your active reading will help you better understand the source, its role in the conversation you've decided to join, and how you might use it in your document.

bedfordresearcher.com
Critical Reading > Active
Reading Strategies

Identify the Genre

One of the most important things to pay attention to as you read is the type of source — or genre — you are reading. If a source is an opinion column rather than an objective summary of an argument, for example, you'll be less likely to be taken in by a questionable use of logic or analysis. If you are reading an annual corporate report for stockholders in a company, you'll recognize that the primary concern of the writers is to present the company in as positive a light as possible. If an article comes from a peer-reviewed scholarly journal, you'll be sure that it's been judged by experts in the field as well founded and worthy of publishing.

Recognizing the type of source you are reading will help you create a context for understanding and questioning the information, ideas, and arguments presented in the source.

Note Illustrations

Illustrations — such as photographs and other images, charts, graphs, tables, animations, audio clips, and video clips — are typically used to demonstrate or emphasize a point, help readers better understand a point, clarify or simplify the presentation of a complex concept, or increase the visual appeal of a document. Illustrations can also serve as a form of argument by presenting a surprising or even shocking set of statistics or setting an emotional tone. As you read, be aware of the types of illustrations and the effects they produce. The types of illustrations you are likely to encounter include the following.

- **Photographs and images,** such as drawings, paintings, and sketches, are frequently used to set a mood, emphasize a point, or demonstrate a point more fully than is possible with text alone.

- **Charts and graphs** provide a visual representation of information. They are typically used to present numerical information more succinctly than is possible with text alone or to present complex information in a compact and more accessible form.

- **Tables** provide categorical lists of information. Like charts and graphs, they are typically used to make a point more succinctly than is possible with text alone or to present complex information in a compact form. Tables are frequently used to illustrate contrasts among groups, relationships among variables (such as income, educational attainment, and voting preferences), or change over time (such as growth in population during the past century).

- **Digital illustrations** are found in sources such as PowerPoint presentations, Web pages, and word processing documents. Illustrations such as audio, videos, and animations differ from photographs, images, charts, graphs, and tables in that they don't just appear on the page — they do things.

You can read more about the uses of illustrations in Chapter 18.

Identify Primary and Secondary Sources

Primary sources are either original works or evidence provided directly by an observer of an event. Primary sources include:

- poems, short stories, novels, essays, paintings, musical scores and recordings, sculpture, and other works of art or literature
- diaries, journals, memoirs, and autobiographies
- interviews, speeches, government and business records, letters, and memos
- reports, drawings, photographs, films, or video and audio recordings of an event
- physical artifacts associated with an event, such as a weapon used in a crime or a piece of pottery found in an archaeological dig

Secondary sources comment on or interpret an event, often using primary sources as evidence (see Table 4.3).

As a research writer, you should attempt to obtain as many primary sources as possible so that you can come to your own conclusions about your issue. Remember that your goal is to develop your own ideas about an issue, so that you can create an original, well-supported contribution to the conversation you've decided to join. If you rely entirely or mostly on secondary sources, you'll be viewing the issue through the eyes of other researchers. Be sure to ask yourself, when you read a secondary source, what factors might have affected the author's argument, presentation, or analysis.

TABLE 4.3 EXAMPLES OF PRIMARY AND SECONDARY SOURCES	
Primary Sources	**Secondary Sources**
A play by William Shakespeare	An article that presents an analysis of the play
A transcript of the statement made by President George W. Bush on September 11, 2001	A recording of an interview in which a historian discusses the significance of the statement
A report of a laboratory study concerning the benefits of strength training for women with osteoporosis	A Web site that presents a review of recent research about prevention and treatment of osteoporosis

Working with Sources

Identify Main Points

Most sources, whether they are informative or argumentative, make a main point that you should pay attention to as you read critically. For example:

- an editorial in a local newspaper urges voters to approve financing of a new school
- an article reports a new advance in automobile emissions testing
- a Web page provides information about the benefits of a new technique for treating a sports injury

Usually, but not always, the main point will be expressed in the form of a thesis statement (p. 201). As you read critically, make sure you understand what the author of the source wants readers to know, accept, believe, or do as a result of reading the document.

Identify Reasons and Evidence

Once you've identified the main point, look for the reasons given to accept it. If an author is arguing, for instance, that English should be the only language used for official government business in the United States, that author might support his or her argument with the following reasons.

The use of multiple languages erodes patriotism.

The use of multiple languages keeps people apart—if they can't talk to one another, they won't learn to respect one another.

The use of multiple languages in government business costs taxpayers money because so many alternative forms need to be created.

Reasons can take a wide range of forms and are often presented in forms that appeal to emotions, logic, principles, values, or beliefs (p. 217). As persuasive as these reasons might seem, they are only as good as the evidence offered to support them. In some cases, evidence is offered in the form of statements from experts on a subject or people in positions of authority. In other cases, evidence might include personal experience. In still other cases, evidence might include firsthand observations, excerpts from an interview, or statistical data.

When you find empirical evidence used in a source, consider where the evidence comes from and how it is being used. If the information appears to be presented fairly, ask whether you might be able to use it to support your own ideas, and try to verify its accuracy by consulting additional sources.

Identify Interpretive Frameworks

Writers frequently analyze and interpret the evidence they've presented. As you read a source, keep in mind that any analysis or interpretation, no matter how well grounded in evidence, is subject to the writer's purpose, interests, values, beliefs, and experiences. Try to understand what sort of interpretive framework

WORKING TOGETHER

Follow the Writer's Argument

Working with a group of classmates, identify the main point, reasons, and evidence in Edwin J. Feulner's article, "The Energy Potential of Fracking," (available at http://www.heritage.org/research/commentary/2013/2/the-energy-potential-of-fracking).

1 List the main point at the top of your page. Determine what the writer is asking you to know, believe, or do.

2 Briefly list each reason to accept the main point in the order in which it appears in the source. You might want to brainstorm lists individually based on your reading of the article and then share your ideas to create the group's list.

3 Once you've agreed on the reasons, work together to identify the most important evidence used to support each reason.

is being used to analyze and make claims about the evidence the writer presents in the document.

An interpretive framework is a set of strategies for identifying patterns. Typically, these frameworks have been used successfully and refined over time by writers interested in a given subject area or working in a particular field. Writers can choose from hundreds (perhaps thousands) of specialized frameworks used in disciplines across the arts, sciences, social sciences, humanities, engineering, and business. A historian, for example, might apply a feminist, social, political, or cultural analysis to interpret diaries written by women who worked in defense plants during World War II, while a sociologist might conduct statistical tests to interpret the results of a survey. As you read sources, pay particular attention to writers who use five broad interpretive frameworks: trend analysis, causal analysis, data analysis, text analysis, and rhetorical analysis.

Trend analysis   Trends are patterns that hold up over time. Trend analysis, as a result, focuses on sequences of events and the relationships among them. It is based on the assumption that understanding what has happened in the past will allow us to make sense of what is happening in the present and to draw inferences about what is likely to happen in the future.

Trends can be identified and analyzed in nearly every field, from politics to consumer affairs to the arts. Economists interested in rising fuel prices, for example, often turn to historical accounts of similar fuel crises in the 1970s to understand recent increases. Sports and entertainment analysts, as well, frequently turn to trend analysis—in attempts to forecast the next NBA champion, for instance, or to explain the reemergence of superheroes in popular culture during the last decade.

As you read sources that use trend analysis, keep in mind that claims based on this form of analysis typically present historical information (sometimes in the form of statistics), argue that a trend exists, and then draw conclusions based on the existence of that trend. Ask yourself, as you read sources using this form of analysis, whether sufficient evidence exists to establish a trend, whether appropriate evidence has been used, and whether alternative conclusions might be drawn from the same evidence.

Causal analysis   Causal analysis focuses on the factors that bring about a particular situation, such as the dot-com collapse in the late 1990s, the rise of terrorist groups, or the impact of calorie restriction on longevity. Writers use causal analysis when they believe that understanding the underlying reasons for a situation will help people address the situation, influence the likelihood of it happening again, or appreciate its potential consequences.

As you read sources that use causal analysis, ask whether the writer has identified multiple causes (since most effects are the result of more than a single cause), whether the writer has identified important causes (since some causes are far more important than others), and whether the writer has confused correlation with causation. Correlation is the observation that two things are related. It's been shown, for example, that people who own large, expensive homes often drive luxury cars. Most people would agree, however, that it would be foolish to think that the best way to get a nice new home is to buy an expensive car. Instead, they'd point out that there are other factors — such as a high income combined with a desire to live in a nice home and drive an expensive car — that are the likely causes.

Data analysis   Data can include a wide range of evidence, including facts, observations, survey responses, statistics, and other forms of numerical information, such as measurements or test scores. Writers frequently use data to make claims about an issue.

Data analysis is something most people do on a regular basis. If you've looked at the percentage of people who favor one particular political candidate over another, for example, you've engaged in data analysis. Similarly, if you've checked your bank account to determine whether you have enough money for a new coat, you've carried out a form of data analysis. Writers typically analyze numerical information to help readers better understand an issue, to look for differences, and to explore relationships.

As you read sources that use this form of analysis, ask whether the writer has presented sufficient evidence to support his or her analysis and whether the reasoning presented by the writer is rigorous and fair. For example, if someone is arguing that a recent survey provides enough evidence for the adoption of a new policy, ask how many people were surveyed and whether they represent a broad cross section of the population. You should also ask whether the writer has described the statistical methods used to make the claim and, if so, whether the methods are appropriate.

Keep in mind as well the common problems that sources relying on data analysis can suffer from, such as base-rate fallacies and cherry picking. An example of a base-rate fallacy would be a claim that drinking a particular drink, such as coffee, can double your risk of developing cancer. If the initial risk was one in ten million, this means that the new risk is two in ten million—far less than the chance of getting in an accident as you drive to the coffee shop. Cherry picking involves selecting only those findings that support a writer's conclusions, rather than reporting all of the relevant findings.

Text analysis Today, the word *text* can refer to a wide range of printed or digital works—and even some forms of artistic expression that we'd be hard pressed to think of as documents. Texts open to interpretation include novels, poems, plays, essays, articles, movies, speeches, blogs, songs, paintings, photographs, sculptures, performances, Web pages, videos, television shows, and computer games.

Many writers use the elements of literary analysis to analyze texts. In this form of analysis, interpreters focus on theme, plot, setting, characterization, imagery, style, and structure as well as the contexts—social, cultural, political, and historical—that shape a work. Writers who use this form of analysis focus both on what is actually presented in the text and what is implied or conveyed "between the lines." They rely heavily on close reading of the text to discern meaning, critique a writer's technique, and search for patterns that will help them understand the text as fully as possible. They also tend to consider and include in their analysis other elements of the wider writing situation in which the text was produced—in particular, the writer's purpose, intended audience, use of sources, and choice of genre.

As you read sources that use text analysis, ask whether the claims made about the text are supported by evidence drawn from the text itself. Be wary of situations in which the writer simply uses the text as a point of departure, rather than offering evidence in the form of quotations, paraphrases, and summaries. Ask as well whether the writer is considering the text in its entirety. In some cases, writers pick and choose from a text and ignore its overall meaning.

Rhetorical analysis In much the same way that writers assess the writing situations that shape work on their documents, they can use rhetorical analysis to contribute to a conversation. In response to the argument in a particular document (written, visual, or some other form), for example, a writer might use rhetorical analysis to explain the origins or purposes of the argument.

As you read sources that use rhetorical analysis, focus on how the various aspects of the rhetorical situation—writers and purpose, writers' roles, readers/audience, sources, and contexts—contribute to the argument used in a document. Determine as well whether the analysis focuses on argument. Many sources that employ rhetorical analysis address the structure of an argument (p. 224), focusing on the writer's use of appeals—such as appeals to logic, emotion, character, and so on (p. 217)—and the quality of the evidence that was provided. Similarly, sources that use rhetorical analysis sometimes criticize an argument by exposing its use of logical fallacies (p. 221). In general, when argument is a key part of a rhetorical analysis, the writer will typically connect the analysis to one or more of the major elements of the rhetorical situation.

II Working with Sources

Identify New and Hard-to-Understand Information

As you read, mark and annotate passages that contain two types of information: new information and information that you initially find hard to understand. Keep track of new information in your research log in the form of a list or as a series of brief descriptions of what you've learned and where you learned it.

You might be tempted, as many writers are, to ignore information that's hard to understand. If you skip over this information, however, you might miss something that is critical to the success of your research project. When you encounter information that's difficult to understand, mark it and make a brief annotation reminding yourself to check it out later.

Sometimes you'll learn enough from your reading of other sources that the passage won't seem as difficult when you come back to it later. And sometimes you'll still be faced with a passage that's impossible to figure out on your own. In this case, turn to other resources or someone else for advice.

Search a database, library catalog, or the Web using words you didn't understand in the source.

Ask your instructor or a librarian for help.

Ask a question about the passage on a newsgroup or electronic mailing list.

Interview an expert in the area.

Identify Similarities and Differences

You can learn a lot by looking for similarities and differences among the sources you read. For example, you might identify a group of authors who take a similar approach to an issue, such as favoring increased government support for research on alternative forms of cancer treatment. You could then contrast this group with other groups of authors, such as those who argue that we should focus on improving conventional treatments and those who believe that government funding would be better spent on seeking cures for cancer. Similarly, you can make note of information in one source that agrees or disagrees with information in another.

CHECKLIST FOR CRITICAL READING

To read critically, pay attention to the following aspects of a source.

✔ Identify the genre.

✔ Note useful illustrations.

✔ Note whether the document is a primary or secondary source.

✔ Identify the main point.

✔ Identify reasons and evidence.

✔ If analysis is used, identify the type of interpretive framework that is used.

✔ Identify new and hard-to-understand information.

✔ Compare the source with the other sources you've read.

These notes can help you build your own argument or identify information that will allow you (and potentially your readers) to better understand the issue.

My Research Project

Note Connections among Sources

In your research log, identify connections among your sources.

1. Do your sources tend to fall into one or more genres, such as scholarly articles, books, blog entries, or Web pages? If so, identify the most common genres.

2. Do your sources tend to be primary or secondary sources, or a mix of the two types? Why do you think you're seeing this pattern?

3. Do the authors of your sources tend to agree with each other? Disagree? Fall into various groups? Describe the pattern you see.

4. Does the information in one or more sources contradict information in other sources? If so, where are you seeing the contradiction and what do you think is causing it?

5. Do authors tend to rely on similar arguments and evidence? If so, describe the arguments and evidence.

6. Are any sources cited frequently by the authors of your sources? If so, identify the source.

7. What interpretive frameworks are found in your sources? Are any of them used in more than one source? If so, why do you think they are relying on this framework or frameworks?

bedfordresearcher.com
My Research Project Activities > Note Connections among Sources

> ## QUICK REFERENCE

Reading Critically and Actively

☑ Read with an attitude, keeping in mind the following: your research question and position statement; your purpose; your readers' needs, interests, knowledge, experiences, values, and beliefs; the type of document you will write and the context in which it will be read; and your requirements and limitations. (p. 68)

☑ Read promising sources multiple times, first skimming, then reading actively, then rereading important passages. (p. 70)

☑ Draft a position statement. (p. 73)

☑ Mark, annotate, and take notes on your sources. (p. 74)

☑ Identify the genre of a source, useful illustrations, primary and secondary sources, main points, reasons and evidence, interpretive frameworks, new and hard-to-understand information, and similarities and differences among sources. (p. 78)

II Working with Sources

Part II
Working with Sources

4	Reading Critically and Actively
5	**Evaluating Sources**
6	Taking Notes
7	Managing Information
8	Avoiding Plagiarism

5

Evaluating Sources

> **Key Questions**
>

At the beginning of a research project, you'll most likely make quick judgments about your sources. Skimming an article, a book, or a Web site might be enough to tell you that spending more time with the source would be wasted effort. As you encounter a new source, determine how well it meets your needs as a research writer and how reliably it presents information, ideas, and arguments.

5a

What factors should I use to evaluate a source?

Evaluating a source means examining its relevance, evidence, author, publisher, timeliness, comprehensiveness, and genre.

Evaluate Relevance   **?**   **WHAT'S MY PURPOSE?**

Relevance is the extent to which a source provides information you can use in your research writing project. The most important questions you should ask to determine the relevance of a source are about your purpose and readers.

In the course of your research, you might find a number of information-filled sources. If the information is not relevant, however, it won't help you fulfill your purpose. For example, a review of Apple's iOS operating system might contain accurate and up-to-date information, but if you're writing about the monopolistic practices of leading hardware manufacturers, this source probably won't be of much use to you.

The information in a source should also be useful to your readers. You might be tempted to include a beautifully worded quotation, but if your readers won't see how it contributes to your document, don't use it. Your readers will expect information that meets their needs. If they want to read about downloading music online, for instance, pass up sources that focus only on traditional music publishers.

Evaluate Evidence

Evidence is information offered to support an author's reasoning about an issue (p. 80). Evidence is connected to reasons through appeals to authority, emotion, principles, values, beliefs, character, and logic. It can also include measurements and observations, typically referred to as empirical evidence. An argument in favor of charging local sales tax on Web-based purchases might use statistics — a form of empirical evidence. It could calculate the revenue a town of fifty thousand might lose if 5 percent of its citizens made fifteen online purchases in a given year. As a research writer, you can evaluate not only the kind of information used in a source but also the quality, amount, and appropriateness of that evidence. Ask the following questions about each source.

- **Is enough evidence offered?** A lack of evidence might indicate fundamental flaws in the author's argument.

- **Is the right kind of evidence offered?** More evidence isn't always better evidence. As you evaluate a source, ask yourself whether the evidence is appropriate for the points being made. Ask as well whether more than one type of evidence is being used. Many sources rely far too heavily on a single type, such as personal experience or anecdotal evidence.

- **Is the evidence used fairly?** Look for reasonable alternative interpretations, questionable or inappropriate use of evidence, and evidence that seems to contradict points made elsewhere in a source. If statistics are offered as evidence, ask yourself whether they are interpreted fairly or presented clearly. If a quotation is used to support a point, try to determine whether it is used appropriately.

- **Is the source of the evidence provided?** Knowing the origins of evidence can make a significant difference in your evaluation of a source. For example, if a source quotes a political poll but doesn't indicate which organization conducted the poll, you might question the reliability of the source.

‖ Working with Sources

Evaluate the Author

In addition to relevance and evidence, you can evaluate a source based on who wrote it. Take, for example, two editorials published in your local newspaper that make similar arguments and offer similar evidence. One is written by a fourteen-year-old middle school student, the other by a U.S. senator. You would certainly favor an editorial written by the senator if the subject was U.S. foreign policy. If the subject was student perceptions about drug abuse prevention in schools, however, you might value the middle school student's opinion more highly.

The importance of authorship as an evaluation criterion varies from source to source. In some cases, including many Web sites, you won't even know who the author is. In other cases, such as signed opinion columns in a newspaper or magazine, your evaluation could be affected by knowing that the author is politically conservative, liberal, or moderate. Similarly, you might find it useful to know that a message published on a Web discussion forum or message board was written by someone who is recognized as an expert in the field.

Ask the following questions about the author of a source.

- **Is the author knowledgeable about the topic?** It can be difficult to judge an author because expertise can be gained in many ways. An author might be an acknowledged expert in a field; he or she might be a reporter who has written extensively about a topic; or he or she might be recounting firsthand experiences. Then again, an author might have little or no experience with a topic beyond a desire to say something about it. How can you tell the difference? Look for a description of the author in the source. If none is provided, see what you can find out about the author by searching the Web (p. 143).

- **What is the author's affiliation?** Knowing the institution, agency, or organization that employs the author or the political party or organizations to which the author belongs can help you evaluate the assumptions that inform a source.

- **How do the author's biases affect the information, ideas, and arguments in the source?** We all have a bias—a set of interests that shapes our perceptions of a topic. As you evaluate a source, consider the extent to which the author's biases affect the presentation of information, ideas, and arguments in the source. To uncover an author's biases, try to learn more about his or her affiliations. You might infer a bias, for instance, if you learn that an author writes frequently about gun control regulations and works for the National Firearms Association.

Evaluate the Publisher

A publisher is a person or group that prints or produces the documents written by authors. Publishers provide access to print or digital sources, including books, newspapers, journals, Web sites, sound and video files, and databases. Some documents—such as personal blog posts or sources obtained through field research—have no publisher.

You can make informed judgments about publishers in much the same way that you can evaluate authors. Ask the following questions about the publisher of a source.

- **How can I locate information about the publisher?** If a publisher is listed in a print document, search for information about the publisher on the Web. You can often tell whether a publisher is reputable by looking at the types of material it publishes. If you are viewing a document on the Web, search for a link to the site's home page.

- **How do the publisher's biases affect the information, ideas, and arguments in the source?** Like authors, publishers have biases. Unlike authors, they often advertise them. Many publishers have a mission statement on their Web sites, while others present information on their Web pages that can help you figure out their bias. You might already know a fair amount about the biases of a publisher, particularly if the publisher is a major newspaper or magazine, such as the *New York Times* (regarded as liberal) or the *Wall Street Journal* (regarded as conservative). If the publisher is a scholarly or professional journal, you can often gain an understanding of its biases by looking over the contents of several issues or by reading a few of its articles.

Evaluate Timeliness

The importance of timeliness — a source's publication date — varies according to your writing situation. If your research project would benefit from sources that have recently been published, then evaluate recent sources more favorably than dated ones. If you're writing an article on the use of superconducting materials in new mass transportation projects, you probably won't want to spend a lot of time with articles published in 1968. On the other hand, if you're writing about the 1968 presidential contest between Hubert Humphrey and Richard Nixon, sources published during that time period will take on greater importance.

Print sources usually list a publication date. It can be more difficult, however, to tell when Web sources were created. When in doubt, back up undated information found on the Web with a dated source.

Evaluate Comprehensiveness

Comprehensiveness is the extent to which a source provides a complete and balanced view of a topic. Like timeliness, the importance of comprehensiveness varies according to the demands of your writing situation. If you are working on a narrowly focused project, such as the role played by shifts in Pacific Ocean currents on snowfall patterns in Colorado in the winter of 2008, you might not find this evaluation criterion as useful as the others. However, if you are considering a broader issue, such as the potential effects of global climate change on agricultural production in North America, or if you are still learning as much as you can about your issue, give preference to sources that provide full treatment.

Evaluate Genre   [FRAMING MY ARGUMENT]

Identifying the genre — or document type — of the source you are evaluating can help you understand a great deal about its intended readers, the kind of appeals and evidence it is likely to use, and the kind of argument it is likely to make. An article in a professional journal, for example, will almost certainly rely on published sources or original research, and it will carefully document its sources so that its readers can locate related documents easily. In contrast, a blog entry is more likely to rely on personal observation and reflection or on responding to events or arguments made in other blogs and is far less likely, as a result, to contain extensive documentation of sources.

Understanding the types of documents that are typically used in the genre you've selected for your project document can help you make an effective argument. By choosing sources that your readers will recognize as appropriate and reasonable, you can increase the chances that your project will be successful. To evaluate a genre, ask the following questions.

- **What style of writing does the genre use?** Ask how formally (or informally) the document is written. Check for the use of specialized terms that might be unfamiliar to general readers. Try to understand how the writer views himself or herself in relation to readers.

- **How is evidence used?** Identify numerical information; quotations and paraphrases; summaries of other documents; charts, graphs, and tables; and images and other illustrations. Ask yourself why the writer would choose the types of evidence you've found in the document.

- **How is the genre organized?** Try to break the document into major sections. Ask whether you've seen this type of organization used in other documents, and think about the purposes of those documents. You'll often find that documents within a genre are organized in similar ways.

- **How is the document designed?** A document's appearance can tell you a great deal about its purpose, intended readers, and likely means of distribution. Ask about its medium — print or digital. Ask whether it uses color, columns of text, images, and other illustrations. Ask what types of readers might appreciate the use of these design elements; then ask what effects these elements might have on potential readers.

As you consider which sources are best suited for your writing project, keep in mind the importance of referring to types of sources that your readers will recognize as relevant, reliable, and authoritative. An important part of your purpose as a writer is to influence your readers, and the sources you use to support your argument will have an impact on them. Featured writer Brandon Tate, for example, might have drawn supporting evidence for his argument about hydraulic fracturing from a wide range of blogs, personal Web sites, discussion forums, and magazine articles. Instead, he chose to rely primarily on government reports, such as an Environmental Protection Agency summary of carbon dioxide emissions, because he knew government reports are generally recognized as credible, reliable, and authoritative (see Figure 5.1).

bedfordresearcher.com
Critical Reading > Reading Visuals: Audience

FIGURE 5.1 Brandon Tate Relied Heavily on Government Reports [U.S. Energy Information Administration.]

CHECKLIST FOR EVALUATING SOURCES

✔ **Determine whether the source is relevant.** Will the source help you accomplish your purpose and address your readers' needs and interests?

✔ **Determine whether the source provides evidence and uses it appropriately.** Is enough evidence of the right kind offered? Is evidence used fairly, is it convincing, and is its source provided?

✔ **Learn about the author of the source.** Ask whether the author is knowledgeable. Try to determine the author's affiliation and consider how the author's biases affect the information, ideas, and arguments in the source.

✔ **Learn about the publisher of the source.** Try to locate information about the publisher, and reflect on how the publisher's biases affect the information, ideas, and arguments in the source.

Working with Sources

✔ **Think about the timeliness of the source** and its impact on and relevance to your project.

✔ **Consider the comprehensiveness of the source** and its impact on and relevance to your project.

✔ **Consider the genre of the source** and its impact on the kind of information included in the source, the manner in which information is used by the author, and the likely audience for which the source was written.

My Research Project

Conduct a Source Evaluation

A source evaluation applies the evaluation criteria you've read about in this chapter to a single source. You should consider each criterion in light of your writing situation and then determine the suitability of the source for your research writing project. To carry out a source evaluation, respond to the following prompts.

1. Provide the complete citation for the source.

2. In what ways are the information, ideas, and arguments in the source relevant to your research writing project?

3. Is the line of argument in the source sound and well supported? In what ways can you use it in your project?

4. What have you learned about the author and publisher that would lead you to accept, question, or reject the line of argument presented in the source?

5. In what ways does the publication date of the source affect your judgment of its usefulness for your project?

6. In what ways does the comprehensiveness of the source affect your judgment of its usefulness for your project?

7. In what ways does the genre of the source affect your judgment of its usefulness for your project?

8. In what ways could this source help you achieve your purpose and address the needs and interests of your readers?

9. How are you likely to use this source in your project?

bedfordresearcher.com
My Research Project Activities > Conduct a Source Evaluation

5b

Should I evaluate all types of sources in the same way?

You can apply the general evaluative criteria discussed in the previous section to most types of sources. As you do so, consider the nature and purpose of the source. And keep in mind the specific challenges that digital and field sources can pose during evaluation. The following discussion highlights additional factors to keep in mind as you evaluate these types of sources.

Consider the Purposes and Audiences of Scholarly, Professional, and Popular Sources

Scholarly, professional, and popular sources differ in ways that can have important implications for your use of these sources in your research writing project. Sources in these three general categories typically are written for distinctly different purposes, directed toward readers who have strikingly different levels of expertise on a subject, and undergo widely varying levels of review by experts on a subject. As you evaluate your sources, consider the characteristics of these three types of publications.

bedfordresearcher.com
Critical Reading > Reading
Visuals: Purpose

Scholarly Publications

- Writers are usually scholars or researchers who have significant expertise in a given field.

- Writers expect readers to possess specialized knowledge about the subject and will typically use jargon and refer to analytical frameworks and research methods without elaboration or explanation.

- Writers typically report original research, review original research, or analyze trends in recent research.

- Scholarly publications are almost always peer-reviewed (evaluated by other experts in the same field). Some introductions to journals, letters, and editorials may not be reviewed.

- Scholarly publications include extensive in-text citations and works cited lists or bibliographies.

- Scholarly publications are useful for gaining a detailed understanding of an issue, for learning about the newest scholarly work or research on an issue, and for identifying related work.

- Examples include journal articles, books published by academic and university presses, and papers presented at conferences.

- Scholarly publications are included in databases that focus on particular disciplines, such as MedLine (medicine), PsychInfo (psychology),

Sociological Abstracts, or MLA International Bibliography (literature, writing, and foreign languages).

Trade and Professional Publications

- Writers are usually professionals in a field who have expertise on an issue, although some writers might be freelancers hired by a company or professional organization.

- Writers expect readers to be members of a profession who have an interest in learning about developments in the field.

- Writers assume that readers will have some knowledge of the field. Because publications often focus on new developments within a field, however, they are not necessarily as technically challenging as scholarly publications.

- Trade and professional publications are sometimes peer-reviewed, but usually are reviewed only by editorial staff.

- Sources are cited, but often less thoroughly than in a scholarly publications.

- Examples include articles in trade and professional journal articles, articles in industry newsletters, blogs, and industry association Web sites.

Popular Publications

- Writers are often reporters who know a great deal about a subject but would be more accurately characterized as generalists. That said, many reporters have deep knowledge of specific areas and issues, such as NPR's Nina Totenberg, who focuses on legal affairs, and CNN's Candy Crowley, who focuses on politics.

- Writers address a general audience. Many popular publications are written at a reading level appropriate for an eighth- to tenth-grade education.

- Popular publications are not peer-reviewed. In many cases, but not all, they are reviewed by editorial staff at a magazine, newspaper, or Web site. You should not assume that popular sources have undergone a careful review.

- Popular publications seldom include citations, although newspaper articles, magazine articles, and blogs often identify sources in general terms. For example, a source might identify the name of a person who has been interviewed or quoted or it might provide a link to a Web site.

- Popular publications usually do not include research findings. Instead, they report or comment on events or activities. Because they often include observations and reports, however, they can be useful for tracking breaking news and current issues and for understanding the effects of an issue. For example, a blog or newspaper article might report comments from people who have been affected by a natural disaster.

- Examples include newspaper and magazine articles, blogs, Web sites, Wikis, YouTube, and other video sharing sites.

Evaluate the Relevance and Credibility of Digital Sources

INFORMATION LITERACY Because anyone can create a Web site, start a blog, contribute to a Wiki, or post a message to a social networking site, email list, Web discussion forum, message board, or comments list approach these sources with more caution than you would reserve for print sources such as books and journal articles, which are typically published only after a lengthy editorial-review process. ■

Web Sites and Blogs To assess the relevance and credibility of a Web site or a blog, examine its domain (.edu, .com, and so on) and look for information about the site (often available through an About page). The tutorial on p. 96 provides information about evaluating Web sites.

Social Networking Sites, Email Lists, Discussion Forums, and Message Boards To assess the relevance and credibility of a message on one of these online forums, try to learn something about the author. On social networking sites, you can usually link back to authors' personal pages. In email lists and discussion forums, check for a "signature" at the end of the message and try to locate a Frequently Asked Questions (FAQ) list. A signature can provide information about the sender, such as a professional title, and the URL for a personal home page where you can learn more about the author. An FAQ can tell you about the purpose of an email list or discussion forum; whether messages are moderated (reviewed prior to posting); and whether membership is open to all or restricted to a particular group. You can use the information you uncover to evaluate the information and ideas you find on the site, list, or forum. It can be useful, for example, to know that the moderator of a discussion forum is a member of an organization frequently discussed in the group. Similarly, it can help to know that a Facebook fan page is run by a corporation whose staff members might delete negative comments or provide potentially misleading responses.

Comments Lists Many articles and blogs allow readers to make comments. If the article or blog addresses a controversial issue, dozens, hundreds, and occasionally thousands of comments might be created. Some of these comments will add new information and insights that you might find useful. Keep in mind, however, that some news and blog sites allow anonymous commenting, which can make it difficult to learn anything about the commenters.

Wikis Wikis are Web sites that can be added to or edited by visitors to the site. Wikis such as Wikipedia (**en.wikipedia.org**) have grown in importance on the Web, and many Wikipedia pages are highly ranked by Web search sites such as Ask, Bing, Google, and Yahoo! Wikis can be good resources as you start a research writing project. In some cases, people who are experts on an issue contribute to Wikis and provide information and analyses that can help you gain an initial understanding of an issue. They also often provide links to other resources that can help you learn about the issue. Unfortunately, it can be difficult to evaluate the credibility of Wiki pages because their creators and editors are often

TUTORIAL

How do I evaluate a Web site?

Because Web sites can be published without having gone through a rigorous review process you'll want to evaluate them carefully. Evaluate a Web site by learning about its author, publisher, purpose, publication date, use of evidence, relevance, timeliness, and credibility. This example shows how you can evaluate a Web page that featured writer Alexis Alvarez found as she explored her topic: steroid use by adolescent girls involved in competitive sports. [Courtesy of UMN News.]

1 Check its domain (.com, .edu, .gov, and so on) to learn about its purpose and publisher:

.biz, .com, .coop	business	**.name**	personal
.edu	higher education	**.net**	network organization
.gov	government	**.org**	nonprofit organization
.mil	military	**.pro**	professional

2 Check the title bar, page header, and page titles to learn about the site's purpose, publisher (p. 88), and relevance (p. 86).

3 Search for information—on the site or through a separate Web search—about the author (p. 88) or publisher (p. 88), if identified.

4 Check timeliness (p. 89) by looking for a publication or a "last modified" date.

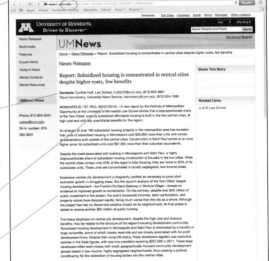

5 Read the body text and review illustrations to evaluate relevance (p. 86), evidence (p. 87), and comprehensiveness (p. 89).

6 Check page footers for information about the publisher and author. Look for About This Site or Contact links (not shown).

difficult to identify and because changes to wiki pages can occur quickly. Some entries are edited so frequently, in fact, that they become the subject of "edit wars," in which edits to a page are undone almost instantly by those who disagree with the edits. The Wikipedia entry on former president George W. Bush, for example, was edited more than 22,000 times during its first ten years of existence, or about six times per day. You'll find similar patterns with other controversial subjects, such as evolution or climate change. In some cases, the entry you found yesterday might have little or no resemblance to the entry you could read today.

With this in mind, it is best to use Wikis when you are beginning to learn about an issue. Avoid citing them as the "last word" on a topic because those last words might change before you submit your final draft.

Evaluate the Relevance and Accuracy of Field Sources

With some adjustment, most of the criteria discussed in this chapter can be applied to field sources such as interviews, correspondence, observations, and surveys. Relevance and the accuracy of the information you collect deserve additional attention. Ask the following questions as you evaluate information collected through field research.

- Are the questions you asked in an interview, a survey, or correspondence still relevant to your research project?

- Is the information you collected in an observation still relevant? Are your observation notes as complete as you had hoped they would be?

- Are the individuals you interviewed or corresponded with as qualified and knowledgeable as you expected?

- Were questions in interviews, surveys, and correspondence answered fully and honestly?

- Did survey respondents have adequate time to complete the survey? Did they appear to believe their privacy would be respected?

My Research Project

Use Evaluation to Trim a Working Bibliography

Use bibliography tools such as those found on the Bedford Researcher Web site at **bedfordresearcher.com** to evaluate sources on the criteria defined in this chapter, enter publication information, create annotations, save text from digital sources, and generate a bibliography.

You can use your evaluations to determine which sources should be added to or removed from your working bibliography. If you decide that a source is no longer relevant to your project, however, don't throw it away. There's always a chance that you'll decide you need it later. Instead of deleting it, put it in a category named "irrelevant," or move it into a new bibliography named "other sources" or "unused sources."

bedfordresearcher.com
My Research Project Activities > Use Evaluation to Trim a Working Bibliography

> **QUICK REFERENCE**

Evaluating Your Sources

☑ Evaluate the relevance, evidence, author, publisher, timeliness, comprehensiveness, and genre of your sources. (p. 86)

☑ Evaluate Web sources for relevance and credibility. (p. 95)

☑ Evaluate field research for relevance and accuracy. (p. 97)

Working with Sources

6

Taking Notes

> **Key Questions**

Taking notes early in your work on a research writing project allows you to keep track of what your sources have to offer. Later, as you begin to focus on planning and drafting your document, you'll be able to review your notes to determine whether to reread a source or set it aside and save time for other, more relevant sources.

6a

Why should I take notes?

Taking notes benefits research writers in two ways. First, it helps you keep track of the most important information, ideas, and arguments you've encountered in your sources. Although you can also do this by saving copies of each of your sources, notes help you zero in on the passages, images, tables, and other parts of your sources that you'll find most useful as you plan and draft your document. If you are working on a project that involves more than a few sources, taking notes will save you a great deal of time searching across your sources for a specific passage.

Second, and more important, taking notes helps you understand your sources more thoroughly than if you simply saved and highlighted copies of them. By paraphrasing or summarizing a source, for example, you force yourself to present passages from the source in your own words (p. 103). This process of putting things into your own words requires you to connect the source to what you already know, which can help you learn more about the issue you're addressing in your research writing project.

Taking notes, as a result, plays a much more vital role in your research writing project than simply keeping track of information. It helps you better understand the issue and lays the groundwork for your own contribution to the conversation you've decided to join.

6b

How can I record useful information, ideas, and arguments in my notes?

Your decisions about how to take notes will affect not only the methods you use but also what you'll focus on as you take them. Your methods—such as using note cards, a paper notebook, a word processing program, Web-based tools, or an app on a smartphone or tablet, for example—should reflect how you like to work with information. If you're uncertain about what might work best for you, talk to other writers, your instructor, or a librarian and then try a few of the most promising methods. You'll find that each method has its own advantages and disadvantages and that no single method is always better than another.

You should take notes when a source:

- features an idea that surprises or interests you or that you think you might want to argue for or against
- provides a statement that would enhance your understanding of the issue
- offers insights into how an authority or expert understands the issue
- provides an understanding of someone else's firsthand experience with an issue or event

As you take notes, remember that they should help you accomplish your purposes as a writer and address your readers effectively. Ensure that you quote your sources accurately, paraphrase passages fairly and appropriately, and sum-marize clearly and fairly. In every case, provide enough source information to allow you to locate the source of the note—useful when you need to check your use of sources for accuracy or want to find additional information.

Choose a Method and Use It Consistently

Some research writers take notes by hand, on note cards, on photocopies of sources, in a notebook, or on loose sheets of paper. Others choose to take notes digitally, in a word processing program, in a database program, in a bibliographic citation program such as EndNote or Reference Manager, in email messages, or in a blog.

Still other research writers have turned to Web-based tools, such as Diigo and Evernote (p. 118), which allow you to create notes, save Web-based materials (including images) for later viewing, and organize notes with folders and labels. Using these kinds of tools, you can save "clips" (all or part of a page) for later viewing, annotate your clips, and create notes to manage your project.

Your notes will be most useful if you take them systematically and consistently. For example, instead of taking some notes on Post-It Notes, some on note cards, and the rest in a word processing file, take all of your notes in one form. This will make it easier to find information later and reduce the time and effort required to organize and draft your document. It will also reduce the chances that you'll plagiarize unintentionally (p. 129).

Quote Directly

A direct quotation is an exact copy of words found in a source. You should take direct-quotation notes in the following cases.

- when a passage in a source features an idea that you want to argue for or against
- when a passage in a source provides a clear and concise statement that would enhance your project document
- when you want to use the exact words of an authority or expert
- when you want to use the exact words of someone who has firsthand experience with the issue you are researching
- when you want to set a mood

You can read about these and other reasons to use quotations in your document in Chapter 17.

Remember that, no matter how you might use a quotation later, your notes must be accurate. When you quote directly in your notes, you should enclose the passage in quotation marks, identify the source, and list the number of the page (or paragraph, if you are using a digital source that does not indicate page numbers) where the quotation can be found. Proofread what you have written to make sure it matches the original source exactly—including wording, punctuation, and spelling.

Using quotation marks as you take notes is critically important. If you don't use quotation marks, you might later think the passage is a paraphrase or summary and unintentionally plagiarize it when you draft your document. To learn more about avoiding plagiarism, see Chapter 8.

In some cases, it makes sense to modify a direct quotation while you're taking notes. You might want to quote only parts of a passage, add clarifying information to a note, or correct an error in the original text.

Modifying a Direct Quotation Using Ellipsis Marks   When only part of a passage relates to your project, you might want to quote only that part in your notes.

To indicate that you have changed a quotation by deleting words, use three spaced periods, or ellipsis marks (. . .). If you don't use ellipsis marks, your readers will assume that a quotation you are presenting is identical to the text found in the source.

Original Passage:

Anderson is convinced that this is the right way to do it because he's seen all of the ways that aren't. A girls' basketball coach for more than two decades, he'd already experienced firsthand all that modern youth sports had to offer. It wasn't pretty: Screaming, red-faced parents who shuffle their children from program to program because Junior or Jane doesn't get enough court time. Elite squads that serve as showcases for a few superstar players trying to attract the attention of a Division 1 program. Eight-year-old prima donnas factory-installed with a sense of entitlement simply because they know their way around a ball and a pair of high-tops.

Source: Eric Dexheimer, "Nothing to Lose," retrieved from http://www.westword .com/issues/2004-05-13/news/sports_print.html, paragraph 15.

Quotation Modified Correctly Using Ellipsis Marks:

"Anderson is convinced that this is the right way to do it because he's seen all of the ways that aren't. A girls' basketball coach for more than two decades, he'd already experienced firsthand all that modern youth sports had to offer. . . . Screaming, red-faced parents who shuffle their children from program to program because Junior or Jane doesn't get enough court time. Elite squads that serve as showcases for a few superstar players. . . . Eight-year-old prima donnas . . . with a sense of entitlement simply because they know their way around a ball and a pair of high-tops" (paragraph 15).

| Four periods indicate the deletion of a full sentence or more. | Three periods indicate material deleted from a sentence. |

Modifying a Direct Quotation Using Brackets   To modify a direct quotation by changing or adding words, use brackets: [ ]. If you don't use brackets when you change or add words, readers will assume the quotation you are presenting is identical to the text found in the source.

Quotation Modified Correctly Using Brackets:

"The [Corporation for National Service] is an independent agency with a 15-member board of directors that is appointed by the president and confirmed by the Senate" (Lenkowsky and Perry 299).

[Corporation for National Service] replaces the original text's use of the acronym CNS.

Remember that using brackets and ellipsis marks does not entitle you to change the meaning of a quotation. Check your notes against the original passages to be sure you aren't misrepresenting the source.

Modifying Quotations Using "Sic"   If a passage you are quoting contains a misspelled word or an incorrect fact, use the word "sic" in brackets to indicate that the error occurred in the original passage. If you don't use "sic," your readers will think that the mistake is yours.

Quotation Modified Correctly Using "Sic":

"George W. Brush's [sic] interest in faith-based initiatives strongly shaped his national service agenda" (Vincent 221).

To avoid unintentional plagiarism when quoting from sources, take careful notes by using the following checklist. Be aware, however, that mistakes can happen, particularly if you are taking notes in a hurry. As you draft your document, remember to look for notes that differ from your usual style of writing. More often than not, if a note doesn't sound like your own writing, it isn't.

CHECKLIST FOR QUOTING

To quote accurately when taking notes, follow these guidelines.

✔ Identify the author, title, and the page or paragraph where the passage can be found.

✔ Avoid unintentional plagiarism by using quotation marks.

✔ Use ellipsis marks, brackets, and "sic" as necessary.

✔ Check your note against the original passage to be sure you aren't introducing errors or misrepresenting the source.

II Working with Sources

Paraphrase

When you restate a passage from a source in your own words, you are paraphrasing the source. Writers use paraphrases in their documents for some of the same reasons they use quotations.

- to illustrate or support points they plan to make in their document
- to cite authorities on an issue
- to share the experiences of people who have been affected by an issue
- to refer to ideas with which they disagree

Using paraphrases in your notes serves three purposes. First, restating a passage in your own words can help you remember it better than if you simply copy and paste a quotation. Second, because paraphrases are written in your own words, they're usually easier to understand later, when you're drafting. Third, paraphrasing as you take notes will help you save time during drafting, particularly if you find—as many writers do—that you don't want to rely exclusively on quotations from your sources.

Paraphrasing is a useful skill that takes practice. The challenges that typically face writers as they paraphrase include mirroring the source material too closely—that is, making such minor changes to the words and sentence structure of a source that the paraphrase remains nearly identical to the original passage—and distorting the meaning of the source.

Consider the differences among the original passage below and the appropriate and inappropriate paraphrases that follow it.

Original Passage:

High school grades and test scores are not the only factors considered by colleges and universities in the admissions process. Other factors that influence college admissions decisions include high school rank, being an athlete, alumni connection, extracurricular activities, special talents, and other personal characteristics of applicants.

Source: William H. Gray III, "In the Best Interest of America, Affirmative Action Is a Must," p. 144.

Appropriate Paraphrase:

William H. Gray III notes that, in addition to high school grades and standardized test scores, most colleges and universities make admissions decisions based on an applicant's participation in sports, involvement in extracurricular activities, personal qualities, talents, relations to alumni, and class rank (144).

Preserves the meaning of the original passage without replicating sentence structure and wording

Inappropriate Paraphrase:

William H. Gray III notes that high school grades and test scores are not the only issues weighed by colleges and universities during college admissions decisions. Other factors that influence those decisions are high school rank, participating in athletics, connections to alumni, out-of-school activities, unique talents, and other personal qualities of applicants (144).

Does not differ sufficiently from original; uses the same sentence structure and changes only some key words

Inappropriate Paraphrase:

William H. Gray III notes that participation in sports and involvement in extracurricular activities are among the most important factors affecting college admissions decisions (144).

Distorts the meaning of the original passage

As you paraphrase, remember that paraphrases are generally about as long as the original passages on which they are based. Keep in mind as well that, even though

---

CHECKLIST FOR PARAPHRASING

To paraphrase, follow these guidelines.

✔ Be sure that you understand the passage by reading it and the surrounding text carefully.

✔ Restate the passage in your own words. Make sure that you do more than simply change a few key words.

✔ Compare the original passage with your paraphrase. Make sure that you've conveyed the meaning of the passage but that the wording and sentence structure differ from those in the original passage.

✔ Note the author, title, and the page or paragraph where the passage can be found.

TUTORIAL

How do I paraphrase a source?

Paraphrasing a source involves restating the ideas and information in a passage in your own words. Use different words and sentence structure to help ensure that your paraphrase isn't too close to the original passage. In this example, Alexis Alvarez identifies a relevant passage in one of her sources and creates a note that paraphrases the passage.

1 Select the passage you want to paraphrase.

Original Passage: Why do athletes risk chronic debilitating diseases and death by taking steroids? Because these drugs work. In very short order, they pack on pounds of muscle and increase strength dramatically. Weight training while using steroids maximizes your gains.

Source: Kendrick, C. (n.d.). Seduced by steroids. Retrieved from http://www.familyeducation.com/drugs-and-alcohol/sports/36182.html.

2 Identify relevant information and ideas in the passage.

Why do athletes risk chronic debilitating diseases and death by taking steroids? Because these drugs work. In very short order, pack on pounds of muscle and increase strength dramatically. Weight training while using steroids maximizes your gains.

3 Draft a paraphrase that identifies the source and includes the information.

Kendrick (n.d.) asks why athletes use steroids, which can lead to serious illness and death. He responds to his own question by noting that steroids increase muscle mass and strength and are particularly effective when used with weight training.

4 Revise the paraphrase so that it uses wording and sentence structure that differs from the original passage.

Kendrick (n.d.) notes that, despite long-term and potentially lethal health risks, athletes use steroids because, in combination with weight training, they can dramatically increase strength and muscle mass.

you are using your own words when you paraphrase, you must still cite the source because the paraphrase presents ideas and information that are not your own.

When paraphrasing, focus on understanding the key ideas in the passage and then restate them in your own words. Begin a paraphrase with the phrase "In other words." This strategy reminds you that it's important to do more than simply change a few words in the passage. You might also want to set the original source aside while you paraphrase so that you won't be tempted to copy sentences directly from it. After you've completed your paraphrase, check it for accuracy.

Summarize

A summary is a concise statement of information in a source. Research writers often summarize an entire source, but they can also summarize lengthy passages. You can write summaries to capture the overall argument and information in a source and to record a writer's argument so that you can later refute it.

Unlike paraphrases, which are generally about as long as the passages on which they are based, summaries are as a rule shorter than the source or passage that is being summarized. Like paraphrases and quotations, you should always cite the source of the summary in your note.

Here is an original passage from *Scientific American*, a source one might consult while researching television addiction. Two notes containing summaries of the passage, one appropriate and the other inappropriate, follow the original.

Original Passage:

What is more surprising is that the sense of relaxation ends when the set is turned off, but the feelings of passivity and lowered alertness continue. Survey participants commonly reflect that television has somehow absorbed or sucked out their energy, leaving them depleted. They say they have more difficulty concentrating after viewing than before. In contrast, they rarely indicate such difficulty after reading. After playing sports or engaging in hobbies, people report improvements in mood. After watching TV, people's moods are about the same or worse than before.

Source: Robert Kubey and Mihaly Csikszentmihalyi, "Television Addiction," p. 76

Appropriate Summary:

Kubey and Csikszentmihalyi, "Television Addiction," p. 76

Kubey and Csikszentmihalyi report that although watching television may relax a viewer, studies have shown it does little to improve a viewer's alertness, energy level, or mood. (summary)

The summary conveys the main point of the article and clearly identifies its authors.

Inappropriate Summary:

Although watching television may relax a viewer, viewers report that turning off the television set makes them feel moody and depressed. (summary)

The summary misrepresents the main point of the article and does not identify the authors.

‖ Working with Sources

CHECKLIST FOR SUMMARIZING

To summarize, follow these guidelines.

✔ Be sure that you understand the source by reading it carefully.

✔ Summarize main points and reasons in your own words. Make sure that you do more than string together a series of close paraphrases of key passages.

✔ Check for unintentional plagiarism by comparing the original source with your summary.

✔ Note the author, title, and, if you are summarizing only part of a source, the page(s) or paragraph(s) where the information can be found.

To avoid unintentional plagiarism when summarizing a source, begin your summary with "The author argues that" or "The author found that." Set the original source aside while you write your summary so that you won't be tempted to copy sentences directly from it. After you've completed your summary, check it for accuracy.

WORKING TOGETHER

Quote, Paraphrase, and Summarize

Form a small group and read Edwin J. Feulner's article, "The Energy Potential of Fracking," (available at http://www.heritage.org/research/commentary/2013/2/the-energy-potential-of-fracking). Each member of the group will be responsible for one of the following activities: identifying useful quotations, creating paraphrases, or summarizing all or part of the article.

1 Read the article.

2 Return to the article and **take notes** in the form of quotations, paraphrases, or summaries.

3 Take turns sharing the notes that were taken. Each group member should explain why the notes were taken and how they might be used in a writing project.

4 As each report is given, the other members of the group should **jot down any new ideas** that emerge from the discussion. Pay attention to useful strategies for identifying useful information, ideas, and arguments and record any good ideas about how to make use of notes.

5 As a group, **prepare a report** that identifies strategies for identifying useful passages; explains how notes can incorporate quotations, paraphrases, and summaries; and reflects on how notes might be used to make progress on a research writing project.

Working with Sources

6c

How can I use my notes to improve my understanding of an issue?

Notes can do far more than record useful information, ideas, and arguments for later use. If only because taking notes requires thought and effort, the process of choosing quotations, creating paraphrases, and summarizing sources can help you gain a deeper understanding of an issue. Yet taking notes can do far more than simply help you remember and understand your sources. It can help you keep track of ideas that occur to you as you work with sources and gain insights into how your sources are related to each other. Taking notes, in a real sense, plays an important role in developing your plan for making a contribution to the conversation you've decided to join.

Record Your Reactions and Impressions

You can use your notes to keep track of your reactions and impressions (see Figure 6.1). If you've read a source before and jotted down brief notes in the margins or added comments using a word processor, look for those now and use them as the basis for a more substantial reflection on the information, ideas, or arguments in a source. For example, you might have written, "This makes sense" in the margin. If so, take some time to create a note that explains why it makes sense and what the source adds to your understanding of the issue. Learn more about annotating sources during critical reading on p. 74.

If you are reading or viewing a source for the first time, use your notes to record your initial impressions, ask questions, and respond to claims made by the author. Then review your notes and expand them by reflecting in more detail on the points raised in your first set of notes.

Compare Sources   ? WHAT'S MY PURPOSE?

Your notes can indicate connections among your sources by identifying relationships among information, ideas, and arguments. Paying attention to your sources as a group—not just to individual sources—helps you gain a more complete understanding of your issue. It also can be useful when you begin planning and organizing your document, since those connections can help you frame your argument. To compare sources, use the following techniques.

- **Look for similarities.** As you gain more familiarity with your issue, you'll start to notice that some sources share the same general approach to the issue. As you take notes, identify similarities among your sources. Later, it can help you define groups of authors that you can use to support your argument, point to as misguided for the same general reason, or use to illustrate a particular point. Featured writer Lauren Mack reviewed her

The title of the source is listed at the top of the note. — Notes on *Blackwater: The Rise of the World's Most Powerful Mercenary Army* by **Jeremy Scahill**

Quotes	Notes and Reactions
The quotation is surrounded by quotation marks. — "On April 28, 2004, the Abu Ghraib prison scandal was blown into the open when CBS's *60 Minutes II* broadcast graphic images depicting U.S. soldiers torturing and humiliating Iraqi prisoners. It soon emerged that private contractors from two U.S. corporations—the San Diego–based firm Titan Corporation and the Virginia-based CACI—were allegedly involved in the torture, having provided interrogators for use at the prison during the period of alleged abuse." (p. 157)	This is a key event in the Iraq War and this passage will surely be a linchpin in the section of my paper regarding PMC malfeasance and crimes.
Nicholas writes down his reactions to the quotations. — "The full magnitude of the industry-wide profits is difficult to gauge because many of the firms, like Blackwater, are ultra-secretive and not publicly traded. But some experts began estimating the value of the industry at $100 billion a year." (p. 158)	A key fact here. This is something I'd like to have another citation to back up, though.
Page numbers follow quotations. — "In late 2006, Senator Lindsey Graham quietly inserted language into the 2007 defense authorization bill, which Bush subsequently signed, that sought to place contractors under the Pentagon's UCMJ [Uniform Code of Military Justice], but what effective impact—if any—this could have remains unclear, with experts predicting resistance from the private war industry." (p. 360)	I'd like to do some more research to see if the UCMJ has been effectively applied to a contractor in the years between the publication of this book and now. Personally, I'd doubt it. This is a powerful industry with plenty of lawyers to challenge this language.

FIGURE 6.1 An Example from Nicholas Brothers's Notes and Reactions [From *Blackwater* by Jeremy Scahill, Copyright © 2007. Reprinted by permission of Nation Books, a member of the Perseus Books Group.]

notes and identified connections she saw between what she'd read on educational Web sites and what she'd learned from her interviews with her colleagues at her New England Aquarium internship. In her interview notes, Lauren added a comparison note: "This ties in with the Smithsonian article."

- **Look for disagreements.** As you learn more about a conversation, you'll begin to understand how writers align themselves. As a result, you'll be prepared to decide which sources might provide support for your argument and which sources will serve best to illustrate alternative approaches to the issue (see Figure 6.2). Taking note of disagreements among your sources can help you determine the sticking points in the conversation you've decided to join. In turn, understanding where your sources

46   THE RISE

The second implication is that this new private military actor is driven by business profit rather than individual profit. PMFs function as registered trade units, not as personal black-market ventures for individual profit or adventure. As firms, they can make use of complex corporate financing, ranging from sale of stock shares to intra-firm trade, meaning that a wider variety of deals and contracts can be worked out. For good reason, individual mercenaries tend only to trust payments in cash and, in turn, cannot be trusted for anything beyond the short-term.

The key is that it is not the person that matters, but the structure that they are within. Many PMF employees have been mercenaries both before and after their employ, but their processes, relationships, and impacts within local conflicts were completely different.

The third distinguishing characteristic of the privatized military industry is that the arena they compete on is the open global market. That is, unlike the activities of the White Legion or similar mercenary units, PMFs are considered legal entities bound to their employers by recognized contracts and in many cases at least nominally to their home states by laws requiring registration, periodic reporting, and licensing of foreign contracts.[17] Rather than denying their existence, private military firms are registered businesses and, in fact, often publicly advertise their services—including many even having corporate websites on the Internet.[18] This status differentiates them not only from mercenaries, who had to hide from the law, but also from past entities, such as the charter companies, that did not coexist with any state law, but rather made their own laws.

New military firms also provide a much wider offering of services and, importantly, to a much wider variety of clients. As the head of Sandline was proud to note, firms in the privatized military industry are "structured organizations with professional and corporate hierarchies . . . We cover the full spectrum—training, logistics, support, operational support, post-conflict resolution."[19] This provides another differentiation from past private military organizations. The goal of PMFs is service provision rather than the exchange of goods—a key distinction from the charter companies. Although one sector exclusively focuses on combat services like contract units and military entrepreneurs, another distinctive development is that PMFs provide military services outside the tactical sphere. Moreover, many are diversified enough to work for multiple (and a wider variety of) clients, in multiple markets and theatres at once—something none of the prior private military actors could do. As previously noted, those that have hired PMFs include other multinational corporations; state regimes—both foreign and the home bases of the firms; international organizations; and even nongovernmental organizations.

> Line up this argument against Scahill's virtually interchangeable use of the terms "private military corporation" and "mercenary"

FIGURE 6.2 An Annotation about a Disagreement among Sources. *Nicholas Brothers reminds himself about the differences among his sources.* [Reprinted from *Corporate Warriors,* by P. W. Singer. Copyright © 2003 by Cornell University. Used by permission of the publisher, Cornell University Press.]

disagree can help you decide where to make your contribution to the conversation.

- **Look for common citations.** As you read your sources, pay attention to the sources they cite. If the majority of your sources refer to a source that you haven't yet consulted, do so. Any source that is being referenced frequently is likely to contain important information, ideas, or arguments. Take note of frequently cited sources and consult them later.

Classify Sources

As you take notes, use them to classify your sources. Among other purposes, you can keep track of sources that might be used to support particular points in your document, that represent various approaches to your issue, and that include important information or ideas. Strategies for classifying sources include tagging, labeling, grouping, listing, and visualizing.

- **Tagging and labeling** *i* **INFORMATION LITERACY** Tags are words or phrases that can be associated with digital notes. When tags are used, it is common to apply more than one tag to a note. Labels, in turn, can be applied to print notes. You can use tags and labels to remind yourself about the purpose or content of a note or to help you remember something about the source. You might tag a note with one of the reasons you're planning to use in your document, for example, or you might label a note as useful for your introduction. Later, as you're working on your introduction or fleshing out that reason, you can quickly call up all of your relevant tagged notes. Similarly, you might label a note to remind yourself about the approach taken in the source to which it refers and later, as you draft, look for notes with that label. ■

- **Grouping** As you read and take notes on your sources, you can begin to classify them into groups—organized, perhaps, by the part of the document in which you plan to refer to the source, the approach advanced in the source, or the kind of evidence contained in the source. If you are working with print notes, you can put them in piles, envelopes, or folders. If you are working with digital notes, you might drag each note into a group (within, for example, a word processing file) or into a folder (if you are saving each note as a distinct file).

- **Listing** Listing is similar to grouping, but it does not require you to move your notes into a particular location. Instead, you can create notes that list your sources. You might, for example, list all of the sources that contain information that might be used to support your position and then list sources that contain information that contradicts your position.

- **Visualizing** You can use the same clustering and mapping techniques as you take notes that you use as you generate ideas and organize your document (p. 23 and p. 113). For example, you can create notes that contain a sketch of the relationships among the sources you've read so far. Or you could draw clusters of sources that support or illustrate a particular approach to your issue and then write brief notes about what they have in common, how the clusters of sources differ from each other, and so on. Similarly, you can draw maps showing the relationships among important ideas addressed in your sources and identify which sources are associated with each idea.

II Working with Sources

Plan Your Document [FRAMING MY ARGUMENT]

Planning notes are directions to yourself about how you might use a source in your project document, how you might organize the document, or ideas you should remember later. You can use planning notes to keep track of your ideas about the role that might be played in your document by the information, ideas, and arguments you encounter. Featured writer Lauren Mack wrote planning notes—such as, "How will this tie in? Use on opening screen?"—as she prepared to write her multimodal essay.

My Research Project

Respond to Sources

As you take notes, you'll gain a deeper understanding of your sources, both individually and collectively. Use your knowledge of your sources to create a response. Your response can be useful later as you plan and draft your project document. Use one or more of the following prompts as the basis for your response.

- What do you agree with in one or more of your sources? Briefly summarize the idea or argument with which you agree and then explain why you agree.

- What do you disagree with in one or more of your sources? Briefly summarize the idea or argument with which you disagree and then explain why you disagree.

- What do you see as the most important idea emerging from your research so far? Briefly summarize the idea and then explain its importance.

- Why do you think one or more of the authors you've taken notes on so far approach the issue as they have? Briefly describe their approaches and then explain why they are taking them.

- What approach do you think should be taken on this issue? Briefly describe the approach and then explain its importance.

bedfordresearcher.com
My Research Project Activities > Respond to Sources

> QUICK REFERENCE

Taking Notes

☑ Decide how you will record your notes; then take notes systematically and consistently. (p. 100)

☑ Take notes to quote passages directly. (p. 101)

☑ Take notes to paraphrase key ideas. (p. 103)

☑ Take notes to summarize whole sources or lengthy passages. (p. 106)

☑ Take notes to record your reactions and impressions. (p. 108)

☑ Take notes to compare the information, ideas, and arguments in sources. (p. 108)

☑ Take notes to classify sources. (p. 111)

☑ Take notes to help plan your document. (p. 112)

Part II
Working with Sources

4	Reading Critically and Actively
5	Evaluating Sources
6	Taking Notes
7	**Managing Information**
8	Avoiding Plagiarism

7

Managing Information

Even with a narrowly defined research question, it's likely that your searches will produce a large number of relevant sources. To use those sources most effectively, decide how to save, organize, and keep track of your sources. Doing so will help you work with your sources more easily as you plan and draft your document.

7a

How can I save and organize the information I find?

As you begin to collect information, spend some time reflecting on how you will save and keep track of it.

Decide How to Save and Organize Print Information

During your research project, you'll accumulate a great deal of print information, such as:

- your written notes (in a notebook, on loose pieces of paper, on Post-It Notes, and so on)
- printouts from Web pages and databases
- articles sent through a library's interlibrary loan service
- printed word processing documents, such as various drafts of your research question and position statement

- books, magazines, newspapers, brochures, pamphlets, and government documents
- photocopies of articles, book chapters, and other documents
- letters, printed email messages, survey results, and so on

Rather than letting all this information build up in messy piles on your desk or stuffing it into folders in your backpack, create a filing system to keep track of your print documents. Filing systems can range from well-organized piles of paper labeled with Post-It Notes to three-ring binders to file cabinets filled with neatly labeled files and folders.

Regardless of the approach you take, keep the following principles in mind.

- **Make it easy to locate your print materials.** Decide whether you want to group material by topic, by date, by pro versus con, by type of material (Web pages, photocopies, original documents, field sources, and so on), or by author.

- **Stick with your organizing scheme.** You'll find it difficult to locate materials if you use different approaches at different points in your research project.

- **Always include complete publication information.** If a source doesn't contain publication information, write it on the document yourself. You'll need it later. Publication information includes author, title, publisher, place and date of publication, and — for a Web source — sponsoring organization and URL.

- **Record the date.** Indicating dates when you recorded information can help you reconstruct what you might have been doing while you took the notes. Dates are also essential for documenting Web sources and other sources obtained online.

- **Write a brief note on each of your print materials.** Indicate how it might contribute to your project.

Decide How to Save and Organize Digital Information *i* INFORMATION LITERACY

As you save digital information, keep it organized. The simplest organizational strategy is to save your work in a single folder (see Figure 7.1). As you save your work, use descriptive file names. Rather than naming a file "Notes 1," for instance, name it "Interview Notes from John Garcia, April 22." Keep in mind that the single-folder approach might not work well for larger projects. At some point, the sheer number of files in the folder makes it difficult to find a single file easily. Rather than scrolling through several screens of files, you might find it more efficient to create multiple folders to hold related files (see Figure 7.2). ■

Downloading Toward the end of your research writing project, particularly when you are drafting your document, you might find yourself wishing that you'd saved all of your digital sources on a hard drive, flash drive, or a network-based

FIGURE 7.1 A Project Workspace Using a Single Folder

service such as DropBox, iCloud, or SkyDrive. Downloading sources allows you to open them in a Web browser or word processor at a later time (see Figure 7.3).

How you save your sources will vary according to the type of digital source you're viewing.

FIGURE 7.2 A Project Workspace Using Multiple Folders

II Working with Sources

- To download entire Web pages, right-click (for Windows), command-click (for Mac), or press and hold a finger (on phones and tablets) on the page and choose the Save or Save as command. Or use the options icon or menu to save the page (see Figure 7.3).

- To download images and other media materials from the Web, click or press and hold on the item you want and select the appropriate command.

- To download records from a database, check the online help pages. Most databases allow you to mark and save records returned by a search. To download full-text sources from databases, you can open and save the file (often a PDF file or a text file) or download it in the same way you would download an image.

Remember that downloading a source does not automatically record the URL or the date on which you viewed the source for the first time. Be sure to record that information in your research log, in your working bibliography (p. 119), or in a document in the folder where you've saved your files.

Copying and Pasting   You can save text from relevant sources as notes in a word processing document. Be sure to keep track of source information, such as the URL and the date you viewed a source, so that you can return to it if necessary and cite it appropriately.

Using Email   You can email yourself messages containing digital documents you've found in your research. Some databases, such as those from EBSCO and OCLC/FirstSearch, allow you to email the text of selected records directly from the database (see Figure 7.4). You can also use email as a form of file folder by sending messages to yourself that include copies of documents in the form of pasted text or attached files. If you use a subject line such as "My Comp 110 Research Project," you can sort your messages by subject line and easily view all of the information you've collected or you can simply search for messages containing the phrase *research project*.

FIGURE 7.3 Downloading a Web Page [Environmental Protection Agency.]

Working with Sources

E-mail Manager

Back

Articles

Number of items to be e-mailed: 8

E-mail from: ephost@epnet.com

E-mail to: nicholas.brothers@statecollege.edu
Separate each e-mail address with a semicolon.

Subject: Sources for Research Assignment

Comments: Sources from Academic Search Premiere, search on "private military corporations"

Format: ● Rich Text ○ Plain Text

Include when sending:

☑ HTML Full Text (when available)
☑ PDF as separate attachment (when available)
○ Standard Field Format
  Detailed Citation and Abstract ▼
● Citation Format
  Chicago/Turabian: Humanities ▼
○ Customized Field Format

Send

☐ Remove these items from folder after e-mailing
For information on e-mailing Linked Full Text, see online help. For information on using Citation Formats, see online citation help

FIGURE 7.4 Sending Email from a Database [Courtesy of EBSCO.]

Taking Photos, Making Recordings, and Saving Notes If you have a smartphone or a tablet, you can record conversations with others, record voice memos that contain ideas about your project, save video, take photos of sources you find in the periodical room (p. 173), and surf the Web to locate sources. Most phone and tablet operating systems provide access to "apps" (or applications), often at no or low cost, that allow you to collect and organize information in the same way you would on a laptop or desktop computer (see Figure 7.5).

A note lists relevant authors

A photo records a location

Voice recording apps can be used to conduct interviews or record ideas

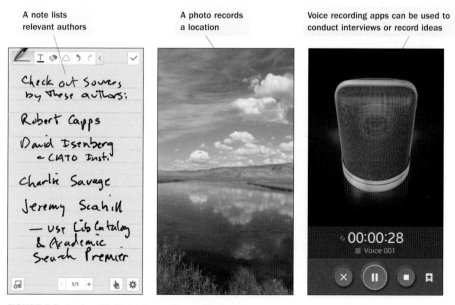

FIGURE 7.5 Saving Digital Information with Apps

As you save information with these tools, keep your work well organized. Use descriptive names, save work in folders or albums, and add information about where and when you found the information. Be sure to talk with other writers about the apps they've found useful and, if they're free, try them out yourself.

Saving Bookmarks and Favorites in Your Browser You can use a Bookmarks or Favorites list in your Web browser to keep track of your sources. Be aware that there are drawbacks to relying on a Bookmarks or Favorites list as a place to "store" your sources. First, pages on the Web can and do change. If you suspect that the page you want to mark might change before you complete your research writing project, download or print it so that you won't lose its content. Second, some Web pages are generated by database programs. In such cases, you might not be able to return to the page using a Bookmarks or Favorites list. A URL like the following usually indicates that a Web page is generated by a database program.

> http://firstsearch.oclc.org/FUNC/QUERY:%7Fnext=NEXTCMD%7F%22/ FUNC/SRCH_RSULTS%22%7FentityListType=0%7Fentitycntr=1%7Fentity ItemCount=0%7F%3Asessionid=1265726%7F4%7F/fsres4.txt

Although this long string of characters starts out looking like a normal URL, the majority of the characters are used by the database program to determine which records to display on a page. In many cases, the URL works only while you are conducting your search. If you add such a URL to your Bookmarks or Favorites list, there's a good chance it won't work later. To avoid this problem, consider downloading Web pages (p. 116) or using Web capture and clipping tools (p. 118).

Keep in mind that Bookmarks and Favorites lists can become disorganized. To avoid this problem, put related items into folders, and give the items on your list descriptive names.

Web Clipping and Content Curation Tools You can also use Web-based tools to save content from online sources. Web clipping tools, which work with your browser as toolbars or "add-ons" (a term used for programs that work within browsers), can be used to copy all or part of a Web page. Leading, free Web capture tools include Diigo (**diigo.com**) and Zotero (**zotero.org**). Content curation tools allow you to create collections of sources and share them—individually or as a group. Scoop.it (**scoop.it**), for example, allows you to save, annotate, and easily revisit Web sites, blogs, and other online content (see Figure 7.6). Although these tools were created largely for commercial purpose (in particular, to help users market products and services), they offer useful tools for writers. Leading, free content curation tools include Listly (**list.ly**) and Paper.li (**paper.li**).

Using Bibliography Tools Use online bibliography tools such as The Bedford Bibliographer at bedfordstmartins.com/bibliographer to save bibliographic information about each of your sources, write a brief note or annotation about each source, evaluate each source, and save text from digital sources. You can also create a bibliography formatted in MLA, APA, *Chicago,* or CSE style. Read more about bibliographies on the following page.

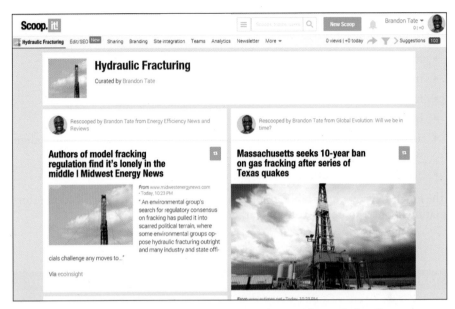

FIGURE 7.6 Scoop.it Allows Writers to Collect, Organize, and Share Online Sources
[Scoop.it! EnergyWire. Peter Andrews/Reuters.]

Backing Up Your Files   Whatever strategies you use to save and organize digital materials, replacing lost information takes time and effort. Avoid the risk of lost information by taking the time to make copies of your digital files and downloads, email messages, saved Web pages and clippings, and Bookmarks or Favorites list.

7b

How can I use a bibliography to organize information?

A bibliography is a list of sources with complete publication information, usually formatted according to the rules of a documentation system such as those created by the Modern Language Association (see Chapter 23), the American Psychological Association (see Chapter 24), or the Council of Science Editors (see Chapter 26), or found in books such as the *Chicago Manual of Style* (see Chapter 25). As you take notes on your sources, use a working bibliography or an annotated bibliography to keep track of the sources you've consulted.

Create a Working Bibliography

A working bibliography is a running list of the sources you've explored and plan to use as you work on your research writing project. Publication information is provided for each source. The organization of your working bibliography can vary according to your needs and preferences. You can organize your sources in any of the following ways.

- in the order in which you collected your sources
- in categories
- by author
- by publication title
- according to how the information, ideas, and arguments in the source align with your position on your issue
- according to an outline of your project document

The entries in a working bibliography should include as much publication information about a source as you can gather (see Table 7.1).

TABLE 7.1 INFORMATION YOU SHOULD LIST IN A WORKING BIBLIOGRAPHY	
Type of Source	**Information You Should List**
All Sources	Author(s) Title Publication year Medium consulted
Book	Editor(s) of book (if applicable) Publication city Publisher Series and series editor (if applicable) Translator (if applicable) Volume (if applicable) Edition (if applicable)
Chapter in an Edited Book	Publication city Publisher Editor(s) of book Book title Page numbers
Journal, Magazine, or Newspaper Article	Journal title Volume number or date Issue number or date Page numbers
Web Page, Blog Entry or Reply, Discussion Forum Post, Email Message, or Chat Transcript	URL Access date (the date you read the source) Sponsoring organization (if listed)
Field Research	Title (usually a description of the source, such as "Personal Interview with Jessica Lynn Richards" or "Observation of June Allison's Class at Tavelli Elementary School") Date (usually the date on which the field research was conducted)

Your working bibliography will change significantly as you work on your research writing project. As you explore your topic and choose an issue, collect sources, read them critically, evaluate them, and take notes, you will add potentially useful sources and delete sources that are no longer relevant. Eventually, your working bibliography will become one of the following.

- a *works cited* or *reference list*—a formal list of the sources you have referred to in a document

- a *bibliography* or *works consulted list*—a formal list of the sources that contributed to your thinking about an issue, even if those sources were not referred to explicitly in the text of the document

Keeping your working bibliography up-to-date is a critical part of your research writing process. It helps you keep track of your sources and increases the likelihood that you will cite all the sources you use in your document—an important contribution to your efforts to avoid plagiarism (see Chapter 8). Bibliography tools allow you to create, organize, and update a working bibliography formatted in styles such as MLA or APA.

The first five sources from Elizabeth Leontiev's working bibliography are found in Figure 7.7.

Entries follow MLA style
(p. 338).

Borwick, Phoebe, and Amy Donohue. "Drugs: Nobody's Winning the War." *Just Focus*. Global Education Centre, 10 Oct. 2006. Web. 5 June 2007.

Forero, Juan. "Coca Advocate Wins Election for President in Bolivia." *New York Times*. New York Times, 19 Dec. 2005. Web. 3 June 2007.

Gordon, Gretchen. "The United States, Bolivia, and the Political Economy of Coca." *Multinational Monitor* 27.1 (2006): 15-20. *Expanded Academic ASAP*. Web. 15 May 2007.

Harman, Danna. "In Bolivia, a Setback for US Anti-Coca Drive." *Christian Science Monitor*. Christian Science Monitor, 22 Dec. 2005. Web. 12 May 2007.

United States. Office of National Drug Control Policy. "Drug Facts: Cocaine." *Office of National Drug Control Policy*. Executive Office of the President of the United States, n.d. Web. 8 June 2007.

When authors are not listed, the sponsoring organization is listed as the author.

FIGURE 7.7 Part of Elizabeth Leontiev's Working Bibliography

Working with Sources

Create an Annotated Bibliography　[FRAMING MY ARGUMENT]

An annotated bibliography provides a brief note about each of the sources you've listed, in addition to its complete citation information. These notes, or annotations, are typically no longer than two or three sentences. The content, focus, and length of your annotations will reflect both your purposes for creating an annotated bibliography and the needs and interests of your readers (see Table 7.2).

TABLE 7.2 PURPOSES AND FEATURES OF ANNOTATED BIBLIOGRAPHIES

	Your Readers			
	Yourself	**An Instructor**	**A Writing Group**	**External Audience**
Purpose	Keep track of sources; plan your document	Show progress on a project; serve as an intermediate assignment	Show how a source might be useful for a group project	Share information about important sources addressing an issue
Features				
Include complete source citation, using proper formatting.	✔	✔	✔	✔
Summarize the source, noting significant findings and key information.	✔	✔	✔	✔
Evaluate the source, including how it is relevant and background information on the author and publisher.	✔	✔	✔	✔
Compare sources.	✔			
Identify passages containing useful information, ideas, and arguments.	✔		✔	
Reflect on how the source could be used in a project document.	✔	✔	✔	
Note how readers might react to information, ideas, and arguments in the document.	✔			
Respond to the source with your own reaction or analysis.	✔			
Create polished, well-crafted sentences.		✔	✔	✔

The following examples show how the same source might be annotated for different readers.

For Yourself:

> This Web page discusses everything about the hydraulic fracturing process and is one of very few sources that gives specific numbers for the amount of water being used in fracking. I will use this information in the section on the disadvantages of fracking.

For an Instructor:

> This Web page provides a great deal of information about the hydraulic fracturing process. It is one of few sources I've found that gives specific numbers about the amount of water being used in fracking. I will use this information to explore some of the environmental and economic disadvantages of fracking.

For Classmates in a Writing Group:

> This Web page discusses everything about the hydraulic fracturing process and is one of very few sources that give specific numbers for the amount of water being used in fracking. We can use this site to get a good understanding of the disadvantages (environmental and economic) of fracking.

For an External Audience, such as Visitors to a Web site:

> The Explore Shale Web page provides an easy-to-understand overview of hydraulic fracking. Its graphical images allow visitors to see how the process works. It also provides details about the hydraulic fracturing process, including the amount of water being used in fracking.

≡ Working with Sources

My Research Project

Create a Working or Annotated Bibliography

Create a bibliography to keep track of your sources as you work on your research writing project. Your bibliography should include complete citation information for the sources you are considering for use in your project. You may also include annotations that contain source descriptions, source evaluations, reflections on the source, and plans for using the source in your project.

You can create a bibliography in print form (such as in a notebook) or in digital form (for example, in a word processing file). You can also use bibliography tools, which allow you to create entries for new sources, annotate sources, evaluate sources, copy and save some or all of the text from a source, and display your working bibliography in various citation styles (see Part V).

bedfordresearcher.com
My Research Project Activities > Create a Working or Annotated Bibliography

Costello, B. (2004, July 4). Too late? Survey suggests millions of kids could be juicing. *New York Post*. Retrieved from http://www.nypost.com

Entries follow APA style (p. 368).

This article discusses steroid and other performance-enhancing drugs used by eighth- through twelfth-grade boys and girls and provides a number of relevant statistics. I'll use this source to support statements about steroid use among young female athletes.

Davies, D., & Armstrong, M. (1989). *Psychological factors in competitive sport.* New York, NY: Falmer Press.

Annotations provide brief summaries of the purpose and content of the sources.

This book addresses various psychological factors in sports including learning, motivation, anxiety, stress, and performance. I'll use it to support my discussion of why sports can have negative effects on girls.

DeNoon, D. (2004, August 4). *Steroid use: Hitting closer to home.* Retrieved from http://webmd.com/fitness-exercise/features/steroid-use-hitting-closer-to-home

Annotations are intended for Alexis and her teacher. They indicate how and where Alexis will use the sources in her document.

This Web page provides information about increasing steroid use in America as well as the latest statistical figures regarding this use. I'll use it for statistical evidence and to drive home the point that this problem needs to be addressed.

Dexheimer, E. (2004, May 13). Nothing to lose: The Colorado Impact teaches girls about life — then hoops. *Denver Westword*. Retrieved from http://www.westword.com

Article about a different way of coaching club basketball focusing mainly on the Colorado Impact club and their policies on practice and community service. I'll use it to provide the basketball coach's viewpoint of club basketball and the effects of it on parents, athletes, etc.

FIGURE 7.8 Part of Alexis Alvarez's Annotated Bibliography, Written for Herself and Her Teacher

An annotated bibliography is a useful tool even if it's not something you'll be expected to submit for a grade or share with other readers. By turning your working bibliography into an annotated bibliography, you can remind yourself of important information, ideas, and arguments in your sources; record your reflections, evaluations, and analyses of each source; note your responses to your sources; and record your ideas about how the source might be used to advance your position on your issue.

> QUICK REFERENCE

Managing Information

☑ Decide how you will save and organize print information. (p. 113)

☑ Decide how you will save and organize digital information. (p. 114)

☑ Create a working bibliography. (p. 119)

☑ Depending on your purpose and audience, create an annotated bibliography. (p. 122)

II Working with Sources

Part II
Working with Sources

4	Reading Critically and Actively
5	Evaluating Sources
6	Taking Notes
7	Managing Information
> 8	**Avoiding Plagiarism**

8

Avoiding Plagiarism

> **Key Questions**

Few writers intentionally try to pass off the work of others as their own. However, deadlines and other pressures can lead writers to take notes poorly and cite sources improperly. In addition, easy access to documents through the Web and full-text databases has made it all too easy to copy and paste work from other writers without acknowledging its source.

Failing to cite your sources can lead to serious problems. Your readers will not be able to determine which ideas and information in your text are your own or which are drawn from your sources. If they suspect you are failing to acknowledge your sources, they are likely to doubt your credibility and suspect your competence, and they might even stop reading your document. More seriously, submitting academic work that does not include proper identification of sources might result in failure in a course or some other disciplinary action.

8a

What is plagiarism?

Plagiarism is a form of intellectual dishonesty. It involves either unintentionally using someone else's work without properly acknowledging where the ideas or information came from (the most common form of plagiarism) or intentionally passing off someone else's work as your own (the most serious form of plagiarism).

Plagiarism is based on the notion of "copyright," or ownership of a document or idea. Like a patent, which protects an invention, a copyright protects an author's investment of time and energy in the creation of a document. Essentially, it assures authors that, when they create a document, someone else won't be able to steal ideas from it and profit from that theft without penalty.

In this sense, plagiarism in academic writing differs in important ways from the kind of mixing and remixing that can take place in popular culture. The expectations of readers of source-based documents differ, for instance, from people who listen to music. While listeners enjoying a song on the radio might not be surprised to hear part of another song added to a mix, readers of an article in *Time* magazine or an academic journal might be alarmed to read an unattributed passage that they recognize as the work of another writer. Context matters, and in this case the context of academic writing differs significantly from that of popular culture.

Unintentional Plagiarism

In most cases, plagiarism is unintentional, and most cases of unintentional plagiarism result from taking poor notes or failing to use notes properly. You are plagiarizing if you:

- quote a passage in a note but neglect to include quotation marks and then later insert the quotation into your document without remembering that it is a direct quotation
- include a paraphrase that differs so slightly from the original passage that it might as well be a direct quotation
- don't clearly distinguish between your ideas and ideas that come from your sources
- neglect to list the source of a paraphrase, quotation, or summary in your text or in your works cited list

Although unintentional plagiarism is, by definition, something that the writer hasn't planned to do, it is nonetheless a serious issue and, when detected, is likely to have consequences. Some instructors might require that an assignment be rewritten; others might impose a penalty, such as a lowered grade or failure on the assignment.

TUTORIAL

How can I avoid unintentional plagiarism?

Unintentional plagiarism is the use of another writer's work without properly acknowledging the source of the ideas or information. Unintentional plagiarism is often the result of rushed work on a project. It can sometimes result from inadequate research writing skills or honest mistakes. In this example, Cori Schmidtbauer checks her rough draft for unintentional plagiarism.

To avoid unintentional plagiarism, follow these steps.

1 Check for a works cited or reference list.

2 Identify each quotation, paraphrase, and summary.

3 Check for appropriate attributions.

4 Check for appropriate in-text citation.

5 Ensure that each source is included in your works cited or reference list.

6 Check for changes in writing style. If you find changes, check your notes to identify the source of the passage and ensure that you haven't neglected to include quotation marks or paraphrased too closely.

Schmidtbauer 7

Works Cited

Abate, Corinne S. "Portia's Wifely Empowerment in *The Merchant of Venice*." *The Merchant of Venice: New Critical Essays*. Ed. John W. Mahon and Ellen Macleod Mahon. New York: Routledge, 2002. Print.

Brannigan, John. *New Historicism and Cultural Materialism*. New York: St. Martin's Press, 1998. Print.

Hebron, Malcolm. *Key Concepts in Renaissance Literature*. New York: Palgrave Macmillan, 2008. Print.

Hopkins, Lisa, and Matthew Steggle. *Renaissance Literature and Culture*. London: Continuum, 2006. Print.

Newman

Shakesp

Tilyard,

Schmidtbauer 4

than deferring to her husband. Initially, Portia fulfills the duties of a Renaissance woman by giving Bassanio her ring, an object that then conveyed ownership as well as commitment. As critic Karen Newman writes in "Portia's Ring: Unruly Women and Structures of Exchange in *The Merchant of Venice*," in bestowing the ring, Portia is providing her new husband a "visual sign of her vow of love and submission" of all she has to give—her body, house, status, fortune, etc. (Newman 260). Yet, Newman explains, by giving herself away into marriage, Portia is bestowing more than Bassanio can reciprocate (261): since Portia is the source of Bassanio's improved standing and newfound wealth, she has the upper hand. Portia demonstrates her ability to manipulate the traditional politics of exchange most vividly in the courtroom scene in Act IV when, posing as the male lawyer "Balthazar," she saves Antonio's life on a legal technicality. In exchange for saving his friend from having to give up a pound of flesh, Bassanio offers "Balthazar" a gift, and the disguised Portia demands that Bassanio hand over the ring. Later, in Act V, Portia (now dressed as herself) derides Bassanio for giving away the object that represents her affection and tells him, "By heaven, I will ne'er come in your bed/ Until I see the ring" (V.i.190–191). With that, she deprives him of what was considered in Renaissance times to be a husbandly right. Through all of these exchanges of the ring, Portia is in complete control; without Bassanio even knowing it, she is able to manipulate the usually male-dominated giver-receiver power dynamic to her own advantage.

Throughout *The Merchant of Venice*, Portia's masculine and manipulative character

Intentional Plagiarism

Intentional plagiarism, although less common than unintentional plagiarism, can lead to academic penalties ranging from a reduced grade on an assignment to failure of a course to expulsion. Intentional plagiarism includes:

- engaging in "patchwork writing," which involves piecing together passages from two or more sources without acknowledging the sources and without properly quoting or paraphrasing
- creating fake citations to mislead a reader about the sources of information used in a document
- copying or closely paraphrasing extended passages from another document and passing them off as the writer's original work
- copying an entire document and passing it off as the writer's original work
- purchasing a document and passing it off as the writer's original work

Plagiarism in Group Projects

Peer review and other collaborative activities raise important, and potentially confusing, questions.

- If another writer suggests changes to your document and you subsequently incorporate them into your document, are you plagiarizing?
- What if those suggestions significantly change your document?
- If you work with a group of writers on a project, do you need to identify the parts that each of you wrote?
- Is it okay to list yourself as a coauthor if another writer does most of the work on a collaborative writing project?

The answers to these questions will vary from situation to situation. In general, it's appropriate to use comments from reviewers in your document without citing them. If a reviewer's comments are particularly helpful, you might acknowledge his or her contributions in your document; writers often thank reviewers in a footnote or endnote or in an acknowledgments section. It is usually appropriate to list coauthors on a collaboratively written document without individually identifying the text that was written by each coauthor, although some instructors ask that individual contributions be noted in the document or on a cover page. If you are uncertain about what is appropriate, ask your instructor.

8b

What are research ethics?

Research ethics are based on the notion that writing—and in particular research writing—is an honest exchange of information, ideas, and arguments among writers and readers who share an interest in an issue. As a research writer, you'll want to behave honestly and ethically. In general, you should:

- acknowledge the sources of the information, ideas, and arguments used in your document—to show respect for the work that others have done before you
- accurately and fairly represent the information, ideas, and arguments—to ensure that you do not misrepresent that work to your readers
- provide citation information for your sources—to help your readers understand how you have drawn your conclusions and where they can locate those sources should they want to consult them

These three rules are the essence of research ethics. Ultimately, failing to act ethically—even when the failure is unintentional—can reflect poorly on you and your document. If your readers suspect that you have acted unethically, they will question the accuracy and credibility of the information, ideas, and arguments in your document. If they suspect you've sacrificed research ethics altogether, they'll probably stop reading your document. Figure 8.1 shows how Cori Schmidtbauer attended to research ethics in her essay about Portia's role in *The Merchant of Venice.*

An attribution is used to identify the source of a paraphrase and subsequent quotation.

than deferring to her husband. Initially, Portia fulfills the duties of a Renaissance woman by giving Bassanio her ring, an object that then conveyed ownership as well as commitment. As critic Karen Newman writes in "Portia's Ring: Unruly Women and Structures of Exchange in *The Merchant of Venice*," in bestowing the ring, Portia is providing her new husband a "visual sign of her vow of love and submission" of all she has to give—her body, house, status, fortune, etc. (Newman 260). Yet, Newman explains, by giving herself away into marriage, Portia is bestowing more than Bassanio can reciprocate (261): since Portia is the source of Bassanio's improved standing and newfound wealth, she has the upper hand. Portia demonstrates her ability to manipulate the traditional politics of exchange most vividly in the courtroom scene in Act IV

Quotation marks and parenthetical source citation indicate partial quotation.

Brannigan, John. *New Historicism and Cultural Materialism.* New York: St. Martin's Press, 1998. Print.

Hebron, Malcolm. *Key Concepts in Renaissance Literature.* New York: Palgrave Macmillan, 2008. Print.

Hopkins, Lisa, and Matthew Steggle. *Renaissance Literature and Culture.* London: Continuum, 2006. Print.

Newman, Karen. "Portia's Ring: Unruly Women and Structures of Exchange in *The Merchant of Venice.*" *Shakespeare Quarterly* 38.1 (1987): 19–33. Print.

Sources are cited in MLA style.

Complete source information is included in the works cited list.

FIGURE 8.1 Attending to Research Ethics

Working with Sources

8c

What is common knowledge?

Although crediting other authors for their work is important, you almost certainly won't need to document every fact and idea used in your document, because some of the information you'll use falls under the category of common knowledge. Common knowledge is information that is widely known, such as the fact that the Declaration of Independence was signed in 1776. Or it might be the kind of knowledge that people working in a particular field, such as petroleum engineering, use on a regular basis.

If you're relatively new to your topic, it can be difficult to determine whether information in a source is common knowledge. As you explore your topic, however, you will begin to identify what is generally known. For instance, if three or more sources use the same information without citing its source, you can assume that the information is common knowledge. If those sources use the information and cite the source, however, make sure you cite it as well.

8d

What is fair use and when should I ask permission to use a source?

The concept of fair use deals with how much of a source you can borrow or quote. According to Section 107 of the Copyright Act of 1976—the fair use provision, available at **copyright.gov/title17/**—writers can use copyrighted materials for purposes of "criticism, comment, news reporting, teaching (including multiple copies for classroom use), scholarship, or research." In other words, writers generally don't need to seek permission to make brief quotations from a source or to summarize or paraphrase a source.

ⓘ **INFORMATION LITERACY** If you are working on an assignment for a course—and do not plan to publish the assignment on the Web or in print—you generally can use material from another source without seeking permission. Remember, however, that in all cases you must still cite the source of the material you use.

Writers who plan to publish their work should seek permission to use material from a source if they want to quote a lengthy passage or, in the case of shorter works such as poems and song lyrics, if they want to quote a significant percentage of the source.

If you seek permission to use a source, explain why and how you want to use it. Many authors and publishers allow academic use of their work but frown on commercial uses. When you contact an author or a publisher, include your name

Dear Ms. Jackson:

I am a student and am completing a research project for my writing class, English Composition 200, at Colorado State University. The research project will be used only for educational purposes and will be distributed only to my instructor and members of my class for a period of three weeks during April and May of this year.

I would like to include in my project the following image, which is displayed on your site at www.westernliving.org/images/2302a.jpg, and would greatly appreciate your permission to do so:

If you are able to grant me the requested permission, please respond to this email message. My deadline for completing my project is April 22nd. I appreciate your quick response.

If you are not the copyright holder or do not have authority to grant this request, I would appreciate any information you can provide concerning the current copyright holder.

Thank you for considering this request.

Sincerely,

Glenn Choi **D**

GlennChoi@students.colostate.edu

(970) 555–1515

FIGURE 8.2 **Sample Permission Request**

A Or "... on the Web at www.myschool.edu."

B Insert or describe passage or image. For example: "paragraphs 3 through 5 of the article," a thumbnail of the image, the URL of a document or image on the Web.

C Or "... sign the enclosed copy of this letter and return it to me."

D Provide contact information, such as name, address, email address, phone number, fax number.

and contact information, the source you wish to use, the purpose for which you will use the source, and the time during which it will be used (see Figure 8.2).

If you contact an author or a publisher by mail, include a self-addressed, stamped envelope. It saves the author or publisher the cost of responding by mail, indicates that you are serious, and, perhaps most important, shows good manners.

8e

How can I avoid plagiarism?

In most cases, writers who plagiarize do so unintentionally. You can avoid unintentional plagiarism by learning how to:

- conduct a knowledge inventory
- take notes carefully
- distinguish between your ideas and those drawn from your sources
- cite sources in the text and in a works cited or reference list
- recognize misconceptions about intentional plagiarism

Conduct a Knowledge Inventory

You can avoid unintentional plagiarism by ensuring that you have a clear understanding of your issue. When you are just beginning to learn about an issue, you might find it difficult not only to express your own ideas clearly and effectively, but also to restate or reframe the information, ideas, and arguments you've encountered in your sources. The result might be a document composed of passages that have been copied without attribution or paraphrased too closely. To address difficulties understanding an issue, conduct a knowledge inventory to gain insights into what you do and don't understand about the issue. Conducting a knowledge inventory involves answering three questions.

1. What do you already know about the issue?
2. What don't you know?
3. What do you want to know?

My Research Project

Conduct a Knowledge Inventory

In your research log, answer the following questions about the issue you've decided to address in your project document.

1. What do I already know about the issue?

2. What don't I know?

3. What do I want to know?

Review your answers and then identify the concepts that, if you understood them more fully, would allow you to work on your assignment more effectively. Learn about those concepts by discussing them with your instructor, a librarian, or someone who knows about or has been affected by the issue.

bedfordresearcher.com
My Research Project Activities > Conduct a Knowledge Inventory

Your answers can provide a starting point for brainstorming, collecting and working with sources, and planning. They can also serve as a guide for discussing the issue with others. Once you've completed your knowledge inventory, meet with your instructor, consult a librarian, or talk with people who are knowledgeable about the issue. Ideally, your discussions will help you determine the most productive way to learn more about your issue. You might, for example, identify key concepts that, if you understood them more fully, would help you write about your issue more effectively.

Take Notes Carefully

Unintentional plagiarism occurs most often when a writer takes poor notes and then uses information from their notes in a document. Notes might contain direct quotations that are not surrounded with quotation marks, paraphrases that differ in only minor ways from the original passage, and summaries that contain original passages from a source. Taking notes accurately and appropriately is the first—and arguably the most important—step in avoiding unintentional plagiarism. For guidance on quoting, paraphrasing, and summarizing during note taking, see Chapter 6. For guidance on integrating quotations, paraphrases, summaries, numerical information, and illustrations into your document, see Chapter 17.

To avoid plagiarizing as you take notes, keep the following guidelines in mind.

- Surround every quotation with quotation marks.
- Ensure that every paraphrase differs in both wording and sentence structure from the original passage.
- Avoid creating summaries that are little more than a patchwork of sentences pulled from the original source.
- Include publication information—in particular, author information and the location of passages that are quoted or paraphrased—about the source on every note.
- Double-check your notes to be sure that they are accurate and do not include problems that might lead to unintentional plagiarism when you integrate source information into your project document.

The tutorial on p. 136 illustrates some of the problems that can arise as you take notes on your sources.

As You Draft, Distinguish between Your Ideas and Ideas in Your Sources   [FRAMING MY ARGUMENT]

To distinguish between your ideas and those obtained through your sources, use attributions—words and phrases that alert your readers to the source of the information or ideas you are using. To avoid plagiarizing as you integrate information from your notes into your document, use these guidelines.

- Look for notes that differ from your usual style of writing. More often than not, if a note doesn't sound like your own writing, it isn't. If you find a note that might be a direct quotation, a close paraphrase, or a patchwork summary, double-check the note against the original source.

- Use author attributions to clearly distinguish information, ideas, and arguments drawn from your sources. Failing to do so is likely to lead your readers to think the information, ideas, and arguments are your own. To avoid this problem, attribute source information using phrases such as "according to Jessica Richards" and "Sandra Chapman argues."

You can learn more about using attributions to identify the origin of quotations, paraphrases, and summaries in Chapter 17.

Identify Sources in Your Document

Include a complete citation for each source you refer to in your document. The citation should appear both in the text of the document (as an in-text citation) and in a works cited or references list.

In the following examples, the writer includes MLA-style parenthetical citations that refer readers to a list of works cited at the end of the document. Note that MLA style, as well as APA, *Chicago*, and CSE styles, allow for a combination of attributions and parenthetical information to refer to sources (see Chapters 23–26).

> Jessica Richards argues, "We need to develop an efficient, cost-effective means of distributing hydrogen fuels before we can move to a hydrogen economy. If we don't we'll be operating in crisis mode when the next serious oil shortage arrives" (322).

> "We need to develop an efficient, cost-effective means of distributing hydrogen fuels before we can move to a hydrogen economy" (Richards 322).

Be sure to cite page or paragraph numbers for paraphrased and summarized information as well as for direct quotations. The following paraphrase of Jessica Richards's comments about energy needs includes the page number of the original passage in parentheses.

> Jessica Richards argues that we need to create an "efficient, cost-effective" system for delivering hydrogen fuel now, instead of while we are facing a critical oil shortage (322).

To learn more about identifying sources in your document, see pp. 262–71 in Chapter 15. To learn how to document sources using the MLA, APA, *Chicago* and CSE documentation systems, see Chapters 23–26.

Understand Why Writers Plagiarize

Although most plagiarism is unintentional, some students do plagiarize deliberately. The causes of intentional plagiarism range from running out of time to seeing little value in a course. The most common reasons offered to explain

II Working with Sources

TUTORIAL

How do I avoid plagiarism as I take notes?

You can avoid plagiarism at the earliest stage of research by taking notes that quote, paraphrase, and summarize sources accurately and by recording the source of the information.

Original Passage: Coral reefs are one of the most important marine habitats in shallow tropical seas. Reefs provide structure and act as focal points for secondary production. As a consequence, coral reefs provide a number of important ecosystem services (Moberg and Folke 1999). Reefs protect shorelines from coastal erosion and provide habitat for fish and millions of other organisms making them the most biodiverse marine ecosystem. These in turn support commercial and recreational fishing, diving and boating activities, tourist activities, shelter harbors and are a source of biomedicinal compounds.
Source: Richard S. Appeldoorn, Paul M. Yoshioka and David L. Ballantine, "Coral Reef Ecosystem Studies: Integrating Science and Management in the Caribbean," p. 134.

1 Quote appropriately by identifying your source, using quotation marks around quoted material, and providing a page number for the quotation.

Quotation

Appropriate

Coral reefs play important roles in the Caribbean ecosystem. As Appeldoorn, Yoshioka, and Ballantine note, "Reefs protect shorelines from coastal erosion and provide habitat for fish and millions of other organisms" (134).

2 Avoid quoting inappropriately by checking your notes for quotation marks and proper citation of the source's information. Be sure that you've quoted the source accurately using ellipsis marks and brackets to show any deletions (p. 101).

Inappropriate

Coral reefs play important roles in the Caribbean ecosystem, since they protect shorelines from coastal erosion and provide habitat for fish and millions of other organisms.

3 When you paraphrase information from a source in your notes, be sure to use your own words to record the meaning of the passage, and provide a page number to help you locate the information (and create a full citation) later on.

Paraphrase

Appropriate

According to Appeldoorn, Yoshioka, and Ballantine, coral reefs play important roles in the Caribbean ecosystem, serving as habitat for a wide range of ocean species and protecting shorelines from erosion (134).

4 Avoid inappropriate paraphrases by reviewing your notes against the source's wording to make sure they aren't a close match. If the source's wording is compelling and you want to capture it, consider using a quotation instead.

Inappropriate

According to Appeldoorn, Yoshioka, and Ballantine, coral reefs protect shorelines from coastal erosion and offer habitat for fish and multitudes of other organisms.

5 When summarizing, use your own words to create an overview of the source's line of argument. Make sure you record the author and title of the source in your notes or following the summary.

Summary

Appropriate

In the article "Coral Reef Ecosystem Studies: Integrating Science and Management in the Caribbean," Appeldoorn, Yoshioka, and Ballantine point out the important roles that coral reefs play in the Caribbean ecosystem. They note that reefs protect shorelines from erosion and provide habitat for fish and a multitude of other aquatic organisms. In addition, they point out, reefs provide important economic and recreational benefits to people, serving as sites for commercial fishing, sources of biomedical compounds, and opportunities for diving, boating, and other tourist activities.

6 Avoid inappropriate summaries by citing the source of your information. Review your notes to be sure you haven't used the source's wording in your summary.

Inappropriate

Coral reefs are one of the most important marine habitats in shallow tropical seas. They provide a number of important ecosystem services, including protecting shorelines from coastal erosion and serving as habitat for fish and millions of other organisms. These in turn support commercial and recreational fishing, diving and boating activities, tourist activities, shelter harbors and are a source of biomedicinal compounds.

II Wroking with Sources

II Working with Sources

intentional plagiarism—and steps you can take to avoid falling victim to its temptation—are listed below.

"It's easier to plagiarize."   Some people believe it takes less work to cheat than to create an original document. That's probably true—but only in the short term. If you are pursuing a college degree, the odds are high that your profession will require writing ability or an understanding of how to work with information. When you're assigned a report or a proposal down the road, you might regret not taking the time to hone your writing and research skills.

"I ran out of time."   Most writers occasionally find themselves wondering where all the time has gone and how they can possibly complete an assignment on schedule. If you find yourself in this situation, contact your instructor about a revised deadline. You might find that you'll face a penalty for turning in work late, but that penalty will almost certainly be less severe than a penalty for intentional plagiarism.

"I couldn't care less about this assignment."   It's not unusual to put off assignments that don't interest you. Rather than avoiding the work, try to approach the assignment in a way that interests you (p. 40). If that fails, contact your instructor to see if you can customize the assignment so that it better aligns with your interests.

"I'm no good at writing."   A lot of people have doubts about their ability to earn a good grade in a writing course. Occasionally, however, some students convince themselves that plagiarizing is a reasonable alternative to writing their own documents. If you lack confidence, seek assistance from your instructor, a campus writing center, a tutoring center, one of the many online writing centers on the Web (such as the Writing@CSU Web site at **writing.colostate.edu**), or a friend or family member. You're likely to find that, even with only modest support, you'll be able to do well.

"I didn't think I'd get caught."   Some students believe—and might even have experiences to support their belief—that they won't get caught plagiarizing. Most writing instructors, however, become familiar with their students' writing styles. If they notice a sudden change in style, or encounter varying styles in the same document, they might become suspicious. The availability of plagiarism detection software also increases the likelihood that plagiarism will be discovered.

"Everybody cheats."   Some people plagiarize because they believe that many of their classmates are doing so. They fear that, if they don't plagiarize, they'll be at a competitive disadvantage. In fact, however, the number of students who plagiarize is quite low. Don't be persuaded by dramatic statistics that plagiarism is the norm in writing classes. The reality is that few students plagiarize intentionally, and those who do still tend to earn lower grades than their peers.

"This course is a waste of my time." If you view a course as little more than a box that needs to be checked, it might seem reasonable to check that box with as little effort as possible. Turning in work that isn't your own, however, can backfire. If you are caught plagiarizing, you'll most likely receive a reduced—or failing—grade for the assignment or the course. Instead of plagiarizing, talk with the instructor or an academic advisor about your lack of interest. You might find that the course actually has some relevance to your interests and career plans.

8f

What should I do if I'm accused of plagiarism?

If your instructor expresses concerns about the originality of your work or the manner in which you've documented your use of information, ideas, and arguments from sources, ask for a meeting to discuss the situation. To prepare for the meeting take the following steps.

- Review your document to identify passages that might have raised suspicions.
- Collect the materials you've used in your writing project, such as copies of your sources, responses to surveys, interview transcripts, and so on.
- Collect materials you've written during the project, such as the results of brainstorming and freewriting sessions; organizational materials you've created, such as clusters, maps, and outlines; and rough and final drafts of your document.
- Reflect on your research writing process.

During the meeting, listen to the concerns of your instructor before responding. It will be natural to feel defensive about the situation, but you'll probably be more comfortable if you take notes and try to understand why your instructor has concerns about your document. Once your instructor is finished expressing his or her concerns, think carefully about what has been said and respond as clearly as possible. You'll probably find that your instructor will have follow-up questions, most likely about the sources you've used, your research writing process, and the document you've written.

If you find that you have engaged in unintentional plagiarism, ask your instructor for guidance about how to avoid it in the future and ask what sort of penalty you will face for your error. Ask, as well, what consequences you might face should it be determined that you have plagiarized intentionally.

If you and your instructor are unable to resolve the situation, you might face a disciplinary process. To prepare for that process, learn as much as you can about the academic integrity policies at your institution.

> **QUICK REFERENCE**

Avoiding Plagiarism

☑ Understand the definition of plagiarism and the concept of copyright. (p. 127)

☑ Understand the meaning of research ethics. (p. 129)

☑ Understand the concept of common knowledge. (p. 131)

☑ Understand the concept of fair use and, if necessary, seek permission to use sources. (p. 131)

☑ Understand how to reduce the chance that you'll plagiarize unintentionally. (p. 133)

☑ Understand why you might be tempted to plagiarize intentionally and reflect on strategies for avoiding temptation. (p. 135)

☑ Understand what to do if you are accused of plagiarism. (p. 139)

The Bedford Researcher

I	Joining the Conversation
II	Working with Sources
III	**Collecting Information**
IV	Creating Your Document
V	Documenting Sources

PART III

Collecting Information

 Searching for Information with Digital Resources   143

 Searching for Information with Print Resources   170

⑪ **Searching for Information with Field Research Methods**   181

Learning how to collect information provides you with the foundation for a successful research project. As you begin to answer your research question, you'll want to know more about how and where to look for useful sources of information. In this section you'll learn how to search for information using digital resources, print resources, and field research methods.

Part III
Collecting Information

> 9   Searching for Information
       with Digital Resources

10   Searching for Information
     with Print Resources

11   Searching for Information
     with Field Research Methods

9

Searching for Information with Digital Resources

The primary challenge you will face as you search for sources is not finding enough sources; it is finding the right sources. This chapter addresses the important differences among library catalogs, databases, Web search sites, and media search sites that you can use to locate relevant, useful information and explains how to use these resources to locate the best sources for your research writing project.

9a

How can I prepare to search?

To increase your chances of obtaining good results from searches of digital resources, reflect on the work you've done so far, identify search terms related to your issue, learn about the types of searches you might conduct, and get feedback on your plans to carry out those searches.

Review Your Research Plan and Proposal   **? WHAT'S MY PURPOSE?**

As you prepared to explore your topic, you might have created an informal research plan. Later, after you chose your issue, you might have created a research proposal (sometimes called a prospectus). If these documents are available, review them. You're likely to find that they'll provide useful guidance for planning your search of digital resources.

You should also spend time reflecting on the progress you've made so far in identifying useful sources. If you searched library catalogs, databases, or the Web, you probably noticed that one or more of these resources produced better results than others. You might also have noticed that some search terms produced better results than others. Be sure to consider what you've learned so far about useful digital resources and promising search terms.

Consider as well potential links between your issue and specific disciplines or professions. An issue of general interest, such as research on stem cells, which raises a host of ethical and moral issues and has been the subject of debate within the popular media, has also been a topic of discussion within the biological sciences, the social sciences, philosophy, and theology, among several others. Exploring discussions taking place within disciplinary and professional publications allows you to examine your topic from important perspectives. In LaunchPad Solo for *The Bedford Researcher*, you'll find starting points for digital searches in a wide range of disciplines and professions.

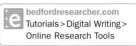
bedfordresearcher.com
Tutorials > Digital Writing >
Online Research Tools

Identify Keywords and Phrases

You can identify useful search terms by using a range of idea-generating techniques, such as brainstorming and clustering, and by building on your research question (p. 45), position statement (p. 70), or thesis statement (p. 201). Brainstorming, freewriting, looping, clustering, and completing sentence starters (pp. 20–26) can help you come up with words and phrases that you can use in your searches. Elizabeth Leontiev, for example, used freewriting to generate ideas for her searches. When she completed her freewriting session, she highlighted promising words and phrases.

> The best source I've read so far is Gutierrez, who said that the best way to improve quality of life for coca farmers is planting alternative crops, like bananas, or even going into dairy farming. There are probably a lot of alternatives — maybe coffee is an option. But there are a lot of obstacles, such as FARC, which is heavily involved in the drug trade, and they prevent farmers from shifting to alternative crops. These groups don't want to lose money by reducing the amount of coca produced. So the farmers find themselves and their families caught between the drug cartels and the government.

You can also generate search terms by using your research question, position statement, or thesis statement as a starting point. Alexis Alvarez, for example, typed her research question in a word processor, formatted the most important words and phrases in the question in boldface, and then brainstormed a list of related words and phrases.

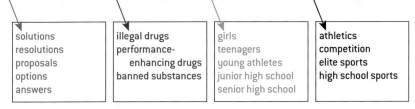

What should be done about **steroid use** by adolescent girls involved in **competitive sports**?

solutions	illegal drugs	girls	athletics
resolutions	performance-	teenagers	competition
proposals	enhancing drugs	young athletes	elite sports
options	banned substances	junior high school	high school sports
answers		senior high school	

My Research Project

Identify Search Terms

To generate keywords for your searches, use one or more of the following strategies.

1. Review your research question, position statement, thesis statement, and working bibliography. Highlight important words and phrases, the names of important authors, and titles of important sources. Create a list of keywords and phrases.

2. Choose one of the words or phrases in your list of search terms and brainstorm about it. Create a list of terms that might be related in some way to the search term you've chosen. Don't worry about how well each new term might work. Instead, jot down ideas as quickly as you can. Then review your list and add the most promising words or phrases to your list of search terms.

3. Choose one of the words or phrases and freewrite about it. Write quickly, without worrying about grammar or mechanics. Then review your freewriting, highlight words and phrases that might serve as search terms, and add them to your list.

↓

4. Try a looping activity by using one of the words or phrases from your free-writing activity as the starting point for a new freewriting session. Repeat the process several times, choosing a promising new word or phrase as a new starting point. At the end of your looping session, highlight promising words and phrases and add them to your list of search terms.

5. Use clustering to general new search terms. Place a word or phrase from your list at the center of a piece of paper, in the middle of a word processing document, in a blank document in an image editor, or in a phone or tablet mind-mapping app such as iThoughtsHD or SimpleMind. Add related terms, and then add terms related to those terms. Add the most promising new words and phrases to your list of search terms.

6. Identify synonyms for words in your list of search terms by using one or more of the following strategies.

   - Open a word processor and use its built-in thesaurus. In Microsoft Word, you can find the thesaurus in the Review ribbon.

   - Visit a Web site such as Thesaurus.com or the Merriam Webster Online Thesaurus (merriam-webster.com/thesaurus/).

   - Search the Web using the search term preceded by the word *synonym* or *define*.

   - Consult a print thesaurus, such as *Roget's 21st Century Thesaurus* or *Webster's New World Pocket Thesaurus*.

7. Use sentence starters, such as the following, to generate additional search terms.

   - The word ___ reminds me of ___.

   - If I were focusing on ___, I would need to think about ___.

   - ___ couldn't happen without ___.

   - The most important aspect of ___ is ___.

   - The most important thing about ___ within my major is ___.

bedfordresearcher.com
My Research Project Activities > Identify Search Terms

Plan Basic Searches

Basic searches consist of entering one or more keywords or phrases in a search field and clicking on the search button. A basic search allows you to look for documents that contain a single word or phrase in the subject, title, text, or in the case of databases, other parts of a database record (see p. 158 for more information about databases). When you enter one or two words in the search field on Google or your library catalog, for example, you are conducting a basic search.

Basic searches can return large sets of results. To increase the odds that your results will be relevant to your subject, consider adding keywords, using exact phrases, and using wildcards.

WORKING TOGETHER

Generate New Search Terms

Work together with your classmates to generate additional keywords and phrases relevant to your issue.

1 **Describe your issue.** Briefly explain what the issue involves, why you are interested in it, and what you think your role might be in the conversation you hope to join (p. 39).

2 **Share your list of search terms.** Ask your classmates to jot down ideas that occur to them as they read your list.

3 **Brainstorm.** Conduct a brief brainstorming session. Listen to your classmates and write down the words and phrases that come up during the session.

4 **Ask questions.** Conduct a brief discussion in which your classmates ask questions about the issue. Keep track of words and phrases that come up during the discussion.

Repeat these activities for each person in the group.

Adding Keywords   In most cases, using several keywords together will limit the number of results returned by your search. This strategy is especially helpful when searching the Web, which tends to produce thousands (sometimes millions) of hits for individual words or phrases (see Figure 9.1).

Adding *competitive* to a search for the keyword *sports* reduces the number of results by roughly 75 percent.

Adding *adolescent* reduces the results by more than 99 percent.

Google sports

About 1,210,000,000 results (0.29 seconds)

Google competitive sports

About 293,000,000 results (0.28 seconds)

Google adolescent competitive sports

About 1,880,000 results (0.31 seconds)

FIGURE 9.1 A Basic Search with Keywords

III Collecting Information

FIGURE 9.2 A Basic Search with Phrases

Searching for Exact Phrases   Sometimes the best way to locate information is to search for an exact phrase. To further refine your search, you might use the phrases *adolescent girls* and *competitive sports* (see Figure 9.2). This would eliminate sources in which the words *adolescent* and *girls* appear but are separated by other words.

Using Wildcards   Sometimes you're not sure what form of a word is most likely to occur. Rather than conducting several searches for *compete*, *competes*, *competitive*, *competition*, and *competitions*, for example, you can combine keywords into a single wildcard search. Wildcards are symbols that take the place of letters or strings of letters. By standing in for multiple letters, they allow you to expand the scope of your search.

The most commonly used wildcard symbols are:

* usually takes the place of one or more characters, such as compet*

? usually takes the place of a single character, such as wom?n

Other wildcard symbols include !, +, #, and $. Consult the help section in a catalog or database or the advanced search page of a Web search engine to learn whether wildcard symbols are supported.

Plan Advanced Searches

In addition to simple searches, most library catalogs, databases, and Web search sites provide an advanced search page. These pages allow you to focus your searches in powerful ways using Boolean operators (which are used to search for all, some, or none of the words in a search box), special symbols (which are used primarily in Web searches), and search limits (such as publication date and document characteristics).

Focusing Searches with Boolean Operators   Boolean operators let you focus a search by specifying whether keywords or phrases can, must, or must not appear in the results. Some Boolean operators also allow you to search for keywords or phrases that appear next to, before or after, or within a certain distance from one another within a document. Table 9.1 lists commonly used Boolean operators and their functions.

TABLE 9.1 COMMONLY USED BOOLEAN OPERATORS

Boolean Operator	Function	Example
AND/&/+	Finds sources that include both terms (either keywords or phrases)	adolescent AND girls adolescent & girls +adolescent +girls
OR/I	Finds sources that include either term	sports OR athletics sports I athletics
NOT/–	Finds sources that include one term but not the other	girls NOT boys girls–boys
ADJ (adjacent)	Finds sources in which the keywords appear next to each other	competitive ADJ athletics
NEAR	Finds sources in which the key-words appear within a specified number of words from each other	adolescent NEAR athlete
BEFORE	Finds sources in which keywords appear in a particular order	competitive BEFORE athletics
Parentheses ( )	Parentheses are used to group keywords and Boolean operators	competitive AND (athletics OR sports) AND (girls NOT boys)

Many databases, library catalogs, and Web search sites include the use of Boolean search terms—typically AND, OR, and NOT or plus (+) and minus (–) signs—in their advanced search forms (see Figure 9.3) or in expert search forms (see Figure 9.4).

FIGURE 9.3 Advanced Search Form Using Boolean Operators [Courtesy of EBSCO.]

Collecting Information

Parentheses group one keyword and a second parenthesis.

OR allows any search terms to be present.

AND requires both sets of search terms to be present.

ProQuest **Sociological Abstracts**

Basic Search | Advanced ▾ | Figures & Tables | About

NOT excludes records that include the search terms in the second set of parentheses.

Command Line Search

Other search options: Advanced Search | Look Up Citation

Enter your search in the box below, using command line syntax. For example, TI(nursing) and AU(smith).
▾ Add search fields

(competitive AND (sports OR athletics)) AND (girls NOT boys)

Search   Clear form

FIGURE 9.4 Expert Search Form Using Boolean Operators [© 2014 ProQuest LLC. All rights reserved.]

Searching: Academic Search Premier | Choose Databases

adolescent girls   TX All Text ▾   Search   Clear   ?

AND ▾ competitive sports   TX All Text ▾

NOT ▾ boys   TX All Text ▾   ⊕ ⊖

Basic Search   Advanced Search   Search History

Search Options

Reset

Search Modes and Expanders

Search modes ?
◉ Boolean/Phrase
○ Find all my search terms
○ Find any of my search terms
○ SmartText Searching Hint

Apply related words
☐

Also search within the full text of the articles
☐

The Limits section provides numerous options for customizing a search.

Limit to documents available in full text

Limit to sources with references

Limit your results

Full Text
☑

References Available
☑

Limit by publication type

Publication

Publication Type
All
Periodical
Newspaper
Book

Document Type
All
Abstract
Article
Bibliography

Language
All
Afrikaans
Arabic
Bosnian

Limit by document type

Number Of Pages
All ▾

Cover Story
☐

Image Quick View
☐

Image Quick View Types
☐ Black and White Photograph   ☐ Chart
☐ Color Photograph   ☐ Diagram
☐ Graph   ☐ Illustration
☐ Map

PDF Full Text
☐

Search

FIGURE 9.5 Advanced Search Using Limits in a Database [Courtesy of EBSCO.]

Limiting Searches   Advanced search forms allow you to limit your searches to documents that have particular characteristics, such as publication date and document type (see Figures 9.5 and 9.6). Search limits allow you to narrow your search in ways that are not available in simple searches. Although the specific limits that are available in an advanced search form vary across databases, library catalogs, and Web search sites, common limits include publication date (or, in the case of Web pages, the date on which a page was last updated), type of document, and the availability of full text (for databases). Many databases and library catalogs also allow you to search within a set of results. This allows you to narrow your results further by adding search terms and setting additional limits.

i INFORMATION LITERACY   As you conduct advanced searches, avoid confusing publication date with what many Web search engines refer to as "modification date," the date on which a particular Web page was most recently updated. Adding an image or changing a single word on a page constitutes a modification. A page created in 1997 will be included in search results for recent sources if a spelling error was corrected last week. Similarly, some Web search engines report a "found on date," which differs from publication date as well. It can take a while for a search site to locate new pages—sometimes as little as an hour after the page is released and sometimes as long as two weeks. In addition, some pages and documents might have been created several years ago but have been found only recently because they have just been made public on a Web site. ▪

FIGURE 9.6 Advanced Search Using Limits on a Web Search Site

TUTORIAL

How do I conduct an advanced search in a database?

Use the advanced search in a database to conduct a Boolean search that includes limits. In this example, Brandon Tate conducted a search in the Academic Search Premier database. [Courtesy of EBSCO.]

1. Use Boolean operators to specify which terms must be in the source (AND), can be in the source (OR), or must not be in the source (NOT).

2. Enter your keywords and phrases. This search looks for articles about hydraulic fracturing and legislation in Colorado that do not involve discussions of lobbying.

3. Choose the database fields that should be searched. Here, the author field is chosen to exclude authors named Drajem, since he already has that source.

4. Set additional limits on your search, such as availability of full text, scholarly journals, and publication date range.

FIGURE 9.7 Searching with Special Operators

Using Special Operators in Web Searches   A number of leading Web sites, such as Google, Yahoo!, Ask, and Bing offer special operators that allow you to fine-tune a Web search (see Figure 9.7). These special operators can be used in combination with keyword, phrase, wildcard, and Boolean searches. Table 9.2 lists several special operators in Web searches.

TABLE 9.2 SPECIAL OPERATORS

Function	Ask	Bing	Google	Yahoo!
Words in Body Text		inbody:steroid	intext:steroid	
Words in Page Title	intitle:steroid	intitle:steroid	intitle:steroid	intitle:steroid
Words in URL	inurl:steroids	inanchor: steroids	inurl:steroids	inurl:steroids
Search a Single Domain	site:www .theantidrug .com	site:www .theantidrug .com	site:www .theantidrug .com	site:www .theantidrug .com
Locate Pages Linking to a Page	inlink:www .theantidrug .com	inbody:www .theantidrug .com	link:www .theantidrug .com	link:www .theantidrug .com
Find Documents in a Specific Format	filetype:pdf	filetype:pdf	filetype:pdf	filetype:pdf

My Research Project
Plan Advanced Searches

If basic searches are likely to result in large sets of results, plan to conduct advanced searches. To get started, review your research plan or research proposal. Then, with your list of potential search terms in mind, consider the following questions.

1. Should I limit my searches to particular types of documents, such as scholarly journals or recent newspaper articles, magazine articles, and blog posts? Should I focus on scholarly books? Should I focus on trade and professional journals? Should I focus on Web discussion forums and email discussion lists? Should I focus on images and video?

III Collecting Information

2. Should I limit my searches to sources published during a certain time period, such as the past two years or between 1960 and 1963?

3. How can I focus my searches by using Boolean search terms?

4. How can I focus my searches of the Web by using special search symbols?

bedfordresearcher.com
My Research Project Activities > Plan Advanced Searches

9b

How can I search for sources with library catalogs?

Library catalogs provide information about the materials in a library's collection. Most libraries provide access to their catalogs through the Web, although some smaller libraries rely on traditional print catalogs. At a minimum, a library catalog will provide information about the author(s), title, publication date, subject, and call number for each source in the library's collection. Often it will also indicate the location of the source in the library and whether the source is available for checkout.

Library catalogs typically help you locate:

- books (print, digital, and audio)
- journals owned by the library (although not individual articles)
- newspapers and magazines owned by the library (although not individual articles)
- documents stored on microfilm or microfiche
- videotapes, audiotapes, CDs, DVDs, and other multimedia items
- maps
- theses and dissertations completed by college or university graduate students

In addition to searching the library catalog at your college or university, you can also benefit from searching other catalogs available on the Web. The Library of Congress catalog, for example, presents a comprehensive list of publications on a particular subject or by a particular author (visit **catalog.loc.gov**). Some sites, such as WorldCat (**worldcat.org**), allow you to locate or search multiple library catalogs. If you find a promising source that your library doesn't own, you can request it through interlibrary loan (p. 172).

Use Search Features

Most library catalogs at colleges and universities allow you to search for sources by author(s), title, keyword, subject, publication date, and call number. You can also create searches that use more than one of these features.

Search by Keyword You can search for a specific word or phrase.

FIGURE 9.8 **Searching by Keyword in a Library Catalog** [Courtesy of Morgan Library, Colorado State University.]

Search by Author If you search by author, you can find sources written by a particular person or organization. Featured writer Cori Schmidtbauer searched for sources written by John Brannigan, one of the writers she'd learned about as she explored her topic.

FIGURE 9.9 **Searching by Author** [Courtesy of Morgan Library, Colorado State University.]

Search by Title If you know the exact title of a source or some of the words in the title, you can search by title to find sources (see Figure 9.10).

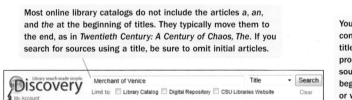

FIGURE 9.10 **Searching by Title** [Courtesy of Morgan Library, Colorado State University.]

Search with Multiple Strategies Library catalogs can help you locate sources quickly, especially when you conduct basic searches, such as an author search by last name. If the last name is a common one such as Smith, Garcia, or Chen, however, your search might produce far more results than you would like. In this case, it might help to use the catalog's advanced search form to search with more than one type of strategy—such as author and keyword—at the same time (see Figure 9.11).

FIGURE 9.11 **Searching with a Combination of Terms** [Courtesy of Morgan Library, Colorado State University.]

Browse by Subject Heading or Call Number

To locate sources related to a promising result, browse by either subject heading or call number (see Figure 9.12).

FIGURE 9.12 **Browsing by Library of Congress Subject Heading** [Courtesy of Morgan Library, Colorado State University.]

To browse directly by subject heading or call number, find out whether your library uses the Library of Congress or Dewey decimal classification systems. Then conduct a call number or subject setting search in your library catalog (the specific options for doing so vary across library catalogs) and enter a main subject heading or call number.

Library of Congress Classification System

A	General Works	K	Law
B	Philosophy, Psychology, Religion	L	Education
C	Auxiliary Sciences of History	M	Music and Books on Music
D	History: General and Old World	N	Fine Arts
E	History: United States	P	Language and Literature
F	History: United States Local and America	Q	Science
G	Geography, Anthropology, Recreation	R	Medicine
H	Social Sciences	S	Agriculture
J	Political Science	T	Technology
		U	Military Science
		V	Naval Science
		Z	Library Science and Information Resources

Dewey Decimal Classification System

000	Computers, Internet, and Systems	500	Science
100	Philosophy	600	Technology
200	Religion	700	Arts
300	Social Sciences, Sociology, and Anthropology	800	Literature, Rhetoric, and Criticism
400	Language	900	History

ⓘ **INFORMATION LITERACY** As you work with subject headings, keep in mind that they differ in important ways from keywords. Subject headings are categories librarians use to organize sources on particular topics. If you search with subject headings in a library catalog, you will find only those sources that have been assigned to that category. If the source is listed under another subject heading, you won't find it even if it contains the same words used in your subject heading search. In contrast, keyword searches will allow you to locate sources that contain the words you are using in your search, but they will not help you find sources that might be relevant to your subject but do not contain those words. In general, it's usually best to search library catalogs in multiple ways. ▪

Collecting Information

My Research Project

Prepare to Search Library Catalogs

As you get ready to search library catalogs, return to your research plan or research proposal and make a list of names, keywords, and phrases. Examine your working bibliography to identify the authors, titles, and subjects of your best sources. Then answer the following questions.

1. What are the names of authors I can use to search by author?

2. What are the titles of works that have been referred to me or that I have found in works cited pages that I can use to search by title?

3. What words and phrases can I use to search by keyword?

4. What words and phrases can I use to search by subject?

5. Does it make sense to search by date? If so, what are the dates I should search within?

6. Would call numbers in the Library of Congress or Dewey decimal classification systems be useful for me to browse? If so, what are these call numbers?

bedfordresearcher.com
My Research Project Activities > Prepare to Search Library Catalogs

9c

How can I search for sources with databases?

Databases operate much like library catalogs, although they focus on a different collection of sources. Whereas a catalog allows you to search for publications owned by the library, a database allows you to search for sources that have been published on a particular subject or in a particular discipline regardless of whether the library owns the sources. Although some databases, such as ERIC, MedLine, and Science Direct, are available publicly via the Web (p. 163), most are available only through library computers or a library Web site.

Libraries subscribe to databases in a manner similar to subscribing to a magazine. Because libraries purchase subscriptions to databases, they typically restrict access to the databases to library patrons, such as students, staff, and faculty.

Databases supply publication information and brief descriptions of the information in a source; some—but not all—provide digital copies of the source. Databases that provide digital copies—sometimes referred to as "full-text" databases—cut out the middle step of needing to search for the source. If you are not sure that your library will own the sources provided by a database, or if you'd simply like to locate them more quickly, consider using full-text databases, such as Academic Search Premier, ERIC, IEEE Xplore, LexisNexis Academic, and ScienceDirect.

If a database does not provide access to digital copies of the source, you can check your library's catalog for the title of the publication in which it appears. If your library does not own the publication, you can request it through interlibrary loan (p. 172).

Databases fall into five general categories.

- **News and information databases** focus on recently published articles in newspapers and popular magazines.

- **Subject databases** focus on a broad subject area, such as education, business, or government.

- **Bibliographies** focus on publications in a specific discipline or profession, such as literary studies, computational linguistics, or the social sciences.

- **Citation indexes** identify sources that have referenced a specific publication, such as an article in a journal or a conference proceeding.

- **Media databases** provide access to images, video, and audio sources.

To search for sources with databases, identify databases that are relevant to the issue you are addressing in your research writing project and then carry out basic and advanced searches. You can identify databases that might be relevant to your issue by reviewing your library's list of databases or consulting a reference librarian.

Search News and Information Databases

If you are focusing on an issue that is likely to have been addressed in recent news coverage, consult news and information databases. Databases in this category, such as ProQuest Newspapers, Alternative Press Index, and Newspaper Source, focus on recently published articles in newspapers, such as the *New York Times*, and popular magazines, such as *Time* and *Newsweek*. Some news and information databases, such as LexisNexis Academic and EBSCOhost Newspaper Source, also allow you to search articles distributed by news services, such as the Associated Press, and transcripts of radio and television programs (see Figures 9.13 and 9.14).

Search Subject Databases

If you are addressing an issue that is related to a broad area of interest, such as business, education, or government, consider searching databases that focus on more general issues, such as Academic Search Premier, Article First, and Catalog of U.S. Government Publications. Subject databases provide information and abstracts (brief summaries) on sources in a given area. WorldCat, for example, identifies sources available in libraries throughout the world, including books and articles as well as media items (see Figure 9.15).

FIGURE 9.13 Searching a News and Information Database [Courtesy of EBSCO.]

Search terms are entered in the search form.

Search is limited by publication date and type.

FIGURE 9.14 Search Results [Courtesy of EBSCO.]

Results are displayed in a list.

Each source can be printed, emailed, or saved.

Full text when available can be viewed in PDF or other formats.

Search terms include two phrases and a keyword.

The search is limited by publication date, language, genre, and availability.

FIGURE 9.15 Searching a Subject Database [© 2014 OCLC Online Computer Library Center, Inc. Used with Permission. WorldCat is a registered trademark/service mark of OCLC.]

Search Bibliographies

If you are contributing to a conversation about an issue within a particular profession or academic discipline, such as literary studies, computational linguistics, or the social sciences, consult bibliographic databases that focus on that area (see Figure 9.16). Many libraries provide advice about databases that are relevant to a particular profession or discipline. For example, if you are interested in an issue related to sociology, you might consult databases such as Family and Society Studies Worldwide, Social Science Abstracts, and Sociological Abstracts. If you are interested in literature or foreign languages, you might consult the MLA International Bibliography.

III Collecting Information

ProQuest **Science & Technology**
Basic Search | Advanced ˅ | Figures & Tables

Advanced Search

Look Up Citation | Command Line

Search terms.

Thesaurus | Field codes | Search tips

| hydraulic fracturing | | | in | Anywhere ˅ |

AND ˅ (Colorado   OR Rocky Mountains   ) in Anywhere ˅

AND ˅ (OR   ) in Anywhere ˅

⊞ Add a row | Remove a row

Search   Clear form

Search results are limited to peer-reviewed articles published in the past three years.

elected databases will return results for this field. View details

Search options

Limit to:
☑ Peer reviewed

Search subject areas

Use search forms customized for each subject

Publication date: Last 3 years ˅

FIGURE 9.16 Searching a Bibliography [Copyright © 2014 ProQuest LLC. All rights reserved.]

FIGURE 9.17 Using a Citation Index [Thomson Reuters.]

A search using the phrase *hydraulic fracturing* and the keyword *government* found a promising article.

Results can be limited by document type (article).

Sources that cite the article are listed in the results.

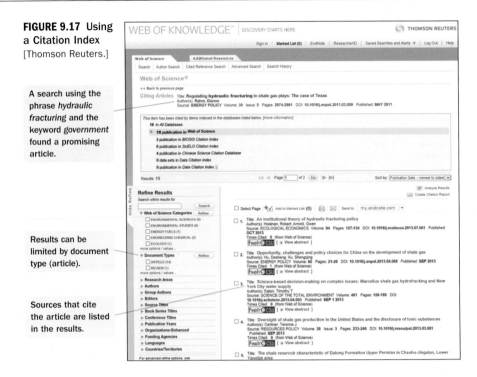

Search Citation Indexes

If you have already located promising sources, you can search citation indexes to identify other sources that refer to those you've located (see Figure 9.17). Depending on the general area you are addressing, you might search databases such as Science Citation Index, Social Sciences Citation Index, or Arts & Humanities Citation Index. Citation indexes provide publication information and abstracts on sources that have referenced a specific publication. A list of these citations can lead you to other relevant sources on your issue, and they can expand your understanding of the conversation you are joining.

ℹ️ **INFORMATION LITERACY** Citation indexes are useful if you have questions about the credibility of a source. Use them to locate the source and determine how other writers have responded to it. Although these databases seldom identify all sources that have cited a source, they can help you understand the role the source is playing in a larger conversation about an issue. ∎

Search Media Databases

If you are seeking non-textual sources, turn to media databases such as ARTstor, AccessScience, or Mountain West Digital Library. Media databases provide access to images, videos, and audio sources. You can use these databases to view historical and contemporary photographs, images of works of art, television shows and movies, and audio recordings of various kinds.

My Research Project

Record Searches

One of the most important research strategies you can use as you collect information is keeping track of your searches. This will save you time, should you need to search again later, and will help determine which keywords and phrases returned the most promising results.

In your research log, record the following information for each of your searches.

1. Resource that was searched

2. Search terms used (keywords, phrases, publication information)

3. Search strategies used (simple search, wildcard search, exact phrase search, Boolean search)

4. Date search was conducted

5. Number of results produced by the search

6. Relevance of the results

7. Notes about the search

bedfordresearcher.com
My Research Project Activities > Record Searches

III Collecting Information

9d

How can I search for sources with Web search sites?

Like library catalogs and databases, Web search sites can help you work with a vast amount of information—in the form of Web pages, blogs, social networking sites, magazine and journal articles, books, music, photos, and videos, etc. Keep in mind, however, that the sources found through Web search sites have not been carefully selected by librarians and editors, as is typically the case with the sources found through library catalogs and databases. Instead, sources found on the Web can be uneven in quality, ranging from peer-reviewed articles in scholarly journals to blogs created by eighth graders.

A surprisingly large number of Web search sites can help you locate sources about the written conversation you've decided to join. Established search sites, such as Ask, Bing, Google, and Yahoo!, constantly compete with new sites, each hoping that you'll turn to them when you wish to conduct a search. To determine which search sites might be best suited to the needs of your research writing situation, consider their areas of emphasis, their range (for example, from general Web searches to such focused areas as blogs or social networking sites), and the tools they offer to support searching and working with results.

Use Web Search Engines

When you use a Web search engine (see Figure 9.18), you obtain information about Web pages and other forms of information on the Internet, including PDF files, PowerPoint files, Word files, blogs, and newsgroups (p. 167). Web search engines keep track of these sources by locating documents on Web sites and entering them in a searchable database. Leading Web search engines include:

AltaVista:	altavista.com
Ask:	ask.com
Bing:	bing.com
Blekko:	blekko.com
DuckDuckGo:	duckduckgo.com
Gigablast:	gigablast.com
Google:	google.com
Lycos:	search.lycos.com
Yahoo! Search:	search.yahoo.com

ⓘ **INFORMATION LITERACY** Keep two cautions in mind as you use Web search engines. First, because most search engines index only a portion of the Web—sometimes as much as 50 percent and sometimes as little as 5 percent—you should use more than one search engine to search the Web. If you don't find what you're

FIGURE 9.18 Google Is the Leading Web Search Engine

Google's "instant search" tool provides search suggestions and shows results as you type. Searches can be limited to types of sources, date, file type, and domain, among other options.

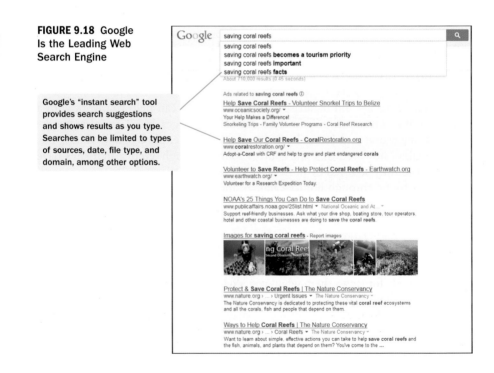

looking for on one, it doesn't mean you won't find it on another. Second, because Web pages can be moved, deleted, or revised, you might find that a search engine's results are inaccurate. Some search sites, such as Google, provide access to cached versions of older Web pages. ▪

Use Web Directories

Unlike Web search sites, Web directories employ human editors to organize information about Web pages into categories and subcategories. Directories allow you to browse lists of Web sites by clicking on general topics, such as Health or Education, and then successively narrow your search by clicking on subtopics. Many directories also permit you to conduct keyword searches within specific categories. This enables you to search within a collection of Web sites that have already been judged by real people to be relevant to your topic. Leading Web directories include:

About.com:	about.com
Best of the Web:	botw.org
ipl2:	ipl.org
Open Directory Project:	dmoz.org
WWW Virtual Library:	vlib.org
Yahoo! Directory:	dir.yahoo.com

Use Meta Search Sites

On a meta search site you can conduct a search on several Web search engines or Web directories at the same time. These sites typically search the major search engines and directories and then present a limited number of results on a single page. Leading meta search sites include:

Dogpile:	dogpile.com
Mamma:	mamma.com
Metacrawler:	metacrawler.com
Search.com:	search.com
Yippy.com:	yippy.com
Zuula:	zuula.com

Use News Search Sites

You can search for news on most major Web search sites and directories, such as Ask, Bing, Google, and Yahoo! In addition, specialized news search sites allow you to conduct focused searches for current and archived news reports, while social news sites such as Digg and StumbleUpon allow you to view news stories and videos that have been recommended by other readers. If you own a

Collecting Information

smartphone, you can also use apps that allow you to view and search news from major newspapers and news sites. Leading news search sites include:

Ask News:	ask.com/news
Bing News:	bing.com/news
Digg:	digg.com
Google News:	news.google.com
StumbleUpon:	stumbleupon.com
World News:	wn.com
Yahoo! News:	news.yahoo.com

Use Reference Search Sites

On a reference search site you can search for information that has been collected in encyclopedias, almanacs, atlases, dictionaries, and other reference resources. Some reference sites, such as Encyclopedia Britannica Online, offer limited access to information from their encyclopedias for no charge and complete access for a fee. Other sites, such as Information Please and Bartleby.com allow unrestricted access to recently published reference works, including the *Columbia Encyclopedia* and *The World Factbook*. If you own a smartphone, you can also use apps developed by Encyclopedia Britannica and Wikipedia to check facts and look up information as you work on your project. Leading reference search sites include:

Bartleby.com Reference:	bartleby.com/reference
Encyclopedia.com:	encyclopedia.com
Encyclopedia Britannica Online:	britannica.com
Information Please:	infoplease.com
Wikipedia:	en.wikipedia.org

i **INFORMATION LITERACY** One widely used reference site, Wikipedia (**en.wikipedia .org**), is collaboratively written by its readers. Because of its comprehensiveness, Wikipedia can serve as a useful starting point for research on a topic. However, because any reader can make changes to the site, it's best to double-check the information you find there. For more information about the drawbacks of relying on Wikis as authoritative sources of information, see p. 95. ■

Use Government Documents Search Sites and Directories

Many government agencies and institutions have turned to the Web as their primary means of distributing their publications. FirstGov, sponsored by the U.S. government, allows you to search the federal government's network of online resources. Government Printing Office Access provides publication information about print documents and links to those publications when they are available online. Sites such as FedStats and USA.gov give access to a wide range of government-related materials. In addition to these specialized government Web sites, you can locate government publications through many Web directories, such as Yahoo! Leading government documents sites include:

About.com's U.S. Government Info:	usgovinfo.about.com
Canadian Government Search Engines:	recherche–search.gc.ca
FedStats:	fedstats.gov
Government Printing Office Access:	gpoaccess.gov
GovSpot.com:	govspot.com
SearchGov.com:	searchgov.com
State and Local Government Directory:	statelocalgov.net
USA.gov:	usa.gov

Use e-Book Sites

In addition to the many e-books available for borrowing from your library, a wide variety of online sites also host books for purchase or free download. You can locate and often preview e-books for your smartphone, tablet, or computer by visiting sites such as:

Amazon:	amazon.com
Barnes and Noble:	bn.com
Google Books:	books.google.com
Internet Archive Community Books:	archive.org/details/texts
Kobo:	kobobooks.com
Online Books Page:	onlinebooks.library.upenn.edu
Project Gutenberg:	gutenberg.org

Use Blog Search Sites

Blogs—short for Weblogs—consist of chronologically ordered entries on a Web site and most closely resemble entries in a diary or journal. Blog entries usually include a title and a text message, but they can also incorporate images, audio, video, and other types of media as well as links to other pages on the Web.

The purposes of blogs vary: Some report on events and issues (see Figure 9.19), some alert readers to information housed elsewhere on the Web, some serve as public relations spaces for institutions and organizations, and some serve largely as a space for personal reflection and expression.

Research writers can use blogs as sources of information and commentary on an issue and as sources of firsthand accounts by individuals involved in or affected by an issue. If you find blogs by experts in the field, you can begin a dialogue with people involved in or knowledgeable about your issue. To locate

FIGURE 9.19 Blog Entry on Protecting Coral Reefs [Reproduced with permission. Copyright © June 2013 *Scientific American*, a division of Nature America, Inc. All rights reserved.]

blogs that are relevant to your research question, use the following blog search sites and directories.

Alltop:	alltop.com
Best of the Web Blogs:	blogs.botw.org
BlogCatalog:	blogcatalog.com
Google Blogsearch:	google.com/blogsearch
IceRocket:	icerocket.com
Technorati:	technorati.com

Use Social Network Search

By searching social networking sites, you can identify individuals who might be knowledgeable about an issue or have been affected by it. You can search social networks using the following sites.

Facebook Search:	facebook.com/search/
Google+ Search:	plus.google.com
LinkedIn Search:	linkedin.com
MySpace Search:	myspace.com

Social Mention: socialmention.com
Twitter Search: twitter.com/search
Tumblr Search: tumblr.com

Use Media Search Sites

The Web is home not only to textual information, such as articles and books, but also to a growing collection of other types of media, such as photographs, podcasts, and streaming video. Image search sites have been available on the Web for years. More recently, search sites have turned their attention to audio and video as well. You can search for media using established search sites, such as Ask, Google, and Yahoo!, as well as a growing number of newer media search sites.

Ask Image Search: ask.com/pictures
Bing Image Search: bing.com/images
Bing Video Search: bing.com/videos/browse
Blinkx: blinkx.com
FindSounds: findsounds.com
Flickr: flickr.com
Google Image Search: images.google.com
Yahoo! Image Search: images.search.yahoo.com
YouTube: youtube.com

III Collecting Information

My Research Project

Discuss Your Research Project with Others

Return to your research log and review what you've learned about your issue. Then ask whether you've taken full advantage of available digital resources. If you are uncertain about how well you've used these resources, discuss your project with a reference librarian or your instructor. Given the wide range of digital resources available, a few minutes of discussion could significantly improve your search for useful sources.

bedfordresearcher.com
My Research Project Activities > Discuss Your Research Project with Others

> **QUICK REFERENCE**

Searching for Information with Digital Resources

☑ Plan your search. (p. 146)

☑ Search your library's catalog. (p. 154)

☑ Identify and search relevant databases. (p. 158)

☑ Identify and use appropriate Web search sites. (p. 163)

Part III
Collecting Information

9   Searching for Information
    with Digital Resources

10 **Searching for Information
    with Print Resources**

11 Searching for Information
    with Field Research Methods

10

Searching for Information with Print Resources

Contrary to recent claims, there is life (and information) beyond the World Wide Web. Print resources can help you locate a wealth of information relevant to your research project. To make the most effective use of the print resources available in a library, ask how the information they can point you toward will help you achieve your purpose as a writer.

10a

Why should I consult print reference works?

Libraries contain a significant collection of print resources designed to help you locate sources. Many of these resources function in a manner similar to that of the databases discussed in Chapter 9. Others offer information that is often not available in digital form, such as reviews of relevant scholarship on various subjects and pointers to other useful resources in an area. Using reference works to locate print resources has several benefits.

- **Most databases have short memories.** Databases seldom index sources published before 1970 and typically index sources only as far back as the mid-1980s. Depending on the conversation you've decided to join, a database might not allow you to locate important sources.

- **Most databases focus on short works.** In contrast, many of the print resources in library reference rooms will refer you to books and longer publications as well as to articles in periodicals.

- **Many library reference resources are unavailable in digital form.** For instance, the *Encyclopedia of Creativity*, which offers more than two hundred articles, is available only in print form.

- **Entries in print indexes are easier to browse.** Despite efforts to aid browsing, databases support searching far better than they do browsing.

ⓘ **INFORMATION LITERACY** If you're working on a research project that has a historical component, as was the case with Elizabeth Leontiev and Cori Schmidtbauer, you'll find that print resources, such as the bibliographies and indexes discussed later in this chapter, can point you toward sources that cannot be located using a database. Moreover, because libraries organize their collections by subject, you can use the sources you locate through print resources as starting points for browsing the library stacks. By relying on the careful selections librarians make when adding to a library collection, you'll be able to find useful, credible sources that reflect your purpose and address your issue. ▪

10b

How can I use the library stacks to locate sources?

The library stacks — or shelves — house the library's collection of bound publications. You can locate publications by browsing the stacks and checking works cited pages for related publications. Once you've decided a source is relevant to your issue, you can check it out or request it through interlibrary loan.

Browse the Stacks

One of the advantages of the classification systems used by most libraries — typically either the Library of Congress or Dewey decimal classification system — is that they are subject-based. As a result, you can browse the stacks to look for sources on a topic because books on similar subjects are shelved together. For example, if your research takes you to the stacks for books about alcohol abuse, you're likely to find books about drug abuse, treatment programs, and codependency nearby.

When you find a publication that seems useful, check the works cited page for related works. The combination of browsing the stacks for sources and checking the works cited pages of those sources can lead you to publications relevant to your issue.

Check Out Books and Periodicals

In some cases, you'll discover that a publication you want is not available because it has been checked out, reserved for a course, or placed in off-site storage. If a publication is checked out, you may be able to recall it — that is, ask that it be returned to the library and held for you. If it has been placed on reserve, you may be able to photocopy or take notes on it. If it has been placed in off-site storage, you can usually request it at the circulation desk.

Use Interlibrary Loan

If you can't obtain the book or periodical you need from your library, use interlibrary loan to borrow materials from another library. Most libraries allow you to request materials in person or on the Web. Some libraries let you check the status of your interlibrary loan request or renew interlibrary loan materials through the Web. You can learn how to use interlibrary loan at your library by consulting its Web site or a librarian.

III Collecting Information

My Research Project

Identify Relevant Disciplinary Print Resources

As you identify print resources, consider connections between your issue and particular professions or disciplines, such as medicine or civil engineering. Many professional organizations, such as IEEE (technology), APA (psychology), and NCTE (English), publish journals and books. These can often be located using publications available in print forms. To get started locating relevant print resources, visit LaunchPad Solo for *The Bedford Researcher*. You'll find starting points for locating print resources in a wide range of disciplines and professions.

bedfordresearcher.com
My Research Project Activities > Identify Relevant Disciplinary Print Resources

10c

How can I use a library periodicals room to locate sources?

Periodicals include newspapers, magazines, and scholarly and professional journals. A periodicals room — or journals room — contains recent issues for library visitors to browse. Many libraries also have a separate room for newspapers published in the last few weeks or months.

i **INFORMATION LITERACY**   To help you locate articles in periodicals, most periodicals rooms provide access to online databases, which are more likely than print indexes and bibliographies to contain listings of recent publications. Once you've identified articles you want to review, you'll need to find the periodicals containing those articles. Most library catalogs allow you to conduct a title search for a periodical in the same way you conduct a title search for a book. The catalog will tell you the call number of the periodical, and most catalogs will give information about its location in the library. In addition, some libraries provide a printed list that identifies where periodicals are located. If you have difficulty finding a periodical or judging which publications are likely to contain articles relevant to your research project, ask a librarian for assistance. ■

Consult Periodicals

To ensure everyone's access to recently published issues, most libraries don't allow you to check out periodicals published within the last year, and they usually don't allow newspapers to be checked out at all. Older periodicals are sometimes placed in bound volumes in the stacks. Few libraries, however, keep back issues of newspapers in paper form. Instead, you can often find back issues of leading newspapers in full-text databases or in microforms. *Microform* is a generic name for both microfilm, a strip of film containing greatly reduced images of printed pages, and microfiche, film roughly the shape and size of an index card containing the same kinds of miniaturized images. You view these images using a microform reader, a projection unit that looks something like a large computer monitor. Many microform readers allow you to print full-size copies of the pages.

Use Works Cited Lists to Find Key Voices   [FRAMING MY ARGUMENT]

Many of the articles you'll find in your library's periodicals room will contain works cited or reference lists. When you find an article that is relevant to your argument, check the list of sources for related articles. As you find new sources, check for authors whose work is cited frequently (see Figure 10.1). This will help identify key voices in the conversation, writers whose work is either controversial, groundbreaking, fundamental, or in some other way central to the conversation.

Collecting Information

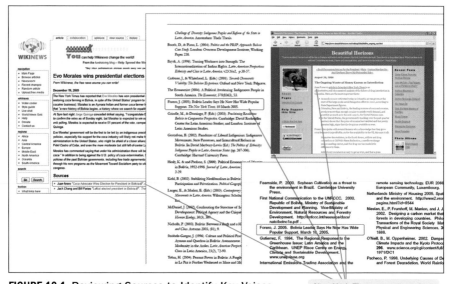

FIGURE 10.1 Reviewing Sources to Identify Key Voices
[Republished with permission of ABC-CLIO, from *The Humanities: A Selective Guide to Information* by Ron Blazek and Elizabeth Aversa, January 1, 2000; permission conveyed through Copyright Clearance Center, Inc.]

New York Times correspondent Juan Forero is a frequently cited source of information about Bolivian politics and efforts to eradicate coca plants.

10d

How can I use a library reference room to locate sources?

Reference rooms contain print resources on a range of topics, from government to finance to philosophy to science. Some of the most important print resources you can consult in a reference room include bibliographies, indexes, biographies, general and specialized encyclopedias, handbooks, almanacs, and atlases. If your library does not have a reference room, you will find these resources in the stacks. A librarian or a member of the library staff at a help desk can help you locate print reference works.

Consult Bibliographies

Bibliographies list books, articles, and other publications that have been judged relevant to a topic. Some bibliographies provide only citations, while others include abstracts—brief descriptions—of listed sources. Complete bibliographies attempt to list all the sources published about a topic, while selective bibliographies attempt to list only the best sources published about a topic. Some bibliographies limit their inclusion of sources by time period, often focusing on sources published during a given year.

Types of Bibliographies   You're likely to find several types of bibliographies in your library's reference room or stacks, including trade bibliographies, general bibliographies, and specialized bibliographies.

- **Trade bibliographies** allow you to locate books published about a particular topic. Leading trade bibliographies include *The Subject Guide to Books in Print, Books in Print,* and *Cumulative Book Index.* Cori Schmidtbauer found a large number of books about *The Merchant of Venice* in the *Annual Bibliography of English Language and Literature* (see Figure 10.2).

- **General bibliographies** cover a wide range of topics, usually in selective lists. For sources on humanities topics, consult *The Humanities: A Selective Guide to Information Sources.* For sources on social science topics, see *Social Science Reference Sources: A Practical Guide.* For sources on science topics, go to bibliographies such as *Information Sources in Science and Technology, Guide to Information Sources in the Botanical Sciences,* and *Guide to Information Sources in the Physical Sciences.*

- **Specialized bibliographies** typically provide lists of sources—often annotated—about a topic. For example, *Art Books: A Basic Bibliography of Monographs on Artists,* edited by Wolfgang M. Freitag, focuses on sources about important artists.

Locating Bibliographies   Although most general and trade bibliographies can be found in your library reference room, specialized bibliographies are likely to be located in your library's stacks. To locate bibliographies, follow these steps.

1. *Consult a cumulative bibliography.* Cumulative bibliographies provide an index of published bibliographies. *The Bibliographic Index: A Cumulative Bibliography of Bibliographies,* for instance, identifies bibliographies on a wide range of topics and is updated annually.

2. *Consult your library's catalog.* When you search your library's catalog, use keywords related to your issue plus the keyword *bibliography.* Cori Schmidtbauer searched her college's catalog using the keywords *Shakespeare* and *bibliography.*

3. *If necessary, seek advice from a reference librarian.* Reference librarians will help you find bibliographies that are relevant to your issue.

Consult Indexes

Indexes provide citation information for sources found in a particular set of publications. Many indexes also include abstracts—brief descriptions—that can help you determine whether a source is worth locating and reviewing. The following types of indexes can be found in libraries.

Periodical Indexes   Periodical indexes list sources published in magazines, trade journals, scholarly journals, and newspapers. Some periodical indexes cover

III Collecting Information

304   SIXTEENTH CENTURY   [2007

The Merchant of Venice ————————————————————————————— The subject
                                                                       heading

5690. BAYNHAM, MATT.   Why is mercy 'twice blest'? NQ (54:3) 2007, 285.

5691. BILELLO, THOMAS C.   Accomplished with what she lacks: law, equity, and
Portia's con. *In* (pp. 109–26) **5221**.

5692. CANTOR, PAUL A.   The shores of hybridity: Shakespeare and the
Mediterranean. LCom (3:4) 2006, 896–913.

5693. CHERNAIK, WARREN.   *The Merchant of Venice.* (Bibl. 2006, 5957.) Rev. by
Willy Maley in MLR (102:4) 2007, 1139–42.

5694. FITZPATRICK, LISA.   Staging *The Merchant of Venice* in Cork: the
concretization of a Shakespearean play for a new society. ModDr (50:2) 2007, Recently
168–83.   published
                                                                                articles
5695. FORKER, CHARLES R.   Marlowe's *Edward II* and *The Merchant of Venice.*
SNL (57:2) 2007, 65, 70.

5696. GROSS, KENNETH.   Shylock is Shakespeare. (Bibl. 2006, 5961.) Rev. by
Katharine Craik in TLS, 21 Sept. 2007, 24; by William J. Kennedy in RQ (60:2)
2007, 665–7; by Martin J. Plax in CompDr (41:2) 2007, 260–4.

5697. HALIO, JAY L.   The study of Shakespearean playbooks. *In* (pp. 38–45) **5409**.

5698. HARRIS, JONATHAN GIL.   The time of Shakespeare's Jewry. SStud (35)
2007, 39–46.

5699. IYENGAR, SUJATA.   Moorish dancing in *The Two Noble Kinsmen.*
See **5885**.

5700. KAPLAN, M. LINDSAY.   Jessica's mother: medieval constructions of Jewish
race and gender in *The Merchant of Venice.* ShQ (58:1) 2007, 1–30.

5701. KOLLMANN, JUDITH.   How 'all that glisters is not gold' became 'all that is
gold does not glitter': Aragorn's debt to Shakespeare. *In* (pp. 110–27) **17430**.

5702. LAKE, JAMES H.   The influence of primacy and recency upon audience
response to Michael Radford's *The Merchant of Venice.* SNL (57:2) 2007, 61, 78.

5703. LEVIN, RICHARD.   Launcelot's and Huck's moral dilemmas. SNL (56:3)
2006/07, 83.

5704. MAGNUS, LAURY.   Michael Radford's *The Merchant of Venice* and the
vexed question of performance. LitFQ (35:2) 2007, 108–20.

5705. MAZER, CARY M.   The intentional-fallacy fallacy. *In* (pp. 99–113) **5412**.

5706. ROSS, CHARLES.   Avoiding the issue of fraud: 4, 5 Philip & Mary c.8 (the
Heiress Protection Statute), Portia, and Desdemona. *In* (pp. 91–108) **5221**.

5707. ROSTON, MURRAY.   Tradition and subversion in Renaissance literature:
studies in Shakespeare, Spenser, Jonson, and Donne. Pittsburgh, PA: Duquesne
UP, 2007. pp. xiii, 258. Rev. by Christopher Baker in RQ (60:4) 2007, 1458–60.

5708. ROTHWELL, KENNETH S.   Trevor Nunn's *The Merchant of Venice*: Portia's
house of mystery, magic, and menace. *In* (pp. 204–16) **5409**.

5709. WILSON, LUKE.   Drama and marine insurance in Shakespeare's London.
In (pp. 127–42) **5221**.

FIGURE 10.2 An Entry from the *Annual Bibliography of English Language and
Literature* on *The Merchant of Venice* [By permission of the Modern Humanities
Research Association.]

Collecting Information

a wide range of periodicals, others focus on periodicals that address a single subject, and still others focus on a small set of or even individual periodicals.

- *The Readers' Guide to Periodical Literature* indexes roughly two hundred general-interest magazines. Updated monthly, the *Readers' Guide* organizes entries by author and subject.
- *Art Index* provides information about sources published only in art magazines and journals. Updated quarterly, *Art Index* organizes entries by author and subject.
- *The New York Times Index* lists articles published only in that newspaper. Updated twice a month, the *Index* organizes entries by subject, geography, organization, and references to individuals.

A student writer used *The Readers' Guide to Periodical Literature* to locate early sources about college admission (see Figure 10.3).

Significant differences can exist between the print and digital database versions of periodical indexes. For example, while the printed *Readers' Guide to Periodical Literature* covers publications since 1900, the *Readers' Guide* database only contains information on articles published since 1983.

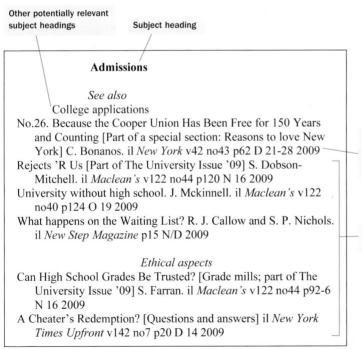

FIGURE 10.3 A Listing in *The Readers' Guide to Periodical Literature* [A listing in *The Reader's Guide to Periodical Literature*, Reprinted from Readers' Guide to Periodical Literature, © H. W. Wilson, a division of EBSCO. Information Services. Used with permission.]

Indexes of Materials in Books   To locate articles in edited books, turn to resources such as the *Essay and General Literature Index*, which indexes nearly five thousand book-length collections of articles and essays in the arts, humanities, and social sciences. You might also find subject-specific indexes of materials in books. The *Cumulative Bibliography of Asian Studies*, for example, covers articles in edited books.

Pamphlet Indexes   Libraries frequently collect pamphlets of various kinds. To help patrons find these materials, many libraries create a pamphlet index. Ask a reference librarian whether your library has a pamphlet index and where it is. You can also consult the *Vertical File Index*. Updated monthly, this index lists roughly three thousand brief sources on ten to fifteen newsworthy topics each month.

Government Documents Indexes   Government documents indexes list documents published by federal, state, and local governments.

- To find documents published by the federal government, consult the *Monthly Catalog of United States Government Publications.*
- To locate documents published by the U.S. Congress, look in the *CIS Index to Publications of the United States Congress.*
- To obtain information about the daily proceedings of the House of Representatives and the Senate, consult the *Congressional Record.*
- For documents published by the Supreme Court, consult *United States Reports*, the cumulative index of the *Official Reports of the Supreme Court.*
- To locate government documents containing statistical information, including census reports, look in the *Statistical Abstract of the United States.*

Many larger college and university libraries serve as depositories of government documents. As a result, indexes to government documents might be found in either the reference room or a separate government documents collection in your library. Ask a reference librarian for help.

Citation Indexes   Citation indexes allow you to determine which publications make reference to other publications, a useful strategy for finding sources that are engaged in the same conversation. To learn which sources refer to an article published in a scientific journal, for example, you could consult the *Science Citation Index*.

Consult Biographies

Biographies cover key figures in a field, time period, or geographic region. *Who's Who in America*, for instance, provides brief biographies of important figures in the United States during a given year, while *Great Lives from History* takes a broader view, offering biographies of key figures in world history.

TUTORIAL

How do I use a bibliography?

Use a bibliography to locate important publications about a subject. In this example, Cori Schmidtbauer used *The Humanities: A Selective Guide to Information Sources* to locate information about William Shakespeare.

1 Locate your subject through the index or page headings, as you would in a phone book.

2 If it is provided, read background information about the subject.

3 Review the bibliography to identify sources that are judged by the author of the subject entry or the editors of the bibliography to be relevant to the subject.

4 Entries in specialized bibliographies are often written by leading scholars. If the author of an entry is identified, search for publications by that author.

Literature ■ *459*

1152. Annual Bibliography of Victorian Studies. Edmonton, Alberta: LITIR Database, 1977– . Ann. ISSN 0227-1400.
The Victorian period is defined as the time period from about 1830 to the beginning of World War I in 1914. This annual bibliography contains English-language materials of various kinds, including books, periodical articles, and reviews relating to that interesting period. It is not limited to literary subjects but attempts to treat the period in its entirety. The work is composed of seven major segments or categories, beginning with general reference works, including fine arts, philosophy and religion, history, social science, and technology. Most important is the section on language and literature, with sections on individual authors. Reviews are cited after the work itself. Indexed by subject, author, title, and reviewer. There is a cumulative index issued as *Victorian Studies* (Indiana University Press, 1957–), a quarterly published an annual bibliography of books and periodical articles since its first Bibliography" serves as a continuation of the list originally published in *M... and was a project of a Committee on Victorian Literature of the Modern L... tion of America. Periodic cumulations of these bibliographies have been... University of Illinois Press as *Bibliographies of Studies in Victorian Litera... (1945; 1945–1954 (1956); 1955–1964 (1967). AMS published the most recent... the periods 1965–1974 (1981), and 1975–1984 (1991).

1153. Interviews and Conversations with 20th-Ce... Writing in English: An Index. Series I–III. Stan A. Vrana... Scarecrow Press, 1982–1990. 3v. ISBN 0-8108-2352-7 (III).
Series II of this work appeared in 1986 and augments the coverage of t... by adding more personalities. In Series I and II, the interviews were publish... and 1980. Series III continues the coverage, indexing interviews published b... 1985. In all the volumes, arrangement is alphabetical by name of the autho... then listed chronologically. These interviews are taken from a variety of sou... and periodicals, both general and literary, from the United States and foreig... included, much to Vrana's credit, are African and Asian titles. Monographi... covered, but are listed separately. About 3,600 interviews are identified i... 4,500 in the second series, and 5,600 in the third series, providing an extrac... venient access tool for this important material.

1154. Shakespeare Survey: An Annual Survey of S... Study and Production. Cambridge, UK: Cambridge Un... 1948– . Ann. ISSN 0080-9152.
This is a highly useful and highly successful annual review of studie... but foremost area of literary research. In the past, it has been under the combi... of several scholarly and cultural organizations: the University of Birmingha... Manchester, Royal Shakespeare Theatre, and the Shakespearean Birthplace... are given to specific themes that provide a focus for the articles of that year o... particular element or feature of Shakespearean study. The scope is internati... are furnished by scholars from a number of countries and regions. Most impo... bibliography is the regular feature "The Year's Contribution to Shakespearea... is a critical survey of research and publication in the field.

1155. The Wellesley Index to Victorian Periodica... Walter E. Houghton, ed. Toronto: University of Toronto Pres... 5v. ISBN 0-4150-3054-4 (v.1).

Author, publisher, and ISBN help locate the source

Literature ■ *471*

as a supplement to the entire set, furnishing excerpts written in the previous ten years and bringing the critical coverage to the 1970s. Volume 5 (1989) is another ten-year supplement. In all volumes, critical studies from both books and periodicals are used.

1188. The Essential Shakespeare: An Annotated Bibliography of Major Modern Studies. 2d ed. Larry S. Champion. New York: G. K. Hall, 1993. 463p. (A Reference Publication in Literature). ISBN 0-8161-7332-X.
An especially useful tool for a student in identifying relevant and important critical studies is this annotated bibliography of more than 1,500 entries, now in its second edition. The coverage is limited to modern criticism, providing references to those studies published only in the twentieth century. Major sections or categories represented are general works, poems and sonnets, English history plays, comedies, and tragedies. Included in the general works section are bibliographies, editions, studies of sources, and film studies. Each of the specialized sections also contains an opening subsection on general studies. Annotations are detailed and furnish scope notes and dominant themes from each work. Although some oversights have been noted in the past edition, the work remains a useful source of information.

*1189. Exploring Shakespeare. Detroit: Gale Research, 1997. (The Gale DISCovering Program). ISBN 0-7876-0913-7. (CD-ROM).
Another in the publisher's program (entries 1255, 1285) presenting a resource kit for teaching/learning consisting of a CD-ROM along with a guide and manual, this is a comprehensive multimedia tool for high school and college students that examines four of the most frequently studied tragedies. Treated here are "Macbeth," "Julius Caesar," "Hamlet," and "Romeo and Juliet"; full text is provided, along with detailed plot summaries with synopses of each act, critical essays, thematic interpretations, and descriptions of historical context. There are listings of characters, related documents, and so forth. A good biography of Shakespeare is provided, as are a time line, notes, and a glossary. Hypertext links bring up relevant full-text documents as well as graphics, audio, and video clips.
*Shakespeare (Creative Multimedia Corporation, 1989) is a CD-ROM publication offering the complete text of all plays, poems, and sonnets in both Queen's English and American English versions. A similar effort is **Complete Works of Shakespeare* (Andromeda Interactive, 1994), which provides full text of plays and sonnets along with numerous images.

1190. The Feminist Companion to Literature in English: Women Writers from the Middle Ages to the Present. Virginia Blain et al. New Haven, CT: Yale University Press, 1990. 1231p. ISBN 0-300-04854-8.
This is the most comprehensive biographical dictionary of its type, covering some 2,700 female writers from the Middle Ages to the mid-1980s who have written in the English language. The work has traded depth for its great breadth, and entries are limited to no more than 500 words. Arrangement is alphabetical by name of writer, with entries providing a biographical sketch, description of important writings, and a brief list of secondary source material for additional reference. Emphasis has been given to inclusion of British writers, although there is representation from the United States, Africa, Asia, the Caribbean, the South Pacific, Australia, and Canada. Novelists, poets, and playwrights are treated along with writers of diaries, letters, biographies, nonfiction, and children's literature. Along with the biographical entries, there are about sixty on topics such as black feminist criticism and science fiction.

Relevant source

Description of source

III Collecting Information

Consult General and Specialized Encyclopedias

General encyclopedias attempt to provide a little knowledge about a lot of things. The idea behind a general encyclopedia, such as the *New Encyclopaedia Britannica*, is to present enough information about a topic to get you started on a more detailed search. Specialized encyclopedias such as *The MIT Encyclopedia of the Cognitive Sciences*, for example, take a narrower focus than general encyclopedias, usually of a field of study or a narrow historical period. In addition, articles in specialized encyclopedias are typically longer than articles in general encyclopedias and offer more detailed coverage of topics.

Consult Handbooks, Almanacs, and Atlases

Like encyclopedias, handbooks provide useful background information about a topic in a compact form. Unlike encyclopedias, most handbooks, such as *The Engineering Handbook*, cover a narrow topic area. Entries in handbooks are also much shorter than the articles found in encyclopedias.

Almanacs contain lists, charts, and tables of information of various types. You're probably familiar with *The Old Farmer's Almanac*, which is known for its accuracy in predicting weather over the course of a year. Information in almanacs can range from the average rainfall in Australia to the batting averages of the 1927 Yankees to the average income of Germans and Poles prior to World War II.

Atlases provide maps and related information about a region or country. Some atlases take a historical perspective, while others take a topical perspective.

My Research Project

Discuss Your Research Project with Others

Return to your research log and review what you've learned about your issue. Then ask whether you've taken advantage of the print resources available in your library reference room. If you're uncertain about how you might use these resources, discuss your project with a reference librarian. Given the wide range of specialized print resources that are available, a few minutes of discussion with a knowledgeable librarian could save you a great deal of time.

bedfordresearcher.com
My Research Project Activities > Discuss Your Research Project with Others

> **QUICK REFERENCE**

Searching for Information with Print Resources

☑ Use the library stacks to locate sources. (p. 171)
☑ Use the periodicals room to locate sources. (p. 173)
☑ Use the reference room to locate sources. (p. 174)

Part III
Collecting Information

9 Searching for Information
   with Digital Resources

10 Searching for Information
    with Print Resources

> **11 Searching for Information
      with Field Research Methods**

11

Searching for Information with Field Research Methods

> **Key Questions**

Published documents aren't the only source of information for a research project. Nor are they always the best. Publications—such as books, articles, Web sites, or television reports—offer someone else's interpretation of an event or an issue. By relying on another person's interpretation, you're looking through that person's eyes rather than through your own.

Experienced research writers know that you don't have to use published reports to find out how an event or issue has affected people—you can ask the people yourself. You don't have to read a review of a concert, movie, or speech— you can go to the event yourself. And you don't have to rely on someone else's survey of public opinion—you can conduct your own.

11a

When should I use field research methods? ❓ WHAT'S MY PURPOSE?

Some research writers think of field research as the next-best thing to learning about an issue through a published source. If they can't find anything relevant in books, in articles, in newspapers, in blogs, or on Twitter, they think, then field research might be worth considering.

These writers misunderstand the value and power of field research. Far from being a good fallback position, field research is sometimes the best way to learn about an issue or collect information to support a position.

Consider using field research methods if you find yourself in one of the following situations.

- If published sources address your issue from a perspective that you don't find useful, field research can provide another way of approaching the issue. For example, most discussions of gun rights and gun control focus on constitutional arguments. If you want to consider the issue from another perspective, such as differences in how people from rural areas and urban or suburban areas understand the issue, you might find it useful to collect information through interviews, surveys, or correspondence.

- If you are interested in an issue that most people think of as settled, published sources are unlikely to include information, ideas, and arguments that might help you challenge the conventional wisdom about the issue. Field research, in contrast, can bring new voices, experiences, and ideas into the conversation.

- If the issue you are addressing is so current that little authoritative information is available, field research can provide needed information about it.

- In some cases, you'll find yourself considering an aspect of an issue that hasn't been addressed so far in your sources. If you come up with a new idea or argument that seems reasonable and obvious, field research can provide a useful reality check, allowing you to explore your idea or argument through interviews, observation, surveys, or correspondence.

- Sometimes you'll find that your line of argument can be strengthened by including primary sources in your document. Information from interviews, correspondence, or observation notes can bring a document to life, providing your readers with firsthand reports from people who know about or have been affected by an issue. Similarly, information from a survey can allow your readers to see trends and differences among groups that might not otherwise be clear.

Thinking carefully about the role field research might play in your research project can help you decide whether and how to conduct it. Sometimes the decision to use a particular field research method is a natural extension of the kind of work you're doing. For example, although Alexis Alvarez was able to find plenty of information from other sources about the pressures that would lead adolescent female athletes to use performance-enhancing drugs, she decided to interview friends and family members who had played competitive sports because she knew that firsthand reports would strengthen her argument.

At other times, the decision to conduct an interview isn't so much the result of careful planning as it is the recognition of an available opportunity. Brandon Tate, who created a Web site about hydraulic fracturing, learned that one of his friends had recently volunteered for a local campaign against fracking. He followed his friend over the course of a day, observing his interactions and the work that he did. Brandon's observations provided him with a personal perspective about fracking that he wouldn't have been able to find through print or digital sources. Similarly, Nicholas Brothers had the opportunity to interview a professor who provided him with valuable insights about his issue, the growing use of private military corporations by the U.S. government.

Whether you rely primarily on field research or use it in combination with information from published sources, remember that field research methods can be powerful tools for exploring your issue and developing your position. As you conduct field research, keep in mind the strategies discussed in Chapter 7 for managing print and digital information. Using those strategies will help you save and organize the information you collect so that you can locate it quickly and easily.

11b

How can I use interviews to collect information?

Interviews — in which one person seeks information from another — can provide firsthand accounts of an event, authoritative interpretations of events and issues, and reactions to an event or issue from the people who have been affected by it. Most interviews follow a question-and-answer format, but some more closely resemble a free-flowing discussion. You can conduct interviews face to face, over the telephone, via email, and even through an instant messaging program.

Plan Your Interview

The most important things to consider as you plan your interview are whom to interview, what to ask, and how to conduct your interview.

Deciding Whom to Interview   Your decisions about whom to interview should be based on the kind of information you want for your research project.

- If you're trying to better understand a specific aspect of a conversation, interview an expert in the field such as a professor, government official, or member of the business community.

■ Collecting Information

- If you want to learn what people in general think about an issue, interview a number of people who are affected by the issue in different ways.
- If you're hoping to collect quotations from people who are authorities on a subject, interview someone who will be recognized as knowledgeable by your readers.

Once you've decided what sorts of people you want to interview, you'll need to identify and contact interview candidates. If you're working on a research project for a class, ask your instructor and classmates for suggestions. Then ask whether they can introduce you to the people they suggest. Before you call to set up an interview, make some preparations.

1. Write a script to help you remember what to say.
2. Prepare a list of dates and times that work for you.
3. Estimate how much time you'll need to complete the interview.
4. Be ready to suggest a location for the interview.
5. Leave your phone number or email address so that your interview candidate can get in touch with you if a conflict arises.

Decide What You Should Ask [FRAMING MY ARGUMENT]

Your interview questions should focus on the issue you want to address in your project. As you prepare your questions, keep the following principles in mind.

1. *Consider your research question*, the role you are adopting, and the kind of information you want to collect. Are you seeking background information, or do you want someone's opinion? An answer to the question, "How did this situation come about?" will be quite different from an answer to the question, "What do you think about this situation?"
2. *Ask questions that require more than a yes or no answer.* You'll learn much more from an answer to a question such as "What factors will affect your vote on referendum X?" than from an answer to "Will you vote for referendum X?"
3. *Prepare a limited number of main questions and many follow-up questions.* Good interviews seldom involve more than eight to ten main questions, but experienced interviewers know that each question can lead to several follow-up questions, such as "Why do you think this has happened?" or "How did your coworkers react to the new policy?"
4. *Be flexible.* Be prepared to tailor your follow-up questions to the interviewee's responses.

Deciding How to Conduct Your Interview
You can conduct interviews face to face, over the telephone, and through a wide range of computer-based tools, such as email, chat, and video communication programs. Each method has advantages and disadvantages.

- Face-to-face interviews conducted in person or through a computer-based video tool such as Skype or Google Voice allow you to carry out a nearly normal conversation with the person you are interviewing. You can rely on your experiences in other conversations to determine whether the interview is effective, whether the person you are interviewing is comfortable, and whether he or she understands your questions. Most interviewees will answer your questions directly, and most will elaborate by giving examples, suggestions about related resources, and so on. If you can see the person you interview, pay close attention to nonverbal cues, such as facial expressions, body positions, and eye contact. Nonverbal cues can help you understand whether your questions are clear, welcome, or surprising and can alert you to opportunities to ask useful follow-up questions.

- Telephone interviews also let you hold a fairly normal conversation, but it's important to ensure that you can carry out your side of the conversation in relative peace and without distractions. You won't have visual cues to help you connect with the person you are interviewing, so be sure to pay attention to pauses, tone of voice, and changes in speaking volume that might indicate surprise, discomfort, or confusion. As in face-to-face interviews, you'll receive fairly direct responses and elaboration to questions.

- Written interviews conducted by email, chat, text messaging, or letter can be a good option if the person you'd like to interview is difficult to reach because of distance or a busy schedule. Written responses to interview questions are generally more precise than spoken responses. Written responses can be reviewed and revised by the person being interviewed to ensure that statements are clear and accurate, while spoken responses are usually more spontaneous.

Deciding Whether to Share Questions in Advance Sharing questions in advance can have benefits and drawbacks. It can allow the person you'll interview to reflect on your questions and prepare a response. If you are interested in seeing candid reactions to a question, however, or if you worry that seeing the questions might make the interviewee reluctant to go through with the interview, don't share them. Ultimately, the decision about whether to share questions in advance depends on your purpose.

Deciding How to Record and Take Notes on Your Interview Recording or saving a transcript of an interview, along with taking notes, provides you with a complete record of what was said, which helps you ensure the accuracy of quotations, paraphrases, and summaries.

- **Recordings** If you plan to record a face-to-face, telephone, or video-based interview, seek permission in advance or at the start of the interview. Remember that some people might be nervous about being recorded, and

III Collecting Information

be prepared to explain how you'll use a recording. If you think someone might be nervous about being recorded, be sure that your initial questions will allow him or her to become comfortable about the interview process.

- **Transcripts** If you are conducting an interview via email (or even via a series of text messages), you'll have a written record of all the responses to your questions. Similarly, you can save a transcript from most chat sessions and even Google Voice conversations, either by saving a file from the chat program or copying and pasting the transcript into a word processing file. Transcripts can be used to create accurate quotations, and they make it relatively easy to review responses to your questions.

- **Taking Notes** You should always take notes during an interview. Recordings and transcripts can be lost through everything from running out of file space on a recorder to computer crashes. More important, taking notes allows you to record your reactions to new information and ideas, to save your thoughts about how you might use all or part of an interview in your document, and to identify important parts of the interview for later review.

Conduct Your Interview

Consult the following checklist before you conduct your interview.

CHECKLIST FOR CONDUCTING INTERVIEWS

✔ **Arrive early and review your questions.** If you are conducting your interview over the phone or via computer, set time aside before the interview to review your questions and then contact the person you are interviewing at the agreed-upon time.

✔ **Introduce yourself and ask for permission to record the interview.** Explain why you are conducting the interview. Ask for permission to record or generate a transcript and ensure that you will be allowed to use quotes from the interview.

✔ **Set up and test your recording equipment or computer.** Ideally, use an audio or video recorder to make a complete record of face-to-face or phone interviews and use the built-in recording or transcript generating features in online communication tools. At a later time, you can review what was said and create exact quotations from the recording or transcript.

✔ **Ask your questions clearly and be ready to respond with follow-up questions.** Allow the person you are interviewing a chance to answer your questions fully and without interruption. Don't insist on strictly following your list of interview questions; if discussion naturally flows in another useful direction, be prepared to shift your line of questioning.

CHECKLIST FOR CONDUCTING INTERVIEWS (continued)

✔ **Take notes, even if you are creating a recording or transcript.** A set of hand-written notes will serve as a backup if there are technical glitches and will help you remember ideas you had during the interview. You should write down key points made during the interview as well as any important ideas that come to mind.

✔ **Be alert for related sources mentioned in the interview.** If specific sources that might be relevant to your research writing project are mentioned during the interview, ask for copies of those sources or for the exact titles and where you might find them.

✔ **Leave your contact information when the interview is over.** Provide a way for the person you interviewed to reach you to change or add anything to his or her comments.

✔ **Send a thank-you note or email message.** Let the person you interviewed know how much you appreciated the opportunity to learn from him or her.

Analyze Your Results

Treat your interview recording or transcript as you would any other source. Read it, listen to it, or view it critically (see Figure 11.1).

- Look for new information, ideas, and arguments.
- Look for statements that confirm or contradict information from your other sources.
- Look for inconsistencies and contradictions within the interview as a whole.
- Ask whether the information, ideas, and arguments are relevant and credible.
- Ask whether you consider the person you interviewed as qualified as you'd expected when you planned the interview.
- Look for statements that might be useful in providing context about the issue.
- Look for statements that might help your readers better understand the issue or that would help them view the issue in a particular way.

Then ask whether you can use the information, ideas, and arguments from the interview in your project document. If not, ask whether it is useful for helping you understand the issue more fully or raises questions that you could investigate in other ways.

Notes on interview with Dr. Jonathan Euchner, assistant professor of political science at Missouri Western State University

Privatization movement began in 1978

- not just military: airline industry too

- privatization gained momentum over Reagan, Bush-41, and Clinton administrations

> Use for section on history of PMCs

PMC contractors mean less bureaucracy and fewer regulations; this is attractive to U.S. military leadership

Said "accountability is key" when it comes to abuses by contractors

> This accountability seems intangible—discuss the continuity issue and the difficulty of terminating contracts with PMCs

Thinks the burden of war in Iraq and Afghanistan has been pushed to relatively few military families

- "The wars are almost an abstraction."

- wars have been paid for with borrowed money

- doesn't think citizens will pay attention to PMCs unless there is a tragic catalyst (like contractors directly responsible for American deaths)

> Good quote to use in conclusion

Stop Outsourcing Security Act

- Missouri's junior senator Claire McCaskill could be a key ally for this bill

> Look up who else supports this act and whether it has gone through Congress

FIGURE 11.1 Annotated Transcript of Nicholas Brothers's Interview with Jonathan Euchner

11c

How can I use observation to collect information?

Like interviewing, observing a setting can provide you with valuable information you would not be able to find in other sources. Although some observations can involve a significant amount of time and effort, an observation need not be complicated to be useful.

Plan Your Observation

As you plan your observation, determine the following.

What You Should Observe and How Often You Should Observe It If, for example, you've decided to observe children in a day-care center, you'll quickly learn that there are not only many day-care providers in your community but also several different kinds of providers. Clearly, observing a large day-care center won't tell you much about what happens in a small center operated out of a home. In addition, there's no guarantee that what you'll see in one day-care center on any given day will be typical. Should you conduct multiple observations? Should you observe multiple types of day-care providers?

The answers to these questions will depend largely on what role the information you collect during your observations will play in your research writing project. If you want to learn more about the topic but don't plan to use anything you observe as a source of evidence in your project, then you might want to conduct a fairly limited observation. If you decide to use evidence from your observations throughout your project, then you will need to conduct multiple observations, possibly in more than one setting. In this case, as you prepare for each observation, review your notes from previous sessions so that you can focus on the most important aspects of what you've observed so far.

What to Look For The biggest limitation of observation is that you can see only one thing at a time. Experienced observers focus their observations on activities that are most relevant to their research projects. As a result, their observations are somewhat selective. Spreading yourself too thin will result in fairly "thin" results. Then again, narrowing in too quickly can mean that you miss important aspects of the setting. Your reasons for conducting an observation and what you hope to gain from it are probably your best guide to what to focus on.

Whether You Need Permission to Observe Seeking permission to observe someone can be complicated. People have expectations about privacy, but people can (and often do) change their behavior when they know they are being observed. As you consider whether to ask for permission, imagine yourself in the position of someone who is being observed. If you are still uncertain, ask your instructor for advice.

If you decide to seek permission to conduct your observations, consider how best to approach the person you'll ask for permission. If you decide to send a letter or an email message, be sure to include a clear description of your research writing project and explanations of why you believe observation will enhance your work on the project, how the observations will be used in your project, and how you will ensure the privacy of the individuals, groups, or organization you observe. If you decide to contact the person by telephone, jot down some notes before you call. In some cases, you might find it useful to use a permission form (see Figure 11.2).

Current School / Program Information

Name _____

Address _____

City _____ State _____

Zip Code _____

Phone _____

Email _____

I, the undersigned, hereby authorize [*observer name*] to observe [*the setting*] for the purposes of completing work on [*name of the research writing project*]. I understand that I may revoke this authorization, in writing, at any time.

Signature: _____

Date: _____

FIGURE 11.2 Sample Permission Form for Observation Sessions

Conduct Your Observation

You'll find a number of similarities between collecting information in an interview and collecting information during an observation. The checklist that follows will help you conduct your observation.

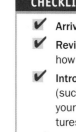

CHECKLIST FOR CONDUCTING OBSERVATIONS

✔ **Arrive early.** Give yourself time to get prepared.

✔ **Review your planning notes.** Remind yourself what you're looking for and how you will record your observations.

✔ **Introduce yourself.** If you have asked for permission to observe a setting (such as a class or a day-care center), introduce yourself before you begin your observation. Use your introduction as an opportunity to obtain signatures or consent forms if you need them.

✔ **Set up your recording equipment.** You'll certainly want to make sure you've got a notepad and pens or pencils. You might also have an audio or a video recorder, a laptop computer, or a smartphone or tablet. Test whatever you've brought with you to make sure it's working properly.

CHECKLIST FOR CONDUCTING OBSERVATIONS (continued)

✔ **Take notes.** As with interviews, take notes during your observation even if you're using an audio or a video recorder. Noting your impressions and ideas while conducting an observation can help you keep track of critical events. In addition, if your recorder doesn't work as expected, a set of notes can mean the difference between salvaging something from the observation and having to do it all over again. If you find yourself in a situation where you can't take notes — such as at a swimming lesson, when you're taking part in the lesson — try to write down your thoughts about what you've observed immediately after the session.

✔ **Leave contact information and send thank-you notes.** If you have asked someone for permission to observe the setting, give the person a way to contact you, and send a thank-you note after you have completed the observation.

Analyze Your Results

Treat your observation notes or recording as you would any other source. Ask whether you observed the setting thoroughly enough to feel confident about moving forward with an analysis. If so, do the following.

- Identify key features and patterns of behavior.
- Identify key individuals and describe their actions.
- Look for unusual and surprising patterns and actions.
- Ask what you've learned about the issue through observation.
- Look for patterns and actions that might be useful in providing context about the issue.
- Look for patterns and actions that, if described, might help your readers better understand the issue or lead them to view the issue in a particular way.

Then ask whether you are confident enough about the results of your analysis to use what you've learned in your project document. If not, ask whether it is useful for helping you understand the issue more fully or raises questions that you could investigate in other ways.

11d

How can I use surveys to collect information?

Surveys allow you to collect information about beliefs, attitudes, and behaviors from a group of people. Typically, surveys help you answer *what* or *who* questions, such as "Who will you vote for in the next election?" Surveys are less useful in obtaining the answers to *why* questions. In an interview, for instance, you can ask, "Why did you vote the way you did in the last election?" and expect to get a reasonably well-thought-out answer. In a survey, however, people often neglect to write lengthy, careful responses. If you conduct a survey, remember to include a copy of your survey questions in an appendix to your project document.

Designing a survey, conducting it, and analyzing the results require a significant investment of time and effort. If you simply want opinions from a handful of people, you can gain that information more efficiently by interviewing or corresponding with them. The information you gain from a well-designed survey, however, may provide insights into an issue that often can't be obtained in other ways.

Plan Your Survey

As you plan your survey, determine the following.

Whom to Survey   You must decide whom and how many people to survey. For instance, if you're interested in what students in a specific class think about an issue, survey all of them. Even if the class is fairly large (say, one hundred students), you probably won't have too much trouble tabulating the results of a brief survey. Keep in mind, however, that most surveys aren't given to everyone in a group. National polls, for instance, seldom survey more than one thousand people, yet they are used to assess the opinions of everyone in the country. So how will you select your representative sample? One way is to choose people from the group at random. You could open your school's directory and then pick, say, every twentieth name. Another option is to stratify your sample. For example, you could randomly select a specific number of first-year, second-year, third-year, and fourth-year students—and you could make sure that the number of men and women in each group is proportional to their enrollment at the school.

What to Ask and How to Ask It with Integrity   Designing effective surveys can be challenging. Understanding the strengths and weaknesses of the kinds of questions that are frequently asked on surveys is a good way to get started. Figure 11.3 illustrates the main types of questions found on surveys. As you consider the types of questions you'll use, keep in mind the importance of asking questions that do not cue the people taking your survey to respond in a particular way. Consider, for example, how you might respond to the following questions.

- Do you support increasing income tax rates to reduce the federal debt?
- Do you support increasing income tax rates to ensure that future generations are not crushed under the burden of a spiraling federal debt?
- Do you support increasing income tax rates to enable the federal government to continue its irresponsible and uncontrolled spending on entitlements?

Whether You Are Asking Your Questions Clearly   Test your survey items before administering your survey by asking your classmates or family members to read your questions. A question that seems perfectly clear to you might con-

Election Survey

Thank you for completing this survey.

A 1. Did you vote in the last presidential election? ☐ yes ☐ no

2. I vote:

In every election	In most elections	In about half of the elections	Rarely	Never
☐	☐	☐	☐	☐

B 3. I have voted in the following types of elections (check all that apply):
   ☐ Regular local elections
   ☐ Special local elections
   ☐ Regular statewide elections
   ☐ National elections

C 4. Voting is a civic duty: ☐ true ☐ false

D 5. All eligible voters should participate in local, state, and national elections:

Strongly Agree	Agree	Not Sure	Disagree	Strongly Disagree
☐	☐	☐	☐	☐

6. Please rate the following reasons for voting on a 1-to-5 scale, in which 5 indicates very important and 1 indicates not at all important:

	1	2	3	4	5
To be a good citizen	☐	☐	☐	☐	☐
To have a say in how government affects my life	☐	☐	☐	☐	☐
To support a particular cause	☐	☐	☐	☐	☐
To vote against particular candidates	☐	☐	☐	☐	☐

E 7. Please rank the following types of elections from most important (4) to least important (1):
   _____ Presidential elections
   _____ Statewide elections
   _____ Local (city and county) elections
   _____ Student government elections

F 8. Please tell us what influenced your decision to vote or not vote in the last election.

FIGURE 11.3 Sample Survey

A Yes/no items divide respondents into two groups.

B Multiple-choice items indicate whether a respondent knows something or engages in specific behaviors. Because they seldom include every possible answer, be careful when including them.

C True/false items more often deal with attitudes or beliefs than with behaviors or events.

D Likert scales measure respondents' level of agreement with a statement, their assessment of something's importance, or how frequently they engage in a behavior.

E Ranking forces respondents to place items along a continuum.

F Short-answer items allow greater freedom of response but can be difficult to tabulate.

III Collecting Information

fuse someone else. Rewrite the questions that confuse your "testers" and then test them again. Doing so will help you improve the clarity of your survey. Consider the evolution of the following question.

Original Question:

What can be done about voter turnout among younger voters?

Revised Question:

In your opinion, what can be done to increase turnout among 18- to 24-year-old voters?

> Does "about voter turnout" mean increasing voter turnout, decreasing voter turnout, or encouraging younger voters to be better informed about candidates? Does the phrase "younger voters" mean 18-year-olds or 30-year-olds?

How to Distribute Your Survey   Surveys are typically distributed via electronic mail, Web pages, or social networking sites, although a number of research writers still conduct paper-based surveys. The advantages of online surveys include the ease of distributing the survey to potential respondents, the growing number of tools that you can use to create surveys (such as SurveyGizmo, SurveyMonkey, Zoomerang, and Quibblo), and the ease of tabulating results with tools that break down responses and create charts from survey data. The disadvantages include the likelihood that the response rates to online surveys will be relatively low (compared to the total number of people who will learn about a survey) and that those who respond will do so because of a specific interest in the issue. In other words, you might find that most of your respondents have some sort of interest or bias that leads them to want to respond and as a result might not form a representative sample of the group you hope to understand.

Paper-based surveys are most useful in situations where you can pass them out to a group, such as students in a class or people attending a meeting. If you are confident that the people in the class or at the meeting are likely to be representative of the group you are seeking to understand, then this can be a useful technique.

Asking people to respond to a survey over the phone tends to result in a low response rate and might be prohibited by local and state laws regarding telephone solicitations. In general, because of the low response rate to telephone surveys, it is seldom a productive tool for collecting survey responses.

Conduct Your Survey

The sheer number of surveys people are asked to complete these days has reduced the public's willingness to respond to them. In fact, a "good" response rate for a survey is 60 percent, and many professional pollsters find lower response rates acceptable.

Analyze Your Results

Once you've collected your surveys, you must tabulate your responses. It's usually best to tabulate survey responses using a spreadsheet program, which provides flexibility when you want to analyze your results. You can also organize

TUTORIAL

How do I write a good survey question?

Developing a good survey question is challenging. The process is similar to writing an essay. The first drafts of survey questions serve to express your thoughts. Subsequent revisions help clarify questions for survey respondents. Keep your purpose in mind to be sure your question will elicit the information you need.

In this example, Brandon Tate devised a survey question to find out how fellow students view hydraulic fracturing—or *fracking*.

1 Write a first draft of the question.

Do you pay attention to television ads about fracking and why or why not?

2 Simplify the question.

Why do you pay attention to — or ignore — television ads about fracking?

3 Consider alternative ways of asking a question—including whether it should be a question.

What are your reasons for paying attention to — or ignoring — televisions ads about fracking?

4 Identify and then clarify keywords and phrases.

List five words to describe television ads about fracking.

5 Ask for feedback from potential respondents. Review and clarify keywords and phrases. Consider potential reactions to phrasing.

Please describe your reaction when you view a television ad about fracking.

III Collecting Information

the results in a table in a word processing program. Once you've tabulated the responses, spend time analyzing the results. You should look for trends in your data. For example, ask whether groups respond differently to particular questions, or whether age or experience seems to predict responses. Look as well for surprising results, such as unexpectedly high levels of agreement or disagreement with Likert-scale items or striking differences in the responses to short-answer questions.

As you conduct your analysis, keep in mind the need to ensure confidentiality for your respondents. Survey respondents usually do not expect their names to be revealed in reports about a survey or to find personally identifiable information in reports. As you review your responses, be on the lookout for information that might help someone identify a particular respondent. A respondent might reveal, for example, that she is the only Iraq War veteran in a particular writing class. If you find this kind of information, do not include it in your report.

CHECKLIST FOR CONDUCTING SURVEYS

✔ **Keep it short.** Surveys are most effective when they are brief. Don't exceed one page.

✔ **Format and distribute your survey appropriately.** If your survey is on paper, make sure the text is readable, there is plenty of room to write, and the page isn't crowded with questions. If you are distributing your survey through email, you can either insert the survey questions into the body of your email message or attach the survey as a word processing file. If you are distributing your survey on the Web, use the formatting tools in your Web survey tool to test out various layouts for your survey questions.

✔ **Explain the purpose of your survey.** Explaining who you are and how you will use the results of the survey in your research writing project can help increase a respondent's willingness to complete and return your survey.

✔ **Treat survey respondents with respect.** People respond more favorably when they think you are treating them as individuals rather than simply as part of a mailing list. Address potential respondents by name in email messages or cover letters. If you are mailing your survey, handwrite the name and address so that your survey doesn't arrive looking like junk mail.

✔ **Make it easy to return the survey.** If you are conducting your survey on the Web or via email, be sure to provide directions for submitting or returning completed surveys. If you are distributing the survey to students in classes, provide a large envelope with your name and contact information into which the surveys can be placed.

11e

How can I use correspondence to collect information?

Correspondence includes any textual communication, such as letters, faxes, and email. Correspondence can also take place through the communication tools available on social networking sites such as Facebook.

Although many research writers benefit from corresponding with experts, correspondence need not be sent only to experts. If you are writing an article about the effects of recent flooding in the Midwest, you could correspond with relatives, friends, or even strangers to ask them about their experiences with the floods. You can use their responses to illustrate the impact of the flood on average folks. You can also correspond with staff at government agencies, corporations, and organizations. Many of these institutions hire public relations personnel to respond to inquiries from the public.

Courtesy is essential when corresponding. Introduce yourself and explain the goals of your research writing project. Make sure that you are clear and ask specific questions. Thank your reader and indicate that you look forward to hearing from him or her. If you decide to send a letter via regular mail, include a self-addressed stamped envelope to increase your chances of getting a response.

11f

How can I use public events and broadcast media to collect information?

Public events, such as lectures, conferences, and public meetings and hearings, often provide research writers with useful information. As with observations, you can record many public events by taking notes or bringing an audio or a video recorder. Be aware, however, that it is unethical to record events that specifically ask that you not do so. If you are asked not to record an event, find out whether a transcript, podcast, or video recording of the event will be available.

Radio and television are sources of information that research writers frequently overlook. News and information programs on television, such as *Nightline* and *60 Minutes*, might provide useful information about the conversation you plan to join. You may want to record the programs in order to examine them in detail. In addition, check the Web for radio programs and transcripts. National Public Radio's news information program *All Things Considered*, for instance, has audio archives going back to January 1996 that you can listen to on the Web (visit **npr.org** and search the program's archives). You can also record local public events that are broadcast on public access cable channels or streamed over the Web.

III Collecting Information

My Research Project

Assess the Relevance of Field Research Methods

Think about whether the field research methods discussed in this chapter might contribute to your research project. If you decide to use observations, interviews, surveys, correspondence, or other forms of field research, seek advice from researchers who have used these methods, or from your instructor or a librarian. Ask questions such as the following.

- How would field research methods help me accomplish my purpose for this project?

- How will my readers react to my use of evidence from field research methods?

- Is evidence from field research typically used in the type of document I plan to write?

In your research log, write down the responses you receive to these and related questions. Then decide whether using field research is a good choice for your project.

bedfordresearcher.com
My Research Project Activities > Assess the Relevance of Field Research Methods

> QUICK REFERENCE

Searching for Information with Field Research Methods

☑ Consider reasons for using field research. (p. 182)

☑ Plan and conduct interviews. (p. 183)

☑ Plan and conduct observations. (p. 188)

☑ Design, conduct, and analyze a survey. (p. 191)

☑ Use correspondence to collect information. (p. 197)

☑ Attend public events and view broadcast media to gather information about your issue. (p. 197)

III Collecting Information

The Bedford Researcher

I	Joining the Conversation
II	Working with Sources
III	Collecting Information
IV	**Creating Your Document**
V	Documenting Sources

PART IV

Creating Your Document

After you have collected information, you'll have a better understanding of the scope of your issue. In the chapters that follow, you'll learn how to use your new knowledge to create a well-written, well-designed document.

12

Developing Your Thesis Statement

> **Key Questions**

As you shift your attention away from collecting and working with sources and toward crafting your own contribution to the conversation about your issue, you'll begin the process of planning your argument. That process begins with reviewing your position statement, your notes, and your purpose in order to draft an effective thesis statement.

12a

How can I prepare to draft my thesis statement?

Your thesis statement provides a clear, focused expression of the main point you want to make. It is, in a nutshell, the most important idea or argument you want to convey to your readers. Your thesis statement should invite your readers to do one of three things: learn something new, change an attitude or belief, or take action. Featured writer Alexis Alvarez, for example, asked her readers to learn something new.

> Although competitive sports can provide young female athletes with many benefits, they can also have negative effects, the worst of which is increasing drug use.

In contrast, featured writer Brandon Tate asked readers to take action to support changes in the regulation of hydraulic fracturing:

> Coloradoans should develop a coordinated response to the growing use of hydraulic fracturing in or near watersheds that supply drinking water to the state.

Your efforts to develop a thesis statement will be influenced by what you've learned about your issue and by your writing situation. Before you begin drafting your thesis statement, review your current position statement, review your notes, and consider your writing situation.

Review Your Position Statement

As you have collected, skimmed, critically read, and evaluated sources, you've almost certainly developed — and perhaps written, reviewed, and revised — a statement defining your position on your issue (p. 70). Now, as you begin the process of deciding what you want to convey to your readers, it is time to reflect on that position. If you have already drafted a position statement, you can turn to it and ask whether it still represents the most important point you want to make about your issue. If you haven't drafted a position statement, do so now. You can use brainstorming, looping, and other idea-generation strategies to help formulate your position statement (p. 20).

Review Your Notes

With your position statement in mind, quickly review your notes. As you review your notes:

- identify important information, ideas, and arguments that you've come across in your reading
- consider whether the information, ideas, and arguments you've identified in your notes will allow you to pursue your personal, academic, and professional interests
- review and elaborate on ideas and arguments that you've come up with as a result of your own thinking about the subject
- consider how your own ideas and arguments might allow you to pursue your interests

As you carry out your review, reflect on your position statement. Ask how well it conveys the information, ideas, and arguments you would most like to address in your document. If you find that it does not fully capture your understanding of the issue — that is, if it doesn't seem to reflect the main point you want to make about your issue — revise your position statement.

Consider Your Purpose and Role 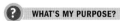 **WHAT'S MY PURPOSE?**

Reviewing your notes will help you deepen your understanding of your issue. That understanding, in turn, is likely to affect how you view your purpose and role as a writer and, by extension, the main point you want to make in your document. Use the following questions to guide how you think about your thesis statement.

- Have your purposes—the reasons you are working on this research writing project—changed since you started? If so, how do you view your purpose now?
- Has your role as a writer—for example, to inform or to solve a problem—changed since you started your research writing project? If so, how do you view your role now?

If your answers to any of these questions suggest that the main point you want to make has changed, revise your position statement.

Reflect on Your Readers

In the same way that you considered your purpose and role, ask whether focusing on a particular main point will help you address your readers' purposes, needs, interests, and backgrounds. If you find that your main point is not well aligned with your readers' concerns, revise your position statement.

12b

How can I develop an effective thesis statement?

To draft your thesis statement, consider what you learned through your reflections on your position statement, notes, and writing situation. Your work on your thesis statement will be affected by the information, ideas, and arguments you've encountered in your reading, the role or roles you are adopting in relation to your readers, and the type of document you plan to write.

Step 1: Identify Important Information, Ideas, and Arguments Associated with Your Position

Begin developing your thesis statement by identifying important information, ideas, and arguments related to your position on your issue. Examine your initial brainstorming or freewriting about your topic and issue. Review your research question and position statement for keywords and phrases. Look through your notes to see how your sources consider questions related to your position. As you review your materials, identify important keywords and phrases; you can use these words and phrases as you draft your thesis statement. Consider the following example, which shows how a writer identified keywords and phrases in her research question, position statement, and notes.

Research Question about Effects of the War on Drugs in South America:

How can we reduce the economic impact of the war on drugs on South American coca farmers?

Position Statement:

The U.S. and South American governments should adopt the "zero cocaine, not zero coca" policy.

Notes on "Bolivia's Knot: No to Cocaine, but Yes to Coca," by Juan Forero:

Newly elected Bolivian president, Evo Morales, is "an Aymara Indian who grew up in poverty in the highlands and became a coca grower" (para. 6). He plans to remove sanctions for growing coca even as he shows "zero tolerance toward trafficking" (para. 6). This is part of his "yes to coca, no to cocaine" campaign. Morales has been a long-time opponent of U.S. efforts to eradicate the coca crop, pointing to its lack of "mind-altering effects" and its use to "mitigate hunger and increase stamina" (para. 7). Morales plans to work with foreign governments to find a market for products made from coca, despite the fact that since 1961 the UN has blacklisted all products made from coca. Those products include soaps, shampoos, toothpaste, flour, and tea, "which is legal and popular in the Andes" (para. 7).

Review the words and phrases you've identified as important and keep them in mind as you begin to draft alternative thesis statements.

Step 2: Focus on Your Role   [FRAMING MY ARGUMENT]

In the same way that your role as a writer—the manner in which you'll relate to your readers—has an impact on your research question (p. 47), your role will shape your thesis statement. Asking your readers to learn something new, as you would be doing if you adopted the roles of observer (reflecting), reporter (informing), interpreter (analyzing), inquirer (developing new knowledge), or evaluator (evaluating), will lead to thesis statements that differ significantly from those that might emerge from roles such as problem solver (to define or solve problems) or advocate (to convince or persuade). Featured writer Nicholas Brothers, for example, adopted the dual roles of interpreter and advocate, first analyzing the U.S. military's growing reliance on private military contractors in the Iraq and Afghanistan wars and then arguing that readers should change their attitudes about—more specifically, to be skeptical of—their use.

> By relying heavily on private military corporations to carry out military operations, the U.S. Department of Defense is undermining its own counterinsurgency efforts in Iraq and Afghanistan.

Had Nicholas adopted the role of informer and simply reported on the growing use of private military contractors, his thesis statement might have resembled the following.

> As the U.S. has expanded its involvement in foreign wars, it has dramatically increased its reliance on private military corporations.

Table 12.1 provides a list of some of the most important roles you might adopt and offers examples of the kinds of thesis statements writers adopting a particular role might use. You can use the sentence starters in the table to generate your ideas for your thesis statement.

TABLE 12.1 THE RELATIONSHIP AMONG ROLES AND THESIS STATEMENTS

Role	Purpose	Sample Sentence Starters
Reporter	To inform	Understanding _____ is essential if we are to _____. The best way to understand _____ is to view it as _____. Understanding _____ can only be achieved by _____.
Inquirer	To create and share new knowledge	_____ causes _____. The most important effects of _____ are _____. _____ can [cure/repair/prevent] _____.
Observer	To reflect	The most important lessons we can learn from _____ are _____. My reflections on _____ have helped me _____. _____ is important because _____.
Evaluator	To evaluate	In general, evaluations of _____ have shown us that it _____. The most important influences on _____ are _____. The best choices available for addressing _____ are _____. _____ has [these strengths and weaknesses].
Interpreter	To analyze	_____ causes _____ because _____. What are the effects of _____? The data suggest that _____ [is/is the result of] a _____. _____ is similar to _____ because _____. _____ differs from _____ because _____.
Problem Solver	To solve problems	_____ is a problem because _____. The solution to _____ is _____. We should adopt _____ as a solution because _____.
Advocate	To convince (change readers' beliefs or attitudes), persuade (cause readers to take action), or mediate (seek to establish common ground among readers)	The origins of this argument are found in _____. The status of this argument is _____. The best argument about _____ is _____. The writers and readers involved in conversation about _____ want to [see/avoid] _____. We should do _____ about _____. We should accomplish _____ by doing _____. We can find common ground about _____ by doing _____.

Step 3: Consider the Type of Document You Plan to Write

An effective thesis statement will reflect the type of document—or genre—you plan to write. Depending on the type of document, your readers will have different expectations about how you present your thesis statement. Readers of an academic essay within a particular discipline, such as philosophy or political science, are likely to expect a calm, clearly written statement of what you want them to learn, believe, or do. Readers of an informative newspaper article will expect you to identify, in a balanced and seemingly unbiased manner, what you want them to learn. Readers of an opinion column will expect you to be more assertive, and perhaps even more entertaining, about your position on an issue. Consider how the following thesis statements, all addressing problems with the recruitment of athletes at a college or university, reflect the type of document the writer plans to draft.

> **Argumentative Academic Essay:**
> The University should ensure that its recruiting practices are fully in compliance with NCAA regulations.
>
> **Informative Newspaper Article:**
> The University is taking steps to bring its recruiting practices in line with NCAA regulations.
>
> **Opinion Column:**
> The University's coaches need to get their act together before the NCAA slaps them with sanctions.

Step 4: Use Your Position Statement to Draft Thesis Statements

As your initial response to your research question, your position statement provides a strong foundation for drafting a set of potential thesis statements. At this state in your research writing process, your position statement is likely to be a fairly general response to your research question. Combined with a role or roles, however, it can help you begin to decide how you want to express your position to your readers. Consider how the following draft thesis statements reflect how you can use a position statement as the basis for asking readers to learn something new, change their attitudes or beliefs, or take action of some kind.

> **Position Statement:**
> The U.S. and South American governments should adopt the "zero cocaine, not zero coca" policy.
>
> **Thesis Statement: Asking Readers to Learn Something New**
> The coca plant, which is used to create cocaine, has numerous economic and medicinal benefits.
>
> **Thesis Statement: Asking Readers to Change Their Attitudes or Beliefs**
> U.S. citizens, long accustomed to equating any form of the coca plant (which is used to manufacture cocaine) as undesirable, will be surprised by its many economic and medicinal benefits.

Thesis Statement: Asking Readers to Take Action
Given the proven economic and medicinal benefits of the coca plant, the United States should rethink its policy toward coca farming in South America.

Step 5: Choose Your Thesis Statement

Review your thesis statements. Ask the following questions about each one.

- Will this thesis statement help me achieve my goals as a writer?
- Do the sources I've read so far give me confidence that I will be able to support the thesis statement?
- Will it address my readers' expectations?
- Will it be consistent with the genre I'm likely to choose?
- Will it sustain my interest in this project?

My Research Project

Generate Draft Thesis Statements

Use the following table to generate draft thesis statements. To complete the activity, identify the role or roles that you are most likely to adopt. Then choose a column, such as "Change Their Attitudes or Beliefs," and generate draft thesis statements. You need not complete every cell in the table, and you can create more than one statement in each cell.

To generate statements, use freewriting or the sentence starters found in Table 12.1.

GOAL: ASKING READERS TO . . .				
Role	Purpose	Learn Something New	Change Their Attitudes or Beliefs	Take Action of Some Kind
Reporter	To inform			
Inquirer	To create and share new knowledge			
Observer	To reflect			
Evaluator	To evaluate			
Interpreter	To analyze			
Problem Solver	To solve problems			
Advocate	To convince, persuade, or mediate			

bedfordresearcher.com
My Research Project Activities > Generate Draft Thesis Statements

IV Creating Your Document

Of these questions, the most important may be the last. Be sure, however, that the thesis statement you choose will help you accomplish your goals, meet the expectations of your readers, and find support from your sources.

Step 6: Refine Your Thesis Statement

Once you've chosen a thesis statement, take time to refine it. As you refine your thesis statement, ask continually how doing so will frame your readers' attention. Consider how the following thesis statement might be refined by adding information, referring to shared assumptions, and narrowing its scope.

> **Draft Thesis Statement:**
> The U.S. government should stop attempting to eradicate coca plants and instead focus on eliminating the manufacture and distribution of cocaine.

Add Information   You can frame your readers' understanding of the issue by incorporating relevant information into your statement.

> **Refined Thesis Statement:**
> Given the failure of the "War on Drugs" to stem the flow of cocaine into the United States, the U.S. government should stop attempting to eradicate coca plants and instead focus on eliminating the manufacture and distribution of cocaine.
>
> Adding information about an area of weakness in the war on drugs directs readers' attention to the need to find an alternative approach.

> **Refined Thesis Statement:**
> The U.S. government should stop attempting to eradicate coca plants, which have been central to the economic well-being of Bolivian farmers for centuries, and instead focus on eliminating the manufacture and distribution of cocaine.

Refer to Shared Assumptions and Common Knowledge   You can refine your thesis statement by calling attention to assumptions that have been made by the community of writers and readers who are addressing your issue, by referring to existing conditions relevant to your issue, or by using conditional words and phrases to set up a main point.

> **Refined Thesis Statement: Referring to Shared Assumption**
> Given our national commitment to economic opportunity and fairness for all, the U.S. government should stop attempting to eradicate coca plants and instead focus on eliminating the manufacture and distribution of cocaine.
>
> The writer calls attention to a widely shared national value.

> **Refined Thesis Statement: Referring to Common Knowledge**
> The U.S. government, recognizing the important role coca farming plays in Bolivia's economy, should stop attempting to eradicate coca plants and instead focus on eliminating the manufacture and distribution of cocaine.
>
> Calling attention to information many writers have referred to frames readers' understanding of the status of the issue.

Refined Thesis Statement: Referring to Existing Conditions

The U.S. government, recognizing its failure to date to eradicate coca plants, should focus on eliminating the manufacture and distribution/of cocaine.

> Referring to the current state of government efforts calls readers attention to a more effective allocation of resources.

You can also use conditional words and phrases to narrow the focus of a thesis statement. You can find a list of these words and phrases on p. 54.

Refined Thesis Statement: Using Conditional Words and Phrases

Although the war on drugs is well intended, it is clear given its lack of results that we should stop attempting to eradicate coca plants and instead/focus on eliminating the manufacture and distribution of cocaine.

> Conditional words and phrases are used to acknowledge good intentions even as they set the stage for an alternative approach.

Narrow the Scope of Your Thesis Statement You can narrow the scope of your thesis statement by looking for vague words and phrases and replacing them with more specific words or phrases.

Draft Thesis Statement:

The U.S. government should focus less on coca plants and more on cocaine.

Refined:

The U.S. government should stop attempting to eradicate coca plants and instead focus on eliminating the manufacture and distribution of cocaine.

Further Refined:

The U.S. government should stop attempting to eradicate coca plants by burning fields and leaving farmers and their families without a means to earn an income and instead focus on eliminating the manufacture and distribution of cocaine, which affect Americans directly.

As you work to refine your thesis statement, keep in mind that it is—and will remain until the late stages of your work on your project—a work in progress. Stay alert to new ideas and information that might change your thinking about your position on your issue. Continue to think about how you might refine or even substantially revise your thesis statement so that you can better frame the issue for your readers.

Table 12.2 presents the featured writers' movements from research question to position statement to thesis statement. Note how each thesis statement answers its research question and directs readers' attention to one aspect of the conversation, encourages them to change their attitudes or beliefs, or urges them to take action of some kind.

TABLE 12.2 THE FEATURED WRITERS' MOVEMENT FROM RESEARCH QUESTION TO THESIS STATEMENT

Featured Writer	Research Question	Position Statement	Thesis Statement
Alexis Alvarez	What are the effects of competitive soccer on adolescent girls?	Steroid use by adolescent girls involved in competitive sports should be addressed by educating athletes, parents, and coaches about health consequences and emphasizing fair play.	Although competitive sports can provide young female athletes with many benefits, they can also have negative effects, the worst of which is increasing drug use.
Nicholas Brothers	What dangers are associated with U.S. reliance on private military corporations in its war on terror?	The overreliance of the United States on private military corporations is a danger to national and international security.	By relying heavily on private military corporations to carry out military operations, the U.S. Department of Defense is undermining its own counterinsurgency efforts in Iraq and Afghanistan.
Elizabeth Leontiev	How can we reduce the economic impact of the war on drugs on South American coca farmers?	The U.S. and South American governments should adopt the "zero cocaine, not zero coca" policy.	The "zero cocaine, not zero coca" policy will boost the Bolivian economy, allow native Andeans to maintain their cultural practices, and reduce cocaine trafficking into the United States.
Lauren Mack	What factors are causing damage to coral reefs?	A combination of human (anthropogenic) and natural factors are causing damage to coral reefs.	The importance of coral reefs to the global environment demands that we take action to protect them.
Cori Schmidtbauer	How does Portia's character in The Merchant of Venice fit in with Elizabethan ideas of women?	Portia appears to rebel against the expectations of Elizabethan culture.	By gaining the upper hand in traditionally male-dominated systems of exchange (notably marriage) and cross-dressing as a male lawyer to defend Antonio in court, Portia assaults the idea of the weak Renaissance woman from every angle. However, a fresh look at The Merchant of Venice reveals that Portia—in a strange way—may have reflected Renaissance culture just as much as she contradicted it.
Brandon Tate	What do we need to know about fracking in order to make responsible decisions about its use?	Fracking has many potential benefits as well as negative consequences, and it should be evaluated alongside other sources of energy.	Fracking encourages reliance on fossil fuels and should be less of a priority than finding sources of renewable energy.
Josh Woelfle	What recent advancements in cancer treatment have been the most promising?	While chemotherapy and radiation have been mainstays of cancer treatment, their side effects can be debilitating, and new forms of treatment are becoming very effective.	Cancer-fighting drugs that focus on growth-signaling enzymes and MDR proteins may soon overtake chemotherapy and radiation as standard cancer treatment.

My Research Project

Refine Your Thesis Statement

In your research log, complete the following activity to refine your thesis statement.

1. I have chosen the following thesis statement:

2. I can refine my thesis statement and frame my readers' understanding of the issue by:

- Adding the following relevant information:
- Referring to the following shared assumptions:
- Referring to the following common knowledge:
- Referring to the following existing conditions:
- Replacing the following vague words and phrases:
- Using the following conditional words and phrases:

bedfordresearcher.com
My Research Project Activities > Refine Your Thesis Statement

---

> QUICK REFERENCE

Developing Your Thesis Statement

✔ Review and reflect on your research question, position statement, notes, and writing situation. (p. 202)

✔ Begin to draft your thesis statement by identifying important information, ideas, and arguments. (p. 202)

✔ Consider your role, the type of document you are writing, and any disciplinary writing conventions. (p. 203)

✔ Generate potential thesis statements. (p. 207)

✔ Choose and refine your thesis statement. (p. 207)

IV Creating Your Document

13

Developing and Organizing Your Argument

> **Key Questions**
>
> **13a. How can I develop my argument?** 213
> Choose reasons to support your main point
> Select evidence to support your reasons
> Decide how to appeal to your readers
> Decide how to address opposing arguments
> Check for logical fallacies
>
> **13b. How can I organize my argument?** 224
> Choose an organizing pattern
> Review and arrange your evidence
> Create an outline

Once you've determined your position on an issue and expressed it as a thesis statement, you've laid the foundation for developing your contribution to the conversation you've decided to join. Developing your argument involves identifying reasons to accept the main point you've advanced in your thesis statement, selecting evidence to support your reasons, deciding how to appeal to your readers, and determining how best to address counterarguments. To improve the overall effectiveness of your argument, you should also assess the integrity of your reasoning and organize your evidence clearly and logically.

13a

How can I develop my argument?

Developing an effective argument involves far more than knowing what you want others to understand or believe or how you want them to act. It requires the development of a strategy to explain and support the main point made in your thesis statement. That strategy should reflect not only your purpose and role but also your readers' needs, interests, values, beliefs, and knowledge of an issue. It should also take into account the conventions typically used in the type of document you plan to write. Most important, it should reflect a willingness to change your argument—from your thesis statement to your reasons and evidence—in response to new information, ideas, and arguments that you might encounter as you work on your research writing project.

Choose Reasons to Support Your Main Point

In longer documents, such as essays, reports, and Web sites, writers usually present several reasons for readers to accept or act on their thesis statements. The kinds of reasons they choose will vary according to the type of document they are writing. In informative articles in newspapers and magazines, for example, writers are likely to focus on the three or four most important aspects of the issue they want readers to understand. In blog posts that analyze an issue, in contrast, writers are likely to choose reasons that help readers understand the results of the analysis. In an argumentative essay, writers usually offer a series of claims that will lead readers to accept their argument or take action in response to it.

To choose reasons to support your main point, consider your readers' expectations.

- Readers of reflective documents, such as some blog posts and academic essays, will expect you to focus on a particular subject. If you are writing a reflective document, ask which of your observations about a subject are most significant and what kind of impression you want to create for your readers.

- Readers of informative documents, such as reports, essays, and articles, expect you to help them understand something about an issue. As you plan an informative document, ask what you want to convey to your readers and what they are most likely to want to know about it.

- Readers of analytical documents, such as some articles in newspapers like the *New York Times* and the *Wall Street Journal*, expect a straightforward and logical presentation of the analysis. To meet readers' expectations about this kind of document, reflect on what your readers are likely to know about the issue, the kinds of questions they might have about it, and the overall conclusion you hope to share with them.

IV Creating Your Document

- Readers of evaluative documents, such as movie and media reviews and progress reports, expect you to provide a reasonable judgment based on a fairly selected set of criteria. As you choose reasons to accept your evaluation, ask what readers will want to gain from reading your document and what you want them to understand about the results of your evaluation.

- Readers of argumentative documents, such as argumentative essays, opinion columns, and blog posts, will expect you to provide a set of reasons for accepting your argument. As you choose your reasons, consider what your readers will know about the issue, how they are likely to respond to your overall argument, and the likely counterarguments they might propose.

As you develop reasons to support your main point, remember that your overall goal is to help your readers pay attention to—and perhaps even to take action in response to—your argument. To guide your efforts, ask questions such as the following, and respond to them by brainstorming, freewriting, looping, clustering, or mapping.

- **Costs.** What costs are associated with not accepting and acting on your main point? Are there monetary costs? Will time and effort be lost or wasted? Will valuable resources be wasted? Will people be unable to lead fulfilling lives? Will human potential be wasted? Will lives be lost?

- **Benefits.** What will be gained by accepting and acting on your main point? Who or what will benefit if your main point is accepted and acted on? What form will these benefits take?

- **Alternatives, choices, and tradeoffs.** In what ways are the potential costs or benefits associated with accepting or acting on your main point preferable to those associated with rejecting your main point or accepting an alternative point?

- **Parallels.** Can you find similarities between the main point you are making about this issue in your thesis statement and claims made about other issues? Can you argue that, if your main point is accepted and acted on, the outcomes will be similar to those found for other issues? What consensus, if any, exists among experts on this issue about what similar situations have led to in the past?

- **Personal experience.** What does your personal experience tell you is likely to happen if your main point is accepted and acted on? What does it tell you might happen if it is rejected?

- **Values and beliefs.** In what ways is your main point consistent with your values and beliefs? With those of your readers? In what ways is it consistent with larger societal and cultural values and beliefs? How might it further those values and beliefs?

Examine the list of reasons you've generated to determine which ones best suit your purpose and will most likely appeal to your readers. Select the reasons that, individually and as a group, best support your main point. If you see inconsistency between the reasons you've chosen and your current thesis statement, consider revising your thesis statement (p. 303).

Decide How Your Reasons Support Your Main Point   Effective arguments make connections (sometimes called *warrants*) between a main point (sometimes called an *overall claim*) and the reasons offered to support it. Sometimes readers accept a connection because they share the writer's values and beliefs or have similar experiences with and knowledge of an issue. In other cases, readers accept a connection because the writer explains it effectively. This explanation (sometimes called *backing*) provides readers with information and analysis that help them understand and accept the connection (see Figure 13.1).

The reasons you choose to support your main point should reflect your understanding of the conversation you've decided to join. Your reasons should emerge from careful thought about the information, ideas, and arguments you've encountered in your reading. Your reasons should reflect your purpose and goals. They should take into account your readers' needs, interests, backgrounds, and knowledge of the issue. And they should be consistent with the conventions of your discipline or profession.

As you consider your reasons, ask how clearly they connect to your main point as it is expressed in your thesis statement. Ask whether you should explain each connection or leave it unstated. Your answers will depend in part on the extent to which your readers share your values, beliefs, experience, and knowledge of the issue. If your readers' background and knowledge differ from yours, connections that make sense to you might not be clear to them.

Select Evidence to Support Your Reasons

For every reason you offer to support your main point, you'll need evidence — such as details, facts, personal observations, and expert opinions — to back up your assertions and help your readers understand your ideas.

You can draw evidence from your sources in the form of quotations, paraphrases, summaries, numerical data, and visual images (p. 90). You can also gather

FIGURE 13.1 Supporting Your Main Point

evidence firsthand by conducting interviews, observations, and surveys, or by reflecting on your personal experience (pp. 183–97).

As you choose evidence to support your reasons, think about whether—and, if so, how—you will show the connections between reasons and evidence. These connections, often called *appeals* (p. 217), help readers understand why a reason is appropriate and valid (see Figure 13.2). Common appeals include citing authorities on an issue; using emotion to sway readers; calling attention to shared principles, values, and beliefs; asking readers to trust the writer; and using logic.

As you select supporting evidence, consider the type of document—or genre—you plan to write. The type of evidence used in various genres can differ in important ways. Articles (p. 294) in magazines, newspapers, and Web sites, for example, are more likely to rely on interviews, observations, and illustrations as primary sources of evidence than are academic essays, whose writers tend to draw information from published sources found in a library or database. Multimodal essays (p. 290), in contrast, are likely to use not only textual information and images but also audio, video, and animation. Evidence also varies widely depending on your discipline or profession, with some relying heavily on textual evidence and others relying on data from original research.

Decide How to Appeal to Your Readers   [FRAMING MY ARGUMENT]

For thousands of years, writers have appealed to readers to accept their ideas as reasonable and valid. Much of the work of ancient Greek and Roman thinkers such as Aristotle and Cicero revolved around strategies for presenting an argument to an audience. Their work continues to serve as a foundation for how we think about conveying information, ideas, and arguments to readers. In particular, the concept of an *appeal* to an audience plays a central role in thinking about how to develop an argument. Essentially, when you ask someone to accept your argument, you are appealing to them—you are asking them to consider what you have to say and, if they accept it as appropriate and valid, to believe or act in a certain way.

You can persuade your readers to accept your argument by appealing to authority, emotion, principles, values, beliefs, character, and logic. Your choice of

FIGURE 13.2 Supporting Your Reasons with Evidence

these appeals should reflect your understanding of your research writing situation and your sense of which appeals might be most effective — individually or in combination — at helping you achieve your goals as a writer.

Appeals to Authority   When you make an appeal to authority, you ask your readers to accept a reason because someone in a position of authority supports it. The evidence used to support this kind of appeal typically takes the form of quotations, paraphrases, or summaries of the ideas of experts on an issue, of political leaders, or of people who have been affected by an issue. As you consider whether your readers will accept a reason, reflect on the notes you've taken on your sources. Ask whether you've identified experts, leaders, or people who have been affected by an issue, and then ask whether you can use them to convince your readers that your reason has merit.

Appeals to Emotion   Appeals to emotion attempt to elicit an emotional response to an issue. The famous "win one for the Gipper" speech delivered by Pat O'Brien, who was playing the part of Notre Dame coach Knute Rockne in the 1940 film *Knute Rockne: All American*, is an example of an appeal to emotion. At halftime during a game against Army, with Notre Dame trailing, he said:

> Well, boys . . . I haven't a thing to say. Played a great game . . . all of you. Great game. I guess we just can't expect to win 'em all.
>
> I'm going to tell you something I've kept to myself for years. None of you ever knew George Gipp. It was long before your time. But you know what a tradition

My Research Project

Select Evidence to Support Your Reasons

Use the following prompts to help identify evidence to support your reasons.

1. List the reasons you are offering to support your main point.

2. Identify relevant evidence, and then list the evidence below each reason. You might need to review your sources to locate additional evidence or even obtain additional sources.

3. Determine whether you are relying too heavily on information from a single source.

4. Determine whether you are relying too heavily on one type of evidence.

5. Determine whether you've chosen evidence that is consistent with the type of document you plan to write.

6. Determine whether the evidence you've collected might lead you to revise the reasons you are offering to support your main point — or whether the thesis statement in which you express your main point should be revised.

bedfordresearcher.com
My Research Project Activities > Select Evidence to Support Your Reasons

he is at Notre Dame. . . . And the last thing he said to me—"Rock," he said, "sometime, when the team is up against it—and the breaks are beating the boys— tell them to go out there with all they got and win just one for the Gipper. . . . I don't know where I'll be then, Rock," he said, "but I'll know about it—and I'll be happy."

Using emotional appeals to frame an argument—that is, to help readers view an issue in a particular way—is a tried and true strategy, especially in advertising, fundraising, and personal communication. But use it carefully, if you use it at all. In some types of documents, such as scholarly articles and essays, emotional appeals are used infrequently, and readers of such documents are likely to ask why you would play on their emotions instead of making a logical appeal or appeals to authority.

Appeals to Principles, Values, and Beliefs   Appeals to principles, values, and beliefs rely on the assumption that your readers value a given set of principles. Religious and ethical arguments are often based on appeals to principles, such as the need to respect God, to love one another, to trust in the innate goodness of individuals, to believe that all of us are created equal, or to believe that security should never be purchased at the price of individual liberty. If you are considering making an appeal to principles, values, or beliefs, be sure your readers are likely to share the particular principle, value, or belief you will use.

Appeals to Character   Writers frequently use appeals to character. When politicians refer to their military experience, for example, they are saying, "Look at me. I'm a patriotic person who has served our country." When a celebrity endorses a product, he or she is saying, "You know and like me, so please believe me when I say that this product is worth purchasing." Appeals to character can also reflect a person's professional accomplishment. When scientists or philosophers present arguments, for example, they sometimes refer to their background and experience, or perhaps to their previous publications. In doing so, they are implicitly telling their readers that they have proven to be accurate and truthful in the past, and that readers can continue to trust them. Essentially, you can think of appeals to character as the "trust me" strategy. As you consider this kind of appeal, reflect on your character, accomplishments, and experiences, and ask how they might persuade your readers to trust you.

Appeals to Logic   When writers talk about logical appeals, they are referring to the concept of reasoning through a set of propositions to reach a considered conclusion. For example, you might argue that a suspect is guilty of murder because police found her fingerprints on a murder weapon, her DNA in blood under the murder victim's fingernails, scratches on the suspect's face, and video of the murder from a surveillance camera. Your argument would rely on the logical presentation of evidence to convince a jury that the suspect was the murderer and to persuade them to return a verdict of guilty. As you develop reasons to support your claim, consider using logical appeals such as deduction and induction.

Deduction is a form of logical reasoning that moves from general principles to a conclusion. It usually involves two propositions and a conclusion.

Proposition 1 (usually a general principle):	Stealing is wrong.
Proposition 2 (usually an observation):	John stole a candy bar from the store.
Conclusion (results of deductive analysis):	John's theft of the candy bar was wrong.

Deduction is often used in arguments about issues that have ethical and moral dimensions, such as birth control, welfare reform, and immigration policy.

Induction is a form of logical reasoning that moves from specific observations to general conclusions, often drawing on numerical data to reveal patterns. Medical researchers, for example, typically collect a large number of observations about the effectiveness and side effects of new medications and then analyze their observations to draw conclusions about the overall usefulness of the medications. Induction is based on probability, that is, it can tell you whether something seems likely to occur based on what has been observed. Three commonly used forms of induction are trend analysis (p. 81), causal analysis (p. 82), and data analysis (p. 82).

My Research Project

Decide How to Appeal to Your Readers

To develop an argumentative strategy, reflect on your purpose, your readers, and your main point. In your research log, record your responses to the following.

1. List each of your reasons.

2. Ask what sorts of appeals are best suited to each reason. Ask, for example, whether appeals to emotion, logic, or character are appropriate for a particular reason.

3. Sketch out promising appeals. Ask, for example, how you would appeal to authority, or how you would appeal to logic.

4. Ask how your readers are likely to respond to a given appeal.

5. Ask whether the kind of document you are writing lends itself to the use of particular appeals.

bedfordresearcher.com
My Research Project Activities > Decide How to Appeal to Your Readers

Decide How to Address Opposing Arguments

If you are writing to convince or persuade your readers, if you are offering an evaluation or analysis that might be challenged by your readers, or if you are proposing a solution to a problem, take the time to identify opposing arguments, or counterarguments. You might assume that calling attention to counterarguments will undermine your argument. Nothing is further from the truth. Identifying counterarguments provides opportunities to test and strengthen your reasons and evidence by comparing them with those put forth by other writers. Considering counterarguments also allows you to anticipate questions and concerns your readers are likely to bring to your document. And later, as you are writing your draft, your responses to these opposing arguments provide a basis for clearly explaining to your readers why your argument, evaluation, analysis, or solution is superior to others.

Remember that if reasonable alternatives to your argument didn't exist, there would be no need for a conversation about the issue in the first place. As a writer contributing to an ongoing conversation, you have a responsibility to indicate that you're aware of what has been said and who has said it. More important, you have a responsibility to consider carefully how your argument improves on the arguments made by other members of the conversation.

Identify Counterarguments   To identify counterarguments, review the sources you encountered as you learned about your issue. Identify the most compelling opposing viewpoints you found, and ask how the reasons and evidence offered to support them compare to yours. Then ask whether you can think of reasonable alternative positions that haven't been addressed in the sources you've consulted. Finally, talk with others about your issue and ask them what they think about it.

Address Counterarguments   To address counterarguments, consider the strengths and weaknesses of each claim in relation to your argument and in relation to the other opposing claims you might have identified. Then decide whether to concede, refute, or ignore each claim.

Concede valid claims   Show your readers that you are being fair—and establish common ground with readers who might otherwise be inclined to disagree with you—by acknowledging opposing points of view and accepting reasonable aspects of counterarguments. For example, if you are arguing that your state government should spend more to repair roads and bridges, acknowledge that this will probably mean reducing funding for other state programs or increasing state taxes.

You can qualify your concession by explaining that although part of a counterargument is sound, readers should consider the argument's weaknesses. You might note, for example, that reducing funding for some state programs could be offset by instituting fees for those who use those programs most.

Refute widely held claims   A counterargument might be widely advocated or generally accepted yet still have significant weaknesses. If you identify widely held claims that have weaknesses such as cost, undesirable outcomes, or logical flaws, describe the counterargument, point out its flaws, and explain why your claim or reason is superior. For example, you might note that, although it is costly to maintain roads and bridges, allowing them to fall into disrepair will cost far more in the long run—in terms of funding, possible injury, or loss of life.

Ignore competing claims Don't assume that addressing counterarguments means giving every competing claim equal time. Some counterarguments will be much stronger than others, and some will be so closely related to one another that you can dismiss them as a group. Once you've addressed valid and widely held competing claims, you can safely ignore the rest. Even though your sense of fairness might suggest that you should address every counterargument, doing so will result in a less effective (and potentially much longer) essay.

Later, as you draft your document, remember to present your discussion of counterarguments using a reasonable and polite tone. You will gain little, if anything, by insulting or belittling writers with whom you disagree, particularly when it's possible that some of your readers think a certain counterargument has merit. You will find it preferable — and generally more effective in terms of achieving your goals as a writer — to carefully and politely point out the limitations of a particular counterargument.

WORKING TOGETHER

Identify and Consider Counterarguments

Working with a group of two or more classmates, carry out a "devil's advocate" exercise to identify and consider opposing claims. First, briefly describe your issue, main point, and reasons. Other members of the group should offer reasonable alternative arguments. One member of the group should serve as a recorder, taking careful notes on the exchange, listing opposing claims, reasons supporting those claims, and your response to the claims. Once the exchange (which might last between three and ten minutes) is completed, switch roles and repeat the activity for every other member of the group.

This activity can be carried out face to face or electronically. If you are working on the activity using a chat program or a threaded discussion forum, you can record your exchange for later review. Most chat programs allow you to create a transcript of a session, and threaded discussion forums will automatically record your exchange.

Check for Logical Fallacies

To ensure the integrity of your argument, acquaint yourself with common logical fallacies — errors in logic that have the potential to undermine readers' willingness to accept an argument. Then check that your argument does not fall victim to them. Some of the most common logical fallacies are described below.

Fallacies Based on Distraction Careful readers will question attempts to divert their attention from the heart of your argument. Avoid the following fallacies:

A red herring is an irrelevant or distracting point. The term originated with the practice of sweeping a red herring (a particularly fragrant type of fish) across the trail being followed by a pack of hunting dogs to throw them off the scent of their prey. For example, the question *Why worry about the rising cost of tuition when the government is tapping our phones?* is a red herring (government surveillance has nothing to do with increases in college tuition).

Ad hominem *attacks* attempt to discredit an idea or argument by suggesting that a person or group associated with it should not be trusted. These kinds of attacks might be subtle or vicious. If you hear someone say that a proposed wind farm should be rejected because its main supporter cheated on her taxes, or that school vouchers are bad because a principal who swindled a school district supports them, you're listening to an *ad hominem* attack.

Irrelevant history is another form of distraction. For example, arguing that a proposal is bad because someone came up with the idea while they were using cocaine suggests that the state of mind of the person who originates an idea has something to do with its merits. It might well be the case that the idea is flawed, but you should base your assessment on an analysis of its strengths and weaknesses. Otherwise, you might as well say that an idea is undoubtedly sound because someone thought of it while he or she was sober.

Fallacies Based on Questionable Assumptions   Guard against the following fallacies by examining the foundations of your argument.

Sweeping generalizations, sometimes known as *hasty generalizations*, are based on stereotypes. Asserting that the rich are conservative voters, for example, assumes that someone who is rich is just like everyone else who is rich. These kinds of arguments don't account for variation within a group, nor do they consider exceptions to the rule.

Straw-man attacks oversimplify or distort another person's argument so it can be dismissed more easily. Just as a boxer can easily knock down a scarecrow, a writer who commits this fallacy might characterize an opposing position as more extreme than it actually is or might refute obviously flawed counterarguments while ignoring valid objections.

Citing inappropriate authorities can take several forms: citing as an authority someone who is not an expert on a subject, citing an authority who has a strong bias on an issue, suggesting that an individual voice represents consensus when that person's ideas are far from the mainstream, or treating paid celebrity endorsements as expert opinion.

Jumping on a bandwagon, also known as *argument from consensus*, implies that if enough people believe something, it must be true. This type of argument substitutes group thinking for careful analysis. The idea of jumping on a bandwagon refers to the practice, in early American politics, of parading a candidate through town on a bandwagon. To show support for the candidate, people would climb onto the wagon.

Fallacies Based on Misrepresentation   Ensure your readers will not question your integrity—or perhaps even call you a liar—by avoiding the following fallacies.

Stacking the deck, often referred to as *cherry picking* or *suppressing evidence*, is the act of presenting evidence for only one side of an argument when sufficient evidence exists for an alternative argument. Most readers will assume that a writer has done this deliberately and will wonder what he or she is trying to hide.

Base-rate fallacies are commonly found in arguments based on statistics. If you read that drinking coffee will triple your risk of developing cancer, you might be alarmed. However, if you knew that the risk rose from one in a billion to three in a billion, you might pour another cup.

Questionable analogies, also known as *false analogies*, make inappropriate comparisons. They are based on the assumption that if two things are similar in one way, they must be similar in others. For example, a writer might argue that the rise in temperatures due to climate change is like a fever, and that just as a fever usually runs its course on its own, so too will the climate recover without intervention.

Fallacies Based on Careless Reasoning   Writers who are rushing to meet a deadline sometimes fall victim to the following fallacies.

Post hoc *fallacies,* formally known as *post hoc, ergo propter hoc* fallacies ("after this, therefore because of this"), argue that because one event happened before a second event, the first event must have caused the second event. For example, a student might conclude that she received a low grade on an essay exam because she argued with an instructor during class. In fact, the real cause might be the poor quality of her exam responses.

Slippery-slope arguments warn that a single step will inevitably lead to a bad situation. For instance, one of the most common arguments against decriminalizing marijuana is that it leads to the use of stronger narcotics. Indeed, some heroin or cocaine addicts might have first tried marijuana, but there is no evidence that *all* marijuana users inevitably move on to harder drugs.

Either/or arguments present two choices, one of which is usually characterized as extremely undesirable. In fact, there might be a third choice, or a fourth, or a fifth.

Non sequiturs are statements that do not follow logically from what has been said. For example, arguing that buying a particular type of car will lead to a successful love life is a non sequitur.

Circular reasoning, also known as *begging the question*, restates a point that has just been made as evidence for itself. Arguing that a decline in voter turnout is a result of fewer people voting is an example of circular reasoning.

IV Creating Your Document

As you build your argument—and in particular, as you consider counter-arguments and check your reasoning for fallacies—you might find that you need to refine your thesis statement and perhaps even your main point. In fact, most writers refine their argument as they learn more about an issue and consider how best to contribute to a conversation. As you prepare to write a first draft of your project document, take another look at your main point, thesis statement, reasons, and evidence. Do they still make sense? Do they stack up well against competing arguments? Do you have enough evidence to meet the expectations of your intended readers? If you answer "no" to any of these questions, continue to develop and refine your argument.

13b

How can I organize my argument?

A well-organized document allows a reader to anticipate—or predict—what will come next. Choose an appropriate organizing pattern by reflecting on your writing situation, main point, thesis statement, reasons, evidence, counterarguments, and appeals. Then use labeling, grouping, clustering, and mapping to arrange your argument and formal and informal outlining strategies to organize your document.

Choose an Organizing Pattern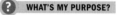

Organizing patterns provide an overall principle for arranging your argument and your research writing project document. Common organizing patterns include the following.

Chronology   The document's organization reflects the sequence in which events occur over time. For example, you might focus attention on a sequence of events in a recent election or during the course of a certain time span. If you are writing an academic essay or developing a multimedia presentation about a historical issue, you might find this organizing pattern useful.

Description   The document provides a point-by-point description of the physical attributes of a subject. For example, you might focus on the typical architectural features of a suburb or use a spatial arrangement that mimics the movement of the human eye as it takes in an image (left to right, top to bottom, near to far, and so on). Description is best for documents that address physical spaces, objects, or people—things that we can see and observe—rather than theories or processes that are not visible.

Definition   The document lays out the distinguishing characteristics of a subject and then provides examples and reasoning to explain what differentiates it from similar subjects. For instance, an essay defining *pride* might begin by stating that it is an emotion and then move on to explain why that particular emotion is not as harmful as many people believe.

Cause/Effect   The document is organized according to factors that lead to (cause) an outcome (effect). For example, you might identify the reasons behind a recent strike by grocery store employees or the health risks that contribute to heart disease.

Process Explanation   The document outlines the steps involved in doing something or explains how something happens. You might, for example, help readers understand the stages of nuclear fission or teach them what steps to take in the event of a meltdown in a nearby power plant.

Pro/Con   Ideas and information are organized to show support for and opposition to an argument or proposal. For example, a writer might organize an analysis of legislation calling for increased reliance on nuclear power by explaining why some groups support the legislation (pro) and others oppose it (con).

Multiple Perspectives   The document arranges information, ideas, and arguments according to a range of perspectives about a subject. Documents using this organizing pattern frequently provide an analysis supporting one perspective. For instance, a document addressing the use of tidal power as an alternative energy source might present the perspectives of utility company executives, environmentalists, oceanographers, legislators, and waterfront residents, ultimately favoring one group over the others.

Comparison/Contrast   The document identifies similarities and differences among the information, ideas, and arguments relevant to a subject. Documents that compare and contrast can be constructed in one of two ways. In the point-by-point approach, the writer presents each relevant point individually and then analyzes how that point operates in the two items being compared. In the whole-by-whole approach, the writer addresses the first item in its entirety, as a whole, and then moves on to the second item. For example, a document analyzing a policy initiative to decriminalize marijuana possession might compare current drug laws to alcohol prohibition or attempt to contrast medical and recreational uses of marijuana.

Strengths/Weaknesses   The document examines positive and negative aspects of a subject, such as increasing federal funding for health care by instituting a national lottery. Documents using this organizing pattern typically work toward a conclusion that one or two considerations outweigh the others.

Costs/Benefits   The tradeoffs associated with a subject, usually a choice or proposal of some sort, are considered in turn. For example, an evaluative essay might discuss why the expenses associated with implementing a particular educational initiative are justified (or not) by the potential for higher test scores.

IV Creating Your Document

Problem/Solution Documents define a problem and discuss the appropriateness of one or more solutions. If multiple solutions are proposed, an argument is usually made for the superiority of one over the others. For instance, an informative article might explain the problem of "brain drain," in which highly educated and skilled workers move out of state, and then argue in support of a proposal to retain and attract more skilled workers.

Your choice of organizing pattern will reflect your purpose and the role or roles you adopt as a writer. If you're adopting the role of *reporter*, for example, you might select chronology, cause/effect, or comparison/contrast. If you're adopting the role of *evaluator*, you're likely to choose from patterns such as strengths/weaknesses, pro/con, comparison/contrast, or multiple perspectives. If you're adopting the role of *problem solver*, you're likely to choose from patterns such as strengths/weaknesses, pro/con, comparison/contrast, or multiple perspectives. If you're adopting the role of *advocate*, you might opt for an organizing pattern that is well suited to argumentation, such as pro/con or strengths/weaknesses.

Your choice of organizing pattern should also reflect the argument you are making in your document and the reasons, evidence, and appeals you use to make your argument. Keep in mind as well that a writer may use more than one organizing pattern in a document. For instance, a process explanation often works in tandem with chronology, since both present steps in a sequence. Similarly, a document presenting multiple perspectives might also adopt a strengths/weaknesses pattern to evaluate the merits of each perspective.

Review and Arrange Your Evidence

Once you have selected an organizing pattern, you can use strategies such as labeling, grouping, clustering, and mapping to determine how to arrange your argument. These strategies will also help you later as you develop an outline for your document.

Label Evidence Labeling can help you understand at a glance how and where you will use evidence from your sources. For example, you might label notes or sources containing the evidence you want to use in your introduction with "Introduction," those that you plan to use to define a concept with the name of that concept, and so on. If you have taken digital notes or saved digital sources, as Brandon Tate did, you have a number of options (see Figure 13.3). Once you've labeled your notes and sources, you can organize them into groups or order them according to the outline you will create.

Group Evidence Grouping involves categorizing the evidence you've obtained from your sources. Paper-based notes and copies of sources can be placed in related piles or file folders; sources and notes in word processing files or a smartphone can be saved in larger files or placed in folders; items in Bookmarks or Favorites lists can be sorted by category.

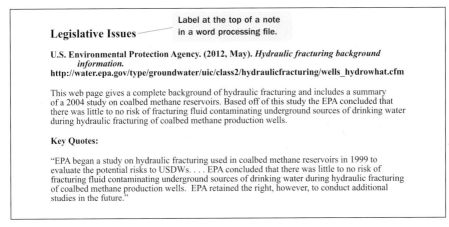

Label at the top of a note in a word processing file.

Legislative Issues

U.S. Environmental Protection Agency. (2012, May). *Hydraulic fracturing background information.*
http://water.epa.gov/type/groundwater/uic/class2/hydraulicfracturing/wells_hydrowhat.cfm

This web page gives a complete background of hydraulic fracturing and includes a summary of a 2004 study on coalbed methane reservoirs. Based off of this study the EPA concluded that there was little to no risk of fracturing fluid contaminating underground sources of drinking water during hydraulic fracturing of coalbed methane production wells.

Key Quotes:

"EPA began a study on hydraulic fracturing used in coalbed methane reservoirs in 1999 to evaluate the potential risks to USDWs. . . . EPA concluded that there was little to no risk of fracturing fluid contaminating underground sources of drinking water during hydraulic fracturing of coalbed methane production wells. EPA retained the right, however, to conduct additional studies in the future."

FIGURE 13.3 Labeling Digital Notes and Sources

Bookmarks can be organized in folders.

Title, URL, and description

FIGURE 13.4 Grouping Electronic Notes and Sources

IV Creating Your Document

Use Clustering   Clustering can be used to explore the relationships among your thesis statement, reasons, and evidence. Clustering involves arranging these elements of your argument visually on a sheet of paper or on a computer screen. By putting your thesis statement at the center of the cluster and your reasons and evidence around it, you can explore how reasons and evidence relate to your main point, and how your reasons relate to each other.

Clustering can be used at several points in a research writing project: as you begin to explore your topic, as you brainstorm to come up with ideas, as you explore relationships among the material you've collected, and now as you begin to arrange your argument (see Figure 13.4).

Use Mapping   You can use mapping to explore sequences of reasons and evidence. For example, you might use mapping to create a timeline or to show how an argument builds on one supporting point after another. This use of mapping

My Research Project

Arrange an Argument by Clustering

Clustering can help you explore the relationships among your main point, thesis statement, reasons, and evidence. To create a cluster:

1. In the middle of a sheet of paper, or in the center of a digital document (word processing file or graphics file), write your main point or thesis statement.

2. Place your reasons around your main point or thesis statement.

3. List the evidence you'll present to support your reasons next to each reason.

4. Think about the relationships among your main point, reasons, and evidence, and draw lines and circles to show those relationships.

5. Annotate your cluster to indicate the nature of the relationships you've identified.

bedfordresearcher.com
My Research Project Activities > Arrange an Argument by Clustering

is particularly effective as you begin to think about organizing your project document, and it often relies on the organizing patterns discussed on pp. 224–26, such as chronology, cause/effect, comparison/contrast, cost/benefit, and problem/solution.

The tutorial on pp. 230–31 shows a map that Nicholas Brothers created to organize his thoughts about the argument in his research essay about U.S. reliance on private military corporations.

Create an Outline

An outline represents the sequence in which your reasons and evidence will appear in your document. As you develop an outline, you'll make decisions about the order in which you will present your reasons and the evidence you'll use to back them up. Later, as you draft, your outline can serve as a plan for creating your document.

Create an Informal Outline Informal outlines can take many forms: a brief list of words, a series of short phrases, or even a series of sentences. You can use informal outlines to remind yourself of key points to address in your document or of notes you should refer to when you begin drafting. Elizabeth Leontiev, who wrote a research essay about the impact of the U.S. war on drugs on South American coca farmers, created the informal outline shown in Figure 13.5. In her outline, each item represents a section she planned to include in her essay.

Nicholas Brothers wrote a "thumbnail outline," a type of informal outline, as he worked on his research essay about private military corporations. Nicholas identified the major sections he would include in his research essay and noted which sources he would use to provide background information and to support his argument (see Figure 13.6).

---

1. *Introduction — what is coca? where is it grown?*

2. *Cultural and economic importance of coca crop*

3. *Evo Morales's plan: "zero cocaine, not zero coca"*
   - *benefits of the Morales plan*

4. *Brief history of other plans and their failures*
   - *U.S. "war on drugs"*
   - *aerial fumigation / coca eradication*
   - *alternative cropping*

5. *Conclusion supporting the Morales plan*

FIGURE 13.5 Elizabeth Leontiev's Informal Outline

Intro

Introduce private military corporations as integral to U.S. military operations. Present the many costs of PMCs to be examined.

Section 1

Explain the history of PMCs, from the Napoleonic era to today. Focus on the post-9/11 era and how privatization of the U.S. military has increased in the last ten years. Key sources: interview transcripts from Brothers and Euchner.

Section 2

Discuss the frequent use of PMCs in Iraq and Afghanistan, as well their diversified functions. Examine the distinction between PMCs and mercenaries. Key sources for background and argument: Scahill and Singer.

Section 3

Give examples of abuses and illegal acts by PMC contractors. Explain why contractors have not been convicted of crimes. Key sources for abuse evidence: Capps, Simpson, and Savage; key sources for lack of legal accountability: Singer, Yeoman, and Risen.

Section 4

Present the view that abuses by contractors undermine the image and goals of the U.S. military. Key sources: the Army Field Manual and the Congressional Research Service report.

Section 5

Discuss other "costs" of PMCs, in particular the amount of taxpayer money spent on them and the brain drain that occurs. Key sources: Stanger, Moshe, and Pelton.

Conclusion

Look at ways Americans can take civic action to end the overreliance on PMCs.

FIGURE 13.6 Nicholas Brothers's Thumbnail Outline

How can I map my argument?

You can map your argument by arranging your reasons and evidence to support your main point. In this example, Nicholas Brothers maps the reasons and evidence in his argumentative essay about U.S. reliance on private military corporations (PMCs) in its war on terror. Later, he will use this map as he develops his outline.

1 List your main point or thesis statement.

2 Review your notes to identify reasons that support your main point.

3 Based on the reasons you will use to help readers accept or act on your main point, choose an organizing pattern (pp. 224–26). Here, the writer chooses a cause/effect pattern to arrange his argument.

4 Use the organizing pattern to map your argument. Here, the writer maps the causes and effects of U.S. reliance on private military corporations.

5 List evidence near supporting points. Here, the writer includes references to sources in parentheses.

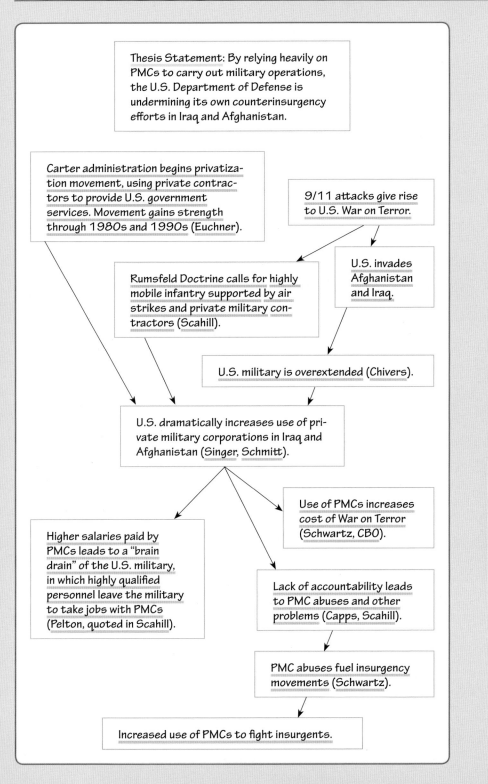

Create a Formal Outline   A formal outline provides a complete and accurate list of the points you want to address in your document. Formal outlines use Arabic numerals, letters, and Roman numerals to indicate the hierarchy of information. An alternative approach, common in business and the sciences, uses numbering with decimal points:

```
I.
      A.
           1.
           2.
      B.
           1.
           2.
II.
```

```
1.
      1.1
            1.1.1
            1.1.2
      1.2
            1.2.1
            1.2.2
2.
```

Writers use formal outlines to identify the hierarchy of information, ideas, and arguments. You can create a formal outline to identify:

- your main point and/or thesis statement
- your reasons
- the sequence in which those reasons should be presented
- evidence for your reasons
- the notes and sources you should refer to as you work on your document

The most common types of formal outlines are topical outlines and sentence outlines.

Topical Outlines present the topics and subtopics you plan to include in your research document as a series of words and phrases. Items at the same level of importance should be phrased in parallel grammatical form.

   In her topical outline for her research essay on steroid use among adolescent girls, Alexis Alvarez includes her thesis statement, suggests the key points she wants to make in her document, maps out the support for her points, and uses a conventional system of numbers and letters (see Figure 13.7).

Sentence Outlines use complete sentences to identify the points you want to cover (see Figure 13.8). Sentence outlines typically serve two purposes.

1. They begin the process of converting an outline into a draft of your document.
2. They help you assess the structure of a document that you have already written.

When you've created your outline, ask whether it can serve as a blueprint for the first draft of your document. Taking the time to create an effective outline now will reduce the time needed to write your first draft later.

Thesis statement: Although competitive sports can provide young female athletes with many benefits, they can also have negative effects, the worst of which is increasing drug use.

I.   **Female Participation in Competitive Athletics**
   A.   Short history and current trends
   B.   Understanding the female athlete
II. **Positive Impact of Competitive Athletics**
   A.   Physiological (Kane & Larkin)
      1.   Reduced risk of obesity and heart disease
      2.   Increased immune functioning and prevention of certain cancers
      3.   Improved flexibility, strength, and aerobic power
   B.   Psychological (Kane & Larkin)
      1.   Improved self-esteem
      2.   Enhanced mental health
      3.   Effective in reducing symptoms of stress, anxiety, and depression
   C.   Sociological
      1.   Expansion of social boundaries
      2.   Teaches responsibility, discipline, and determination
      3.   Educational asset
III. **Negative Impact of Competitive Athletics**
   A.   Physiological (Graham)
      1.   Overtraining
      2.   Eating disorders
      3.   Exercise-induced amenorrhea and osteoporosis

FIGURE 13.7 Part of Alexis Alvarez's Topical Outline

Thesis statement: Although competitive sports can provide young female athletes with many benefits, they can also have negative effects, the worst of which is increasing drug use.

   I.   Society has been concerned with the use of performance-enhancing drugs among younger male athletes, but many don't know that these drugs are also used by younger female athletes.
      A.   Women began participating in sports in the mid-19th century, although participation was not encouraged until recently. Millions of girls are involved in a wide range of physical activities and are participating in school-sponsored sports.
      B.   In response to pressures of competitive sports, girls' steroid use has increased and younger and younger girls are taking steroids.
   II. Sports can benefit a girl's growth and development physiologically as well as psychologically and sociologically.
      A.   Participation in sports has a wide range of positive physiological effects on adolescent girls.
         1.   Studies have shown that participation in sports can reduce the risk of obesity and heart disease.
         2.   Studies have shown that participation in sports appear to increase immune functioning and prevent certain cancers.
         3.   Participation in sports has also been linked to improved flexibility, strength, and aerobic power.

FIGURE 13.8 Part of Alexis Alvarez's Sentence Outline

My Research Project

Create and Review Your Outline

In your word processing program or in your research log, create an outline. If your word processing program has an outlining tool, use it to create a formal outline. In Microsoft Word, use Outline View (available in older versions of Word through the View Outline menu command) to view your document in outline mode. Use the Promote and Demote buttons on the outlining toolbar to set the levels for entries in your outline. Use the Collapse and Expand buttons to hide and show parts of your outline.

Review your outline by asking yourself the following questions.

1. Does my outline provide an effective organization for my document?

2. Have I covered all of my key points?

3. Have I addressed my key points in sufficient detail?

4. Do any sections seem out of order?

bedfordresearcher.com
My Research Project Activities > Create and Review Your Outline

---

> **QUICK REFERENCE**

Developing and Organizing Your Argument

☑ Identify reasons to accept your thesis statement. (p. 213)

☑ Select evidence to support your reasoning. (p. 215)

☑ Decide how to appeal to your readers. (p. 217)

☑ Consider and address counterarguments. (p. 219)

☑ Check for logical fallacies. (p. 221)

☑ Choose an organizing pattern for your argument. (p. 224)

☑ Arrange your evidence. (p. 226)

☑ Create an outline. (p. 228)

IV Creating Your Document

14

Drafting

Key Questions

If you're new to research writing, you might be surprised at how long it's taken to get to the chapter about writing your document. If you are an experienced research writer, you know that you've been writing it all along. Research writing isn't so much the act of putting words to paper or on screen as it is the process of identifying and learning about an issue, reflecting on what you've learned, and contributing to the conversation about your issue.

14a

How can I help my readers follow my argument?

After all the work you've done learning about your issue and formulating your ideas about what you want to share with your readers, you still need to write an effective document—one that your readers will find easy to read and understand. To help your readers follow your argument, work from an outline, write effective paragraphs, use transitions and cues to move your readers through your document, and integrate information from sources effectively.

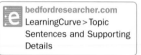
bedfordresearcher.com
LearningCurve > Topic
Sentences and Supporting
Details

Work from an Outline

Your outline provides a framework you can use to draft your document. Your outline likely includes your plans for

- the points you will include in your document
- the order in which you will make your points
- the evidence you will use to support each point

As you review your outline, check whether you have organized your points in a way that will allow you to achieve your purpose and whether you are addressing the needs, interests, values, and beliefs of your readers.

If you have listed information about the sources you will use to support your points, you can check whether you are

- providing enough evidence to support your points
- relying too heavily on a limited number of sources
- relying too heavily on support from sources that favor one side of the conversation

As you prepare to draft your document, you might find it necessary to reorganize your ideas to achieve your purpose.

If you created an informal outline, it can be the skeleton of your document, and you can now begin fleshing out sections. Translate a bulleted list of items, for instance, into a series of brief sentences, or write paragraphs based on the key points in the outline. If you created a formal outline, such as a topical outline or a sentence outline, you can use each main point in the outline as a topic sentence for a paragraph. For example, you can form supporting sentences from the subpoints under each main point.

If your outline contains references to specific notes or sources, make sure that you use those notes in your draft. Take advantage of the time you spent thinking about which sources are most appropriate for a particular section of your document.

As you work on your document, you might find it necessary to reorganize your ideas. Think of your outline as a flexible guide rather than a rigid blueprint.

TUTORIAL

How do I use an outline to draft my document?

Use your outline as the "skeleton" of the first draft of your document. In this example, Alexis Alvarez expands her outline into a rough draft.

1 Save your outline with a new name, such as Draft1.doc.

2 Turn major headings in your outline into headings and subheadings in your draft.

3 Convert lower-level entries into topic sentences for paragraphs.

4 Use lists of items as sentences in each paragraph.

5 Locate evidence to support your points. Quote, paraphrase, and summarize sources identified in your outline.

1. Benefits of Sports for Girls
   a. Physical Health Benefits
      i. Reduces risks of adult-onset coronary disease and some cancers (Kane & Larkin, 1997)
      ii. Enhances immune system, posture, strength, flexibility, and heart-lung endurance (Kane & Larkin, 1997; "Sports in America," 1994)
   b. Mental Health Benefits (Kane & Larkin, 1997; Orozco interview)
      i. Positive body image
      ii. Confidence and self-esteem
      iii. Sense of control
   c. Social benefits (Orozco and Alvarez interviews)
2. Problems Caused by Sports for Girls
   a. Physical side effects

Girls and Sports: The Upside

According to Kane and Larkin (1997), adolescent girls who exercise regularly can lessen their risks for adult-onset coronary disease and certain cancers. Girls' involvement in sports and exercise also tends to improve immune functioning, posture, strength, flexibility, and heart-lung endurance (Kane & Larkin, 1997; "Sports in America," 1994).

In addition, competitive athletics can enhance mental health by offering adolescent girls positive feelings about body image; tangible experiences of competency, control, and success; improved self-esteem and self-confidence; and a way to reduce anxiety (Kane & Larkin, 1997). Juan Orozco, who has coached competitive soccer for nine years at the adolescent female level, confirmed that making a competitive sports team is a privilege that many girls work toward with determination and longing and that being picked to participate encourages these young athletes to believe in themselves and their abilities (personal interview, Sept. 22, 2004).

A final benefit is that sports expand social boundaries and teach many of the personal and social skills girls will need throughout their lives. According to Orozco, through competitive athletics girls learn a crucial lesson in how to

Create Paragraphs That Focus on a Central Idea

Writers use paragraphs to present and develop a central idea. Depending on the complexity of your argument and the type of document you are writing, a single paragraph might be all you need to present your reasoning and evidence—or it might play only a small role in conveying your thinking about an issue. You can create effective paragraphs by ensuring that they are focused, organized, and well developed. You can help readers follow your argument by using transitions that clearly convey the relationships among paragraphs.

Paragraphs often have a topic sentence in which the writer makes an assertion, offers an observation, or asks a question. The rest of the sentences in the paragraph elaborate on the topic. Consider the following paragraph, drawn from Nicholas Brothers' research essay.

> Given the potential costs in justice and national security, why hire contractors at all? Ironically, perhaps the most often-cited reason for using private contractors is that using these corporations saves the taxpayer money since the government can hire them on an as-needed basis and does not have to pay for contractors' training, health care, or pensions. Professor Allison Stanger of Middlebury College challenges this notion in her 2009 book *One Nation Under Contract: The Outsourcing of American Power and the Future of Foreign Policy* when she points out that nearly all private contractors previously served in the military, meaning that many of them are receiving pension payments anyway. Stanger writes that "the federal government is effectively paying for the training and retirement of the contractors it hires, all appearances to the contrary, as well as paying double or triple the daily rate for their services." Therefore the Department of Defense would actually save taxpayers money by reversing the trend of privatization.

The central idea of the paragraph follows an initial question.

The third and fourth sentences use evidence from a source to show the real cost of hiring contractors.

The final sentence draws a conclusion that supports the essay's thesis statement.

Create Paragraphs That Use Appropriate Organizing Patterns

Effective paragraphs follow an organizing pattern, often the same one that the document as a whole follows, such as chronology, description, or costs/benefits (pp. 224–26). These common patterns help readers anticipate what you'll say. Readers who recognize a pattern, such as problem/solution, will find it easier to focus on your ideas and argument if they understand how you are organizing your paragraph. Note how the following paragraph, drawn from featured writer Alexis Alvarez's essay, uses the problem/solution organizing pattern.

> What can we do to help adolescent female athletes avoid illicit drug use? How can we help them avoid the pitfalls of competitive athletics? Parents, coaches, and the athletes themselves all play a crucial role in averting bad choices. First, parents and coaches need to be aware that performance-enhancing drugs are a problem. Some adults believe that steroid use is either

The paragraph begins by restating the problem.

The central idea of the paragraph is provided in the third sentence.

One part of the solution to the larger problem is provided in the fourth sentence.

minimal or nonexistent among teenagers, but one study concluded that "over half the teens who use steroids start before age
16, sometimes with the encouragement of their parents. . . .
Seven percent said they first took 'juice' by age ten" (Dudley,
1994, p. 235).

> The fifth sentence provides evidence from a
> source to illustrate the nature of the problem.

Create Transitions Within and Between Paragraphs

Transitions help readers understand the relationships among sentences, paragraphs, and even sections of a document. Essentially, they smooth the way for
readers, helping them understand how information, ideas, and arguments are
related to one another. Transitions are most effective when they don't call attention to themselves, but instead move the reader's eye along to the next sentence,
paragraph, or section. Consider the following examples of the steps involved in
preparing fish.

No Transitions:
Catch the fish. Clean the fish. Filet the fish. Cook the fish. Eat the fish. Catch
another fish.

Inconsistent Transitions:
First, catch the fish. Secondly, clean the fish. When you've done that, filet the fish.
Next, cook the fish. Fifth, eat the fish. After all is said and done, catch another fish.

Consistent Transitions:
First, catch the fish. Second, clean the fish. Third, filet the fish. Fourth, cook the
fish. Fifth, eat the fish. Finally, catch another fish.

Transitions frequently appear as words and phrases, such as those used in the previous example. They can also take the form of sentences and paragraphs. Transitional sentences, such as the following, often appear at the end or beginning of
paragraphs and serve to link two paragraphs.

> . . . . a series of tests. The results of the tests revealed a surprising trend.

> Incredibly, the outcome was far better than we could have hoped. After
> reviewing . . .

Transitional paragraphs, such as the following example, call attention to a major
shift in focus within a document.

> In the next section, we explore the reasons behind this surprising development. We
> focus first on the event itself. Then we consider the reasons underlying the event.
> Our goal is to call attention to the unique set of relationships that made this
> development possible.

As you create transitions, pay attention to the order in which you introduce new
information and ideas in your paragraphs. In general, it is best to begin a sentence with a reference to information and ideas that have already been introduced and to introduce new information and ideas at the end of a sentence. For
example, consider the following examples, which begin a new paragraph.

Introducing New Information First:
Admissions staff look at the kind of courses students are taking, in addition to looking at grades.

Building on Information That Has Already Been Introduced:
And it's not just grades that matter; admissions staff also look at the kind of courses students are taking.

The second example, by referring to information that has been introduced in the previous paragraph, provides an effective transition to a new paragraph, even as it introduces new information about additional college admissions criteria. In contrast, readers of the first example would not have the benefit of seeing how the new information fits into what they've already read.

Common transitions and their functions are presented below.

To Help Readers Follow a Sequence
furthermore
in addition
moreover
next
first/second/third

To Elaborate or Provide Examples
for example
for instance
such as
in fact
indeed
to illustrate

To Compare
similarly
in the same manner
like
as in

To Contrast
however
on the other hand
nevertheless
nonetheless
despite
although/though

To Signal a Concession
I admit that
of course
granted

To Introduce a Conclusion
as a result
as a consequence
because of
therefore
thus
for this reason

Provide Cues to Keep Your Readers on Track

A document that is well organized and well designed allows a reader to antici-pate—or predict—what will come next, which helps readers understand your goals more easily and stay within the frame you've provided. The test is whether your readers can move smoothly through your document without wondering, "Where did that come from?" As you draft, check whether your document is organized and designed consistently and predictably. You might find the follow-ing techniques useful.

Provide Forecasts and Cross-References A forecast is a type of transitional sentence that prepares your readers for a shift in your document, such as the boundary between one section and the next. Cross-references tell your readers that they can find related information in another section of the document or let them know that a particular issue will be addressed in greater detail elsewhere. On a Web site, forecasts and cross-references might take the form of small images, flags, or statements such as "Continue to next section" or "Follow this link for more information."

Use Headings and Subheadings You can help your readers keep their place in your document by using headings and subheadings. Your formatting should distinguish between headings (major sections) and subheadings (subsections).

Use a Menu If you are writing a digital document such as a Web site or a multimodal essay, you can add a menu on the side, top, or bottom of your pages that readers can see as they work through your site. Brandon Tate provided a menu on every page of his site (see Figure 14.1).

Pay Attention to Design Principles As you draft your document, pay attention to the principles of effective design. Using a readable body font that is clearly different from the font used for headings and subheadings, for example, can improve readability significantly. Similarly, breaking out information using bulleted and numbered lists, providing descriptive page headers or footers, and integrating illustrations effectively into your text can greatly enhance readability. If you are drafting a digital document, keep in mind the uses of digital illustrations. You can read more about design in Chapters 16 and 18.

Integrate Information from Sources Effectively

Information from sources can be used to introduce an important concept, establish the strength of a writer's argument, and elaborate on the central ideas in your document. Writers frequently state a point, offer a reason to accept it, and support their reasoning with evidence from a source, typically in the form of quotations, paraphrases, and summaries. In the following example, drawn from Brandon

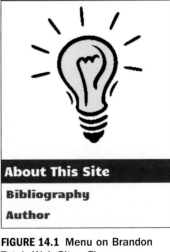

Learn More

The Pros

Environmental Benefits

Economic Benefits

The Cons

Impact on Water

Impact on Air Quality

The Conclusion

About This Site

Bibliography

Author

FIGURE 14.1 Menu on Brandon Tate's Web Site *The menu helps readers understand the organization of the site and move to pages within it.*

IV Creating Your Document

Tate's Web site, a quotation and a paraphrase are used to support a point introduced in the first sentence of the paragraph.

> In fact, pollution from power plants may worsen as the demand for electric power continues to increase. The U.S. Department of Energy (2012b) notes that "it is likely that the nation's reliance on fossil fuels to power an expanding economy will actually increase over at least the next two decades even with aggressive development and deployment of new renewable and nuclear technologies" (para. 1). Moreover, demand in developing nations is expected to increase even more dramatically. Of the nearly 1,200 conventional, coal-fired power plants now on the drawing board worldwide, most are in developing countries (Plumer, 2012). The addition of so many new plants will almost certainly lead to more global air pollution in the near term.

By quoting an authority on the issue, the U.S. Department of Energy, Brandon strengthens his argument. The quotation, along with a subsequent paraphrase of a passage from another source, provides evidence to support his point. He follows the quotation and paraphrase with a sentence that restates the main point of the paragraph. (See Chapter 15 for more about integrating information from sources.)

14b

How can I write with style and engage my readers?

As you draft your document, consider how you'll keep your readers' attention — and be aware of how the construction of your sentences and paragraphs can affect their willingness to keep reading.

Use Details to Capture Your Readers' Attention

An effective paragraph does more than simply convey information — it provides details that bring an issue to life. Consider the differences between the following paragraphs.

Example 1: Minimal Details
Hydraulic fracturing has recently become a growing controversy in the United States of America. This is because many people believe that the environmental harms of this oil and gas drilling technique outweigh its benefits. Others, in contrast, argue that it has helped sustain our use of natural gas and petroleum.

Example 2: Extensive, Concrete Details
Hydraulic fracturing, also known as fracking, has recently become a growing controversy in the United States of America. This is because many people believe that its environmental harms outweigh any possible benefits it may offer. According to the U.S. Environmental Protection Agency [EPA] (2012), fracking is used to "maximize the extraction of underground resources." The horizontal drilling technique involves pumping water, chemicals, and specialized sand into shale formations deep down inside the Earth at intense pressure (EPA, 2012). This creates

fractures in the formations allowing the bounded resources such as natural gas and petroleum to be released. Combined, these two fossil fuels generate roughly 60% of all energy consumed in the United States (U.S. Energy Information Administration [EIA], 2012).

Both examples, drawn from Brandon Tate's Web site on hydraulic fracturing, convey the same main point. The first example, however, does little more than state the facts. The second example provides details from sources published by the U.S. Environmental Protection Agency and the U.S. Energy Information Administration. The details drawn from these sources allow readers to gain a more complete, and more concrete, understanding of the issue.

Write Clearly and Concisely

Readers don't want to work any harder than necessary to follow the information, ideas, and arguments in a document. To keep your readers from setting your document aside, write clearly and concisely. Consider, for example, the following passages.

> Please join me, Dr. Watson. I have concluded that I am in a situation in which I require your assistance.

> Come here, Dr. Watson. I need you.

> Help!

The second passage, reputed to be the first words ever spoken on a telephone, was spoken by Alexander Graham Bell after he'd spilled acid on his pants. Had he spoken the first passage instead, he might have wasted crucial time while he waited a few extra seconds for his assistant to figure out what he was being asked to do. The simple exclamation of "Help!" might have been even more effective and would certainly have taken less time to utter. Then again, it might have been too vague for his assistant to figure out just how he needed to act and what sort of help was required.

In general, if two sentences provide the same information, the briefer sentence is usually easier to understand. In some cases, however, writing too little will leave your readers wondering what you are trying to get across.

The following techniques can help you write clearly and concisely.

- **Avoid unnecessary modifiers.** Unnecessary modifiers are words that provide little or no additional information to a reader, such as *fine, many, somewhat, great, quite, sort of, lots, really,* and *very.*

  Example Sentence with Unnecessary Modifiers:
  The Lincoln MKZ serves as a really excellent example of a very fine performance sedan.

  Revised Example:
  The Lincoln MKZ serves as an excellent example of a performance sedan.

- **Avoid unnecessary introductory phrases.** Avoid phrases such as *there are, there is, these have, these are, here are, here is, it has been reported that, it* *has been said that, it is evident that, it is obvious that,* and so on. Sentences beginning with *It goes without saying,* for example, allow you to emphasize a point, but you can often recast such sentences more concisely by simply stating the point.

Example Sentence with Unnecessary Introductory Phrase:
It goes without saying that drinking water should be clean.

Revised Example:
Drinking water should be clean.

- **Avoid stock phrases.** As you draft, express yourself clearly by avoiding the use of stock phrases, such as the following.

Stock Phrase	Alternative
as a matter of fact	in fact
at all times	always
at that point in time	then
at this point in time	now, currently
at the present time	now, currently
because of the fact that	because
by means of	by
due to the fact that	because
in order to	to
in spite of the fact that	although, though
in the event that	if

Example Sentence with Stock Phrase:
Call the security desk in the event that the alarm sounds.

Revised Example:
Call the security desk if the alarm sounds.

Write Actively (Most of the Time)

One of the easiest things you can do to engage your readers is to write in the *active voice.* A sentence written in active voice specifies an actor—a person or thing—who carries out an action.

Active Voice:
Juan took an exam.

The tornado leveled the town.

Kevin Love scored the game-winning basket with .2 seconds remaining in overtime.

> bedfordresearcher.com
> LearningCurve > Active and Passive Voice

In contrast, a sentence written in *passive voice* indicates that something was done, but it does not necessarily specify who or what did it.

IV Creating Your Document

Passive Voice:
The exam was taken by Juan.

The town was leveled.

The game-winning basket was scored with .2 seconds remaining in overtime.

In general, you'll want to emphasize the actor, because sentences written in active voice are easier to understand and provide more information—not only *what* was done, but also *who* did it. Passive voice, however, can be effective when active voice would require the inclusion of unnecessary information. For example, many scientific experiments are conducted by large teams of researchers. Few readers would want to know which members of the team carried out every task discussed in an article about the experiment. Rather than using active voice (for example, "Heather Landers, assisted by Sandy Chapman and Shaun Beaty, anesthetized the mice, and then Greta Steber and Justin Switzer examined their eyes for lesions"), you can use passive voice ("The mice were anesthetized, and their eyes were examined for lesions"). In this case, the sentence written in passive voice is clearer, easier to understand, and free of unnecessary information.

Passive voice is also useful if you wish to emphasize the recipient of the action, rather than the person or thing carrying out the action. Police reports, for example, often use passive voice ("The suspect was apprehended at the corner of Oak and Main Streets").

Adopt a Consistent Point of View

Writers typically adopt a particular point of view as they write:

- first person: *I*, *we*
- second person: *you*
- third person: *she*, *he*, *it*, *one*, *they*, or nouns that describe a particular group or an individual, such as *doctors*, *teachers*, *engineer*, *lawyer*, *Mr. Smith*, or *Lee Chen*

When writers shift their point of view within a sentence, readers notice—and sometimes have to stop and ask themselves what just happened. Consider the following example.

Shift in Point of View:
After the climbers reached the summit in record time, we burst into song.

The sentence begins with a third-person point of view (*the climbers*) and then shifts to first-person (*we*). The sentence would be easier to understand if it were written in either first- or third-person.

Consistent Point of View:
After the climbers reached the summit in record time, they burst into song.

After we reached the summit in record time, we burst into song.

To keep your readers engaged—or, more accurately, to avoid disrupting the smooth reading of your document—ensure that you adopt a consistent point of view.

Vary Your Sentence Structure

Understanding the types of sentences that you can write and the types of sentence structures you can use can help you create a document that will maintain your readers' interest. You can begin to accomplish this by understanding the four basic types of sentences.

Statements:	Dick runs quickly.
Questions:	How quickly did Dick run?
Commands:	Run, Dick, run.
Exclamations:	Way to go, Dick!

You can continue by understanding the four basic sentence structures, which are distinguished by the types and numbers of *clauses* they contain. A clause—a sequence of words containing a subject and a verb—can be either *independent* or *dependent*. (Sometimes these types of clauses are referred to as *main* and *subordinate*, respectively.) The primary difference between these types of clauses is that independent clauses can function on their own as a complete sentence, while dependent clauses cannot.

Simple (a single independent clause):
Jane runs quickly.

> ▦ Independent clause
> ▨ Dependent clause

Compound (two or more independent clauses):
Jane runs quickly, but she doesn't run as quickly as Dick.

Complex (an independent clause and a dependent clause):
Although Jane runs quickly, Dick is quicker.

Compound-Complex (two or more independent clauses and at least one dependent clause):
All things considered, the Dick and Jane readers were wildly successful, but they have faded into the comfortable oblivion of history.

Mixing sentence types and structures will help you produce an appealing rhythm in your writing. If you neglect to vary your sentences, on the other hand, your readers are likely to find your document monotonous and boring. To keep your readers' interest, vary your sentence type, structure, and length. Consider the following examples.

Similar Sentence Structure and Length:
We decided to spend the morning at El Rastro. El Rastro is a Sunday morning flea market extraordinaire. We decided to take the subway to get there. A man stood quite close as we got on. I found this strange in an uncrowded subway station. Then I felt his hand in my left pocket. I also felt his hand on my back. It's a good thing that I'm ticklish. I instinctively shrugged away from his hands. Then I swore loudly and imaginatively at him. (It's inappropriate to swear on a Sunday in Spain. I wouldn't have done it under normal circumstances.) He had almost gotten away with my sunglasses. This would almost certainly have disappointed him. I know it would have inconvenienced me.

Each sentence uses the same sentence type (statements) and the same simple sentence structure. Sentence length ranges from seven to nine words.

> **Varied Sentence Structure and Length:**
> We decided to spend the morning at El Rastro, a Sunday morning flea market extraordinaire. As we got on the subway to get to El Rastro, I noticed that a man was standing quite close to me—strange, since the subway wasn't crowded. Then I felt his hand in my left pocket and his hand on my back. (Fortunately, I'm ticklish.) "What the heck?" I thought, instinctively shrugging away and swearing at him (an inappropriate thing to do on a Sunday morning in Spain, but I was caught off guard). He had almost gotten away with my sunglasses, which would have disappointed him and inconvenienced me.

Sentence types include statements and questions. Sentence structures include simple, compound, and complex. Sentence length ranges from three to twenty-eight words.

Choose Your Words Carefully   **?**   **WHAT'S MY PURPOSE?**

The reading process can be disrupted—and sometimes stopped altogether—by shifts in formality or the introduction of surprising or hard-to-understand words. As you draft your document, pay attention to level of formality and the extent to which specialized terms are used in the conversation about your issue. Pay attention as well to the variety and specificity of your words.

Formality   Your reading of other documents that contribute to the conversation about your issue will give you insights into the level of formality you should strive for when you draft your document. Some written conversations, such as those conducted on blogs and Web discussion forums, are relatively informal and can even show evidence of lack of respect for the opinions of other participants in the discussion. Others, such as those conducted through scholarly journals in the sciences or the arts and humanities or through magazines such as the *Nation* or *The Atlantic*, adopt a formal, restrained tone. Still others, such as those conducted through many popular media outlets, are casual but respectful. As you read about your issue, note the level of formality and the manner in which writers refer to ideas and arguments in other sources.

> **Informal Writing:**
> It was awesome to see how well the U.S. soccer team did in the last World Cup.

> bedfordresearcher.com
> **e** LearningCurve >
> Appropriate Language

> **Formal Writing:**
> The performance of the U.S. soccer team in the most recent World Cup was gratifying.

Specialized Language   Specialized language, sometimes called *jargon*, can allow writers and readers to communicate effectively and efficiently—but only if both parties are familiar with the terms. If you are contributing to a conversation in which specialized language is used heavily, familiarize yourself with the terms your readers will expect you to use. For example, if you plan to write an article for a Web site that focuses on motorcycle touring, you can write more concisely and with greater accuracy if you use the proper terminology.

Ineffective Use of General Language:
Braking that involves a mechanism that coordinates proportionally the amount of pressure applied to your front and rear brakes during turns that get progressively tighter can be hazardous if you fail to initiate the turn properly.

Effective Use of Specialized Language:
Linked braking during decreasing-radius turns can be hazardous if you fail to initiate the turn properly.

In contrast, readers who are unfamiliar with specialized language will find it more difficult to understand your point. Most people in the United States, for example, have at least a passing familiarity with basketball, but many would find it difficult to understand the following statement.

Ineffective Use of Specialized Language for a General Audience:
Box-and-one defenses are largely ineffective against well-executed pick-and-roll plays that result not in shots, but in skip passes, particularly if the pick-and-rolls are initiated on the baseline.

Variety   Variety is not only the spice of life—it's also the key ingredient in an effective, engaging document. Even a well-conceptualized and thoroughly supported argument can fail to impress if it's presented in dull, monotonous language. Consider the differences between the following examples.

Lack of Varied Word Choice:
The U.S. space program has benefited the United States in more ways than most U.S. government programs, largely because of the important technologies that have found their way into the U.S. economy.

Varied Word Choice:
NASA has benefited the nation in more ways than most federal programs, largely because of the important technologies that have found their way into the U.S. economy.

Avoid Sexist Language

It is still technically correct to use male pronouns, such as *he*, *him*, and *his*, when the gender of a noun, such as *doctor* or *nurse*, is unspecified. Most readers, however, object to this assumption—or they are at least sensitive to it. Readers are even more likely to object if you make the mistake of referring to representatives of particular professions using gender-specific pronouns.

When describing your symptoms to a doctor, be sure to tell him everything that's relevant. Similarly, when a nurse is taking your blood pressure, feel free to let her know how you feel.

By implying that all doctors are male and all nurses are female, the writer of this passage plays into common stereotypes. The result is that many readers will form a negative opinion of the writer.

To avoid sexist language, recast your sentences so that generic references, such as *a doctor*, are plural, such as *doctors*, as in the following example.

Sexist Language:
A doctor who pursues an advanced specialization might need to spend as many as 15 years of study before he can go into practice on his own.

Nonsexist Language:
Doctors who pursue advanced specializations might need to spend as many as 15 years of study before they can go into practice on their own.

Consult a Good Handbook

The strategies discussed in this chapter provide a good starting point for improving your style. Your decisions about style, however, are likely to touch on a far wider range of concerns than are addressed here. As you work to improve your writing, consult a good handbook. There you'll find detailed discussions and numerous examples of strategies you can use to polish your style.

14c

How can I use my introduction to frame my issue? [FRAMING MY ARGUMENT]

All readers expect documents to include some sort of introduction. Whether they are reading a home page on a Web site or an opening paragraph in a research report, readers want to learn quickly what a document is about. Your introduction, as a result, is a logical and appropriate place to begin framing your issue.

As you begin to draft your introduction, consider strategies you might use to frame your issue and introduce your main point. Keep track of those strategies so that you can revise your introduction later on. Many writers find that crafting an effective introduction is the most challenging part of drafting. If you run into difficulties, put your introduction aside and come back to it after you've made more progress on the rest of the document. There's no law that says you have to write the introduction first.

Call Attention to an Aspect of the Issue

Your introduction provides a framework within which your readers can understand and interpret your contribution to the conversation about your issue. By calling attention to a specific situation, by asking a particular question, or by conveying a carefully chosen set of details, you can help your readers view the issue in a particular way. Consider, for example, the differences between two introductions to an essay about buying habits among younger Americans.

Introduction 1:
In the face of an all-too-slowly recovering economy, frugality is undergoing a revival in America. Young people are cutting up their credit cards, clipping coupons, and sticking to detailed budgets. In effect, they're adopting the very habits

IV Creating Your Document

they mocked during the heady days of easy credit and weekend shopping sprees. Second-hand stores and thrift stores like Goodwill or the Salvation Army are drawing record numbers of customers, while once stable retail giants such as Circuit City and the Sharper Image have gone out of business (*Wall Street Journal*). In fact, retail sales during the Christmas season were down 2.8% last year, the lowest since 1995 (CNNMoney.com). The causes of this sea change in the spending habits of young Americans are complex and varied: high rates of unemployment, fewer jobs for recent college graduates, difficulty securing credit, and that elusive factor economists call "consumer confidence."

Introduction 2:
The new frugal spending habits of American consumers between the ages of 18 and 34 are endangering the very individuals who are trying to save money. Plagued by an economy that stubbornly refuses to rebound, with prolonged high unemployment rates and a tight credit market, young Americans are naturally turning to their spending habits as one area they can control. They are cutting down on how much money they spend in restaurants, bars, retail stores, and entertainment venues. As a result, usually robust Christmas sales were down an alarming 2.8% last year, the lowest since 1995 (CNNMoney.com). Even once stable retail giants such as Circuit City and the Sharper Image have gone out of business (*Wall Street Journal*). While the desire to hold onto their money is logical, all this coupon clipping, budgeting, and thrift-store shopping threatens the key to economic recovery, what economists call "consumer confidence." If we don't loosen our grip on our wallets and inject some much-needed cash into the system, we will face far more dire economic consequences in the years to come.

The first introduction frames the subject as an explanation of why younger Americans have changed their buying habits. The second introduction frames the subject as a warning that these changing habits might be causing more harm than good. While each introduction draws on the same basic information about current rates of spending, and while both will do a good job of introducing the essay, they ask readers to focus their attention on different aspects of the subject.

You can frame your discussion by calling attention to specific aspects of a topic, including:

- The agent: a person, an organization, or a thing that is acting in a particular way
- The action: what is being done by the actor
- The goal: why the actor carried out the action
- The result: the outcome of the action

Introduction 2:
The new frugal spending habits of American consumers between the ages of 18 and 34 are endangering the very individuals who are trying to save money. Plagued by an economy that stubbornly refuses to rebound, with prolonged high unemployment rates and a tight credit market, young Americans are naturally turning to their spending habits as one area they can control. They are cutting down on how much

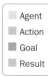

- Agent
- Action
- Goal
- Result

money they spend in restaurants, bars, retail stores, and entertainment venues. As a result, usually robust Christmas sales were down an alarming 2.8% last year, the lowest since 1995 (CNNMoney.com). Even once stable retail giants such as Circuit City and the Sharper Image have gone out of business (*Wall Street Journal*). While the desire to hold onto their money is logical, all this coupon clipping, budgeting, and thrift-store shopping threatens the key to economic recovery, what economists call "consumer confidence." If we don't loosen our grip on our wallets and inject some much-needed cash into the system, we will face far more dire economic consequences in the years to come.

Choose an Appropriate Strategy for Your Introduction

Your introduction offers probably the best opportunity to grab your readers' attention and shape their response to your ideas. You can frame your readers' understanding of your issue by choosing one of several introductory strategies.

State the Topic   Tell your readers what your issue is, what conversation you are focusing on, and what your document will tell them about it, as in the following introduction.

> Artists and their artwork do not exist in a vacuum. The images artists create help shape and in turn are shaped by the society and culture in which they are created. The artists and artworks in the Dutch Baroque period are no exception.

Establish the Context   In some cases, you'll want to give your readers background information about your subject or an overview of the conversation that has been taking place about it. Notice, for example, how Mark Hemingway sets up his article in *National Review Online* in response to media coverage of private military contractors.

> In the reams of media coverage surrounding the Blackwater incident last week one curious detail remains virtually unreported. The general theme of the coverage remains that private military contractors are somehow "above the law," but almost no media sources have referred to the fact that, as of last fall, contractors are subject to the same Uniform Code of Military Justice that governs U.S. soldiers.

State Your Thesis   If your research document presents an argument, evaluation, solution, or interpretation, use your introduction to get right to your main point. In other words, lead with a thesis statement, as in the following introduction.

> While the private tragedies of its central characters have public implications, William Shakespeare's *Julius Caesar* is more about personal struggles than political ambition. It is easy to see the play as one whose focus is the political action of public events. The title character, after all, is at the height of political power. However, the interior lives of Julius Caesar, Marcus Brutus, and their wives offer a more engaging storyline. Shakespeare alternates between public and private scenes throughout the play to emphasize the conflict between duties of the Roman citizenry and the feelings and needs of the individual, but it is the "private mind and heart of the individual" (Edwards 105) that the reader is compelled to examine.

Define a Problem   If your research has led you to propose a solution to a problem, you might begin your document by defining the problem. Alexis Alvarez used this strategy to introduce her essay.

> Almost daily, headlines and newscasters tell us about athletes' use of performance-enhancing drugs. Indeed, stories of such drug use seem to increase each year, with investigations of possible steroid use by college football players, by major league baseball players, and even by Olympic gold medalists. It is easy to gain the impression that many adult athletes, particularly males, may be using drugs in order to improve their performance and physical appearance. What may be surprising and even shocking to most of us, however, is that these drugs, especially anabolic steroids, are increasingly used by adolescent athletes and that girls are just as likely as boys to be users.

Read Alexis Alvarez's research essay on p. 388.

Make a Surprising Statement   Grab your readers' attention by telling them something they don't already know. It's even better if the information is shocking, unusual, or strange.

> What is the most common cause of hunger in the world? Is it drought? Locusts? Crop diseases? Nope. Most hunger in the world has absolutely nothing to do with food shortages. Most people who go to bed hungry, both in rich and in poor countries, do so in places where markets are filled with food that they cannot have.

Ask a Question   Asking a question invites your readers to become participants in the conversation. At the end of her introduction, Alexis Alvarez encouraged her readers to take an interest in the problem of steroid use by adolescent female athletes by asking a question.

> What role is competitive sports playing in this dangerous trend? Why are some girls feeling the need to ingest performance-enhancing drugs?

Tell a Story   Everyone loves a story, assuming it's told well and has a point. This writer began her newspaper article about the benefit of writing by hand with a story of a young boy who struggles to master the skill.

> Ask preschooler Zane Pike to write his name or the alphabet, then watch this 4-year-old's stubborn side kick in. He spurns practice at school and tosses aside workbooks at home. But Angie Pike, Zane's mom, persists, believing that handwriting is a building block to learning. She's right. Using advanced tools such as magnetic resonance imaging, researchers are finding that writing by hand is more than just a way to communicate. The practice helps with learning letters and shapes, can improve idea composition and expression, and may aid fine motor-skill development.

Provide a Historical Account   Historical accounts can help your readers understand the origins of a situation and how the situation has changed over time. A Web site focusing on relations between the People's Republic of China and Taiwan used this historical account.

> On February 21, 2000, the People's Republic of China (PRC) shocked the world with its release of the white paper "The One-China Principle and the Taiwan

Issue." In this 18-page document, the Chinese government outlined its case that, in keeping with the "One China" principle to which the United States and Taiwan had allegedly agreed, Taiwan is the rightful property of the People's Republic of China, and revealed that it intended to use force if Taiwan did not move to reunite with the mainland.

Draw a Contrast   Drawing a contrast asks your readers to begin making a comparison. Elizabeth Leontiev began her essay by contrasting what the word *cocaine* means to U.S. citizens and South American coca farmers.

> To most Americans, the word *cocaine* evokes images of the illegal white powder and those who abuse it, yet the word has a completely different meaning to the coca farmers of South America.

Read Elizabeth Leontiev's research essay on p. 363.

Lead with a Quotation   A quotation allows your readers to learn about the issue from someone who knows it well or has been affected by it, as in the following introduction.

> "Without a few lucky breaks, we'd still be bagging groceries at Albertsons," says lead singer Rickie Jackson of the recent Grammy winning band, Soft Affections.

Provide a Map   The most direct way of framing an issue and signaling the organization of your document is to provide a map, or preview, of your supporting points in your introduction.

> This report will cover three approaches to treating cancer of the bladder: chemotherapy, a combination of chemotherapy and radiation, and surgical removal of the organ.

14d

How can I use my conclusion to frame my issue?

Your conclusion provides an opportunity to reinforce your message. It offers one last chance to achieve your purpose as a writer and to share your final thoughts about the issue with your readers.

Reinforce Your Argument

At a minimum, your conclusion should summarize the reasons you've offered to support your thesis statement. You might also want to restate your thesis (in different words) to reinforce the main idea for readers. If you didn't include a thesis statement in your introduction, consider stating your main idea in your conclusion. Ending with a clear indication of what you want someone to think, believe, or do as a result of reading your document gives you one final opportunity to influence your readers.

Elizabeth Leontiev concluded her analysis of the impact of Evo Morales's vision for South American coca farmers like this.

> Through his bold program of "zero cocaine, not zero coca," Morales aims to improve the lives of Andean farmers and the economies of South American countries, while still remaining committed to controlling the illegal drug trade. Morales's example illustrates that it is time to work *with* coca farmers, rather than against them.

Select an Appropriate Strategy for Your Conclusion

Conclusions that simply summarize a document, like Elizabeth's, are common — and sometimes effective, especially when the writer has presented complex concepts. But a conclusion can do much more than simply restate your points. It can also give your readers an incentive to continue thinking about what they've read, to take action about the subject, or to read more about it.

As you draft, think about what you want to accomplish. You can choose from a range of strategies to write an effective conclusion.

Offer Additional Analysis Extend your discussion of the issue by supplying additional insights. In a Web site about wind-generated electrical power, one writer concluded a discussion of wind power and the environment by linking wind power to the production of hydrogen gas.

> Another promising area — in terms of wind power's contribution to clean energy — is the role it can play in a "hydrogen economy." Because hydrogen gas, when burned, does not produce carbon dioxide (its only emission is water vapor), some legislators and environmentalists are looking to hydrogen as a replacement for fossil fuels. Generating hydrogen gas, however, requires power, and a number of plans to generate it rely on coal-powered plants. Wind-power advocates argue, instead, that wind turbines can supply the power needed to produce hydrogen gas. Recent government studies support this approach ("Wind Power Facts," 2004).

Speculate about the Future Reflect on what might happen next. The author of an essay about the potential use of hydrogen as a fuel source, for example, might use this technique.

> It is certain, though, that at some point the fossil fuels that have sustained our society's electricity and run our motor vehicles for over a century will run out — or become so expensive that they'll no longer provide an economically viable source of energy. Whether that day comes in five years or fifty, we need to shift to a new energy source — one that is practical, economical, and environmentally friendly. Hydrogen has demonstrated great promise as a new candidate for fuel. To realize that promise, however, we must work to remove the barriers that currently prevent hydrogen's emergence as a mainstay of our future economy.

Close with a Quotation Select a quotation that does one of the following.

- offers deeper insight into the points you've made in your document
- sums up the points you've made in your document

- points to the future of the issue
- suggests a solution to a problem
- illustrates what you would like to see happen
- makes a further observation about the issue
- presents a personalized viewpoint from someone who has experienced the issue you are addressing

Alexis Alvarez used a quotation from a personal interview to underscore her main point about the use of steroids among adolescents girls involved in competitive sports.

> In short, these athletes have not lost sight of the true objective of participating in sports — they know that their success is due to their efforts and not to the effects of a performance-enhancing drug. When asked what she would say to athletes considering steroid use, Melissa Alvarez said:
>
> > If you are training and doing your best, you should not have to use steroids. At the end of the day, it is just a game. You should never put your health at risk for anything, or anyone. It should be your top priority. (personal communication, September 26, 2004)

Close with a Story Tell a story about the issue you've discussed in your document. The story might suggest a potential solution to the problem, offer hope about a desired outcome, or illustrate what might happen if a desired outcome isn't realized. This writer concluded his newspaper article by continuing a story he used in his introduction.

> So [Scott] struggles to get a foothold in the civilian work force. His brother in Boston lost his roommate, and early last month Scott moved into the empty bedroom, with his parents paying Scott's share of the $2,000-a-month rent until the lease expires on Aug. 31. And if Scott does not have a job by then? "I'll do something temporary; I won't go back home," Scott said. "I'll be a bartender or get work through a temp agency. I hope I don't find myself in that position."

Close with a Question Questions provide an effective means of inviting readers to consider the implications of the ideas explored in a document. After summarizing his position in his argumentative essay, Nicholas Brothers included a compelling question in his closing paragraph.

> In the end, we as voters and taxpayers must ask ourselves, who do we want to carry out U.S. defense missions abroad: those accountable to the U.S. military, or those beholden to private corporations?

Read Nicholas Brothers' argumentative essay on p. 417.

Call Your Readers to Action Make a recommendation or urge your readers to do something specific. For example, you might ask them to participate in solving a problem by donating time, money, or effort to a project. Or you might ask them to write to someone, such as a politician or corporate executive, about an issue. Calls to action ask readers to do more than simply accept what you've written;

they ask readers to do something. Nicholas Brothers used this strategy in an earlier draft of his argumentative essay.

> On her Web site, Jan Schakowsky urges Americans to contact their representatives to co-sponsor the legislation and become citizen co-sponsors of the Stop Outsourcing Security Act themselves. Political action may be the most powerful remedy to our current state of apathy.

Link to Your Introduction   This technique is sometimes called a "bookends" approach because it positions your introduction and conclusion as related ends of your document. The basic idea is to turn your conclusion into an extension of your introduction.

- If your introduction used a quotation, end with a related quotation or respond to the quotation.
- If your introduction used a story, extend that story or retell it with a different ending.
- If your introduction asked a question, answer the question, restate the question, or ask a new question.
- If your introduction defined a problem, then you can provide a solution to the problem, restate the problem, or suggest that readers need to move on to a new problem.

> QUICK REFERENCE

Drafting

- ✔ Use your outline to begin drafting your document. (p. 236)
- ✔ Draft focused, well organized paragraphs. (p. 238)
- ✔ Include effective transitions, signals, and cross-references. (p. 239)
- ✔ Keep readers on track with the use of headings, menus, and effective design. (p. 241)
- ✔ Integrate information from sources clearly. (p. 241)
- ✔ Use details to engage your readers. (p. 242)
- ✔ Write with style by writing clearly and concisely, using active voice, adopting a consistent point of view, varying your sentence structure, choosing your words with care, avoiding sexist language, and consulting a handbook. (p. 243)
- ✔ Use your introduction to frame your issue. (p. 249)
- ✔ Use your conclusion to reinforce your argument. (p. 253)

15

Using Sources Effectively

> ## Key Questions

15a. How can I use sources to accomplish my purposes as a writer?   258
Introduce an idea or argument
Contrast ideas or arguments
Provide evidence for your argument
Align your argument with an authority
Define a concept, illustrate a process, or clarify a statement
Set a mood
Provide an example
Amplify or qualify a point

15b. How can I integrate sources into my draft?   262
Identify your sources
Quote strategically
Paraphrase information, ideas, and arguments
Summarize
Present numerical information
Use images, audio, video, and animations

15c. How should I document my sources?   271
Choose a documentation system
Provide in-text references and publication information

15d. How can I ensure I've avoided unintentional plagiarism?   273
Quote, paraphrase, and summarize accurately and appropriately
Distinguish between your ideas and ideas in your sources
Check for unattributed sources in your document

As you draft your document, remember the range of strategies you can use to support your points, convey your ideas, and illustrate positions taken by other authors. This chapter discusses how you can use source information to meet the needs of your writing situation and addresses the primary techniques for integrating source information into your document: quotation, paraphrase, and summary. It also looks at techniques for working with numeric information, images, audio, video, and animations.

Much of the information in this chapter is based on MLA style, which is commonly used in the humanities. See Chapter 20 for more on MLA style and Chapters 21–23 for guidelines on APA, *Chicago*, and CSE styles.

15a

How can I use sources to accomplish my purposes as a writer?

Your sources can help you introduce ideas, contrast the ideas of other authors with your own, provide evidence for your points, align yourself with an authority, define concepts, illustrate processes, clarify statements, set a mood, provide an example, and qualify or amplify a point. You can present information from sources in several ways.

- as a quotation, paraphrase, or summary
- as numerical information
- as illustrations such as images, audio, video, and animations

As you draft your document, consider how your use of sources can lead your readers to view your issue in terms that are most favorable to your purposes. By selecting source information carefully, you can make your point more directly than you might want to using your own words. Calling opponents of a proposal "inflexible" and "pig-headed," for example, might signal your biases too strongly. Quoting someone who uses those terms, however, allows you to get the point across without undermining an otherwise even and balanced tone.

The following are some of the most effective ways to use information, ideas, and arguments from sources to contribute to a written conversation about an issue.

Introduce an Idea or Argument   [FRAMING MY ARGUMENT]

You can use a quotation, paraphrase, or summary to introduce an idea or argument to your readers. As you choose a quotation, paraphrase, or summary, keep in mind that it will call your readers' attention to particular aspects of your argument.

Consider how the following quotation, for instance, leads readers to view a public debate about education reform as a battle between reformers and an entrenched teachers union.

> "The teachers union has balked at even the most reasonable proposals for school reform," said Mary Sweeney, press secretary for Save Our Schools, which has

sponsored a referendum on the November ballot calling for funding for their voucher plan. "We believe
the November election will send a wake-up call about
the need to rethink their obstructionist behaviors."

> Phrases such as "balked at even
> the most reasonable proposals"
> and "their obstructionist
> behaviors" place the blame for
> the problem on the teachers
> union.

    If Sweeney and supporters of Referendum D are
successful, the educational landscape in . . .

In contrast, note how the following quotation frames the debate as a question of
how best to spend scarce education funds.

"In the past decade, state and local funding of public
education in real dollars has declined by 7.2 percent,"
said Jeffrey Allister, state chair of the governor's Special Commission on Education Reform. "Referendum
D, if passed, would further erode that funding by
shifting state dollars to private schools." As the state

> Phrases such as "funding
> of public education in real
> dollars has declined" and
> "further erode that funding"
> call attention to the financial
> challenges faced by schools.

considers the merits of Referendum D, which would institute the first statewide
voucher program in the United States, opponents of the measure have . . .

Contrast Ideas or Arguments

When you want to indicate that disagreement exists on an issue, you can use
source information to illustrate the nature and intensity of the disagreements.
The following example uses partial quotations (p. 264) to highlight differences in
proposed solutions to a problem.

> Solutions to the state's higher education funding shortfall range from traditional
> approaches, such as raising taxes, to more radical solutions, among them privatiz-
> ing state colleges and universities. Advocates of increased taxes, such as Vincent
> Richards of the Higher Education Coalition, argue that declines in state funding
> of higher education "must be reversed immediately or we will find ourselves in a
> situation where we are closing rural community colleges and only the wealthiest
> among us will have access to the best education" (A4). Those in favor of privatiz-
> ing higher education suggest, however, that free market approaches will ultimately
> bring about "a fairer situation in which the poor, many of whom have no interest
> in higher education, are no longer asked to subsidize higher and higher faculty
> salaries and larger football stadiums" (Pieters 23).

Base your choices about how to contrast ideas and arguments on the clarity and
conciseness of your sources and on the effects you hope to achieve. If you want
to express complex ideas as concisely as possible, you might use paraphrase and
summary. If you want to convey the emotional qualities of an author's position
on an issue, use quotations.

Provide Evidence for Your Argument

Arguments that consist of a series of unsupported assertions amount to little
more than a request for a reader's trust. Even when the writer is eminently trust-
worthy, most readers find such arguments easy to dismiss. In contrast, providing
evidence to support your assertions increases the likelihood that your readers will
accept your argument. Note the differences between the following passages.

IV Creating Your Document

Unsupported Assertion:

Given a choice between two products of comparable quality, reputation, and cost, American consumers are far more likely to purchase goods that use environmentally friendly packaging. Encouraging the use of such packaging is a good idea for America.

No evidence is provided to support the writer's assertion.

Supported Assertion:

Given a choice between two products of comparable quality, reputation, and cost, American consumers are far more likely to purchase goods that use environmentally friendly packaging. A recent study by the High Plains Research Institute found that the shelf life of several biodegradable plastics not only exceeded the shelf life of the products they were used to package, but also cost less to produce (Chen and Lohann 33). In addition, a study by the Consumer Products Institute found that, when made aware that products were packaged in environmentally friendly materials, consumers were more likely to buy those products.

Summaries of the results of two studies provide evidence for the assertion made in the first sentence.

Similarly, visual sources can lend support to an assertion. For example, an assertion about the unintended consequences of military action might be accompanied by a photograph of a war-torn street or a wounded child.

Align Your Argument with an Authority

Aligning an argument with an authority—such as a subject matter expert, a scientist, a politician, or a religious figure—allows you to borrow someone else's credibility and status. Start by making an assertion and follow it with supporting information from a source, such as a quotation, paraphrase, or source summary.

Although voice recognition appears to be a promising technology, challenges associated with vocabulary, homonyms, and accents have slowed its widespread implementation. "The computer right now can do a very good job of voice recognition," said Bill Gates, co-founder and former chairman of Microsoft Corporation. "It certainly will re-define the way we think of the machines when we have that voice input" (Gates, par. 42).

Define a Concept, Illustrate a Process, or Clarify a Statement

Writers commonly turn to information from sources when that information is clearer and more concise than what they might write themselves. You might define a concept by quoting or paraphrasing a dictionary or an encyclopedia, or use an illustration to help readers understand a complex process, such as the steps involved in cellular respiration.

Writers also use information from sources to clarify their statements. A writer might amplify a statement by providing examples from sources or qualify a statement by noting that it applies only to specific situations and then use a quotation or paraphrase from a source to back that up.

Studies have found connections between weight loss and coffee intake. This doesn't mean that drinking a couple of cups of coffee each day leads to weight loss. However, three recent studies reported that individuals who increased their coffee intake from fewer than three cups to more than eight cups of coffee per day experienced weight losses of up to 7 percent over a two month period (Chang, Johnson and Salazar, Neiman). "It may be that increased caffeine intake led to a higher metabolic level, which in turn led to weight loss," noted John Chang, a senior researcher at the Centers for Disease Control. "Or it might be that drinking so much coffee depressed participants' appetites" (232).

Set a Mood

You can also choose quotations and illustrations with an eye toward establishing an overall mood for your readers. The emotional impact of images of a celebration at a sporting event, an expression of grief at a funeral, or a calming mountain vista can lead your readers to react in specific ways to your document. Similarly, a striking quote, such as "The screams of pain coming out of that room will stay with me as long as I live," can evoke a specific mood among your readers.

Provide an Example

It's often better to *show* with an example than to *tell* with a general description. Examples provide concrete evidence in your document. Note how the writer of the following passage used an example from a well-known film to illustrate a point about her family's relationship with food.

> And the obsession with eating! My grandmother feeds us constantly. My dad and I always laugh at that scene in *Goodfellas* where the mobsters show up at two in the morning after killing someone, and one mobster's mother whips up a full pasta meal for them. We know that my grandmother would do the same thing: "Are you hungry? Here, sit, eat!" Grandma holds interventions over pasta. If she is unhappy with something someone in the family is doing, she invites everyone over for pasta and we hash it out together.

Amplify or Qualify a Point

You can use amplification to expand the scope of a point. Consider how information from a source is used in the following example to broaden a discussion of the dangers football players face when they add bulk.

> NFL offensive linemen who weigh less than 300 pounds are often described as "undersized," so it's no surprise that young football players are getting the message that bigger is better — and bulking up. A recent study of high school linemen in Iowa showed that 45% were overweight and 9% were severely obese, while only 18% of other young males were overweight; even more troubling, a study in Michigan revealed that among football players from ages 9 to 14, 45% could be considered overweight or obese (as cited in Longman, 2007).

Qualifications, in contrast, allow you to narrow the scope of a statement, reducing the possibility that your readers might misunderstand your meaning. Note how the writer made it clear that deaths related to weight gain are a rare occurrence in football.

> Although such fatalities are unusual, a growing number of doctors believe that use of dietary supplements increases the risk of heat stroke among football players.

IV Creating Your Document

15b

How can I integrate sources into my draft?

You can integrate information, ideas, and arguments from sources into your draft by quoting, paraphrasing, summarizing, presenting numerical information, and using illustrations. As you do so, make a point of distinguishing your ideas and information from those found in your sources.

Identify Your Sources

You should identify the sources of information in your document for several reasons. First, doing so fulfills your obligation to document your sources. Second, it allows you (and your readers) to recognize the boundaries between your ideas and those borrowed from sources. Third, it can help you strengthen your document by calling attention to the qualifications or experiences of the person whose ideas you are incorporating.

Use Attributions and In-Text Citations   Whenever you quote, paraphrase, or summarize, distinguish between your ideas and information obtained through your sources by using attributions—brief comments such as "according to" or "as the author points out"—to alert your readers that the point is not your own.

Writers who use MLA or APA documentation format also provide citations—or acknowledgments of source information—within the text of their document to indicate where borrowed material ends. These citations, in turn, refer readers to a list of works cited or a list of references at the end of the document.

Note the following examples, which use attributions and in-text citations.

MLA Style:
Pamela Coke argues, "Education reform is the best solution for fixing our public schools" (22).

> Attributions identify the author of the quotations.

"Education reform is the best solution for fixing our public schools" (Coke 22).

> MLA-style in-text citations include the author's name and exact page reference.

APA Style:
Pamela Coke (2008) has argued, "Education reform is the best solution for fixing our public schools" (p. 22).

> APA-style in-text citations include the author's name, publication date, and exact page reference.

"Education reform is the best solution for fixing our public schools" (Coke, 2008, p. 22).

As you acknowledge material you've borrowed from sources, you'll want to vary the wording of your attributions. As you do, be aware of the way that the verbs in attributions can convey important shades of meaning—for example, the difference between writing that someone "alleged" something and someone "confirmed" something. The form your attributions take will depend on your use of citation style. MLA recommends present tense ("the author points out"), while

APA recommends past tense ("the author pointed out") or present perfect tense ("the author has explained").

Some Common Attributions

according to	claimed	expressed	reported
acknowledged	commented	inquired	said
affirmed	confirmed	interpreted	stated
alleged	declared	mused	suggested
asked	denied	noted	thought
asserted	described	observed	wondered
assumed	disputed	pointed out	wrote
believed	emphasized	remarked	

You can learn more about in-text citations and the MLA, APA, *Chicago*, and CSE documentation systems in Part V.

Provide a Context   Skilled writers know the importance of providing a context for the source information they include in their documents. It's not enough to simply put text within two quotation marks and move on. Such "orphan quotations"—quotations dropped into a paragraph without any introduction—are confusing. Worse, paraphrases and summaries inserted without context can easily be mistaken for the writer's own work, leading to accusations of plagiarism.

To provide a clear context for your source information, establish why the quotation, paraphrase, or summary is reliable by identifying the source's credentials. In addition, indicate how it relates to your main idea and what it contributes to the point you are making. If you don't, readers will wonder why it's there.

However, Wechsler et al. (2003) of the Harvard School of Public Health analyzed trends at schools using social norms marketing and revealed that the campaigns did not necessarily decrease student drinking; in some cases, schools even reported higher alcohol consumption, according to seven criteria that measured whether students drank, how much, and how often. As the researchers explained, "individual students' drinking behaviors align more closely to the drinking behaviors of their immediate social group rather than to the overall student population at a given school" (pars. 30–33).

> Attribution identifies the source as experts.

> Writer follows APA style; parenthetical citation identifies the paragraph numbers where the quotation was found.

Quote Strategically

A well-chosen quotation can have a powerful impact on your readers' perception of your argument and on the overall quality of your document. Quotations can also add a sense of immediacy by bringing in the voice of someone who has been affected by an issue or can lend a sense of authority to your argument by conveying the words of an expert. Quotations can range in form from brief, partial quotations to extended, block quotations. As you integrate quotations into your document, remember that you might need to modify them to suit your purpose and fit the flow of your sentences. When you do, be careful to punctuate them properly.

Use Partial, Complete, and Block Quotations   Quotations can be parts of sentences (partial), whole sentences (complete), or long passages (block). When you choose one type of quotation over another, consider the length and complexity of the passage as well as the obligation to convey ideas and information fairly.

Partial Quotations can be a single word, phrase, or most of a sentence. They are often used to convey a well-turned phrase or to complete a sentence using important words from a source, as in the following example.

> Nadine K. Maxwell, a guidance services coordinator in Fairfax, Virginia, says that students' chances of being admitted can be greater if they apply early, although this varies from school to school and year to year and "may depend upon the applicant pool at the school where they are applying" (32).

Quotation marks indicate the borrowed phrase.

Source information, including the number of the page containing the quotation, is clearly identified.

Complete Quotations are typically one or more complete sentences and are most often used when the meaning of the passage cannot be conveyed adequately by a few well-chosen words, as in the following example.

> I smiled when I read Elizabeth Gilbert's memoir *Eat, Pray, Love.* She writes, "The Neapolitan women in particular are such a gang of tough-voiced, loud-mouthed, generous, nosy dames, all bossy and annoyed and right up in your face just trying to friggin' *help* you for chrissake, you dope — *why they gotta do everything around here?*" (78).

Since the source of the quotation is identified in an attribution ("Elizabeth Gilbert's memoir . . ."), only the page number appears in the citation at the end of the sentence.

Block Quotations are extended quotations (usually more than four typed lines) that are set off in a block from the rest of the text. In general, use a colon to introduce the quotation, indent the entire quotation one inch from the left margin, and include source information according to the documentation system you are using (such as MLA, APA, *Chicago,* or CSE). Since the blocked text indicates to your readers that you are quoting directly, you do not need to include quotation marks.

In the article "In the Best Interest of America, Affirmative Action in Higher Education Is a Must," William H. Gray III states:

Quotation marks are not used to surround block quotations.

> High school achievement and test scores are considered to be very important criteria in the admissions process by most of the four-year public degree-granting colleges and universities. Nonetheless, high school grades and test scores are not the only factors considered by colleges and universities in the admissions process. Other factors that influence college admissions decisions include high

school rank, being an athlete, alumni connections, extracurricular activities, special talents, and other personal characteristics of applicants. (par. 5)

In block quotations, the citation information is placed after the period.

A paragraph number is provided for an online source.

Modify Quotations Appropriately You can modify quotations to fit your draft. It is acceptable, for example, to delete unnecessary words or to change the tense of a word in a partial quotation so that it fits your sentence. For example, if you wanted to change the tense of a verb in a partial quotation so that it fits the sentence, you would use brackets to indicate the change.

Original Quotation:
"They treated us like family and refused to accept a tip."

Quotation Modified Using Brackets:
It's a place where the staff treats you "like family and [refuses] to accept a tip," said travel writer Melissa Ancomi.

Brackets indicate a word that has been changed.

Keep in mind, however, that research writers have an obligation to quote sources accurately and fairly. You should indicate when you have added or deleted words, and you should not modify quotations in a way that distorts their meaning.

The most useful strategies you can use to modify quotations include using ellipsis marks (. . .) to indicate deleted words, using brackets [ ] to clarify meaning, and using "sic" to note errors in a source. You can learn more about modifying quotations using these strategies on pp. 101–03.

Punctuate Quotations Correctly The rules for punctuating quotations are as follows.

- Use double quotation marks (" ") around partial or complete quotations. Do not use quotation marks for block quotations.

- Use single quotation marks (' ') to indicate quoted material within a quotation.

    "The hotel manager told us to 'make ourselves at home.'"

- Place commas and periods inside quotation marks.

- Place question marks and exclamation points outside quotation marks if the punctuation pertains to the entire sentence rather than the quotation. In the following example, the original quotation is not a question, so the question mark should be placed after the quotation mark.

    But what can be gained from following the committee's recommendation that the state should "avoid, without exceptions, any proposed tax hike"?

- Place question marks and exclamation points inside quotation marks if the punctuation pertains to the quotation itself.

    Dawn Smith asked an important question: "Do college students understand the importance of avoiding running up credit card debt?"

- Place colons and semicolons outside quotation marks.

  > Many young consumers consider themselves "free at last"; all too often, however, they find that freedom has its costs.

- When citation information is provided after a quotation, place the punctuation mark (comma, period, semicolon, colon, or question mark) after the parenthetical citation.

  > "Preliminary reports have been consistent," Yates notes. "Without immediate changes to current practices, we will deplete known supplies by mid-century" (335).

- At the end of a block quotation, place the final punctuation before the parenthetical citation.

- Use three spaced periods (an ellipsis mark) to indicate an omission within a sentence.

  > According to critic Joe Robinson, Americans are overworked: "Ask Americans how things are really going and you'll hear stories of . . . fifty- and sixty-hour weeks with no letup in sight" (467).

- Place a period before the ellipsis mark to indicate an omission at the end of a sentence:

  > The most recent information indicates, says Chen, that "we can expect a significant increase in costs by the end of the decade. . . . Those costs, however, should ramp up slowly" (35).

CHECKLIST FOR INTEGRATING QUOTATIONS INTO A DOCUMENT

✔ Identify the source of the quotation.

✔ Punctuate the quotation appropriately.

✔ Use ellipsis marks, brackets, and "sic" as necessary.

✔ Check each quotation against the source to be sure you aren't introducing errors or misrepresenting the source.

✔ Use transitions and attributions to integrate the quotation effectively into your document.

✔ Ensure that the source is cited in your works cited or references list.

Paraphrase Information, Ideas, and Arguments

A paraphrase is a restatement, in your own words, of a passage from a source. Unlike summaries, which are shorter than the text being summarized, paraphrases are about as long as the text on which they are based. Paraphrases can be used to illustrate or support a point you make in your document or to illustrate another author's argument about an issue.

TUTORIAL

How do I integrate a quotation into my draft?

After you select a passage to quote, you'll need to acknowledge the source, punctuate the quotation properly, and provide a context for the information. This example uses MLA style; be sure to follow the guidelines for the documentation style you are using.

Original Passage

1 Locate the passage you want to quote and identify the text you want to include in the quotation.

2 Add quotation marks or, if the quotation is long, set the text in a block (p. 264). If you modify the passage, use ellipsis marks and brackets appropriately (p. 265).

3 Identify the source of the quotation and the location, such as the page number. Give the author's qualifications in an author tag if you haven't already done so for this source in your document.

4 Avoid "orphan quotations" by providing a context for your quotation. Introduce the quotation and indicate how it relates to your argument.

One clear warning from both resilience theory and practical experience is that prevention is better than cure. The empirical evidence is unambiguous: the trajectory of reef condition is declining globally; because once a reef is degraded it usually stays that way (but see below). Interventions need to focus (a) on reversing interacting slow drivers, particularly overfishing, pollution and greenhouse gas emissions, to avoid transgressing thresholds leading to phase-shifts, and (b) on promoting processes like coral recruitment and herbivory that maintain the coral-dominated states of healthy reefs.

Source: Hughes, Terry P., et al. "Rising to the Challenge of Sustaining Coral Reef Resilience." *Trends in Ecology and Evolution* 25.11 (2010): 619–680. Print.

"One clear warning . . . is that prevention is better than cure. . . . Interventions need to focus (a) on reversing interacting slow drivers . . . and (b) on promoting processes like coral recruitment and herbivory that maintain the coral-dominated states of healthy reefs."

In their article "Rising to the Challenge of Sustaining Coral Reef Resilience," Terry P. Hughes et al. note, "One clear warning . . . is that prevention is better than cure. . . . Interventions need to focus (a) on reversing interacting slow drivers . . . and (b) on promoting processes like coral recruitment and herbivory that maintain the coral-dominated states of healthy reefs" (638).

It is not enough to try to rehabilitate damaged reefs. In their article "Rising to the Challenge of Sustaining Coral Reefs," Terry P. Hughes et al. note, "One clear warning . . . is that prevention is better than cure. . . . Interventions need to focus (a) on reversing interacting slow drivers . . . and (b) on promoting processes like coral recruitment and herbivory that maintain the coral-dominated states of healthy reefs" (638). Sustaining coral reefs involves protecting existing coral in healthy reef environments.

IV Creating Your Document

Your notes are likely to include a number of paraphrases of information, ideas, and arguments from your sources. (See Chapter 6 to learn how to write a paraphrase.) To integrate these paraphrases into your document, begin by making sure your paraphrase is an accurate and fair representation of the source. Reread the source to double-check the accuracy and fairness of your paraphrase, and then revise the paraphrase so that it fits the context and tone of your document. Use attributions to ensure a smooth transition from your ideas to the ideas found in the source.

In the following example, note how Alexis Alvarez lets her readers know where her statement ends and where the support for her statement, in the form of a paraphrase, begins.

> Competitive sports also teach athletes how to cope with failure — **Alexis's idea.**
> as well as success. In the best of situations, as Sieghart (2004)
> noted, athletes are able to assess their achievements realistically, — **The source of paraphrase is cited per APA style.**
> letting neither winning nor losing consume their reality.

An attribution marks transition from Alexis's idea to source ideas.

CHECKLIST FOR INTEGRATING PARAPHRASES INTO A DOCUMENT

✔ Identify the source of the paraphrased material.

✔ Compare the original passage with your paraphrase. Make sure that you have conveyed the meaning of the passage but that the wording and sentence structure differ from those in the original passage.

✔ Use transitions and attributions to integrate the paraphrase smoothly into your document.

✔ Ensure that the source is cited in your works cited or references list.

Summarize

A summary is a concise statement, written in your own words, of information found in a source. (See below to learn about summarizing entire sources and lengthy passages within a source.) When you integrate a summary into your draft, review the source to make sure your summary is an accurate and fair representation of the ideas in the original source. Be careful, as well, to identify the source and include a citation. You can summarize an entire source, parts of a particular source, or a group of sources to support your argument.

Summarize an Entire Source   Research writers frequently summarize an entire work. In some cases, the summary might occupy one or more paragraphs or be integrated into a discussion contained in one or more paragraphs. In other cases, the summary might be as brief as a single sentence.

Alexis Alvarez summarized a report issued by the Centers for Disease Control and Prevention in her research essay about steroid use by adolescent girls involved in competitive sports.

In May 2004, the Centers for Disease Control and Prevention (CDC) published its latest figures on self-reported drug use among young people in grades 9 through 12. The CDC study, "Youth Risk Behavior Surveillance — December 2003," found that 6.1% of its survey participants reported using steroids at least once, up from 2.2% in 1993. The report also showed that use of steroids appears to be increasing among younger girls: While only 3.3% of 12th-grade girls reported using steroids, 7.3% of 9th-grade girls reported using them. Moreover, girls might be starting to use steroids at a higher rate than boys. The CDC study indicated that 9th-grade girls had reported slightly higher rates of steroid use than boys (7.3% and 6.9% respectively), while 10th-, 11th-, and 12th-grade girls all reported lower use than boys.

> The author, title, and publication date are identified in the text, so parenthetical citation is not required for either MLA or APA style.

> The main point of the report.

> Additional information from the report.

In contrast, Alexis offered a much briefer, "nutshell" summary of a related source.

A 2003 article in *Drug Week* stated that girls who participate in sports more than eight hours a week are at considerable risk for taking many illicit drugs: The higher the level at which athletes compete, the higher their risk for substance abuse ("Sporting Activities").

Summarize Specific Ideas and Information from a Source   You can also use summaries to convey key information or ideas from a source. In his research essay, Nicholas Brothers summarized a section of a book about private military corporations.

A look at definitions in Singer's *Corporate Warriors* reveals that PMCs and traditional mercenaries differ in several key ways. Perhaps the most important difference is that a private military corporation is just that: a legal corporate entity[10] (as opposed to the illegal adventurer or rag-tag squad evoked by the word "mercenary"). Another significant distinction is that PMCs offer a wide range of services ... while mercenaries can rarely do more than engage in combat.

> The summary is introduced with the author and specific source of the ideas.

> Per *Chicago* style, a citation appears as a numbered footnote.

Summarize a Group of Sources   In addition to summarizing a single source, research writers often summarize groups of sources. It's not unusual, for instance, to encounter in research documents phrases such as "Numerous authors have argued ..." or "The research in this area seems to indicate that. . . ." Such collective summaries allow you to establish a point briefly and with authority. They are effective particularly at the beginning of a document, when you are establishing a foundation for your argument, and can serve as a transitional device when you move from one major section of the document to another.

When you are summarizing a group of sources, separate the citations with a semicolon. MLA guidelines require including author and page information, as in the following example.

Several critics have argued that the Hemingway code hero is not always male (Graulich 217; Sherman 78; Watters 33).

APA guidelines require including author and date information, as in the following example.

> The benefits of early detection of breast cancer have been well documented (Page, 2007; Richards, 2007; Vincent, 2008).

CHECKLIST FOR INTEGRATING SUMMARIES INTO A DOCUMENT

✔ Identify the source you are summarizing.

✔ Ensure that you have summarized the source in your own words. Make sure that you do not merely string together a series of close paraphrases of key passages.

✔ Use transitions and attributions to integrate the summary smoothly into your document.

✔ Ensure that the source is cited in your works cited or references list.

Present Numerical Information

If it suits the issue you are addressing, you might use numerical information, such as statistics, in your document. You can present this information within sentences, or you might use tables, charts, or graphs, as Brandon Tate did on his Web site about hydraulic fracturing (see Figure 15.1). Keep in mind that you still need to accurately and fairly present the numerical information in your document and clearly identify the source of the information, just as you would for textual information. For more information about using tables, charts, and graphs, see pp. 285–86.

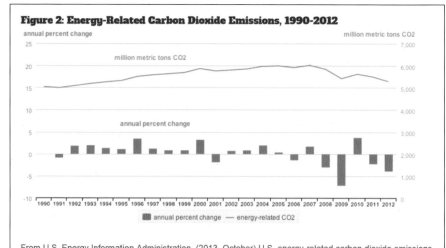

Figure 2: Energy-Related Carbon Dioxide Emissions, 1990-2012

From U.S. Energy Information Administration. (2013, October) U.S. energy-related carbon dioxide emissions, 2012. Retrieved from http://www.eia.gov/environment/emissions/carbon/

FIGURE 15.1 Chart on Brandon Tate's Web Site

Use Images, Audio, Video, and Animations

Including images in your print document and images, audio, video, or animation files in your electronic document can enhance its effectiveness. Use caution, however, when taking images and audio, video, or animations from other sources. Simply copying a photograph into your document might be a form of plagiarism. The same is true of audio, video, and animations files.

Lauren Mack carefully documented the sources of the images, audio clips, and video clips she used in her multimodal research essay. Since she was writing an academic essay—rather than a document intended for publication and wide distribution—she did not seek permission to use the images, audio, and video that she had found in other sources. (In contrast, the publisher of this book sought and received permission to publish those materials.)

i **INFORMATION LITERACY** If you are creating a digital document, such as a Web page or a multimedia presentation, use the following approach to integrating digital illustrations.

- Make a link between your document and a document that contains an image, sound clip, or video clip—rather than simply copying the image and placing it in your document.

- If it isn't possible or appropriate to create a link to another document, you should contact the owner of the image, sound clip, or video clip for permission to use it.

- If you cannot contact the owner, review the fair use guidelines discussed on p. 131 for guidance about using the material.

As you've done for the other sources you cite in your document, make sure you fairly present images, audio, or video and identify their author or creator. ▨

15c

How should I document my sources?

You should cite your sources within the text of your document as well as provide complete publication information for each source you've used. Fully documenting your sources in this way can help you achieve your purpose as a writer, such as establishing your authority and persuading your readers. Documenting your sources also helps you avoid plagiarism, gives credit to others who have written about an issue, and creates a record of their work that your readers can follow and build upon.

Choose a Documentation System

The documentation systems most commonly used in academic disciplines are the following.

- **MLA** This style, from the Modern Language Association (MLA), is used primarily in the humanities—English, philosophy, linguistics, world languages, and so on. See Chapter 20.

- **APA** This style, from the American Psychological Association, is used mainly in the social sciences—psychology, sociology, anthropology, political science, economics, education, and so on. See Chapter 21.

- *Chicago* Developed by the University of Chicago Press, this style is used primarily in history, journalism, and the humanities. See Chapter 22.

- **CSE** This style, from the Council of Science Editors (formerly the Council of Biology Editors), is used mainly in the physical and life sciences—chemistry, geology, biology, botany, and so on—and in mathematics. See Chapter 23.

Your choice of documentation system will be guided by the discipline or field within which you are writing and by any requirements associated with your research writing project. If your project has been assigned to you, ask the person who assigned it or someone who has written a similar document which documentation system you should use. If you are working on a project for a writing class, your instructor will most likely tell you which documentation system to follow.

Your choice will also be guided by the genre you have chosen for your document. For example, while academic essays and articles appearing in scholarly journals typically use a documentation system such as MLA or APA, newspaper and magazine articles often do not; instead, they identify sources in the main text of the document rather than in a works cited or references list. If you write a digital document that cites other online sources, you might simply link to those sources.

Provide In-Text References and Publication Information

The specific format of your in-text citations will depend on the documentation system you use. If you use MLA or APA style, you'll cite—or formally acknowledge—information in the text using parentheses and add a list of sources to the end of your document. Key publication information is usually provided in a works cited list (MLA and CSE), reference list (APA), or bibliography (*Chicago*). This list appears at the end of the document and includes the following information about each source.

- author(s) and/or editor(s)
- title
- publication date
- publisher and city of publication (for books)
- periodical name, volume, issue, and page numbers (for articles)
- URL and access date (for online publications)

Each documentation system creates an association between citations in the text of a document and the works cited or reference page. See Part V for documentation models.

15d

How can I ensure I've avoided unintentional plagiarism?

Because plagiarized material will often differ in style, tone, and word choice from the rest of your document, your readers are likely to notice these differences and wonder whether you've plagiarized the material—or, if not, why you've written a document that has so many stylistic inconsistencies. If your readers react negatively, it's unlikely that your document will be successful.

You can avoid unintentional plagiarism by quoting, paraphrasing, and summarizing accurately and appropriately; distinguishing between your ideas and ideas in your sources; and checking for unattributed sources in your document.

Quote, Paraphrase, and Summarize Accurately and Appropriately

Unintentional plagiarism usually occurs when a writer takes poor notes and then uses the information from those notes in a document. As you draft, do the following.

- Look for notes that differ from your usual style of writing. More often than not, if a note doesn't sound like your own writing, it isn't.
- Place quotation marks around any direct quotations, use ellipsis marks and brackets appropriately (see pp. 264–66), and identify the source and the page or paragraph number of the quotation.
- Make sure that paraphrases differ significantly in word choice and sentence structure from the passage being paraphrased, and identify the source and page or paragraph number from which you took the paraphrase.
- Make sure that summaries are not just a series of passages or close paraphrases copied from the source.

> bedfordresearcher.com
> Tutorials > Do I Need to Cite That?

Distinguish Between Your Ideas and Ideas in Your Sources

Failing to distinguish between your ideas and ideas drawn from your sources can lead readers to think other writers' ideas are yours. Examine how the writer of the following passage might have failed to distinguish his ideas from those of Joel Levine and Lawrence May, authors of a source used in the essay.

Failing to Credit Ideas to a Source:
According to Joel Levine and Lawrence May, authors of *Getting In*, entrance exams are an extremely important part of a student's college application and carry a great deal of weight. In fact, a college entrance examination is one of the two most significant factors in getting into college. The other, unsurprisingly, is high school grades.

IV Creating Your Document

Because the second and third sentences fail to identify Levine and May as the source of the information about the second important factor affecting admissions decisions—high school grades—the passage implies that the writer of the research essay is the source of that information.

In contrast, the writer actually included the following passage in the essay.

Giving Credit to the Source:

According to Joel Levine and Lawrence May, authors of *Getting In*, entrance exams are an extremely important part of a student's college application and carry a great deal of weight. In fact, they claim that a college entrance examination is "one of the two most significant factors" in getting into college (the other, unsurprisingly, being high school grades).

> The attribution, "they claim," credits Levine and May as the source of the information.
>
> Quotation marks are used to indicate a partial quotation.

To distinguish between your ideas and those obtained through your sources, use attributions—words or phrases that alert your readers to the source of the ideas or information you are using. As you take notes and draft your document, use the name of an author or the title of the source you're drawing from each time you introduce ideas from a source.

Examples of Attributions

According to Scott McPherson . . .

Jill Bedard writes . . .

Tom Huckin reports . . .

Kate Kiefer observes . . .

Bob Phelps suggests . . .

In the words of Pamela Coke . . .

As Ellen Page tells it . . .

Reid Vincent indicates . . .

Jessica Richards calls our attention to . . .

Check for Unattributed Sources in Your Document

You should include a complete citation for each source you refer to in your document. The citation should appear in the text of the document (as an in-text citation, footnote, or endnote) or in a works cited list, reference list, or bibliography.

In the following MLA-style examples, the writer includes parenthetical citations that refer readers to a list of works cited at the end of the document. Note that MLA style allows for a combination of attributions and parenthetical information to refer to sources.

Reid Vincent argues, "We must explore emerging energy technologies before we reach a peak oil crisis" (322).

"We must explore emerging energy technologies before we reach a peak oil crisis" (Vincent 322).

> MLA-style in-text citations include the author's name and exact page reference.

> QUICK REFERENCE

Using Sources Effectively

☑ Use source information to accomplish your purpose. (p. 258)

☑ Integrate quotations appropriately. (p. 262)

☑ Integrate paraphrases appropriately. (p. 266)

☑ Integrate summaries appropriately. (p. 268)

☑ Integrate numerical information appropriately. (p. 270)

☑ Integrate images, audio, video, and animations appropriately. (p. 271)

☑ Choose a documentation system. (p. 271)

☑ Provide in-text references and a works cited or reference list. (p. 272)

☑ Check for unintentional plagiarism by checking your quotations, paraphrases, and summaries; checking for unattributed sources; and distinguish between your work and information, ideas, and arguments from your sources. (p. 273)

IV Creating Your Document

16

Designing Documents

> **Key Questions**

Many writers think of designing a document as something that comes at the end of the writing process, after drafting, revising, and editing are complete. In fact, design can be a powerful tool during the planning and drafting stages. By considering design as you plan and work on your draft, you can create a document whose appearance helps you achieve your purpose, address your readers effectively, and take advantage of the context in which it will be read.

16a

What role does design play in my document?

Your decisions about the design of your document, from choosing appropriate fonts to presenting information in charts and tables to selecting compelling illustrations, can have powerful effects on how you shape and present your ideas and how your readers understand and react to your document. Understanding design principles and elements, as well as the design conventions of documents typically assigned in college courses, can help you craft a unique and substantial contribution to a conversation.

Understand Design Principles [FRAMING MY ARGUMENT]

Before you begin formatting text and inserting illustrations, consider how the document design principles of *balance, emphasis, placement, repetition,* and *consistency* can help you accomplish your goals as a writer.

Balance Balance is the vertical and horizontal alignment of elements on your pages (see Figure 16.1). Symmetrical designs create a sense of rest and stability and tend to lead the reader's eye to focus on a particular part of a document. In contrast, asymmetrical—or unbalanced—designs suggest movement and guide the reader's eye across the page.

FIGURE 16.1 Symmetrical (left) and Asymmetrical (right) Layouts [U.S. Department of Energy.]

IV Creating Your Document

Emphasis   Emphasis is the placement and formatting of elements, such as headings and subheadings, so they catch your readers' attention. You can emphasize an element in a document by using a color or font that distinguishes it from other elements, by placing a border around it and adding a shaded background, or by using an illustration, such as a photograph, drawing, or graph.

Placement   Placement is the location of elements on your pages. Placing elements next to or near each other suggests that they are related. Illustrations, for example, are usually placed near the passages in which they are mentioned.

Repetition   Repetition is the use of elements, such as headers and footers, navigation menus, and page numbers, across the pages in your document. As readers move from page to page, they tend to expect navigation elements, such as page numbers, to appear in the same place. In addition, repeated elements, such as a logo or Web navigation menu, help establish a sense of identity across the pages in your document.

Consistency   Consistency is the extent to which you format and place text and illustrations in the same way throughout your document. Treating each design element—such as illustrations, headings, and footnotes—consistently will help your readers recognize the different roles played by the elements in your document and, by extension, help them locate the information they seek. A consistent design can also convey a sense of competence and professionalism to your readers, increasing their confidence in the quality and credibility of your document.

You should also keep two other principles in mind: *moderation* and *simplicity*. An overly complex design can work against the effectiveness of a document by obscuring important ideas and information. Using design elements moderately to create simple yet effective designs is the best approach.

Design for a Purpose   ❓ WHAT'S MY PURPOSE?

A well-designed document presents your information, ideas, and arguments in a manner that helps you accomplish your purpose. Your purpose, as a result, should inform your design decisions.

You might use design to achieve any of the following goals.

- **Setting a Tone.** One of the most powerful tools writers have for accomplishing their purpose is establishing an emotional context for their readers. Drawing on the design principles of balance and placement, you can set a tone by using a particular color scheme, such as bright, cheerful hues, or by selecting photographs or drawings with a strong emotional impact.

- **Helping Readers Understand a Point.** You might use the design principles of emphasis and placement to introduce and help readers understand your points. Headings or pull quotes can call your readers' attention to important ideas and information. To introduce a main point, you might use a contrasting font or color to signal the importance of the information. To highlight a definition or an example, you might use borders or place the

FIGURE 16.2 Using Images to Create an Emotional Impact
How is the photograph likely to influence the reader's response to the headline? [Wired Magazine/Adam Rogers/Condé Nast. AP Photo/Ariana Cubillos.]

passage in a pull quote. You can also help readers understand a point by using illustrations.

- **Convincing Readers to Accept a Point.** The key to convincing readers is providing them with appropriate, relevant evidence. Drawing on the principles of emphasis and placement, you can use illustrations, marginal glosses, pull quotes, and bulleted lists to call attention to that evidence.

- **Clarifying Complex Concepts.** Sometimes a picture really is worth a thousand words. Rather than attempting to explain a complex concept using text alone, use an illustration. A well-chosen, well-placed photograph, flow chart, diagram, or table can define a complex concept such as photosynthesis in far less space, and in many cases far more effectively, than a long passage of text. You can also clarify the key elements of a complex concept with bulleted and numbered lists.

Design for Your Readers

A well-designed document helps readers understand the organization of the document, locate information and ideas, and recognize the function of parts of the document. It is also easy on your readers' eyes: Readers working with a well-designed document will not have to strain to read the text or discern illustrations. Use document design to do the following.

IV Creating Your Document

FIGURE 16.3 Headings and Subheadings in an Essay   *Use of a contrasting font and color helps readers understand the document's organization.*

Help Readers Understand the Organization of a Document   You can use headings and subheadings to signal the content of each part of the document. If you do, keep in mind the design principles of emphasis and consistency: Format your headings in a consistent manner that helps them stand out from other parts of the document (see Figure 16.3).

Help Readers Locate Information and Ideas   Many longer print documents use tables of contents and indexes to help readers locate information and ideas. Web sites typically provide a mix of menus and navigation headers and footers to help readers move around the site. When these navigation aids are integrated into pages, they are often distinguished from the surrounding text by the use of bordered or shaded boxes or through the use of contrasting fonts.

Help Readers Recognize the Function of Parts of a Document   If you include passages that differ from the main text of your document, such as sidebars and "For More Information" sections, help readers understand their function by designing them to stand out visually. Using emphasis, for example, you might format a sidebar in an article with a shaded or colored box. Similarly, you might format a list of related readings or Web links in a contrasting font or color.

Design to Address Genre Conventions

Understanding the design conventions of the type of document you plan to write will help you create a document that meets the expectations of your readers. Genres are characterized not only by distinctive writing styles, types of evidence, and organizing patterns, but also by distinctive types of design. An article in a magazine such as *TIME* or *Rolling Stone*, for example, is characterized by the use of columns, headings and subheadings, pull quotes, and illustrations, while an academic essay is characterized by wide margins, double-spaced lines, and comparatively restrained use of color and illustrations. Your readers will expect your document to be similar in design to other examples of that genre. This doesn't mean that you can't depart from those conventions should the need arise, but it does mean that you should take their expectations into account as you design your document.

16b

What design elements can I use?

Understanding the range of design elements at your disposal will enable you to decide which of these options to use as you design your document. These elements include fonts, line spacing, and alignment; page layout strategies; color, shading, borders, and rules; and illustrations.

Use Fonts, Line Spacing, and Alignment

Fonts, line spacing, and alignment choices are the most common design decisions made by writers. They are also among the most important, since poor choices can make a document difficult to read. The following examples provide an overview of the key features of fonts and the uses of fonts, line spacing, and alignment.

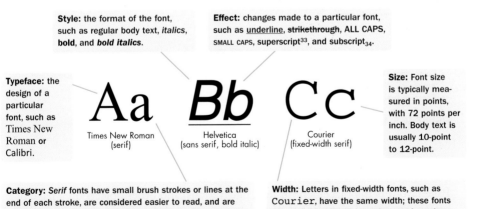

Style: the format of the font, such as regular body text, *italics*, **bold**, and ***bold italics***.

Effect: changes made to a particular font, such as underline, ~~strikethrough~~, ALL CAPS, SMALL CAPS, superscript[33], and subscript[34].

Typeface: the design of a particular font, such as Times New Roman or Calibri.

Times New Roman (serif)

Helvetica (sans serif, bold italic)

Courier (fixed-width serif)

Size: Font size is typically measured in points, with 72 points per inch. Body text is usually 10-point to 12-point.

Category: *Serif* fonts have small brush strokes or lines at the end of each stroke, are considered easier to read, and are often used for body text. *Sans-serif* fonts lack serifs and are often used for headings and subheadings. Other categories include *decorative* (Limehouse Roman, **Mambo Bold**) and symbol (Wingding: ✈📖■☆📖✿♌).

Width: Letters in fixed-width fonts, such as Courier, have the same width; these fonts are useful for displaying columns of numbers. Letters in variable-width fonts, such as Times New Roman and Helvetica, have different widths; these fonts are better suited to body text and headings.

FIGURE 16.4 Font Basics

Line spacing refers to the amount of space between lines of text. Larger line spacing appears easier to read, so you'll often find increased line spacing used in introductory paragraphs, executive summaries (which provide an overview of a longer document), and sidebars (see p. 293). When text is crammed together vertically, it is difficult to read and add comments. Keep this in mind if you are creating a document such as an essay on which someone else might write comments.

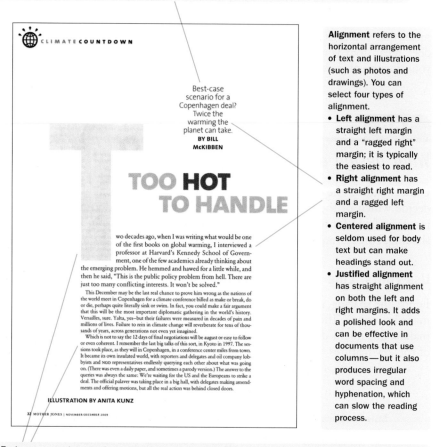

Alignment refers to the horizontal arrangement of text and illustrations (such as photos and drawings). You can select four types of alignment.

- **Left alignment** has a straight left margin and a "ragged right" margin; it is typically the easiest to read.
- **Right alignment** has a straight right margin and a ragged left margin.
- **Centered alignment** is seldom used for body text but can make headings stand out.
- **Justified alignment** has straight alignment on both the left and right margins. It adds a polished look and can be effective in documents that use columns—but it also produces irregular word spacing and hyphenation, which can slow the reading process.

Fonts are a complete set of type of a particular size and typeface. As you choose fonts, consider the following.
- **Select fonts that are easy to read.** For body text, avoid decorative fonts and italics.
- **Select fonts that complement each other.** A serif body font, such as Times New Roman or Garamond, works well with a sans serif heading font, such as Arial, Helvetica, or Calibri.
- **Exercise restraint.** Generally, use no more than four different fonts in a document.

FIGURE 16.5 Using Fonts, Line Spacing, and Alignment [Courtesy of Mother Jones.]

Use Page Layout Elements

Page layout is the placement of text, illustrations, and other objects on a page or screen. Successful page layout draws on a number of design elements, including white space, margins, columns, headers and footers, page numbers, headings, lists, captions, marginal glosses and pull quotes, and sidebars. Figure 16.6 on page 283 illustrates these design elements.

White space—literally, empty space—frames and separates elements on a page.

Columns generally appear in newspaper and magazine articles—and, to a growing extent, in articles published on the Web. Essays, on the other hand, are typically formatted in a single column. Columns can improve the readability of a document by limiting the eyes' physical movement across the page and by framing other elements.

Margins are the white space between the edge of the page or screen (top, bottom, right, and left) and the text or graphics in your document.

Headings and subheadings identify sections and subsections, serve as transitions, and allow readers to locate information more easily.

Marginal glosses are brief notes in a margin that explain or expand on text in the body of the document.

Captions and callouts describe or explain an illustration, such as a photograph or chart.

Headers, footers, and page numbers appear at the top or bottom of the page, set apart from the main text. They help readers find their way through a document; they provide information, such as the title of the document, its publication date, and its author; and they frame a page visually.

Pull quotes (not shown) highlight a passage of text—frequently a quotation—through the use of borders, white space, distinctive fonts, and contrasting colors.

Numbered and bulleted lists (not shown) display brief passages of related information using numbers or symbols (usually round "bullets"). The surrounding white space draws the eye to the list, highlighting the information for your readers, while the brief content in each entry can make concepts or processes easier to understand.

Sidebars (not shown) are brief discussions of information related to, but not a central part of, your document. Sidebars simplify the task of integrating related or supporting information into the body of the article by setting that information off in a clearly defined area.

FIGURE 16.6 Using Page Layout Elements [Reproduced with permission. Copyright © February 2012. *Scientific American*, a division of Nature America, Inc. All rights reserved. Illustration: Thomas Fuchs; Photo: Don Farrell/Digital Vision/Getty Images.]

Use Color, Shading, Borders, and Rules

Color, shading, borders, and rules (lines running horizontally or vertically on a page) can increase the overall attractiveness of your document, call attention to important information, help readers understand the organization of your document, help readers recognize the function of specific passages of text, and signal transitions between sections (see Figure 16.7). As you use these design elements,

Signal the organization of a document. In a longer print document, headers, footers, headings, and subheadings might be formatted with a particular color to help readers recognize which section they are reading. On a Web site, pages in each section could share the same background or heading color.

Call attention to important information. Color, borders, shading, and rules can subtly yet clearly emphasize an illustration, such as a table or chart, or an important passage of text, by distinguishing it from the surrounding body text.

Signal the function of text. A colored or shaded background, as well as colored type, can be used to differentiate captions and pull quotes from body text. Rules can also separate columns of text on a page or screen.

Be consistent. Use the same colors for top-level headings throughout your document, another color for lower-level headings, and so on. Use the same borders and shading for sidebars. Use rules consistently in pull quotes, headers, and footers. Don't mix and match.

Understand the effects of color. Some effects are physical. Bright yellow, for example, can tire your readers' eyes. Other effects are emotional—and are often linked to readers' cultural backgrounds. In many cultures, green is regarded as soothing because it is associated with nature and growth. Red, in contrast, is often associated with danger. As a result, it tends to attract attention.

FIGURE 16.7 Using Color, Shading, Borders, and Rules [Copyright © Rolling Stone LLC 2010. All Rights Reserved. Used by Permission. Top: Dan Monick/Corbis Outline; middle: Mick Rock/Retina; bottom: © DreamWorks/courtesy Everett Collection.]

IV Creating Your Document

exercise restraint. Avoid using more than three colors on a page unless you are using a photograph or work of art. Be cautious, as well, about using multiple styles of rules or borders in a document.

Use Illustrations   [FRAMING MY ARGUMENT]

Illustrations — charts, graphs, tables, photographs and other images, animations, audio clips, and video clips — can expand on or demonstrate points made in the text of your document. They can also reduce the text needed to make a point, help readers better understand your points, and increase the visual appeal of your document.

Photographs and Other Images   Photographs and other images, such as drawings, paintings, and sketches, are frequently used to set a mood, emphasize a point, or demonstrate a point more fully than is possible with text alone.

Charts and Graphs   Charts and graphs represent information visually. They are used to make a point more succinctly than is possible with text alone or to present complex information in a compact and more accessible form. They frequently rely on numerical information.

Tables   Like charts and graphs, tables can present complex information, both textual and numerical, in a compact form.

Other Digital Illustrations   Digital publications allow you to include a wider range of illustrations that bring sound and movement to your document, including audio, video, and animations.

As you work with illustrations, keep the following guidelines in mind.

- **Use an illustration for a purpose.** Illustrations are best used when they serve a clear function in your document. Avoid including illustrations simply because you think they might make your document "look better."

- **Place illustrations near the text they illustrate.** In general, place illustrations as close as possible to the point where they are mentioned in the text. If they are not explicitly mentioned (as is often the case with photographs), place them at a point where they will seem most relevant to the information and ideas being discussed.

- **Include a title or caption that identifies or explains the illustration.** The documentation style you are using, such as MLA or APA, will usually offer advice on the placement and format of titles and captions. In general, documentation systems suggest that you distinguish between tables and figures (which include other illustrations), number tables and figures in the order in which they appear in the document, and use compound numbering of tables and figures in longer documents (for example, the second table in Chapter 5 would be labeled "Table 5.2"). Consult the documentation system you are using for specific guidelines on illustrations.

16c

How can I design my document?

Although essays are perhaps the most commonly used assignments in writing courses, you might have the opportunity to decide which genre you'll use to make your contribution to a conversation. Or you might be asked to adapt the contents of an academic essay for presentation in another genre, such as a brochure or Web page. As you consider your choices, you'll find a wide array of documents that you can use to reach your readers. In this chapter, you'll find discussions of how to design some of the most important print and digital genres.

Design an Academic Essay

Some writers might be surprised to see *design* and *academic essay* used in the same sentence. They're aware, of course, that they should use wide margins, readable fonts, and double-spaced lines, and they generally understand that they should do this to help readers—typically an instructor—read and respond to their work. Beyond these elements, however, they think of design as having little or no role in their essays.

They're wrong. Thoughtful design can help you achieve your goals, address your readers' expectations, and adapt to the context in which your essay will be written and read.

Ask How Design Elements Can Help You Achieve Your Writing Goals   Traditionally, essay assignments have focused on the written expression of ideas and arguments. As a result, writers have tended to use images sparingly, if at all, and to make limited use of design elements such as color, shading, borders, and rules in their academic essays. Writers have also tended to avoid the use of tables and charts, perhaps thinking that these kinds of design elements would be more appropriate for genres such as reports and professional articles.

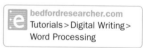

bedfordresearcher.com
Tutorials > Digital Writing >
Word Processing

Yet these design elements can help you present complex information and ideas more clearly, distinguish between items considered in an evaluation, illustrate the aspects of a particular problem, or frame your argument by calling readers' attention to particular information and ideas. As you draft your essay, consider how the wide range of design elements discussed on pp. 281–85 might help you accomplish your goals as a writer. As you consider your options, keep in mind your instructor's preferences regarding the use of these elements. If you are uncertain about your instructor's preferences, ask for guidance.

Consider Reader Expectations   Readers approach an essay with a set of writing and design conventions in mind. They expect you to make a main point, to support your point with reasons and evidence, and to identify the sources you've drawn on in your essay. They also expect you to follow generally accepted design conventions, such as the guidelines provided by the documentation systems published by groups such as the MLA and APA (see Part V). You'll frequently find guidance on how to format an academic essay in your assignment. You can also consult your instructor if you have any questions.

As you design your essay, consider not only what your readers expect, but also how you can build on those expectations to accomplish your goals as a writer. You can use design elements such as fonts, color, shading, borders, and rules to help readers anticipate and more easily follow the organization of your essay. You can use tables, charts, and figures to let your readers view, understand, and carry out their own analysis of the information you include in your essay. If you are distributing your essay in digital format, you can help readers access related information, such as video clips, audio clips, animations, and related data sets, via links—or you can embed these materials directly in your essay. You can read more about how these design elements can help you in these areas on pp. 281–85.

View an Essay   The following pages are from an essay written by college freshman Gaele Lopez for his composition class. They reflect his awareness of his instructor's expectations about line spacing, margins, documentation system, page numbers, and inclusion of a title page.

You can view other essays formatted in MLA, APA, *Chicago*, and CSE styles in Part V.

CHECKLIST FOR DESIGNING ACADEMIC ESSAYS

Consider the following design conventions associated with academic essays.

✔ Cover page or essay header, depending on your instructor's preferences or documentation style formatting requirements

✔ Readable body font (example: 12-point Times New Roman)

✔ Double-spaced lines

✔ Wide margins, one inch or larger

✔ Consistent use of assigned documentation system

✔ Headers and footers in a readable font distinct from body font

✔ If used, headings and subheadings formatted in fonts and colors that distinguish them from the body text and show relative importance of heading levels

✔ If used, illustrations labeled and placed either within the text near relevant passages or in an appendix, according to instructor's preferences

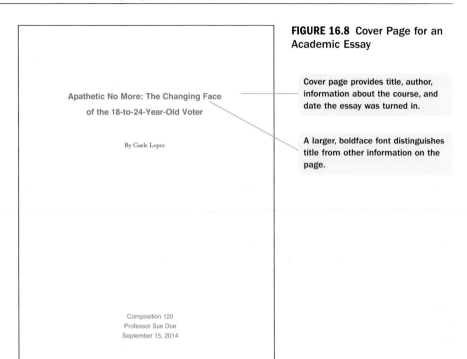

FIGURE 16.8 Cover Page for an Academic Essay

Cover page provides title, author, information about the course, and date the essay was turned in.

A larger, boldface font distinguishes title from other information on the page.

FIGURE 16.9 First Page of an Academic Essay

A header with writer's last name and page number is repeated at the top of each page.

Title is repeated on first page of essay in a larger, colored, sans serif font that distinguishes it from the body text.

Body text is set in a serif font, which is more readable than most sans serif fonts.

All body text is formatted consistently.

One-inch margins and double-spaced lines provide space for the teacher to write comments.

A graph appears near its mention in the text, supporting claims made there.

FIGURE 16.10 Interior Page
of an Academic Essay

Lopez 3

In the 2008 primaries, turnouts among younger voters doubled, tripled, and
in some case quadrupled the turnouts recorded in any previous primary (Pew
Charitable Trust, par. 2). Analysts – even some of those who had suggested
raising the voting age – quickly began to investigate why younger voters were
turning out in such unprecedented numbers, what impact their votes would
have on the upcoming presidential election, and what this change in behavior
would have on future elections.

Factors Contributing to the Change in Voting Behaviors

Why the sudden change? Or is it as sudden as it seems? Analysts
Mark Hugo Lopez, Emily Kirby, and Jared Sagoff, writing after the 2004
presidential elections, pointed to "the confluence of extensive voter outreach
efforts, a close election, and high levels of interest in the 2004 campaign"
as factors that drove turnout among younger voters to "levels not seen since
1992" (1). They cautioned, however, that it was unclear whether the 2004
results were indicators of a significant change or simply an aberration.

It would appear, based on patterns seen in the 2006 mid-term elections and
in the 2008 presidential primaries, that there really is evidence of a change.
In its report on record turnout in the 2008 primaries and caucuses, the Pew
Charitable Trust notes,

> The research showed that college students are deeply concerned
> about issues, involved personally as volunteers and ready to consider
> voting. But they want political leaders to be positive, to address real
> problems and to call on all Americans to be constructively involved
> (par. 5).

As we look toward the fall 2008 elections, it seems clear that young voters
will not only play an important role in the election, but might in fact play the
deciding role. Voters such as Reid Vincent,

A heading, formatted in blue and
using a sans serif font that differs
from the serif body font, calls
attention to a shift in Gaele's
argument.

Block quotation is set off by indent-
ing the margins on both sides.
Quotation marks are not needed
for block quotations.

FIGURE 16.11 Works Cited Page
of an Academic Essay

Reference page is titled "Works
Cited" per MLA style.

MLA format is used to cite sources.
Entries are double-spaced and have
a hanging indent.

Lopez 4

Works Cited

Lopez, Mark Hugo, Emily Kirby, and Jared Sagoff. "Fact Sheet: The Youth Vote 2004."
www.civicyouth.org. The Center for Information and Research on Civic Learning and
Engagement, July 2005. Web. 20 Aug. 2008.

Margnarelli, Margaret. "Young Voter Apathy: Will America's Youth Go to the Polls?"
GovSpot.com. StartSpot Media Works, n.d. 22 Aug. 2008.

"Record Youth Voter Turnout for '08 Presidential Primaries and Caucuses." *Pew Charitable
Trust*. Pew Charitable Trust, 13 June 2008. Web. 27 Aug. 2008.

United States. Bureau of the Census. *United States Census Bureau Population Reports: Voting
and Registration in the Election of November 1996, P20-504*. By Lynne M. Casper and
Loretta E. Bass. July 1998. Web. 27 Aug. 2008.

Vincent, Reid. Personal Interview. 28 Aug. 2008.

Design a Multimodal Essay

Multimodal essays are characterized by their essayistic form and their use of multiple types of illustrations. As essays, they present information in a linear sequence, one idea after another. As multimodal documents, they combine text with images, animation, sound, and/or video to establish a line of argument and support the writer's points.

Consider Your Purpose and Role   Multimodal essays require careful selection and organization of sources not only for their content, but also for the manner in which they appeal to readers. Depending on your argument, you might find that an embedded video clip is likely to be more effective than an audio clip or image. In each case, your purpose and role as well as your understanding of your readers' needs, interests, values, beliefs, experiences, and knowledge of the issue will affect your decisions about content and design.

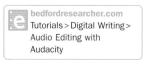

bedfordresearcher.com
Tutorials > Digital Writing >
Photo Editing Basics
with GIMP

Consider Reader Expectations about Design   Multimodal essays have emerged quite recently as a distinct genre. Your readers are likely to expect only that you'll provide a linear document that contains one or more types of embedded media; uses fonts, colors, borders, and lines consistently and effectively; and is designed to be viewed on a computer screen or tablet. If you develop an extended essay, such as the multimodal essay created by Lauren Mack, your readers are also likely to expect you to provide navigation aids such as tables of contents and page links that will allow them to move easily to different parts of the essay.

Choose Your Composing Tools   Multimodal essays vary widely not only in form, but also in the software used to create them. You can create multimedia essays using a word processing program such as Microsoft Word or Apple Pages, a multimedia presentation program such as PowerPoint or KeyNote, or Web site development programs such as Dreamweaver. As you choose your design tools, consider how their distinctive features will help you accomplish your goals as a writer. A word processing program might be a better choice than a multimedia presentation program, for example, if you plan to rely more heavily on text than on images and video. In contrast, a program such as PowerPoint offers more options for including multimedia elements than most word processing or Web development programs.

bedfordresearcher.com
Tutorials > Digital Writing >
Audio Editing with
Audacity

ⓘ **INFORMATION LITERACY**   Microsoft PowerPoint and other multimedia presentation programs, such as Apple Keynote, Google Slides, or OpenOffice Impress, offer a set of tools that are well suited to integrating multimedia sources with text. The Insert Toolbar in PowerPoint, for example, allows you to add images, audio, video, and other media sources along with tables, text boxes, and links. To get started, create a new presentation and click on the Insert menu in the command ribbon.

FIGURE 16.12 PowerPoint's Insert Ribbon

Using a multimedia presentation program to create a multimedia essay invites you to think of the program not as a set of bulleted slides, but as a group of pages that can be filled with various types of media. If you look at each page as a blank canvas, you can see how you might design an essay containing pages that look like those you might find in a magazine or on the Web.

FIGURE 16.13 *Text, a video, and images are used on a multimedia presentation slide.*

View a Multimodal Essay The following examples are drawn from the multimodal essay written by Lauren Mack. Lauren developed her essay using PowerPoint. Note her use of text, illustrations, color, headings and subheadings, and menus to clearly convey her argument about the impact of climate change on coral reefs.

IV Creating Your Document

An image draws the reader's eye and sets the tone for the presentation.

Coral Reefs

The title and author are presented in readable fonts that stand out against the background.

A Presentation by Lauren Mack

FIGURE 16.14a Pages from a Multimodal Essay

Threats to Coral Reefs

Coral reefs were once a resilient ecosystem, easily overcoming natural disasters like hurricanes and tsunamis. Lately, coral reefs have been faced with much tougher challenges. Many human activities, such as fishing and tourism, impact reefs in a negative way. One of the biggest threats to coral reefs, especially in the U.S., is **pollution** [4][8].

Body text is presented in a readable sans-serif font that contrasts with the background.

Fig. 5: Reefs around the world are at risk for a variety of reasons.
Source: www.coralreef.noaa.gov

FIGURE 16.14b

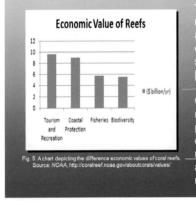

Importance to Humans

Coral reefs have an estimated worth of **$30 billion** worldwide [9]. Should coral reefs disappear, it is likely that there would be a significant backlash in the fishing industry since a large portion of marine life that we eat such as snapper, grouper, scallop, and many more are found in those habitats [2].

Economic Value of Reefs

Those in the fishing industry aren't the only ones making a living off these beautiful ecosystems. In addition to providing food, they also boost their local economies by providing jobs in ecotourism through scuba diving, snorkeling, and recreational fishing [9][1].

Coral reefs also have a reputation for saving us in more ways than one. Not only do reef structures protect our shoreline communities from maritime destruction, but scientists have also discovered that reefs hold a huge potential for medical advancements with compounds found only in coral reef environments [1].

Fig. 5: A chart depicting the difference economic values of coral reefs. Source: *NOAA*, http://coralreef.noaa.gov/aboutcorals/values/

Images illustrate key ideas in the text.

Source information and credits are provided for images.

FIGURE 16.14c

Page headings are formatted consistently throughout the presentation.

Pollution Problems

Pollution has led to events such as global climate change and rising ocean temperatures, making it one of the major factors contributing to the loss of coral reef ecosystems [14].

Some reef problems associated with pollution include:

* Bleaching
* Ocean Acidification
* Marine Debris

A bulleted list previews upcoming points in the presentation.

FIGURE 16.14d

IV Creating Your Document

CHECKLIST FOR CREATING MULTIMODAL ESSAYS

✔ Use your experiences writing academic essays as a foundation for your work on a multimodal essay.

✔ Reflect on your purpose and role, the expectations of your readers, and the context in which your essay will be written and read.

✔ Choose your composing tools, keeping in mind their appropriateness for your writing situation and their tendency to drive design decisions in particular directions.

✔ Develop an appropriate and consistent design for your document, paying particular attention to issues such as the following:

- Consistent use of fonts, colors, shading, borders, and rules

- Readable heading and subheading fonts (example: 16-point Times New Roman or Verdana)

- Readable body font designed for onscreen reading (example: 11-point Calibri or Georgia)

- Placement of titles, text, and illustrations, with illustrations labeled and located near relevant text passages

- If used, transitions between pages (dissolves, page flips) quick and not distracting

- If used, background images and sounds chosen to enhance rather than obscure the elements on each page

✔ Create navigation tools such as next and previous buttons, links, menus, and tables of contents.

Design an Article

Articles appear in a wide range of publications, including newspapers, magazines, scholarly and professional journals, and Web sites, among others. Articles rely heavily on information obtained from sources such as books, Web sites, government reports, interviews, surveys, and observation. Article writers should consider several factors that affect design: the overall design of the publication in which they hope to place their article, the audience the publication addresses, the subjects typically written about in the publication, and the style and tone used in other articles in the publication.

Consider Your Purpose and Role Articles are written for a wide range of purposes, from informing to evaluating to entertaining to persuading or convincing. As you consider potential design choices, keep your purpose and role in mind. If you are informing your readers about a complex concept, for example, you might use a diagram or chart to convey information in a way that would be difficult to do through words alone. If you are trying to persuade your readers to take action, you might select a color scheme that sets a particular mood or insert an image that evokes a strong emotional response.

Consider Reader Expectations about Design   Because most articles are written for a specific publication, writers typically have a clear picture of their readers (age, income, education, hobbies, and so forth) and can develop a line of argument that directly addresses their needs and interests. An article about an election, for example, might report on turnout among younger voters, offer a profile of a recently elected senator from the Midwest, or describe the activities of an organization such as the League of Women Voters.

Depending on the publication you are targeting, your article might use headings and subheadings, columns, sidebars, pull quotes, and a wide array of illustrations. To gain an understanding of your readers' expectations about the design of your article, scan other articles in the publication. Take note of the range of design choices in the articles. Then read a few of the articles more closely to gain insights into the choices the writers made as they wrote and designed their articles.

Your analysis of your target publication can help you gain an overall understanding of the type of publication that might publish your article. You're likely to find, of course, that there's quite a bit of variety in articles that appear in even the most narrowly focused publication. But understanding your potential readers and the subjects they seem to care about can help you compose a better article. Similarly, applying what you've learned about the writing and design conventions of articles that have appeared in the publication will show its editors — the people who ultimately decide what is accepted for publication — that you have tailored your article to their needs.

My Research Project

Analyze a Target Publication

Analyzing a publication involves asking questions about its readers, the subject its articles address, its writing conventions, and its design. To locate a print publication, visit your library's periodical room (p. 173) or consult a reference librarian. You can also search for information about the publication on the Web (p. 163) or in databases (p. 158). To locate information about a digital publication, such as *Slate*, visit its Web site, conduct database searches, or consult a reference librarian.

In your research log, record your answers to the following questions about the publication to which you will submit your article.

Readers

Examine the publication as a whole to learn what you can about its readers.

- Can you find a "letters to the editor" section? If so, reading the letters and any responses from the editors might give you insights into who reads the publication and why they read it.

- If there are advertisements in the publication, do they tell you anything about the readers? Who advertises in the publication? What products or services do they offer or what issues or problems do they address?

↓

IV Creating Your Document

- What can you learn about the readers from the range of subjects or issues addressed in articles and other parts of the publication?

- Can you find any information about the publisher? Can you tell whether it is a commercial enterprise, a government agency, a non-profit organization, a scholarly or professional organization, or an individual? Does the publication have a mission statement? Does it describe its purpose or goals, the audience it hopes to reach, or its origins? If so, what does it tell you about the target audience?

Subjects

Look at recently published articles in the publication. You can often find them in tables of contents, indexes, and archives. Depending on the publication, you might also be able to search a full-text database (p. 158) or search the Web for archived articles.

- What issues and subjects are addressed in articles?

- How long are the articles? What are the shortest? What are the longest? Where do they fall on average?

- What do you think is the purpose of the publication? Is its goal to inform, to advocate, to address problems? Or does it address a range of purposes?

Writing Conventions

Study the articles in the publication to learn about its writing conventions.

- How would you characterize the style and tone of the articles? Is it generally formal, informal, or somewhere in between? Are contractions (*can't, won't, isn't*) used? Are individuals identified by their full names and titles (Dr. Shaun Beaty)?

- How are sources identified? Do the articles use an in-text citation system, such as MLA, APA, *Chicago*, or CSE (see Part V)? Do they use footnotes or endnotes? Do they link directly to the source? Do they informally identify the source?

- What do the authors of articles seem to assume about their readers? Do they use specialized language (or jargon)? Do they expect you to know a great deal about the subject? Do you think the authors expect you to be an expert in the field to understand their articles?

Design

To gain an understanding of your readers' expectations about the design of your article, scan articles in the publication, read a few carefully, and take notes.

- Would you characterize the articles as heavy on text? Or are images, tables, charts, figures, and other illustrations used? If the article is published in a digital format, does it include audio or video clips? Does it include other digital illustrations, such as animations or apps that a reader could work with?

- How is color used in the article, if at all? Does the article make use of borders, rules, and shading?

- Does the article use headings and subheadings? If so, how are they formatted? What kinds of fonts are used? Is there much variety in the fonts?

- How is the article laid out? Does it use columns? Sidebars? Block quotes?

bedfordresearcher.com
My Research Project Activities > Analyze a Target Publication

View an Article   The articles that follow were published in *Indiana Daily Student*, the student newspaper at Indiana University. Paired with photos, the articles make use of font formatting and visual elements to set a mood, call attention to key points, and convey information.

FIGURE 16.15 Front Page of a Student Newspaper
[Courtesy of Indiana University, June 19, 2014.]

INDIANA DAILY STUDENT | THURSDAY, JUNE 19, 2014 | IDSNEWS.COM

'Light Totem' to return with color

A large headline contrasts with the text and the headlines for individual articles.

BY VICTORIA LUTGRING
vlutgrin@umail.iu.edu

Bylines are set in bold and sans serif to differentiate them from main body text.

Newspaper articles are formatted in columns.

Captioned photos add visual interest and information.

See Weekend, page 7, to revisit your IU bucket list, including the 'Light Totem'

Callouts in large, sans serif font highlight key ideas and information in the article.

IU ranks No. 6 in attendance

FROM IDS REPORTS

Your guide to this weekend's events, pages 9 and 10

Rankings for other Big Ten teams
No. 7 Wisconsin
No. 8 Ohio State
No. 13 Nebraska
No. 17 Iowa
No. 18 Michigan State
No. 23 Purdue
No. 24 Michigan
No. 32 Minnesota
No. 72 Northwestern
No. 83 Penn State

CHECKLIST FOR DESIGNING ARTICLES

With the results of your publication analysis in mind, consider the following design conventions.

✔ Column layout appropriate for target publication and target audience

✔ Line spacing typically single-space

✔ Readable body font (example: 10- or 11-point Century Schoolbook)

✔ Color, borders, shading, and rules used appropriately

✔ Heading and subheadings formatted in fonts and colors that distinguish them from body text and show the relative importance of heading levels

✔ Illustrations labeled and placed near relevant passages

Design a Web Site

Web sites consist of linked pages, typically organized through a home page and navigational devices such as menus, tables of contents, indexes, and site maps. The main pages of Web sites usually provide broad overviews of the topic, and related pages add detailed information.

Consider Your Purpose and Role   Web sites are able to engage readers in ways that print documents cannot: They can link directly to related sites, allow visitors to access video and audio files, and support communication among the site's readers and writers. This wealth of design and navigation options, however, carries significant design challenges for writers. As you consider your purpose in developing a Web site, you must reflect not only on what you hope to accomplish—informing or persuading readers, for example—but also on design elements that can help you achieve your purpose. Key considerations include helping readers move easily through your site, formatting text to highlight important information and ideas, and selecting effective digital illustrations.

Consider Reader Expectations about Design   Given the wide range of individuals with access to the Web, writers must anticipate the needs of a much more diverse group of readers than is the case with documents distributed in print. Designers of Web sites, as a result, typically attempt to provide their readers with a significant amount of guidance about the purpose, content, and organization of their sites on the pages readers usually visit first. This guidance can include site menus, tables of contents, links to pages that provide information about the site, and links to pages that provide contact information (see Figures 16.16–16.18).

Over the past decade, the appearance of many Web sites has grown similar to that of magazines, with a heavy use of images and other illustrations. Writers typically design a Web site with many of the same considerations they apply to the pages in a magazine article, choosing a unified color scheme, formatting headings and subheadings consistently across pages, and using borders, shading, and rules in a manner similar to that of many print publications. They must also address, however, the placement and appearance of navigation menus and digital illustrations, such as audio and video clips, animations, and embedded programs and downloadable files.

View Pages from a Web Site

A large heading identifies the issue addressed by the site.

A side menu provides links to pages on the site.

Search allows readers to locate information on the site.

'ormation about the author is provided. A list of sources eferenced n the site available.

Body text is formatted in a serif font that is easy to read.

A bulleted list calls attention to important information.

FIGURE 16.16 Web Site Home Page

A link to the site main page is provided on all pages.

Headings use a larger font and a contrasting color.

The side menu appears in the same place on every page.

A title appears above a chart.

A chart illustrates a key point raised in the body text.

Source information is provided. The font uses a contrasting color.

FIGURE 16.17 Web Site Content Page
[U.S. Energy Information Administration.]

Extra space after each paragraph helps differentiate one from another.

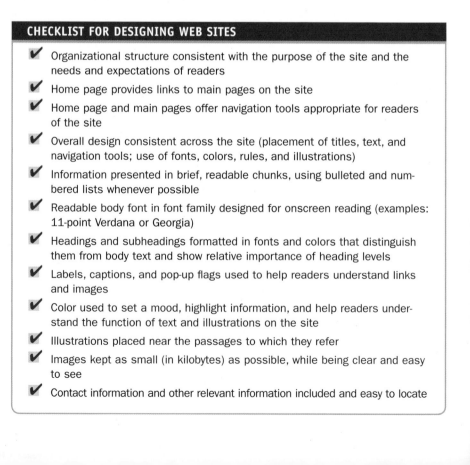

FIGURE 16.18 Annotated Bibliography Web Page

CHECKLIST FOR DESIGNING WEB SITES

✔ Organizational structure consistent with the purpose of the site and the needs and expectations of readers

✔ Home page provides links to main pages on the site

✔ Home page and main pages offer navigation tools appropriate for readers of the site

✔ Overall design consistent across the site (placement of titles, text, and navigation tools; use of fonts, colors, rules, and illustrations)

✔ Information presented in brief, readable chunks, using bulleted and numbered lists whenever possible

✔ Readable body font in font family designed for onscreen reading (examples: 11-point Verdana or Georgia)

✔ Headings and subheadings formatted in fonts and colors that distinguish them from body text and show relative importance of heading levels

✔ Labels, captions, and pop-up flags used to help readers understand links and images

✔ Color used to set a mood, highlight information, and help readers understand the function of text and illustrations on the site

✔ Illustrations placed near the passages to which they refer

✔ Images kept as small (in kilobytes) as possible, while being clear and easy to see

✔ Contact information and other relevant information included and easy to locate

> **QUICK REFERENCE**

Designing Documents

✔ Understand the design principles of balance, emphasis, placement, repetition, and consistency. (p. 277)

✔ Design to achieve your purposes. (p. 278)

✔ Design to address your readers' needs, interests, values, and beliefs. (p. 279)

✔ Design to address genre conventions. (p. 280)

✔ Use design elements—such as fonts, line spacing, alignment, page layout, color, shading, borders, rules, and illustrations—effectively and appropriately to increase the readability and effectiveness of your document. (p. 281)

✔ Consider purpose, role, and reader expectations to design academic essays, multimodal essays, articles, and Web sites. (p. 286)

IV Creating Your Document

17

Revising and Editing

When writers revise and edit, they evaluate the effectiveness of their drafts and, if necessary, work to improve them. Although the two processes are related, they focus on different aspects of a document. To revise is to assess how well a document responds to a specific writing situation, makes an argument, presents reasons, and uses evidence. To edit is to evaluate and improve the expression—at the sentence and word levels—of the information, ideas, and arguments in the document.

17a

What should I focus on as I revise my document?

Revising involves rethinking and re-envisioning your document. It focuses on such big-picture issues as whether the document you've drafted is appropriate for your writing situation; whether your argument is sound and well supported; whether you've organized and presented your information, ideas, and arguments clearly and effectively; and whether you've made appropriate decisions about genre and design.

Consider Your Writing Situation ❓ WHAT'S MY PURPOSE?

As you revise, ask whether your document helps you achieve your purpose. If your goal is to inform readers about a particular subject, ask whether you've provided appropriate information, whether you've given enough information, and whether that information is presented clearly. If your purpose is to convince or persuade your readers in some way, ask whether you have chosen appropriate reasons and evidence and presented your argument as effectively as you can.

Review as well your readers' needs, interests, values, beliefs, and knowledge of the issue. It's useful during revision to imagine how your readers will react to your document by asking questions such as these.

- Will my readers trust what I have to say? How can I establish my credibility?
- Will my readers have other ideas about how to address this issue? How can I convince them that they should believe what I say?
- Will my readers find my evidence appropriate and accurate? Is my selection of evidence consistent with their values and beliefs?

Finally, identify your requirements, limitations, and opportunities. Ask yourself whether you've met the specific requirements of the assignment, such as length and number of sources. Evaluate your efforts to work around limitations, such as lack of access to information. Think about whether you've taken full advantage of your opportunities and any new ones that have come your way.

Consider Your Argument and Ideas [FRAMING MY ARGUMENT]

As you revise, ask how well you are conveying your argument and ideas to your readers. First, check the clarity of your thesis statement. Is it phrased in a way that is compatible with the needs, interests, values, and beliefs of your readers? Second, ask whether the argument and ideas in your document help your readers understand and accept your thesis statement. As you make this assessment, keep in mind the role or roles you've decided to adopt — such as informing your readers, interpreting or analyzing, or advocating for a particular position.

IV Creating Your Document

Consider Your Use and Integration of Sources

Think about how you've used source information in your document. First, review the amount of support you've provided for your points and the appropriateness of that support for your purpose and readers. Then, if you are arguing about an issue, determine whether you've identified and addressed reasonable opposing viewpoints.

It's also important that you integrate your sources effectively into your document and acknowledge them according to the documentation system you are following. Ensure that you have cited all your sources and that you've clearly distinguished between your ideas and those of other writers. Review your works cited or reference list for completeness and accuracy. Remember that improper documentation can reduce your document's effectiveness and your credibility.

Consider the Structure and Organization of Your Document

Your readers should be able to locate information and ideas easily. As you read your introduction, ask whether it clearly and concisely conveys your main point and whether it helps your readers anticipate the structure and organization of your document. Reflect on the appropriateness of your organizing pattern (p. 224) for your purpose and readers. If you've used headings and subheadings, evaluate their effectiveness.

Make sure your document is easy to read. Check for effective paragraphing and paragraph structure. If you have a number of small paragraphs, you might combine paragraphs with similar ideas. If you have a number of long paragraphs, break them up and add transitions. Finally, ask whether your conclusion leaves your readers with something to think about. The most effective conclusions typically provide more than a document summary.

Consider Genre and Design

Consider both the genre—or type—of document that you are writing (p. 280) and your use of design principles and elements (see Chapter 16). Since you are writing in a particular genre, such as a source-based argumentative essay or an article for a popular magazine, ask whether the choices you've made about the content and style of your document are consistent with your readers' expectations about that type of document. Be sure to consider, for example, issues such as level of formality, accepted sources of evidence, and organization.

Take a careful look, as well, at how you've designed your document. Does it resemble what your readers will expect? For example, if you're writing an academic essay, have you double-spaced your lines, used a readable font, and set wide margins? If you are creating a Web site, have you made it easy for your readers to find their way around? Have you used design principles and elements to achieve your purpose and address the needs and interests of your readers?

17b

What strategies should I use to revise?

As you revise, you can draw on strategies for reviewing and improving your document. These strategies range from saving multiple drafts of your document to assessing its argument and organization to obtaining feedback from others.

Save Multiple Drafts

You might not be happy with every revision you make. To avoid wishing that you hadn't made extensive revisions to a draft of your document, save a new copy of your draft before every major revising session. Name your drafts by number—as in Draft1.doc, Draft2.doc, and so on—or by date, as in Draft-April6.doc and Draft-April10.doc. Or come up with a naming system that works for you. What's important is that you save multiple versions of your drafts in case you don't like the changes you've made.

Highlight Your Main Point, Reasons, and Evidence

As you revise, ensure that your main point (usually expressed as a thesis statement), reasons, and evidence are fully developed. An effective way to do this is to identify and examine each element in your draft, both individually and as a group of related points. If you are working with a printed document, use a highlighter, colored pens or pencils, or sticky notes. If you are working in a word processing program, use the highlighting tools to mark the text. You might use different colors to highlight your main point, supporting points, and evidence. If you are focusing solely on the evidence in your document, use different colors to highlight evidence from different sources (to help you check whether you are relying too heavily on a single source) or to differentiate the type of evidence you are using (such as quotations, paraphrases, summaries, and numerical data).

Challenge Your Assumptions

It's easy to agree with an argument that you've developed. Challenge your main idea, reasons, and evidence by using one of the following strategies. Keep track of your challenges by using the Comment tool in your word processor.

- **Put yourself in the place of your readers.** As you read, pretend that you are one of your readers. Try to imagine a single reader—or, if you're ambitious, a group of readers. Ask questions they might ask. Imagine concerns they might bring to their reading of your document. A reader interested in solving a problem might ask, for example, whether a proposed solution is cost effective, is more appropriate than alternative solutions, or has unacceptable side effects. As you revise, take these questions and concerns into account.

- **Play devil's advocate.** A devil's advocate raises reasonable objections to ideas and arguments. As you review your document, identify your key claims and pose reasonable objections to them. Make note of these potential objections and take them into account as you revise.

- **Play the "so what?" game.** As you read your document, ask why readers would care about what you are saying. By asking "so what?" questions, you can gain a better understanding of what your readers are likely to care about and how they might respond to your arguments and ideas. Make note of your responses to these questions and consider them as you revise.

Scan, Outline, and Map Your Document

i **INFORMATION LITERACY** Use the following strategies to review the structure and organization of your document.

- **Scan headings and subheadings.** If you have used headings and subheadings, they can help you track the overall flow of your argument and ideas. Ask whether the organization they reveal is appropriate for your writing situation and your role as a writer.

- **Scan the first sentence of each paragraph.** A quick reading of the first sentence in each paragraph can reveal points at which your argument shifts. As you note these shifts, think about whether they are appropriate and effective.

- **Outline Your Document.** Create a topical or sentence outline of your document (p. 228) to assess its structure and organization. This strategy, sometimes called a *reverse outline*, helps you identify the sequence of your points and amount of space you've devoted to each aspect of your document. If you are viewing your document in a word processor, use the Styles tool to assign levels to headings in your document and then view it in outline view.

- **Map Your Document.** On paper, in a word processor, or in a graphics program, draw a map of your document. Like an outline, a map can help you identify the organization of your points and the amount of evidence you've used to support them.

As you review the organization and structure of your document, reflect on whether it is appropriate given your purpose, readers, argument, and available information.

Ask for Feedback

After spending long hours on a project, you may find it difficult to identify problems your readers might have with your draft. You might read the same paragraph eight times, failing to notice that the evidence you are using to support a point actually contradicts it. Or you might not notice that your document's

How do I strengthen my argument during revision?

By this point in your research writing process, you are probably quite comfortable with your argument. But what would a reader with fresh eyes think? Imagine that you are a reader encountering this essay for the first time, and then respond as the author.

	Reader's Comments	**Author's Responses**
1 Look for confusing or unclear points. As you read the essay, do any questions form in your mind? Write down your questions, then—wearing your author's hat again—consider how your essay can address them more fully.	—You mention mercenaries, but it's not clear how they're different from contractors. —You say that contractors are under different rules than members of the military, but it's not clear why.	—Must distinguish the two roles more clearly; maybe provide a historical look at the differences and do a direct comparison —Need to sort out the reasons behind the different codes of justice and make these more clear
2 Play devil's advocate. Identify your key claims and pose reasonable objections to them. Consider how you could address them in your essay.	—You claim that contractors have abused their power, but haven't there been cases of soldiers committing crimes?	—Need to include this point—and talk about accountability of military vs. contractors
3 Play the "so what?" game. As a reader, consider why you should care about this topic. Then respond to help readers identify the significance of your issue.	—What if I'm not interested in private military corporations? Why should I pay attention?	—Talk about the "brain drain" on our armed forces—good soldiers going to PMCs rather than continuing to serve in the military —Address national security threats made worse by PMCs

---

CHECKLIST FOR REVISING

✔ **Review your research writing situation.** Ask whether your document helps you achieve your purposes; addresses your readers' needs, interests, values, and beliefs; meets your requirements; effectively works around limitations; and takes advantage of opportunities. (p. 303)

✔ **Evaluate your argument and ideas.** Ask whether your document provides a clear and appropriate thesis statement and whether your argument and ideas support your thesis statement and are consistent with your roles. (p. 303)

✔ **Assess your use and integration of sources.** Ask whether you have offered adequate support for your points, considered reasonable opposing viewpoints, integrated and acknowledged your sources, and distinguished between your work and that of other writers. (p. 304)

✔ **Examine the structure and organization of your document.** Ask whether the introduction is clear and concise, clearly conveys your main point, and helps your readers anticipate the structure of your document. Also think about whether the organizational structure is easy to follow, paragraphs are easy to read, and transitions are effective. Ask whether the conclusion provides more than a summary of the document. (p. 304)

✔ **Evaluate genre and design.** Ask whether the genre you've created helps you accomplish your purpose. Check that you've followed the style and design conventions associated with the type of document you've created. (p. 304)

✔ **Use effective revision strategies.** Create multiple drafts to preserve earlier work; review your document to assess its argument and organization; get feedback from other writers. (p. 305)

---

organization could confuse your readers. You can ask for feedback on your draft from a friend, relative, colleague, or writing center tutor. It's generally a good idea to ask for help from someone who will be frank as well as supportive and to be specific about the kinds of comments you're looking for. Hearing "It's just fine" from a reviewer will not help you to revise.

WORKING TOGETHER

Use Peer Review to Improve Your Document

One of the biggest challenges writers face is reading a draft of their own work as a reader rather than as the writer. Because you know what you're trying to say, you find it easy to understand your draft. To determine how you should revise your draft, ask a friend or classmate to read your essay and consider the questions below.

Purpose

1 What do you see as the purpose of the document? Did you learn anything new? Did it change your understanding of or attitudes toward the issue? Did it make you want to take action on the issue?

2 Is the design of the document appropriate for its purpose? How could it be improved?

Readers

3 Did you find the document interesting, persuasive, or otherwise useful? Why or why not?

4 Do the information, ideas, and arguments included in the document seem to take into account readers' needs, interests, values, beliefs, knowledge, and experience? How could this be improved?

5 Does the document seem fair? Did you detect any bias or agenda in the way information, ideas, and arguments were presented?

6 Did you find the reasons and evidence in the document convincing? What could I change to improve my argument?

7 Did you find the appeals appropriate? Effective? How could they be improved?

8 Did you notice any logical fallacies or other problems in reasoning?

Source

9 Does the document make sense? Can anything be added, clarified, or rearranged to help you understand the issue better? Do you think any of the details are unnecessary?

10 Do the sources strike you as reliable and appropriate? Does any of the information included in the document seem questionable?

Context

11 Is the subject sufficiently narrow and focused? Is the thesis statement clear?

12 Would any of the information be better presented in visual form?

13 Is the physical appearance of the document appropriate? Did you find the font easy to read? Did you find it easy to make comments?

For each of the points listed above, ask your reviewers to provide concrete advice about what you should do to improve your draft. It can help if you ask them to adopt the role of an editor—someone who is working with you to improve your draft.

IV Creating Your Document

17c

What should I focus on as I edit my document?

Before you begin to edit, remember that editing involves assessing the effectiveness, accuracy, and appropriateness of the words and sentences in a document, not its overall structure or ideas. If you're uncertain about whether you've organized your document as effectively as possible or whether you've provided enough support for your argument, deal with those issues first. In the same way that you wouldn't start painting a house until you've finished building the walls, hold off on editing until you're confident that you're finished revising.

Focus on Accuracy

You'll risk damaging your credibility if you provide inaccurate information in your document. To reduce this risk, do the following.

- **Check your facts and figures.** Your readers might think you're deliberately misleading them if you fail to provide accurate information. As you edit, return to your original sources or your notes to check any facts and figures.

- **Check every quotation.** Return to your original sources or consult your notes to ensure that you have quoted each source exactly. Make sure that you have noted any changes to a quotation with ellipsis marks or brackets (p. 265), and make sure that those changes haven't altered the original meaning of the passage. Make sure you have cited the source in the text and in a works cited or reference list.

- **Check the spelling of every name.** Don't rely on spelling checkers, which provide the correct spelling for only the most common or prominent names.

Focus on Economy

Editing for economy involves reducing the number of words needed to express an idea or convey information to your readers. Removing unnecessary modifiers and wordy introductory or stock phrases can make your writing more concise and to the point (p. 243). Editing for economy generally makes it easier for your readers to understand your meaning. However, you should use care when you edit for economy; your readers still need to understand the point you are trying to make.

Focus on Consistency

Editing your project document for consistency helps you present information in a uniform way. Use the following techniques to edit for consistency.

- **Treat concepts consistently.** Review your document for consistent treatment of concepts, information, ideas, definitions, and anecdotes.

- **Use numbers consistently.** Check the documentation system you are using for its guidelines on the treatment of numbers. You might find that you should spell out the numbers zero through ten and use Arabic numerals for numbers larger than ten.

- **Treat your sources consistently.** Avoid referring to some sources using first names and to others using honorifics, such as *Dr.*, *Mr.*, or *Ms.* Also check that you have cited your sources appropriately for the documentation style you are using, such as MLA or APA. Review each reference for consistent presentation of names, page numbers, and publication dates.

- **Format your document consistently.** Avoid any inconsistencies in your use of fonts, headings and subheadings, and tables and figures.

Focus on Style

Your readers will judge you—and what you have to say—not only on what you say but on how you say it. Edit for matters of style by choosing the right words, using active and passive voice appropriately, adopting a consistent point of view, rewriting complex sentences, varying your sentence length and structure, providing transitions, and avoiding sexist language (see Chapter 14).

Focus on Spelling, Grammar, and Punctuation

Poor spelling doesn't necessarily affect your ability to get your point across—in most cases readers will understand even the most atrociously spelled document—but it does affect what your readers think of you. Ignore enough spelling errors in your document and you'll erode their confidence in your ability to present information or make an argument. The same goes for grammar and punctuation. If you haven't made sure that subjects and verbs agree and that sentences end with the appropriate punctuation, a reader might not trust that you have presented your facts correctly.

17d

What strategies should I use to edit?

Thorough editing involves making several passes through your document to ensure that you've addressed accuracy, economy, and consistency; style; and spelling, grammar, and punctuation. The following tips can make that process both easier and more productive.

Read Carefully

As you've worked on your document, you've become quite familiar with it. As a result, it can be easy to read what you meant to write instead of what you actually wrote. The following strategies can help you read with fresh eyes.

IV Creating Your Document

- **Set your document aside before you edit.** If time permits, allow a day or two to pass before you begin editing your document. Taking time off between revising and editing can help you see your writing with new eyes.

- **Pause between sentences for a quick check.** Avoid getting caught up in the flow of your document—where the meaning takes precedence over the structure and expression of your sentences—by stopping after each sentence. Slowing down can help you identify problems with your text.

- **Read aloud.** Reading your document aloud can help you find problems that might not be apparent when it's read silently.

- **Read in reverse order.** To check for problems with individual sentences, start at the end of your document and read the last sentence first, then work backward through the document. To check for problems at the word level, read each word starting with the last one in the document. Disrupting the normal flow of your document can alert you to problems that might not stand out when it's read normally.

Mark and Search Your Document

i INFORMATION LITERACY   Use the following marking and searching strategies to edit for accuracy, consistency, and use of sexist language.

Mark Your Document   As you read, use a highlighting pen or the highlighter tool in your word processor to mark errors or information that should be double-checked. Consider using different colors to highlight specific types of problems, such as sexist language or inconsistent use of formal titles.

Use the Find and Replace Tools   Use your word processor to edit concepts, names, numbers, and titles for consistency and accuracy. Once you've identified a word or phrase that you'd like to check or change, you can search for it throughout your document. If you are referring to sources using a parenthetical style, such as MLA or APA, use the Find tool to search for an opening parenthesis. If you discover that you've consistently misspelled a word or name, use the Replace tool to correct it throughout your document.

Use the Split Window Tool   Some word processors allow you to split your window so that you can view different parts of your document at the same time. Use this tool to ensure that you are referring to a concept in the same way throughout your document or to check for consistent use of fonts, headings, subheadings, illustrations, and tables. ■

Use Spelling, Grammar, and Style Tools with Caution

i INFORMATION LITERACY   Most word processors provide tools to check spelling, grammar, punctuation, and style. Used with an awareness of their limitations, these tools can significantly reduce the effort required to edit a document. Spelling checkers have two primary limitations. First, they can't identify words that are spelled correctly but misused—such as *to/two/too*, *their/they're/there*, and *advice/advise*. Second, spelling checkers are ineffective when they run into a word they don't recognize, such as proper names, technical and scientific terms, and unusual words. To compound this problem, spelling checkers often suggest replacement words. If you take the advice, you'll end up with a paper full of incorrect words and misspelled names.

The main limitation of grammar, punctuation, and style checkers is inaccurate advice. Although much of the advice they offer is sound, a significant proportion is not. If you are confident about your knowledge of grammar, punctuation, and style, you can use the grammar and style-checking tools in your word processor to identify potential problem areas in your document. You'll find that these tools can point out problems you might have overlooked, such as a subject-verb disagreement that occurred when you revised a sentence. However, if you don't have a strong knowledge of grammar, punctuation, and style, you can easily be misled by inaccurate advice.

If you have any doubts about advice from your spelling checker, consult an up-to-date dictionary. If you have concerns about the suggestions you receive from your grammar, punctuation, and style checker, consult a good handbook. ▪

Ask for Feedback

One of the biggest challenges writers face is reading a draft of their own work as a reader rather than as the writer. Because you know what you're trying to say, you'll find it easy to understand your draft. And because you've read and reread your document so many times, you're likely to overlook errors in spelling, punctuation, and grammar. After you've edited your document, ask a friend, relative, or classmate to proofread it and to make note of any problems.

> **QUICK REFERENCE**

Editing

☑ Ensure your document is accurate. Check facts and figures, quotations, and spelling of names. (p. 310)

☑ Strive for economy. Remove unnecessary modifiers, eliminate unnecessary introductory phrases, and avoid use of stock phrases. (p. 310)

☑ Ensure that your document is consistent. Use concepts, numbers, and source information consistently. Check your document for consistent use of formatting and design. (p. 310)

☑ Use appropriate tone and style. Use appropriate words, rewrite overly complex sentences, and vary sentence length and structure. (p. 311)

☑ Check for correct spelling, grammar, and punctuation. Use your word processor's spelling, grammar, punctuation, and style tools; consult a handbook and dictionary; and ask someone to proofread your draft. (p. 312)

18

Presenting Your Work

> **Key Questions**

Writers are frequently asked to present their work to others. In some cases, a presentation accompanies a formal written document, such as a report or a proposal. In other cases, it takes the place of a written document. Traditionally, presentations have involved some form of oral presentation to an audience—anything from a casual talk to a formal address. It is now common, however, to find writers presenting their work in the form of a recorded talk, a set of multimedia slides, or a print or digital portfolio. In this chapter, you'll find discussions of strategies for presenting your work in face-to-face and online settings.

How can I make an oral presentation?

Writers are often asked to make a presentation, lead a discussion, or share their thoughts through speaking rather than writing. The ability to present your ideas through an oral presentation is an important skill that you'll use not only in your courses, but also throughout your professional and personal life.

Designing an effective oral presentation involves much more than simply taking what you've written and reading it aloud. When you're physically present to share your ideas, your ability to connect personally with your audience is affected by your choice of words, your physical appearance, your use of gestures and other forms of nonverbal communication, your ability to maintain eye contact, and variation in your tone of voice. In addition, your connection with your audience is affected by their ability to follow your line of argument. As you design your presentation, remember that most people find it more difficult to understand complex information, ideas, and arguments when they hear them than when they read (or reread) them. As a result, you should focus on how you can help your listeners follow your line of argument and see you as a credible presenter.

Consider Your Purpose and Audience   (?) WHAT'S MY PURPOSE?

The most important thing to remember about designing an oral presentation is engaging your audience and keeping them interested in your ideas. As you plan your presentation, ask what you want to accomplish, what your audience expects to hear, and how you can balance your purpose with their needs and interests. The answers to these questions will shape everything in your speech, from language choices to visual aids.

Narrow Your Scope

It is important to consider how much your audience knows about your topic. With their knowledge and expertise in mind, focus on a few key points and decide how much detail you'll need to provide to help them follow your line of argument. If you have already drafted a written document, use it as the basis for your presentation, but don't try to cover every point and every piece of supporting evidence you've included in your document.

Draw on your thesis statement (p. 207), reasons and evidence (p. 213), and conclusions to create a brief overview of your presentation that you can use in your introductory remarks. This "preview statement" will help your audience gain an understanding of your line of argument and the organization right from the start.

Create a Barebones Outline   [FRAMING MY ARGUMENT]

Once you've developed a focus for your presentation and determined its main point and general organization, you can create an outline. It's a good idea to begin with a basic outline that includes the following.

- an opening line that captures the attention of your audience
- a statement of your main point, typically in the form of a thesis statement
- a sentence establishing your credibility and purpose; your audience should understand that you care about and understand the issue, either through personal experience or through research, and that they can trust what you have to say
- two to four key points
- evidence to support your key points
- transition statements to guide your audience through your talk
- a conclusion that reinforces your audience's understanding of the main ideas they should take away from your talk
- a closing line or an invitation to ask questions that makes it clear to your audience that you have finished your presentation

WORKING TOGETHER

Develop Guidelines for Group Work

Group presentations are a common occurrence in college classrooms and the workplace. Unfortunately, many writers can look back at a group project and find something they didn't like about the experience. They might have been in a group dominated by an ineffective leader. They might have had to do far more than their fair share on a project. At the last minute, they might have been left in the lurch by someone who failed to deliver a critical part of the project. Whatever the reason, many writers often prefer to work alone. Yet group work can be productive and satisfying, and most experienced writers can point to a wide range of situations in which working with other writers significantly improved their work on a writing project.

To get ready to work with other writers, reflect on your experiences with group work. Then, working with the members of your group, develop a set of guidelines that would improve the quality of group work. To carry out this activity, follow these steps.

1 Individually, spend five minutes brainstorming (p. 20) or freewriting (p. 22) about your experiences with collaborative work. List both positive and negative experiences.

2 As a group, discuss your experiences. Each person should note the advantages and disadvantages of collaborative work.

3 As a group, identify the most significant challenges to working together effectively.

4 As a group, create a list of guidelines that would address these challenges.

Once you've completed the activity, share your guidelines with other groups in the class. As a class, create a list of guidelines for collaborative work in your course.

Think about Language

In an oral presentation, you'll use spoken language to connect personally with your audience. Through your choice of words, phrases, metaphors, imagery, and turns of speech, you'll engage your listeners in your argument and ideas. Your choices about how to address your audience should be made with the goal of engaging them in your issue. For example, you might talk about how your issue affects "us" and ask them to consider what "we" should do to address it.

As you consider your language choices, keep in mind that spoken language is usually more casual than written language. If you adopt the formal tone of an academic essay, you might sound stiff and unnatural. Keep in mind, as well, the power of repetition in oral presentations. You'll help your audience follow your line of argument by stating important points more than once and in different ways. Finally, consider the role of emotional appeals in your presentation (p. 217). To connect personally with your audience and to engage your audience with your issue, you should explore the use of vivid descriptions, surprising statistics, and humor. Don't rely heavily on emotional appeals, however. To maintain your credibility, you'll want to balance emotional appeals with logic by presenting sound reasoning and support for your argument (p. 213).

> **e** bedfordresearcher.com
> Tutorials > Digital Writing >
> Presentations

Design Speaker's Notes

Although many speakers write their presentations word for word, this strategy usually does not produce outstanding results. It's better to develop a set of speaker's notes to prompt yourself as you present your points. Using notes, instead of a word-for-word speech, will force you to speak directly to your listeners. Many seasoned speakers use note cards for their speaker's notes, as they are easy to hold in one hand and are not as distracting as fluttering paper. As you prepare your notes, make sure that they are easy to read, so that you can view your next point with a quick glance. You should include the following information in your speaker's notes.

- your opening line, written out in full, in case your mind goes blank due to nervousness
- your preview statement
- any statements that you need to give word for word, such as carefully worded observations about a controversial point or clear descriptions of a complex concept
- your supporting points and reminders of important evidence, including direct quotes, statistics, and names of important people
- transition sentences from one part of the presentation to the next
- memory prompts for parts of your presentation that you've found yourself forgetting as you practice
- reminders to use a visual aid, such as a chart

IV Creating Your Document

Engage with Your Audience

When you give an oral presentation, *how* you say something is almost as important in getting your message across as *what* you say. Important parts of your delivery include the following.

- **Maintain eye contact with your audience.** Eye contact communicates that you know your topic and that you care about making sure the audience understands your argument.

- **Vary the pitch of your voice.** Speaking in a monotone is the fastest way to put your audience to sleep. When you mention a startling statistic, raise your pitch. To demonstrate weight and importance, go to a lower register in your voice. Practice using vocal variety to make sure that it sounds natural.

- **Speak loudly.** You might feel like you're yelling, but the audience will let you know (by looking surprised) if you are too loud. Speakers rarely are.

- **Articulate every word clearly.** Consonants are often dropped in casual conversation, so you should pay attention to making them clearer than you would in normal speaking.

- **Slow down.** Most presenters speak much too quickly. Slow down your normal rate of speaking to make sure that the audience has time to process your words. As you practice, note where you tend to speed up and add a comment, such as "Slow Down!", to your speaker's notes.

View Speaker's Notes

Figures 18.1 through 18.3 show speaker's notes from Alexis Alvarez's oral presentation on the use of steroids by adolescent girls involved in sports.

1: Intro

Barry Bonds, A-Rod, Marion Jones, Lance Armstrong—what do all of these big names have in common? (**pause, wait for audience response**)

Include nonverbal cues in your note cards. This will remind you to interact with your audience.

1. **All accused of using performance-enhancing drugs**

2. **Used to seeing athletes break records, find out later about steroid use**

Use short phrases to cue your thoughts.

3. **Happening for younger athletes—including young women**

FIGURE 18.1 Note Card with a Nonverbal Cue

2: Establish Credibility & Preview

- My background as an athlete
- Explain why I care about the topic

SLOW DOWN!

Preview:

(1) First, I am going to talk about the positive impact that competitive athletics can have on young women.

(2) Then, I'll go over some of the negative consequences of competitive athletics on these young women, including steroid use.

(3) Finally, I want to talk about what parents and coaches can do to help create a positive athletic experience for these young women.

> Use brief reminders about nonverbal communication. Format your nonverbal cues in a different color so you don't accidentally speak them out loud.

> Write your preview statement word for word in your notes.

FIGURE 18.2 Note Card with a Preview Statement

3: Positive Impact of Competitive Athletics on Young Women

- President's Council on Physical Fitness and Exercise—ways sports impact young athletes

For the body:

- Less risk of heart disease and certain cancers as adults
- Improves:
  - Immune system
  - Posture
  - Strength
  - Flexibility
  - Endurance

Internal Transition: Also improves mental health

> Include your source citations. Refer to your sources to establish your credibility.

> Use internal transition cues to provide time for you to switch to your next note card as your audience thinks about the point.

FIGURE 18.3 Note Card with a Transition Cue and a Source Citation

IV Creating Your Document

CHECKLIST FOR DESIGNING ORAL PRESENTATIONS

✔ Determine the presentation's purpose.

✔ Narrow your presentation's scope to between two and four key points.

✔ Write a preview statement.

✔ Choose supporting evidence for your key points.

CHECKLIST FOR DESIGNING ORAL PRESENTATIONS (continued)

✔ Create a basic outline of your presentation.

✔ Prepare speaker's notes that you can read easily and quickly.

✔ Consider how the size and physical arrangement of the room will affect your ability to interact with your audience.

✔ Practice your presentation and ask for feedback from your practice audience.

✔ Arrive early to ensure adequate time for setup.

✔ During the presentation, observe and respond to your audience.

✔ Vary the pitch of your voice, speak loudly, and clearly articulate your words.

18b

How can I give a multimedia presentation?

Multimedia presentations allow you to illustrate points using more than spoken words alone, enabling your audience to follow your argument more easily and to understand complex ideas better. During these presentations, slides containing text or graphics are projected on a screen and, in some cases, audio, video, or animations are played. Multimedia presentations can also include links to the Web and embedded applications, such as spreadsheets. Some multimedia presentations are created for delivery via the Web, allowing a larger audience to access the presentation. Web-based multimedia presentations can be designed so that the speaker either appears in a smaller video window next to the presentation slides or provides a voiceover for each slide.

With multimedia presentation programs such as PowerPoint, Keynote, Impress, and Google Presentations, writers can create well-designed presentations. More specialized programs are also available for particular types of presentations. Prezi (**prezi.com**), for example, allows you to create "zooming" presentations that can be useful for creative purposes such as digital storytelling. Emaze (**emaze.com**), in contrast, offers a Web-based tool that stands out because of its innovative templates.

Consider Your Purpose   ? WHAT'S MY PURPOSE?

A strong multimedia presentation highlights your points without stealing the show. When used with moderation and created according to good design principles, multimedia elements can add credibility to a presentation, aid your ability to make your argument, and help your audience better understand complex ideas. A presentation on recent changes in education policy, for example, might include video clips in which students, teachers, parents, and community members discuss the effects of those policies or the reasons leading to their development. A presentation on social networking might include links to social networking sites, a chart illustrating the growth in use of such sites over the past decade, or screenshots showing a range of purposes for which such sites are used.

Consider Audience Expectations about Design

Poorly designed multimedia presentations sometimes seem as numerous as grains of sand on a Caribbean beach. Audiences in settings ranging from business meetings to conferences to lecture halls have been subjected to them, and perhaps you have been too. If so, you'll be aware of the benefits of keeping in mind the following design guidelines.

- Keep text to a minimum. A general rule is six words per bullet point, six bullet points per slide, and no more than six slides in a row of all text.
- Use readable fonts, such as 44-point Corbel for headings and 28-point Calibri for body text.
- To enhance the readability of slides, use either a light background with dark text or a dark background with light text.
- Choose a color scheme that reflects the purpose and tone of your line of argument. Use bright colors, for example, for a light-hearted topic. Use neutral colors for a serious presentation.
- Use audio, video, and animation with moderation. Generally, clips should run no longer than one minute each.
- Be consistent in your choice of fonts, colors, and page layout.
- Avoid the use of slow or overly complex transitions between slides.
- Avoid the use of distracting sound effects on slides or during slide transitions.

CHECKLIST FOR DESIGNING MULTIMEDIA PRESENTATIONS

✔ Create an outline of your presentation, focusing on the line of argument you want to present to your audience.

✔ Identify points that would benefit from multimedia illustrations.

✔ Follow effective design principles regarding color scheme, fonts, and page layout.

✔ Use multimedia elements in moderation.

✔ To ensure that your slides are readable and well designed, preview your presentation on a screen similar in size to what you will be using during your talk.

✔ Face your audience as you make your presentation.

✔ Use multimedia elements to advance your line of argument, pointing out important information and illustrations on slides.

✔ Create a backup plan in case technology fails. Consider using handouts as a backup.

IV Creating Your Document

View a Multimedia Presentation

Figures 18.4 through 18.7 show slides from a multimedia presentation designed by Elizabeth Leontiev.

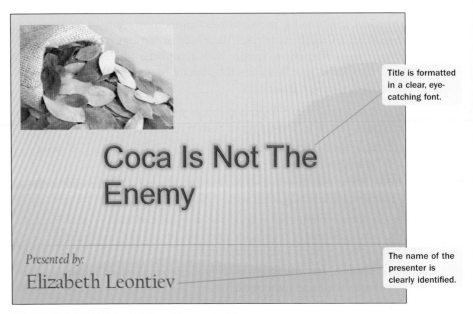

FIGURE 18.4 Title Slide [Ildi Papp/Shutterstock.]

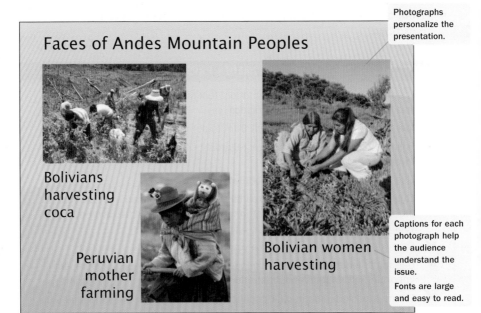

FIGURE 18.5 Slide with Photographs and Captions [Top left: AP Photos/Scott Dalton; bottom left: Sean Sprague/age footstock © Paolo Aguilar/epa/Corbis; right: © Paolo Aguilar/epa/Corbis.]

FIGURE 18.6 Slide Supporting the Writer's Presentation [Left: Gayvoronskaya-Yang/Shutterstock; right: Joerg Reuther/Shutterstock.]

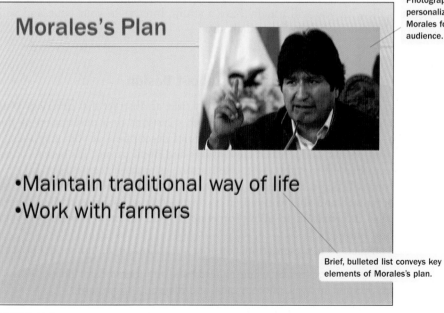

FIGURE 18.7 Slide with a Bulleted List [AP Photos/Juan Karita.]

IV Creating Your Document

18c

How can I create a poster presentation?

Poster presentations are often given at conferences, workshops, or symposiums for particular disciplines and professions. Most poster exhibitions involve numerous presenters, typically in a large room or hallway, and audience members who look for posters that interest them.

Consider Your Purpose and Audience   ❓ **WHAT'S MY PURPOSE?**

Your audience will usually have some background knowledge in the discipline or area that your presentation addresses. For example, if you are giving a poster presentation at a microbiology conference, it is safe to assume that the individuals who stop to talk with you will have at least a basic understanding of the central terminology and research methods used in the discipline. You should expect that most members of your audience will spend about five minutes talking with you about a poster. Be prepared, as a result, to provide a brief overview of your project, its key findings, and their significance. You might find it useful to create speaker's notes that you can view between discussions to remind yourself of the key points you want to make.

Be prepared, as well, for likely questions and challenges. The individuals who stop to talk with you will usually have a strong interest in your issue and will want to know what you've learned about it.

Consider Audience Expectations about Design

Posters typically include a large, explanatory title; an abstract that describes your study and its findings; a list of key research questions or a description of the problem or issue that you've addressed; a brief description of your methods; a summary of results; and a list of conclusions and implications. It's best to organize your poster left to right and top to bottom, as most of the people who view your poster will begin reading in the upper left corner. Your poster should be clearly organized and able to stand on its own — that is, your poster should have just enough information to allow someone to gain an understanding of your project and findings.

As you plan your presentation, consider the following design guidelines.

- Limit your use of text by using bulleted and numbered lists, tables, charts, graphs, images, photographs, and diagrams to present information.

- Format your poster so that all text and illustrations can be read from four feet away.

- Use a limited number of complementary fonts.
- Use empty space (sometimes called "white space") to reduce clutter and help your audience identify important information.
- Choose a color scheme that is consistent with your purpose.
- Use color to create interest and capture audience attention.

View a Poster

Figure 18.8 shows a poster developed by Nicholas Brothers about private military corporations.

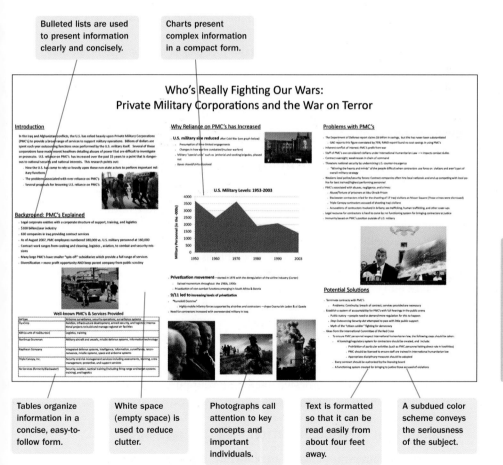

FIGURE 18.8 Poster for a Presentation [Top left: John Moore/Getty Images News; center left: © Ali Haider/epa/Corbis; bottom left: © Jim Young/Reuters/Corbis; bottom left: © Jim Young/Reuters/Corbis; top center: © Bettmann/Corbis center center: Source: U.S. State Department; bottom center: © Laszlo Balogh/Reuters/Corbis; top right: © Larry Downing/Reuters/Corbis; bottom right: © Bernd Obermann/Corbis.]

CHECKLIST FOR DESIGNING POSTER PRESENTATIONS

✔ Narrow your focus. Determine what absolutely needs to be included for a knowledgeable audience to understand your issue.

✔ Prepare a list of likely questions and your responses.

✔ Practice your presentation with a professor, an advisor, a friend, or a family member.

✔ Check for guidelines on poster size (many conferences have specific requirements).

✔ Plan for the physical setup of your poster. Will you need some sort of stand, or are you mounting your material on a board that stands on its own?

✔ Consider how to transport your poster to the site.

✔ During your presentation, remember that most questions are posed out of curiosity, not to catch you off guard. Be polite and professional, and avoid becoming defensive.

✔ Be prepared to share a handout about your project or even a complete written document.

18d

How can I develop a portfolio?

Portfolios are collections of written documents, reflections on the development of those documents, and related materials such as sources, notes, outlines, and brainstorming documents. They are typically, but not always, distributed via the Web. Widely used digital portfolio tools (typically referred to as e-Portfolios) include the Blackboard e-Portfolio system tools (available as part of these widely used course management systems) and the Writing Studio's free e-Portfolio tool (**writing .colostate.edu**). Some writers use programs such as PowerPoint or Dreamweaver to create portfolios that can be presented on a flash drive or some other form of offline storage. Still others use free Web tools such as Google Sites (**sites.google .com**) and Zeeblio (**zeeblio.com**) to create Web sites to present their portfolios.

Most of these tools allow you to add documents, develop a table of contents, and choose a design template. As you create a portfolio, you should consider a number of issues that affect design, including your purpose for sharing your work and the expectations of your readers.

Consider Your Writing Situation   WHAT'S MY PURPOSE?

Portfolios are sometimes created to showcase a writer's work, as might happen when you are seeking a job or wish to share your work with friends and family. Portfolios are also created in response to class assignments and institutional assessment plans. Some colleges and universities, for example, ask students to create portfolios so that they can measure the overall writing ability of their students.

Readers are likely to expect your portfolio to communicate clearly its purpose and content and make it easy to locate and view the documents you've provided. They are also likely to expect you to make it easy to get in touch with you. A well-designed portfolio should provide, as a result, something like a table of contents and your contact information. In an e-Portfolio, this might consist of a navigation menu or a set of links on the main page. In a print portfolio, this information might appear on the first or second page.

Select Your Materials

A writing portfolio typically includes some or all of the following materials.

- Your contact information (email address, phone number, and/or mailing address)
- An introduction to the portfolio that addresses its purpose and contents
- Final drafts of documents
- A reflection on the documents in the portfolio, on your growth as a writer, and on your goals as a writer. This often takes the form of a letter, statement, or brief essay. In an e-Portfolio, you could also share your reflections through video or audio clips.

A writing portfolio might include any of the following materials.

- Rough drafts of documents, often with comments from instructors or other writers
- Sources used in a particular writing project, along with any notes or source evaluations
- Planning notes, freewriting and other forms of idea generation, and maps or outlines
- Your comments on the work of other writers
- Grades and comments from instructors

Choose a Publishing Tool

As with other types of documents, your choice of tools for composing and publishing your portfolio will affect not only how you present your materials but also your understanding of what is possible to present. If you create a print portfolio, you can collect and bind your work, place all of your work in a folder, or simply clip it together and share it with a reader. If some of your work turns out to be difficult to include in a print portfolio, as might be the case with note cards or pages in a journal, you might photograph or scan them, print them, and include them with the rest of your work. If you create an e-Portfolio, you have many other options. You can distribute an e-Portfolio as:

- a single word processing or PDF file
- a collection of word processing or PDF documents

- a PowerPoint or Keynote presentation
- a Web site or blog
- a work in an e-Portfolio tool

Each of these tools offers possibilities quite different from what you can accomplish with a print portfolio. Even more important, the possibilities associated with each of these tools—and the experiences they can offer your readers—differ in striking ways from each other. Some tools will allow you to use video and audio clips while others will give you more control over the kind of navigation menus and links you can create. Some programs, such as PowerPoint and Keynote, will make it relatively easy to use page transitions and animations or to switch easily from one color scheme to another. Your decisions about the tool you use to create your portfolio, as a result, should reflect your purpose and an awareness of what a particular tool allows you to do.

Design Your Portfolio

As you design your portfolio, keep the principles of simplicity and consistency in mind. You should develop a consistent look and feel for your portfolio, focusing in particular on issues such as color and font scheme, page layout, and navigation tools. It is likely, of course, that the individual documents in your portfolio will have their own distinctive designs. Readers will expect this and, if the design of these documents is essential to their effect, you should not redesign them. However, if you are working with a set of essays in which your design decisions are

CHECKLIST FOR DEVELOPING PORTFOLIOS

✔ Reflect on your writing situation, paying particular attention to the purposes of the portfolio, your readers' expectations, and the context in which your portfolio will be read.

✔ Select materials for your portfolio.

✔ Choose a tool to compose and publish your portfolio.

✔ Choose an organizing pattern for your portfolio.

✔ Develop a simple, consistent design for your portfolio. Pay particular attention to:

- font scheme
- color scheme
- page layout
- navigation tools

✔ Create an introduction that calls attention to particular aspects of your portfolio.

✔ Reflect on the materials presented in your portfolio, calling attention to key issues and offering evidence to support your conclusions.

less important than what you've written, you might consider reformatting them so that they follow the design you've chosen for the portfolio as a whole.

You should also spend some time thinking about how your readers will work with your portfolio. If you are creating a print portfolio, you might use a table of contents to help readers see how your portfolio is organized. You might also attach colored tabs to pages to help them find the start of each document. If you are creating an e-portfolio, you might think about the type of navigation tools you might provide, such as tables of contents and menus, and you might consider the use of hyperlinks to help readers move from one part of the e-portfolio to another.

Your design decisions should help your readers work easily and quickly with the materials you've included in your portfolio. In general, simple, uncluttered designs that use readable fonts and consistent colors will allow your readers to work through your portfolio without distraction.

 QUICK REFERENCE

Presenting Your Work

- ✔ Make an oral presentation. (p. 315)
- ✔ Give a multimedia presentation. (p. 320)
- ✔ Create a poster presentation. (p. 324)
- ✔ Develop a portfolio. (p. 326)

IV Creating Your Document

The Bedford Researcher

I	Joining the Conversation
II	Working with Sources
III	Collecting Information
IV	Creating Your Document
V	**Documenting Sources**

PART V

Documenting Sources

As you complete your work on your research writing project, you can turn your attention fully to the task of citing and documenting your sources. This section discusses reasons to document your sources and describes four major documentation systems: MLA, APA, *Chicago*, and CSE.

19

Understanding Documentation Systems

Key Questions

19a. What is a documentation system and which one should I use? 333

19b. How should I document my sources? 335

Research writers document their sources to avoid plagiarism, give credit to others who have written about an issue, and create a record of their work that others can follow and build upon. These reasons illustrate the concept of writing as participation in a community of writers and readers. By documenting your sources, you show that you are aware that other writers have contributed to the conversation about your issue and that you respect them enough to acknowledge their contributions. In turn, you expect that writers who read your document will cite your work.

Documenting your sources can help you achieve your purpose as a writer, such as establishing your authority and persuading your readers. If your readers find that you haven't documented your sources, they'll either suspect that you're careless or decide that you're dishonest. In either case, they won't trust what you have to say.

19a

What is a documentation system and which one should I use?

Many professional organizations and publications have developed their own rules for formatting documents and citing sources. As a result, writers in many disciplines know how to cite their sources clearly and consistently, and their readers know what to expect. For example, imagine that a psychologist is writing an article for the *Journal of Counseling Psychology*. The writer is likely to know that submissions to the journal go through a rigorous review for substance and style before being accepted for publication. Among its expectations, the journal requires that writers use the documentation system created by the American Psychological Association (APA). Given the high level of competition for space in the journal, the writer knows that even if the article is substantive and compelling, it will not be accepted for publication if it does not use APA style appropriately. After ensuring the article is clearly written and well argued, the writer double-checks the article to ensure it follows the formatting and source citation guidelines specified by the APA documentation system.

Several of the documentation systems most commonly used in the various academic disciplines are covered in this book.

- **MLA** This style, from the Modern Language Association, is used primarily in the humanities—English, philosophy, linguistics, world languages, and so on. See Chapter 20.

- **APA** This style, from the American Psychological Association, is used mainly in the social sciences—psychology, sociology, anthropology, political science, economics, education, and so on. See Chapter 21.

- *Chicago* Developed by the University of Chicago Press, this style is used primarily in history, journalism, and the humanities. See Chapter 22.

- **CSE** This style, from the Council of Science Editors (formerly the Council of Biology Editors), is used mainly in the physical and life sciences—chemistry, geology, biology, botany, and so on—and in mathematics. See Chapter 23.

Your choice of documentation system will be guided by the discipline or field within which you are writing and by any requirements associated with your research writing project. If your project has been assigned to you, ask the person who assigned it or someone who has written a similar document which documentation system you should use. If you are working on a project for a writing class, your instructor will most likely tell you which documentation system to follow.

If you don't have access to advice about which documentation system is best for your project, consider the discipline in which you are writing. In engineering and business, for example, a wide range of documentation styles are used, with most of them specific to scholarly journals or specializations within the discipline. Consider as well the genre you have chosen for your project document. The manner in which sources are cited can vary widely from one type of document to another. For example, while academic essays and articles appearing in scholarly journals typically use a documentation system such as MLA, APA, *Chicago*, or CSE, newspaper and magazine articles often do not and rely instead on identification of sources in the main text of the document rather than in a works cited or reference list.

19b

How should I document my sources?

How you document sources will depend on your writing situation. Most often, you will:

1. provide a reference to your source within the text
2. provide a complete set of citations, or formal acknowledgments, for your sources in a works cited or reference list

The specific format of your in-text citations will depend on the documentation system you use. If you use MLA or APA style, you'll cite — or formally acknowledge — information in the text using parentheses and add a list of sources to the end of your document. If you use the *Chicago* notes style, you'll acknowledge your sources in footnotes or endnotes and supply a bibliography at the end of your document. If you use the CSE citation-sequence style, you will number the citations in your text and list your sources in the order in which they are referenced. If you write a digital document that cites other online sources, you might simply link to your sources.

ℹ INFORMATION LITERACY Many digital resources — such as library catalogs, databases, and Web sites — provide quick links that attempt to demonstrate the citation for a given source. Use caution when relying on these citation generators, which may not exactly match the style of the documentation system you are using. ▪

Table 19.1 presents examples of in-text citations and works cited or reference list entries for each of these major documentation styles. As Table 19.1 shows, although each style differs from the others, especially in the handling of in-text citations, they share a number of similarities.

With the exception of Web style, key publication information is usually provided in a works cited list, reference list, or bibliography. These lists appear at the end of the document and include the following information about each source.

- author(s) and/or editor(s)
- title
- publication date
- publisher and city of publication (for books)
- periodical name, volume, issue, and page numbers (for articles)
- URL and access date (for online publications)

Each documentation system creates an association between citations in the text of a document and the works cited page.

V Documenting Sources

My Research Project

Review Your Working Bibliography

Start by reviewing the source citations in your working bibliography. Make sure that you've used the appropriate documentation system and entered sufficient source information to fully document your sources.

bedfordresearcher.com
My Research Project Activities > Review Your Working Bibliography

TABLE 19.1 EXAMPLES OF IN-TEXT CITATIONS AND BIBLIOGRAPHIC ENTRIES FOR MAJOR DOCUMENTATION STYLES

Style	In-Text Citation	Works Cited or Reference List Entry
MLA Style	Over the past few years, the Bolivian government has not seen much economic growth (Gordon 16).	Gordon, Gretchen. "The United States, Bolivia, and the Political Economy of Coca." *Multinational Monitor* 27.1 (2006): 15–20. Print.
APA Style	Over the past few years, the Bolivian government has not seen much economic growth (Gordon, 2006, p. 16).	Gordon, G. (2006). The United States, Bolivia, and the political economy of coca. *Multinational Monitor, 27*(1), 15–20.
***Chicago* Style: Notes System**	Over the past few years, the Bolivian government has not seen much economic growth.[3] 3. Gretchen Gordon, "The United States, Bolivia, and the Political Economy of Coca," *Multinational Monitor* 27, no. 1 (2006): 16.	Gordon, Gretchen. "The United States, Bolivia, and the Political Economy of Coca." *Multinational Monitor* 27, no. 1 (2006): 15–20. *Note: The citation is placed in a footnote or endnote, and again in the bibliography.*
CSE Style: Citation-Sequence System	Over the past few years, the Bolivian government has not seen much economic growth.[3]	3. Gordon G. The United States, Bolivia, and the political economy of coca. Multinational Monitor. 2006;27(1):15–20. *Note: Numbered citations are placed in the reference list in the order in which they appear in the text.*
Web Style	Gordon notes that, over the past few years, the Bolivian government has not seen much economic growth.	Many Web documents will link directly to a cited work, as shown here. Or they may use a style such as MLA, APA, *Chicago*, or CSE.

> QUICK REFERENCE

Understanding Documentation Systems

☑ Choose an appropriate documentation system. (p. 333)

☑ Document your sources in your text and, depending on the documentation system, create a works cited list, reference list, or bibliography. (p. 335)

☑ Review your sources for accuracy and completeness. (p. 336)

20

Using MLA Style

> **Key Questions**
>
> **20a. How do I cite sources within the text of my document?**   341
>
> **20b. How do I prepare the list of works cited?**   344

Modern Language Association (MLA) style, used primarily in the humanities, emphasizes the authors of a source and the pages on which information is located in the source. Writers who use the MLA documentation system cite, or formally acknowledge, source information within their text using parentheses, and they provide a list of sources in a works cited list at the end of their document.

For more information about MLA style, consult the *MLA Handbook for Writers of Research Papers*, Seventh Edition. Information about the MLA Handbook can also be found at **mla.org**.

To see featured writer Elizabeth Leontiev's research essay, formatted in MLA style, turn to p. 363.

CITATION TUTORIALS FOR COMMON WORKS CITED ENTRIES

CITATIONS WITHIN YOUR TEXT

ENTRIES IN YOUR WORKS CITED LIST

Books, Conference Proceedings, and Dissertations

Sources in Journals, Magazines, and Newspapers

20a

How do I cite sources within the text of my document?

MLA style uses parentheses for in-text citations to acknowledge the use of another author's words, facts, and ideas. When you refer to a source within your text, place the author's last name and specific page number(s)—if the source is paginated—within parentheses. Your reader then can go to the works cited list at the end of your document and find a full citation there.

1. Basic Format for Direct Quotation Often you will want to name the author of a source within your sentence rather than in a parenthetical citation. By doing so, you create a context for the material (words, facts, or ideas) that you are including and indicate where the information from the author begins. When you are using a direct quotation from a source and have named the author in your sentence, place only the page number in parentheses after the quotation. The period follows the parentheses.

> Vargas reports that "each year, unintentional drownings kill more than 830 children younger than 14 and cause, on average, 3,600 injuries" (B01).

When you have not mentioned the author in your sentence, you must place the author's name and the page number in parentheses after the quotation. Again, the period follows the parentheses.

> After car accidents, "drowning is the second-leading cause of unintentional deaths" among toddlers (Vargas B01).

When you are using a block (or extended) quotation, the parenthetical citation comes after the final punctuation and a single space.

If you continue to refer to a single source for several sentences in a row within one paragraph—and without intervening references to another source—you may reserve your reference to the end of the paragraph. However, be sure to include all of the relevant page numbers.

2. Basic Format for a Summary or Paraphrase When you are summarizing or paraphrasing information gained from a source, you are still required to cite the source. If you name the author in your sentence, place only the page number in parentheses after the paraphrase or summary. Punctuation marks follow the parentheses. When you have not mentioned the author in your sentence, you must place the author's name and the page number in parentheses after the quotation.

> Vargas points out that drowning doesn't happen in the manner you might expect; children slip under water quietly, making very little noise to alert unsuspecting parents or guardians (B01).

3. Entire Source   If you are referring to an entire source rather than to a specific page or pages, you will not need a parenthetical citation.

> The explorations of race in ZZ Packer's *Drinking Coffee Elsewhere* can be linked thematically to the treatment of immigrants in Lahiri's work.

4. Corporate or Group Author   Cite the corporation or group as you would an individual author. You may use abbreviations for the source in subsequent references if you add the abbreviation in parentheses at the first mention of the name.

> The Brown University Office of Financial Aid (BUOFA) has adopted a policy that first-year students will not be expected to work as part of their financial aid package (12). BUOFA will award these students a one-time grant to help compensate for the income lost by not working (14).

5. Unknown Author   If you are citing a source that has no known author, such as the book *Through Palestine with the 20th Machine Gun Squadron*, use a brief version of the title in the parenthetical citation.

> The members of the squadron rode horses while the cooks were issued bicycles, requiring the cooks to exert quite a lot of effort pedaling through the desert sand (*Through Palestine* 17).

6. Two or More Works by the Same Author   For references to authors with more than one work in your works cited list, insert a short version of the title between author and page number, separating the author and the title with a comma.

> (Ishiguro, *Unconsoled* 146)

> (Ishiguro, *Remains* 77)

7. Two or More Authors with the Same Last Name   Include the first initial and last name in the parenthetical citations.

> (G. Martin 354)

> (F. Martin 169)

8. Two or Three Authors   Include the last name of each author in your citation.

> Casting physically attractive actors wins points with film audiences: "Primitive as the association between outward strength and moral force may be, it has its undeniable appeal" (Clarke, Johnson, and Evans 228).

9. Four or More Authors   Use only the last name of the first author and the abbreviation "et al." (Latin for "and others"). Note that there is no comma between the author's name and "et al."

> (Barnes et al. 44)

10. Literary Work   Along with the page number(s), give other identifying information, such as a chapter, scene, or line number, that will help readers find the passage.

> The sense of social claustrophobia is never as palpable in *The Age of Innocence* as when Newland realizes that all of New York society has conspired to cover up what it believes to be an affair between him and Madame Olenska (Wharton 339; ch. 33).

11. Work in an Anthology   Cite the author of the work, not the editor of the anthology. (See also #34 on p. 348.)

> In "Beneath the Deep, Slow Motion," Leo says, "The Chinese call anger a weary bird with no place to roost" (Barkley 163).

12. Sacred Text   Give the name of the edition you are using along with the chapter and verse (or their equivalent).

> He should consider that "Where no counsel is, the people fall: but in the multitude of counselors there is safety" (*King James Bible*, Prov. 11.14).

> In the Qu'ran, sinners are said to be blind to their sins ("The Cow" 2.7).

13. Two or More Works   Use a semicolon to separate entries.

> Forethought is key in survival, whether it involves remembering extra water on a safari trail or gathering food for a long winter in ancient times (Wither and Hosking 4; Estes and Otte 2).

14. Source Quoted in Another Source   Ideally, you will be able to find the primary, or original, source for material used in your research project document. If you quote or paraphrase a secondary source — a source that contains information about a primary source — use the abbreviation "qtd. in" (for "quoted in") when you cite the source.

> MIT professor Richard Lundgren has stated, "global warming is small and magnified by the alarmists with deeply compromised political pressure, data fudging, and out and out guesswork" (qtd. in de Garmo A13).

15. Print Source without Page Numbers   If no page numbers are provided, list only the author's name in parentheses.

> Although his work has been influenced by many graphic artists, it remains essentially text based (Fitzgerald).

16. Digital or Nonprint Source Give a page, section, paragraph, or screen number, if used, in the parenthetical citation.

Teters believes the mascots dehumanize Native Americans, allowing spectators to dismiss the Native Americans' true culture as well as their hardships (Saraceno, par. 20).

20b

How do I prepare the list of works cited?

MLA-style research documents include a reference list titled "Works Cited," which begins on a new page at the end of the document. If you wish to acknowledge sources that you read but did not cite in your text, you may title the list "Works Consulted" and include them. The list is alphabetized by author. If the author's name is unknown, alphabetize the entry using the title of the source. To cite more than one work by the same author, use the author's name in the first entry. Thereafter, use three hyphens followed by a period in place of the author's name; list the entries alphabetically by title. All entries in the list are double-spaced, with no extra space between entries. Entries are formatted with a hanging indent: The first line of an entry is flush with the left margin and subsequent lines are indented one-half inch or five spaces.

In longer documents, a list of works cited may be given at the end of each chapter or section. In digital documents that use links, such as a Web site, the list of works cited is often a separate page to which other pages are linked. To see a works cited list in MLA style, see p. 367.

Books, Conference Proceedings, and Dissertations

17. One Author

Kolbert, Elizabeth. *The Sixth Extinction: An Unnatural History*. New York: Henry Holt, 2014. Print.

18. Two or Three Authors List all the authors in the same order as on the title page, last name first for only the first author listed. Use commas to separate authors' names.

Brynjolfsson, Erik, and Andrew McAfee. *The Second Machine Age: Work, Progress, and Prosperity in a Time of Brilliant Technologies*. New York: W. W. Norton, 2014. Print.

Datta, Sona, Pratapaditya Pal, and Rivka Israel. *Urban Patua: The Art of Jamini Roy*. Mumbai: Marg, 2010. Print.

How do I cite books using MLA style?

When citing a book, use the information from the title page and the copyright page (on the reverse side of the title page), not from the book's cover or a library catalog. Consult pp. 341–44 for additional models for citing books.

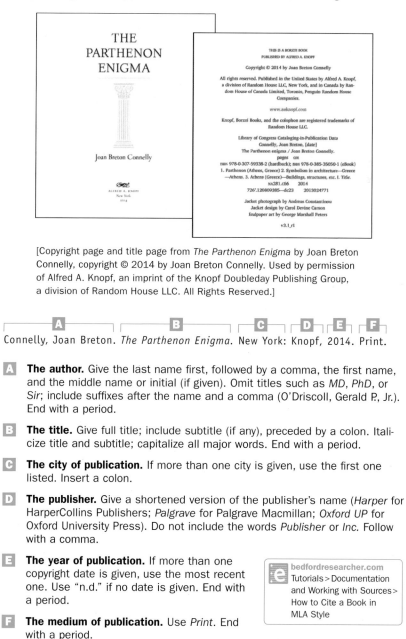

[Copyright page and title page from *The Parthenon Enigma* by Joan Breton Connelly, copyright © 2014 by Joan Breton Connelly. Used by permission of Alfred A. Knopf, an imprint of the Knopf Doubleday Publishing Group, a division of Random House LLC. All Rights Reserved.]

A **B** **C** **D** **E** **F**

Connelly, Joan Breton. *The Parthenon Enigma*. New York: Knopf, 2014. Print.

A **The author.** Give the last name first, followed by a comma, the first name, and the middle name or initial (if given). Omit titles such as *MD*, *PhD*, or *Sir*; include suffixes after the name and a comma (O'Driscoll, Gerald P., Jr.). End with a period.

B **The title.** Give full title; include subtitle (if any), preceded by a colon. Italicize title and subtitle; capitalize all major words. End with a period.

C **The city of publication.** If more than one city is given, use the first one listed. Insert a colon.

D **The publisher.** Give a shortened version of the publisher's name (*Harper* for HarperCollins Publishers; *Palgrave* for Palgrave Macmillan; *Oxford UP* for Oxford University Press). Do not include the words *Publisher* or *Inc.* Follow with a comma.

E **The year of publication.** If more than one copyright date is given, use the most recent one. Use "n.d." if no date is given. End with a period.

F **The medium of publication.** Use *Print*. End with a period.

> bedfordresearcher.com
> Tutorials > Documentation and Working with Sources > How to Cite a Book in MLA Style

19. Four or More Authors   Provide the first author's name (last name first) followed by a comma, and then the abbreviation "et al." (Latin for "and others").

Levin, Miriam, et al. *Urban Modernity: Cultural Innovation in the Second Industrial Revolution*. Cambridge: MIT P, 2010. Print.

20. Corporate or Group Author   Write out the full name of the corporation or group, and cite the name as you would an author. This name is often also the name of the publisher.

National Geographic. *In Focus: National Geographic Greatest Portraits*. Washington: Natl. Geographic, 2010. Print.

21. Unknown Author   When no author is listed on the title or copyright page, begin the entry with the title of the work. Alphabetize the entry by the first word of the title other than *A, An,* or *The*.

The Book of Nature. Munich: Kunth, 2010. Print.

22. Two or More Books by the Same Author   List the entries alphabetically by title.

Pollan, Michael. *Cooked: A Natural History of Transformation*. New York: Penguin, 2013. Print.

---. *Food Rules: An Eater's Manual*. New York: Penguin, 2009. Print.

23. Editor(s)   Use the abbreviation "ed." or "eds."

Olson, Gregory Allen, ed. *Landmark Speeches on the Vietnam War*. College Station: Texas A&M UP, 2010. Print.

24. Translated Book   List the author first and then the title, followed by the name of the translator and publication information. Use the abbreviation "Trans."

Eco, Umberto. *History of Beauty*. Trans. Alastair McEwen. New York: Rizzoli, 2010. Print.

25. Book in a Language Other than English   You may give a translation of the book's title in brackets.

Márquez, Gabriel García. *Del amor y otros demonios* [*Of Love and Other Demons*]. New York: Vintage, 2010. Print.

26. Edition Other than the First   Include the number of the edition and the abbreviation "ed." after the title.

Gmelch, George, Robert V. Kemper, and Walter P. Zenner. *Urban Life: Readings in the Anthropology of the City.* 5th ed. Long Grove: Waveland, 2010. Print.

27. Multivolume Work Include the total number of volumes and the abbreviation "vols." after the title.

Chapman, Roger, and James Ciment, eds. *Culture Wars in America: An Encyclopedia of Issues, Viewpoints, and Voices.* 2nd ed. 3 vols. Armonk, NY: M.E. Sharpe, 2014. Print.

If you have used only one of the volumes in your document, include the volume number after the title. Then list the total number of volumes after the medium of publication.

Di Berardino, Angelo, et al. *Encyclopedia of Ancient Christianity.* Vol. 2. Downers Grove, IL: InterVarsity, 2014. Print. 3 vols.

28. Book in a Series If a series name and/or number appears on the title page, include it at the end of the citation, after the medium. If the word "Series" is part of the series name, use the abbreviation "Ser."

Hernández, Felipe, Peter Kellett, and Lea K. Allen, eds. *Rethinking the Informal City: Critical Perspectives from Latin America.* New York: Berghahn, 2010. Print. Remapping Cultural History 11.

29. Republished Book Indicate the original date of publication after the title.

Melville, Herman. *Bartleby, the Scrivener: A Story of Wall-Street.* 1853. Champaign: Book Jungle, 2010. Print.

30. Book with a Title within the Title

Stuckey, Sterling. *African Culture and Melville's Art: The Creative Process in* Benito Cereno *and* Moby-Dick. New York: Oxford UP, 2009. Print.

31. Author with an Editor Include the name of the editor (first name first) after the title.

Mathews, John Joseph. *Twenty Thousand Mornings: An Autobiography.* Ed. Susan Kalter. Norman: U of Oklahoma P, 2012. Print.

32. Anthology To cite an anthology of essays, stories, or poems or a collection of articles, list the editor or editors first (as on the title page), followed by the abbreviation "ed." or "eds."

Knox, Peter E., and J. C. McKeown, eds. *The Oxford Anthology of Roman Literature.* New York: Oxford UP, 2013. Print.

33. Foreword, Introduction, Preface, or Afterword Begin with the author of the part you are citing and the name of that part. Continue with the title of the work and its author (first name first), following "By." At the end of the entry, list the inclusive page numbers on which the part of the book appears.

Burns, Ken. Foreword. *David's Inferno: My Journey through the Dark Wood of Depression.* By David Blistein. Hobart, NY: Hatherleigh, 2013. xi–xii. Print.

If the author of the foreword or other part is also the author of the work, use only the last name after "By."

Olson, Gregory Allen. Introduction. *Landmark Speeches on the Vietnam War.* By Olson. College Station: Texas A&M UP, 2010. 1–12. Print.

If the foreword or other part has a title, include the title in quotation marks between the author and the name of the part.

Walker, Alice. "Learning to Dance." Preface. *Hard Times Require Furious Dancing.* By Walker. Novato: New World, 2010. xv–xvi. Print.

34. Chapter in an Edited Book or Selection in an Anthology Begin your citation with the author and the title of the chapter or selection. Follow this with the title of the anthology or collection, the abbreviation "Ed." (meaning "Edited by"), and names of the editors (first name first) as well as publication information. At the end of your entry, give the inclusive page numbers for the selection or chapter.

Dugan, Máire A., and Dennis Carey. "Toward a Definition of Peace Studies." *Three Decades of Peace Education around the World: An Anthology.* Eds. Robin J. Burns and Robert Aspelagh. New York: Routledge, 2013. 79–96. Print.

35. Two or More Works from One Anthology To avoid repeating the same information about the anthology several times, include the anthology itself in your list of works cited.

Fishkin, Shelley Fisher, ed. *The Mark Twain Anthology: Great Writers on His Life and Works.* New York: Lib. Classics, 2010. Print.

In the entries for individual selections or chapters, list the author and title of the selection (in quotation marks) and cross-reference the anthology by giving the editor's name and the page numbers on which the selection appears, with no comma between them. Do not include the medium of publication.

Eliot, T. S. "Huck and Oliver." Fishkin 246–51.

Kipling, Rudyard. "On the Art of Mark Twain." Fishkin 66–77.

36. Screenplay

Cholodenko, Lisa, and Stuart Blumberg. *The Kids Are All Right: The Shooting Script*. New York: Newmarket, 2011. Print.

37. Published Proceedings of a Conference
Provide information as you would for a book, adding information about the conference after the title: the date, sponsors, and location of the conference. Then add the publication data as for a book. End with the medium.

Davis, Susan, ed. *Future Nature, Future Culture(s): Proceedings for Balance — Unbalance 2013 International Conference*. 31 May–2 Jun 2013, Noosa Biosphere Limited and Central Queensland University. Noosa, Australia: Central Queensland U, 2013. Print.

38. Paper Published in Proceedings of a Conference
Treat a selection from conference proceedings as you would a selection in an edited collection.

Chang, Charles B. "Learning to Produce a Multidimensional Laryngeal Contrast." *New Sounds 2010: Proceedings of the 6th International Symposium on the Acquisition of Second Language Speech*. Ed. K. Dziubalska-Kołaczyk, M. Wrembel, and M. Kul. 1-3 May 2010, School of English, Adam Mickiewicz University. Poznan: Adam Mickiewicz University. 89–94. Print.

39. Sacred Text
Include the title of the version as it appears on the title page. If the title does not identify the version, place that information directly after the title.

Holy Bible: New Revised Standard Version. Nashville: Abingdon, 2010. Print.

40. Published Dissertation or Thesis
Cite as you would a book, with the title in italics, but include information specific to the dissertation, such as the school and the year the dissertation was accepted.

Hitotsubashi, N. S. *The Life and Times of* Beowulf: *Monsters and Heroes in the Named Lands of the North*. Diss. Wheaton College, 2013. Norton, MA: Wheaton College, 2013. Print.

41. Unpublished Dissertation or Thesis
Place the title of the thesis or dissertation in quotation marks and add information about the type of dissertation, the school, and the date.

Higgins, Wayne C. "Urban Regeneration: Enabled by Mobility Centric Architecture." MA thesis. MIT, 2010. Print.

42. Abstract of a Dissertation or Thesis Treat an abstract as you would an article in a journal. First give the information for the dissertation. Then add the source, abbreviated either *DA* or *DAI* (for *Dissertation Abstracts* or *Dissertation Abstracts International*), volume number, year (in parentheses), and item number page numbers.

Bruce, La Marr Jurelle. "'The Domain of the Marvelous': Madness, Blackness, and
    Radical Creativity." Diss. Yale U, 2013. *DAI* 74.11 (2014): 3572026. Print.

Sources in Journals, Magazines, and Newspapers

43. Article in a Journal Paginated by Volume Most journals continue pagination for an entire year, beginning again at page 1 only in the first volume of the next year. After the journal title (omit introductory articles such as *The*), list the volume number and issue number (if any) with a period between them, the year of publication in parentheses, a colon, and inclusive page numbers. End with the medium.

Kinzser, Charles K. "Considering Literacy and Policy in the Context of Digital
    Environments." *Language Arts* 88.1 (2010): 51–61. Print.

44. Article in a Journal Paginated by Issue Some journals begin at page 1 for every issue. After the volume number, add a period and the issue number, with no space.

Love, Jessica. "They Get to Me: A Young Psycholinguist Confesses Her Strong
    Attraction to Pronouns." *American Scholar* 79.2 (2010): 64–71. Print.

45. Article That Skips Pages Give only the first page number and a plus sign (+), with no space between.

Mahler, Jonathan. "The Second Coming." *New York Times Magazine* 15 Aug. 2010:
    30+. Print.

46. Article with a Quotation in the Title Enclose the quotation in single quotation marks within the article title, which is enclosed in double quotation marks.

Díaz, Isabel González. "Enriching the 'Rags-to-Riches' Myth." *Black Scholar*
    43.1/2 (2013): 43–51. Print.

47. Article in a Monthly or Bimonthly Magazine After the author's name and title of the article, list the title of the magazine, the date (use abbreviations for all months except May, June, and July), and the inclusive pages.

McArdle, Megan. "The Freeloaders: How a Generation of File-Sharers Is Ruining
    the Future of Entertainment." *Atlantic* May 2010: 34–35. Print.

TUTORIAL

How do I cite articles from periodicals using MLA style?

Periodicals include journals, magazines, and newspapers. This page gives an example of a citation for a print journal article. Models for citing articles from magazines and newspapers are on pp. 350–53.

If you need to cite a periodical article you accessed electronically, follow the guidelines below and see also p. 361. [Chris Lezotte, Born to take the highway: Women, the automobile, and rock n roll. Published 6 Sept 2013 in The Journal of American Culture 36:3. Republished with permission of John Wiley & Sons Limited conveyed through Copyright Clearance Center, Inc.]

> bedfordresearcher.com
> Tutorials > Documentation and Working with Sources > How to Cite an Article in MLA Style

Lezotte, Chris. "Born to Take the Highway: Women, the Automobile, and Rock 'n' Roll." *Journal of American Culture* 36.3 (2013): 161–76. Print.

A   The author. Give last name first, followed by a comma, first name, and middle initial (if given). Omit titles such as *MD*, *PhD*, or *Sir*; include suffixes after the name and a comma (O'Driscoll, Gerald P., Jr.). End with a period.

B   The article title. Give the full title; include the subtitle (if any), preceded by a colon. Enclose the title and subtitle in quotation marks, and capitalize all major words. Place a period inside the closing quotation mark.

C   The periodical title. Italicize the periodical title; exclude any initial *A*, *An*, or *The*; capitalize all major words.

D   The volume number and issue number. For journals, include the volume number; if the journal uses issue numbers, include a period (no space) and then the issue number as well.

E   The date of publication. For journals, give the year in parentheses followed by a colon. For monthly magazines, don't use parentheses; give the month and year. For weekly magazines and newspapers, don't use parentheses; give the day, month, and year (in that order). Abbreviate the names of all months except May, June, and July.

F   Inclusive page number(s). For numbers 100 and above, give only the last two digits and any other preceding digits if different from the first number (22–28, 402–10, 1437–45, 592–603). If an article continues on non-consecutive pages, include the first page number followed by a plus sign. Include section letters for newspapers, if relevant. End with a period.

G   The medium of publication. For print publications, use *Print*. End with a period.

48. Article in a Weekly or Biweekly Magazine Give the exact date of publication, inverted.

Greider, William. "The Federal Reserve at 100 and Why It Needs a Total Overhaul."
   Nation 3 Mar. 2014: 12–19. Print.

49. Article in a Daily Newspaper If the title of the newspaper begins with *The*, omit the word. If the newspaper is not a national newspaper (such as the *Wall Street Journal*, *Christian Science Monitor*, or *Chronicle of Higher Education*) or the city of publication is not part of its title, give the name of the city in square brackets [Cincinnati] after the title. List the date in inverted order and, if the masthead indicates that the paper has more than one edition, give this information after the date ("natl. ed.," "late ed."). Follow with a colon and a space, and end with the page numbers (use the section letter before the page number if the newspaper uses letters to designate sections). If the article does not appear on consecutive pages, write only the first page number and a plus sign (+), with no space between.

Eisenberg, Anne. "The Path to Reading a Newborn's DNA Map." *New York Times*
   9 Feb. 2014: B3. Print.

50. Unsigned Article in a Newspaper or Magazine Begin with the title of the article. Alphabetize by the first word other than *A*, *An*, or *The*.

"FDA Sends e-Cigarette Companies a Warning." *Detroit News* 10 Sept. 2010: A22.
   Print.

51. Editorial in a Newspaper Include the word "Editorial" after the title.

"Fixing Immigration, in Principle." Editorial. *New York Times* 31 Jan. 2014: A20.
   Print.

52. Letter to the Editor Include the word "Letter" after the title.

Hasl, Rudy. "Jefferson's Mammoth." Letter. *Smithsonian* June 2010: 6. Print.

53. Review Give the author name and title of the review if provided, then include the words "Rev. of," followed by the title of the work under review; a comma; the word "by" (for a book) or "dir." (for a play or film); and the name of the author or director. Continue with publication information for the review.

Hornaday, Ann. "A Tough Tale Told with Tenderness." Rev. of *The Fighter*, dir.
   David O. Russell. *Washington Post* 17 Dec. 2010: T23. Print.

Johnson, Bethany. Rev. of *Lotions, Potions, Pills, and Magic: Health Care in Early
   America*, by Elaine G. Breslaw. *North Carolina Historical Review* 90.4 (2013):
   416–17. Print.

54. Published Interview Begin with the person interviewed. If the published interview has a title, give it in quotation marks. If not, write the word "Interview" (no quotation marks or italics). If an interviewer is identified and relevant to your project, give that name next. Then supply the publication data.

Kelley, Kitty. "The Secret Sharer." Interview by Deborah Solomon. *New York Times Magazine* 11 Apr. 2010: MM18. Print.

55. Article in a Special Issue After the author and the title of the article (in quotation marks) include the title of the special issue (in italics), then write the words "Spec. issue of" before the regular title of the periodical.

Redd, Steven B., and Alex Mitz. "Policy Perspectives on National Security and Foreign Policy Decision Making." *2013 Public Policy Yearbook.* Spec. issue of *Policy Studies Journal* 41.S1 (2013): S11–S37. Print.

Print Reference Works

56. Encyclopedia, Dictionary, Thesaurus, Handbook, or Almanac Cite as you would a book (see p. 345).

57. Entry in an Encyclopedia, Dictionary, Thesaurus, Handbook, or Almanac In many cases, the entries and articles in reference works are unsigned. Therefore, begin your citation with the title of the entry in quotation marks, followed by a period. Give the title of the reference work, italicized, and the edition and year of publication. If a reference work is not well known (perhaps because it includes highly specialized information), provide the editor's name as well as all of the bibliographic information. If the entries in the work are arranged alphabetically, you may omit the volume and page numbers.

"Aboriginal English." *A Dictionary of Varieties of English.* Ed. Raymond Hickey. West Sussex, UK: Wiley, 2014. Print.

If you cite a specific definition, include that information after the title of the entry, adding the abbreviation "Def." and the number of the definition.

"Heterodox." Def. 1. *Oxford English Dictionary.* 3rd ed. 2010. Print.

58. Map or Chart Generally, treat a map or chart as you would a book without authors. Give its title (italicized), the word "Map" or "Chart," and publication information. For a map in an atlas, give the map title (in quotation marks) followed by publication information for the atlas and page numbers for the map. If the creator of the map or chart is listed, use his or her name as you would an author's name.

Benchmark Recreation Map: Oregon. Map. Chicago: Rand, 2010. Print.

"Africa: Political." Map. *Oxford Atlas of the World.* 17th ed. New York: Oxford UP, 2010. 255. Print.

59. Government Publications   In most cases, cite the government agency as the author. If there is a named author, editor, or compiler, provide that name after the title. Use the abbreviations "Dept." for department, "Cong." for Congress, "S." for Senate, "H." or "HR" for House of Representatives, "Res." for resolution, "Rept." for report, "Doc." for document, and "GPO" for Government Printing Office.

United States. Cong. House. Committee on Science and Technology. *America*
    Competes: Big Picture Perspectives on the Need for Innovation, Investments
    in R&D, and a Commitment to STEM Education. 111th Cong., 2nd sess. Serial
    no. 111-70. Washington: GPO, 2010. Print.

For congressional bills (not reports or resolutions), do not include a period after the abbreviations "S" or "HR".

If you are citing from the *Congressional Record,* the entry is simply *Cong. Rec.* followed by the date, a colon, and the page numbers.

60. Pamphlet   Format the entry as you would for a book (see p. 345).

Florida Power and Light. *Safety Planning Information for Neighbors of FPL's*
    St. Lucie Nuclear Power Plant. Miami: FPL, 2013. Print.

Field Sources

61. Personal Interview   Place the name of the person interviewed first, words to indicate how the interview was conducted ("Personal interview," "Telephone interview," or "E-mail interview"), and the date. (Note that MLA style is to hyphenate "e-mail.")

Parlon, Charisse. Personal interview. 4 Feb. 2014.

62. Unpublished Letter   If written to you, give the writer's name, the words "Letter to the author" (no quotation marks or italics), and the date the letter was written. End with the form of the material: use "MS" (for manuscript) for a letter written by hand and "TS" (for typescript) for typed letters.

Boyd, Edward. Letter to the author. 11 Aug. 2014. TS.

If the letter was written to someone else, give that name rather than "the author."

63. Lecture or Public Address   Give the speaker's name and the title of the lecture (if there is one). If the lecture was part of a meeting or convention, identify that event. Conclude with the event data, including venue, city, and date. End with the appropriate label ("Lecture," "Panel discussion," "Reading").

Joseph, Branden. "1962." Dept. of Art History, U of Chicago, Cochrane Art
    Center, Chicago. 11 Mar. 2010. Lecture.

Media Sources

64. Film or Video Recording   Generally begin with the title of the film or recording (italicized). Always supply the name of the director (following the abbreviation "Dir."), the distributor, and the year of original release. You may also insert other relevant information, such as the names of performers or screenplay writers, before the distributor.

Saving Mr. Banks. Dir. John Lee Hancock. Perf. Tom Hanks and Emma Thompson.
     Disney, 2013. Film.

If you wish to emphasize an individual's role in the film or movie, such as the director or screenplay writer, you may list that name first.

Olivier, Laurence, dir. and perf. *Hamlet*. Paramount, 1948. Film.

For media other than film (such as videotape and DVD), cite it as for a film but identify the medium at the end.

Guess Who's Coming to Dinner. Dir. Stanley Kramer. 1967. Sony Pictures Home
     Entertainment, 2008. DVD.

65. Television Program   If the program has named episodes or segments, list those in quotation marks. Then include the title of the program or series (italicized), the network, the station's call letters and city (if any), and the date on which you watched the program. If there are relevant persons to name (such as an author, a director, a host, a narrator, or an actor), include that information after the title. Add the medium at the end.

"The Sign of Three." *Sherlock*. BBC. 26 Jan. 2014. Television.

66. Radio Program   Cite as you would a television program.

"A Closer Look at How Corporations Influence Congress." *Fresh Air*. Host Terry
     Gross. Natl. Public Radio. WHYY, Philadelphia. 13 Feb. 2014. Radio.

67. Radio or Television Interview   Provide the name of the person interviewed and the title of the interview. If there is no title, write "Interview" and, if relevant, the name of the interviewer. Then provide the name of the program, the network, the call letters of the station, the city, and the date.

Assange, Julian. Interview by Katie Couric. *CBS Evening News*. CBS. KCTV, Kansas
     City. 20 Dec. 2010. Television.

68. Sound Recording   Begin with the name of the person whose work you want to highlight: the composer, the conductor, or the performer. Next list the title, followed by names of other artists (composer, conductor, performers), with abbreviations indicating their roles. The recording information includes the manufacturer and the date. Add the medium of the recording at the end (CD, LP, Audiocassette, Audiotape, or MP3 file).

Kuroda, Takuya. *Rising Son*. Prod. José James. Blue Note, 2014. CD.

If you wish to cite a particular track on the recording, give its performer and title (in quotation marks) and then proceed with the information about the recording. For live recordings, include the date of the performance between the title and the recording data.

Cash, Johnny. "Folsom Prison Blues." *The Great Lost Performance*. Rec. 27 July
   1990. Island, 2007. MP3 file.

69. Musical Composition   Give the composer and title. Italicize the title unless it identifies the composition by form ("symphony," "suite"), number ("op. 39," "K. 231"), or key ("E flat").

Berlioz, Hector. Symphonie Fantastique. op. 14.

If you are referring to a published score, provide publication data as you would for a book. Insert the date of composition between the title and the publication information and capitalize the abbreviations *no.* and *op.*

Minchin, Tim. *Roald Dahl's Matilda — the Musical*. 2012. London: Wise-Music
   Sales. 2013. Print.

70. Live Performance   Generally, begin with the title of the performance (italicized). Then give the author and director; the major performers; and theater, city, and date.

1776. By Peter Stone. Dir. Jon Huffman. Perf. Peter Riopelle, Mark Sawyer-Daily,
   and Mason Stewart. Bomhard Theatre, Louisville. 27 June 2010. Performance.

71. Work of Art   Give the name of the artist, the title of the work (italicized), the date of composition, the medium of composition, and the name of the collection, museum or owner, and the city. If you are citing artwork published in a book, add the publication information for the book and the medium of publication ("Print") at the end.

Barlow, Phyllida. *Broken Upturned House,* 2013. Steel armature, polystyrene,
   cement, scrim, paint, PVA, plywood, timber, polyfiller, varnish. Norton Mus.
   of Art, West Palm Beach.

72. Advertisement   Provide the name of the product, service, or organization being advertised, followed by the word "Advertisement." Then provide the usual publication information.

Bose. Advertisement. *Sports Illustrated* 4 Oct. 2010: 69. Print.

73. Cartoon Treat a cartoon like an article in a newspaper or magazine. Give the cartoonist's name, the title of the cartoon if there is one (in quotation marks), the word "Cartoon," and the publication data for the source.

Chast, Roz. "Dadonomics." Cartoon. *New Yorker* 1 Nov. 2010: 75. Print.

Digital Sources

74. Article from an Online Database or Subscription Service Cite it as you would a print article, then give the name of the database in italics, the medium consulted ("Web"), and the date you accessed the article. (See also p. 358.)

Gregory, Alice. "Perfect Imperfection." *American Photo* 24.2 (2014): 38–46. *Art Full Text*. Web. 23 Mar. 2014.

75. Abstract from an Online Database Provide the publication information for the source, followed by the word "Abstract," the name of the database, the medium ("Web"), and the date you accessed it.

Ashley, Seth. "The Closing of the Ether: Communication Policy and the Public Interest in the United States and Great Britain, 1921–1926." *Communication Law and Policy* 18.1 (2013): 36. Abstract. *LexisNexis Academic*. Web. 29 Jan. 2014.

76. Entire Web Site Provide the name of the Web site in italics, the sponsor or publisher, the date of publication or last update, the medium, and the date of access.

Solar System Exploration. NASA, 5 Mar. 2014. Web. 6 Mar. 2014.

77. Work from a Professional or Commercial Web Site Include the author (if available), the title of the document in quotation marks, and the title of the Web site in italics. Then give the sponsor or publisher, the date of publication or last update, the medium, and the access date. (See also p. 360.)

"Davenport City Profile." *CityForward*. IBM Corp. 2014. Web. 23 Feb. 2014.

78. Academic Course or Department Web Site For a course page, give the name of the instructor, the course title in italics, a description such as "Course home page," the course dates, the department, the institution, the medium, and the access date. For a department page, give the department name, a description such as "Home page," the institution, the date of the last update, the medium, and your access date.

Global Studies Dept. *Crossing Borders: Islam and the West*. Course home page. Spring 2011. International Programs, Alfred U. Web. 20 Jan. 2014.

Coll. of Health and Human Sciences. Home page. Colorado State U, 2014. Web. 24 Feb. 2014.

TUTORIAL

How do I cite articles from databases using MLA style?

Libraries subscribe to services such as LexisNexis, InfoTrac, and EBSCOhost that provide access to databases of digital texts. The databases provide publication information, abstracts, and complete text of documents in a specific subject, discipline, or profession. (See also Chapter 9.) [Courtesy of EBSCO.]

A ⌐ ⌐**B**

Mackey, Allison. "Troubling Humanitarian Consumption: Reframing Relationality

C **D**

in African Child Soldier Narratives." *Research in African Literatures* 44.4

E **F** **G** **H** **I**

(2013): 99–122. *Academic Search Premier*. Web. 22 Feb. 2014.

A **The author.** Give the last name first, followed by a comma and the first name. Omit titles such as *MD*, *PhD*, or *Sir*; include suffixes after the name and a comma (O'Driscoll, Gerald P., Jr.). End with a period.

B **The article title.** Give the title and subtitle (if any), preceded by a colon. Enclose the full title in quotation marks, and capitalize all major words. Place a period inside the closing quotation mark.

C **The periodical title.** Italicize the periodical title; exclude any initial *A*, *An*, or *The*; capitalize all major words.

D **The volume number and issue number if appropriate.** For journals, give the volume number; if the journal uses issue numbers, include a period (no space) and then the issue number as well.

E **The date of publication.** For journals, give the year in parentheses, followed by a colon. For monthly magazines, don't use parentheses; give the month and year. For weekly magazines and newspapers, give the day, month, and year.

F **Inclusive page number(s).** For numbers 100 and above, give only the last two digits and any other preceding digits if different from the first number (22–28, 402–10, 1437–45, 592–603). Include section letters for newspapers, if relevant.

G **The name of the database.** Italicize the name of the database, followed by a period.

H **The medium consulted.** Use "Web" followed by a period.

I **The date of access.** Use the day-month-year format; abbreviate all months except May, June, and July. End with a period.

bedfordresearcher.com
Tutorials > Documentation and Working with Sources > How to Cite a Database in MLA Style

79. Work from a Personal Web Site   Include the name of the person who created the site. If the site has no title, give a description such as "Home page." Then follow with the sponsor of the Web site (if any), the date of the last update, the medium ("Web"), and your date of access.

Kennedy, Pagan. Home page. 27 Aug. 2012. Web. 27 Feb. 2014.

80. Message Posted to a Newsgroup, Email List, or Online Discussion Forum Cite the name of the person who posted the message; the title (from the subject line, in quotation marks); if the posting has no title, add the phrase "Online posting"; then add the name of the Web site (italicized), the sponsor or publisher, the date of the message, the medium ("Web"), and the date you accessed the posting.

McKinney, Julie. "Proposed Updates to Food Labels." *Learning Disabilities*
   Discussion List. Natl. Inst. for Literacy, 5 Mar. 2014. Web. 30 Mar. 2014.

81. Article Posted on a Wiki

"Pointillism." *Wikipedia*. Wikimedia Foundation, 23 Feb. 2014. Web. 24 Feb. 2014.

82. Entire Blog   To cite an entire Weblog, give the author (if available), the title of the Weblog (italicized), the sponsor or publisher (if none, use "N.p."), the date of publication or last update, the medium ("Web"), and the date of access.

Castrodale, Beth. *Small Press Picks: Favorite New Fiction from Small and Micro*
   Publishers. N.p. 3 Feb. 2014. 28 Feb. 2014.

83. Entry or Comment Posted on a Blog   To cite an entry or a comment on a Weblog, give the author of the entry or comment (if available), the title of the entry or comment in quotation marks, the title of the blog (italicized), the sponsor or publisher, the date the material was posted, the medium, and the access date.

Lalami, Laila. "Quotable: Cormac McCarthy." *Laila Lalami*. Laila Lalami, 28 Apr.
   2010. Web. 17 Aug. 2014.

84. Email message   Cite the sender of the message; the title (from the subject line, in quotation marks); "Message to" the recipient of the message; the date of the message; and the medium ("E-mail"). (Note that MLA style is to hyphenate "e-mail.")

Martin, Adrianna. "Re: Questions about the District Budget." Message to the
   author. 19 Jan. 2014. E-mail.

Pabon, Xavier. "Brainstorming for Essay." Message to Brayden Perry. 24 Apr. 2014.
   E-mail.

TUTORIAL

How do I cite works from Web sites using MLA style?

You will likely need to search the site to find some of the citation information you need. For some sites, all of the details may not be available; find as many as you can. Remember that the information you provide should allow readers to retrace your steps electronically to locate the sources. Consult pages 357–62 for additional models for citing Web sources. [Laila Alawa and Wardah Khalid/Patheos.com.]

A B

Alawa, Laila, and Wardah Khalid. "The Problem with Petitions — For Muslim

C

School Holidays and Otherwise." *Altmuslim: Global Perspectives on Muslim*

D E F G

Life, Politics, and Culture. Patheos, 29 Jan. 2014. Web. 13 Mar. 2014.

A **The author of the work.** Give the last name first, followed by a comma, the first name, and the middle initial (if given). Omit titles such as *MD*, *PhD*, or *Sir*; include suffixes after the name and a comma (O'Driscoll, Gerald P., Jr.,). Insert a period. If no author is given, begin with the title of the work.

B **The title of the work.** Give the full title; include the subtitle (if any), preceded by a colon. Enclose the title and subtitle in quotation marks, and capitalize all major words. Place a period inside the closing quotation mark. If you are citing an entire Web site, begin with the title of the Web site.

C **The title of the Web site.** Give the title of the entire site italicized. If there is no clear title and it is a personal home page, use "Home page" without italicizing it. End with a period.

D **The name of the sponsoring organization.** Look for the sponsor's name at the bottom of the site's home page. Follow with a comma.

E **The date of publication or most recent update.** Use the day-month-year format; abbreviate all months except May, June, and July. End with a period.

F **The medium consulted.** For works found online, use "Web" followed by a period.

G **The date you accessed it.** Give the most recent date you accessed the site. End with a period.

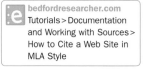

bedfordresearcher.com
Tutorials > Documentation and Working with Sources > How to Cite a Web Site in MLA Style

85. E-Book   Cite an e-book as you would a print book; then give the title of the format, database, or Web site (italicized), the medium ("Web"), and the access date (see also #17 on p. 344).

Selingo, Jeffrey J. *College (Un)Bound: The Future of Higher Education and What It*
    Means for Students. Boston: New Harvest–Houghton Mifflin, 2013. *Kindle*
    Book. Web. 1 Feb. 2014.

86. Article in an Online Periodical   Provide the author, the title of the article (in quotation marks), and the name of the Web site (in italics). Then add the publisher or sponsor, the date of publication, the medium, and your date of access (see also #43 on p. 350).

Hurley, Dan. "Nicotine, the Wonder Drug?" *Discover.* Kalmbach Publishing Co.,
    Mar. 2014. Web. 3 Apr. 2014.

87. Online Poem   Cite an online poem as you would a print poem, followed by the name of the site, the sponsoring organization (if any), the date of publication or latest update, the medium, and the date of access.

Shumate, David. "If You Hire a Poet to Draw a Map." *Kimonos in the Closet.*
    Pittsburgh: U of Pittsburgh P, 2014. *Verse Daily.* Verse Daily, 2 Mar. 2014.
    Web. 24 Apr. 2014.

88. Online Editorial or Letter to the Editor   Include "Letter" or "Editorial" after the title (if any). Follow with the title of the Web site, the sponsor or publisher, the date of publication, medium, and date of access (see also #51 and #52 on p. 352).

Quigley, Richard J. "Russia's Image versus Reality." Letter. *Chicago Tribune.*
    Chicago Tribune, 21 Feb. 2014. Web. 17 Mar. 2014.

89. Online Review   (See also #53 on p. 352.)

Freeman, Dyson. "The Case for Blunders." Rev. of *Brilliant Blunders,* by Mario
    Livio. *New York Review of Books.* NYREV, 6 Mar. 2014. Web. 12 Apr. 2014.

90. Entry in an Online Reference Work   (See also #57 on p. 353.)

"Wali." *Banglapedia: National Encyclopedia of Bangladesh.* 2nd ed. Banglapedia,
    2012. Web. 20 Apr. 2014.

91. Online Film, Television Program, or Video Clip   (See also #64 and 65 on p. 355.)

"Pray the Devil Back to Hell." *Women War and Peace.* Creators Abigail Disney,
    Pamela Hogan, and Gini Reticker. PBS, 18 Oct. 2011. Web. 15 Mar. 2014.

DeGeneres, Ellen. "It Gets Better." *YouTube.* YouTube, 30 Sept. 2010. Web.
    22 Feb. 2014.

92. Online Work of Art or Image   Cite like a work of art but omit the medium of composition, and after the location, add the title of the Web site or database (italicized), the medium consulted ("Web"), and your date of access. (See also #71 on p. 356.)

Johns, Jasper. *Perilous Night.* 1982. Natl. Gallery of Art, Washington. *National Gallery of Art.* Web. 10 Mar. 2014.

Gardner, Alexander. *President Lincoln on Battle-field of Antietam.* Oct. 1862. *Flickr.com.* Web. 26 Mar. 2014.

93. Online Map or Chart   (See also #58 on p. 353.)

"Fisherman's Wharf, San Francisco." Map. *Google Maps.* Google, 2014. Web. 19 Apr. 2014.

94. Online Advertisement   Give the item or organization being advertised followed by the word "Advertisement." Then add the information about the Web site. (See also #72 on p. 356.)

Akron-Canton Regional Food Bank. Advertisement. *Ohio.com.* Ohio.com, 2014. Web. 6 Mar. 2014.

95. Other Online Sources   For other online sources, adapt the guidelines to the medium. Include as much information as necessary for your readers to easily find your source. The examples below are for a radio program available in an online archive, and an online archive of oral-history interviews.

"True Urban Legends." Host Ira Glass. *This American Life.* Chicago Public Radio. WBEZ, Chicago. 23 Apr. 2010. MP3 file. 18 Mar. 2014.

Bruno, Angelo, and Eddie Nieves. "I Think I Could Have Done Another 31 Years." *StoryCorps.* StoryCorps, n.d. Web. 2 Mar. 2014.

96. CD-ROM   Treat a CD-ROM as you would a book, noting "CD-ROM" as the medium.

Orman, Suze. *Stop Identity Theft Now Kit.* Salt Lake City: TrustID, 2008. CD-ROM.

97. Multidisc CD-ROM   Either give the total number of discs or, if you used only one of the discs, give the number of that disc.

Lindley, Philip, and Alex Moseley. *English Parish Churches.* Turnhout: Brepols, 2007. CD-ROM. Disc 2.

98. Computer Software or Video Game   Cite computer software as you would a book. Provide additional information about the medium on which it is distributed (CD-ROM, Xbox 360, etc.) and the version.

Uncharted: Drake's Fortune. Foster City: Sony Computer Entertainment, 2007. CD-ROM.

MLA-Style Research Essay

Elizabeth Leontiev

Professor Lynda Haas

WR 39C

10 June 2010

Coca Is Not the Enemy

To most Americans, the word *cocaine* evokes images of the illegal white powder and those who abuse it, yet the word has a different meaning to the coca farmers of South America. *Erythroxylum coca*, or the tropical coca plant, has been grown in the mountainous regions of Colombia, Bolivia, and Peru since 3000 BC. The coca plant has been valued for centuries by indigenous South American cultures for its ability to alleviate pain and combat fatigue and hunger (Forero, "Bolivia's Knot"). Just as many Americans drink coffee every day, natives of the Andes Mountains chew coca leaves and drink coca tea for a mild stimulant effect. Easy to grow, not addictive, and offering many medicinal benefits, coca is part of the everyday lives of the people in this region.

Aside from its medicinal and cultural value, coca is also important to Andean farmers economically, as a result of a long history of illegal drug trafficking. Dried coca leaves mixed with lime paste or alkaline ashes produce cocaine—a highly addictive substance that delivers euphoric sensations accompanied by hallucinations (Gibson). Supplying the coca for the illegal drug trade accounts for a tremendous portion of the Bolivian, Peruvian, and Colombian economies. In Bolivia, for example, it has been estimated that coca makes up anywhere from one-third to three-quarters of the country's total exports (Kurtz-Phelan 108). In 1990 the Bolivian president even asserted that 70% of the Bolivian gross domestic product was due to the coca trade (Kurtz-Phelan 108).

Despite such statistics, for most farmers in the region growing coca is about making a living and supporting their families, not becoming wealthy or furthering the use of cocaine. More than half of Bolivians live in poverty, with a large portion earning less than $2 a day (U.S. Foreign Affairs, Defense, and Trade Div. 2). In the words of one coca farmer, "'The U.S. says 'Coca is cocaine, coca is cocaine,' but it isn't,' says Argote. 'Coca is the tree of the poor'" (Schultz and Gordon). Can we reduce cocaine trafficking without eliminating coca? Evo Morales, the current president of Bolivia, believes the answer is

The heading includes writer's name, instructor's name, course, and date.

Title is centered, and essay is double-spaced with one-inch margins.

Elizabeth's introduction provides important context.

MLA-style in-text citations include author and page number.

Elizabeth cites an indirect source: words quoted in another source.

"yes" and has advocated a "zero cocaine, not zero coca" policy in his country. This policy would allow native Andeans to maintain their cultural practices, boost South American economies, and channel coca into a new market, away from cocaine traffickers. For all of these reasons, the Morales plan should become a model for other coca-growing countries.

Morales gained recognition for his "zero cocaine, not zero coca" program during his 2005 presidential campaign. His policy aims to legalize the coca crop but not the cocaine that is produced from that crop. He also expressed a desire to get the United Nations to rescind its 1961 convention declaring coca an illegal narcotic. In December 2005, Morales won the election with more than 50% of the vote, and he made history as the first indigenous Bolivian president (Forero, "Coca").

> A brief title distinguishes two sources by the same author.

Morales's plan promotes the best interests of the Andean farmers and offers multiple economic and social benefits. First, South American countries would be able to export non-narcotic coca-based products, such as soaps, toothpaste, tea, alcohol, and candies (Logan). Products like these are already being produced for local use in Bolivia, and manufacturers would like to seek an international market for them. These new coca products would stimulate the Bolivian economy and put money in the pockets of coca growers to support their families, rather than in the pockets of the drug lords. Second, if the market for legal coca were to increase, farmers would be able to make a legal living from a crop that has long been a mainstay of their culture. With legal coca products, the indigenous people of the Andes would not have to sacrifice their way of life. Finally, an increase in the demand for legal coca products might also result in less cocaine being trafficked illegally around the world, since more of the raw material for cocaine will be used for new legal coca products.

> Elizabeth addresses counter-arguments and provides support for her assertion.

In order to understand the benefits of Morales's plan, we must first investigate the failures of the alternatives. The United States has been waging various "wars on drugs" for decades, spending up to $1 billion trying to control cocaine trafficking from South America (Forero, "Bolivia's Knot"). In the 1990s the United States shifted its efforts from fighting the trafficking of cocaine to eliminating the source of the drug—the coca plants growing in Bolivia, Colombia, and Peru. Coca eradication has taken two main forms. In Bolivia, bands of soldiers move through the countryside using machetes to hack away coca plants (see Fig. 1). This process is slow and dangerous, and there have been reports of human rights abuses and extreme violence against the peasant farmers who grow coca (Gordon 16). In nearby

> Reference to a photograph included in the essay.

Leontiev   3

Colombia, the United States funded aerial fumigation programs to
poison the coca fields; native farmers complain that the herbicide
used in the fumigation is causing health problems and environmental
pollution ("US Weighs Cost"). By destroying coca plants in Colombia,
the United States has "left 500 million people poorer" (Padgett 8). It
is unclear whether fumigation results in any benefit, since farmers
respond by moving farther and farther into the jungle and replanting
their crops there (Otis). Such dense areas are harder to see and
therefore harder to fumigate effectively.

FIG. 1. Manual eradication of a coca field in Chapare, Bolivia.
United Nations Office on Drugs and Crime. [© Courtesy of
United Nations Office on Drugs and Crime.]

Caption includes figure number and source information.

Another U.S. effort encouraged farmers to replace coca with
other crops, like coffee, bananas, and pineapples. Alternative crop
programs seem like a good idea because they will get rid of the coca
farms, but they have their own drawbacks. First, as coca grower
Leonida Zurita-Vargas noted in her 2003 *New York Times* opinion
column, transporting heavy fruits like pineapples from the mountainous
coca-growing regions is expensive and difficult. Second, growers are
seldom willing to give up coca farming because they can make more
money by selling coca than any other crop. Even with government
incentives for alternative cropping, coca remains more profitable, a big
inducement for poor farmers who can barely support their families and
send their children to school. The *Houston Chronicle* reports that even
in areas where farmers have planted alternative crops, the farmers are
being lured back to the coca plant by larger profits (Otis). One coca
farmer asserted that by growing coca, he could "make ten times what

The in-text citation provides just the author's name, since the online source did not include page numbers.

Leontiev   4

he would make by growing pineapples or yucca" (Harman). Ultimately, alternative cropping means less coca production overall, which will drive up coca prices and encourage more farmers to abandon their alternative crops and return to coca.

After decades of legislation and various eradication programs, cocaine trafficking remains a major problem. The most recent data show that coca cultivation throughout the region remains steady (see Fig. 2). Contrary to dire predictions, there has been no major spike in Bolivian coca production since Morales was elected at the end of 2005. Furthermore, critics argue that cocaine is no less available in the United States than before eradication began, and street prices remain low (Forero, "Colombia's Coca"). Instead of curbing cocaine trafficking, America's war on drugs has turned out to be a war against the peasants of Colombia, Bolivia, and Peru.

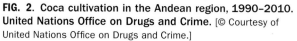

FIG. 2. Coca cultivation in the Andean region, 1990–2010. United Nations Office on Drugs and Crime. [© Courtesy of United Nations Office on Drugs and Crime.]

Throughout the years, the various wars on drugs have failed to produce effective results for the United States. The programs of alternative cropping and eradication did not succeed due to the legislators' inability to see life through the eyes of the coca farmers— something Evo Morales is able to do. In 2006, Morales addressed the UN General Assembly and waved a coca leaf in the air: "[This] is a green coca leaf, it is not the white of cocaine. [T]his coca leaf represents Andean culture; it is a coca leaf that represents the environment and the hope of our peoples." Through his bold program of "zero cocaine, not zero coca," Morales aims to improve the lives of Andean farmers and the economies of South American countries, while still remaining committed to controlling the illegal drug trade. Morales's example illustrates that it is time to work *with* coca farmers, rather than against them.

The conclusion reinforces Elizabeth's thesis statement.

MLA

V Documenting Sources

Leontiev 5

Works Cited

Forero, Juan. "Bolivia's Knot: No to Cocaine, but Yes to Coca." *New York Times*. New York Times, 12 Feb. 2006. Web. 3 June 2007.

- - -. "Coca Advocate Wins Election for President in Bolivia." *New York Times*. New York Times, 19 Dec. 2005. Web. 3 June 2007.

- - -. "Colombia's Coca Survives U.S. Plan to Uproot It." *New York Times*. New York Times, 19 Aug. 2006. Web. 3 June 2007.

Gibson, Arthur C. "Freud's Magical Drug." *The Mildred E. Mathias Botanical Garden*. UCLA, 1999. Web. 22 Apr. 2007.

Gordon, Gretchen. "The United States, Bolivia, and the Political Economy of Coca." *Multinational Monitor* 27.1 (2006): 15-20. *Expanded Academic ASAP*. Web. 15 May 2007.

Harman, Danna. "In Bolivia, a Setback for US Anti-Coca Drive." *Christian Science Monitor*. Christian Science Monitor, 22 Dec. 2005. Web. 12 May 2007.

Kurtz-Phelan, Daniel. "'Coca Is Everything Here': Hard Truths about Bolivia's Drug War." *World Policy Journal* 22.3 (Fall 2005): 103-12. *Academic OneFile*. Web. 22 Apr. 2007.

Logan, Sam. "De-Vilifying the Coca Leaf." *Andean Information Network*. Andean Information Network, 12 Mar. 2007. Web. 3 June 2007.

McCausland, Greg. "Coca Leaves in Context." *Devotion Frees*. N.p., 21 Aug. 2010. Web. 3 June 2014.

Otis, John. "Officials Urge Farmers to Try Alternative to Coca Crop." *Houston Chronicle*. Houston Chronicle, 14 July 2000. Web. 23 Apr. 2014.

- - -. "Officials Urge Farmers to Try Alternative to Coca Crop." *Houston Chronicle*. Houston Chronicle, 14 July 2000. Web. 23 Apr. 2007.

Padgett, Tim. "Taking the Side of the Coca Farmer: A Maverick Politician Stirs a Continent and Puts Washington's Drug War at Risk." *Time* 5 Aug. 2002: 8. Print.

Schultz, Jim, and Gretchen Gordon. "'Coca Is the Tree of the Poor': Indigenous People Leap Forward in Bolivia." *New America Media*. Pacific News Service, 20 Dec. 2005. Web. 20 May 2007.

United Nations. Office on Drugs and Crime. *Bolivia: Coca Cultivation Survey for 2006*. June 2007. Web. 22 May 2007.

United States. Foreign Affairs, Defense, and Trade Div. *Bolivia: Political and Economic Developments and Relations with the United States*. By Clare M. Ribando. 26 Jan. 2007. Web. 22 Apr. 2007.

"US Weighs Cost of Plan Colombia." *BBC News*. BBC, 5 July 2005. Web. 20 May 2007.

Zurita-Vargas, Leonida. "Coca Culture." *New York Times*. New York Times, 15 Oct. 2003. Web. 21 May 2007.

Part V
Documenting Sources

21

Using APA Style

 Key Questions

21a. How do I cite sources within the text of my document?   370

21b. How do I prepare the reference list?   373

American Psychological Association (APA) style, used primarily in the social sciences and in some of the natural sciences, emphasizes the author(s) and publication date of a source. Writers who use the APA documentation system cite, or formally acknowledge, information within their text using parentheses and provide a list of sources, called a reference list, at the end of their document. For more information about APA style, consult the *Publication Manual of the American Psychological Association,* Sixth Edition, and the *APA Style Guide to Electronic References.* Information about these publications can be found on the APA Web site at **apa.org**. To see Alexis Alvarez's research essay, formatted in APA style, turn to p. 388.

CITATION TUTORIALS FOR COMMON REFERENCE LIST ENTRIES

- Books   375
- Articles from periodicals   379
- Articles from databases   383
- Works from Web sites   385

CITATIONS WITHIN YOUR TEXT

1. Basic format for direct quotation   370
2. Basic format for summary or paraphrase   371
3. Two authors   371
4. Three, four, or five authors   371
5. More than five authors   372
6. Corporate or group author   372
7. Unknown author   372
8. Two or more works   372
9. Source quoted in another source   372
10. Source with no page numbers   373

APA

v Documenting Sources

21a

How do I cite sources within the text of my document?

APA uses an author-date form of in-text citation to acknowledge the use of another writer's words, facts, or ideas. When you refer to a source, insert a parenthetical note that gives the author's last name and the year of the publication, separated by a comma. Even when your reference list includes the day or month of publication, the in-text citation should include only the year. For a quotation, the citation in parentheses also includes the page(s) on which the quotation can be found, if the source has page numbers. Note that APA style requires using the past tense or present perfect tense to introduce the material you are citing: *Renfrew argued* or *Renfrew has argued.*

1. Basic Format for Direct Quotation   When you are using a direct quotation from a source and have named the author in your sentence, place the publication date in parentheses directly after the author's last name. Include the page number (with "p." for *page*) in parentheses after the quotation.

> Yousafzai (2013) wrote that the door to her all-girls school in Swat "was like a magical entrance to our own special world" (p. 2).

If you are using a direct quotation from a source and have not mentioned the author's name in your sentence, place the author's last name, the publication date, and the page number in parentheses.

> (Yousafzai, 2013, p. 86).

2. Basic Format for Summary or Paraphrase   When you are summarizing or paraphrasing, place the author's last name and date either in the sentence or in parentheses at the end of the sentence. Include a page or chapter reference if it would help readers find the original material in a longer work.

> Baker (2011) questions how advances in artificial intelligence might undermine the value of human intelligence and knowledge in some realms (p. 15).

> As the Watson experiment demonstrates, even the physical appearance of artificial intelligence devices is shaped by human preconceptions — and fears — of technology (Baker, 2011, p. 112).

3. Two Authors   List the last names of both authors in every mention in the text. If you mention the authors' names in a sentence, use the word "and" to separate the last names, as shown in the first example. If you place the authors' names in the parenthetical citation, use an ampersand (&) to separate the last names, as shown in the second example.

> Drlica and Perlin (2011) wrote that "although many infections tend to occur in persons having weakened immune systems, MRSA can infect anyone" (p. 3).

> Everyone is susceptible to MRSA, not just those who are already weak or ill (Drlica & Perlin, 2011, p. 3).

4. Three, Four, or Five Authors   In parentheses, name all the authors the first time you cite the source, using an ampersand (&) before the last author's name. In subsequent references to the source, use the last name of the first author followed by the abbreviation "et al." (Latin for "and others").

> Visual illusions serve an important scientific purpose in illustrating the brain's processes (Macknik, Martinez-Conde, & Blakeselee, 2010).

> Neuroscientists have found much value in studying magic and how it subverts the brain's expectations of visual input (Macknik et al., 2010).

5. More Than Five Authors   In all references to the source, give the first author's last name followed by "et al."

> Coles et al. (2011) demonstrated the correlation between prenatal alcohol exposure, smaller brain size, and diminished memory function.

6. Corporate or Group Author   In general, cite the full name of the corporation or group the first time it is mentioned in your text. If you add an abbreviation for the group in square brackets the first time you cite the source, you can use the abbreviation in subsequent citations.

> Reactions to the idea of global climate change vary widely and are subject to many influences, including personal beliefs and cultural values (American Psychological Association [APA], 2010, p. 6). Similarly, the psychosocial effects of the signs of climate change, such as fear and anxiety over dwindling natural resources or unusual weather patterns, are functions of individual and cultural contexts (APA, 2010, p. 7).

7. Unknown Author   Sources with unknown authors are listed by title in the list of references. In your in-text citation, shorten the title as much as possible without introducing confusion. Add quotation marks to article titles, and italicize book titles.

> The debate over evolution and creationism continues in the wake of recent scientific discoveries ("Fossil," 2011).

If a source identifies its author as "Anonymous," use that word to cite the author of the source.

> The rise in coastal water levels has been referred to as a national crisis (Anonymous, 2011).

8. Two or More Works   List the sources in alphabetical order and separate them with semicolons. If you are referring to two or more sources by the same author, order those sources chronologically.

> While the rush of adrenaline experienced during combat can be life saving at the time, adrenaline levels in combat veterans can remain high even after their return home, resulting in an array of stress-related health problems (Friedman & Sloane, 2008; Hoge, 2010).

9. Source Quoted in Another Source   Ideally, you will be able to find the primary, or original, source for material used in your research writing project document. If you quote or paraphrase a secondary source—a source that contains information about a primary source—mention the primary source and indicate that it was cited in the secondary source. Include the secondary source in your reference list.

In discussing the need for child protection in Romania, Tabacaru (2011) argued, "If conditions are not in place for foster care, they will all go to institutions" (as quoted in Nelson, Fox, & Zeanah, 2014, p. 61).

10. Source with No Page Numbers Many Web sources lack stable page numbers. If the source has numbered paragraphs, include the paragraph number using the abbreviation "para." If the paragraphs are not numbered, include the section heading and indicate which paragraph in that section you are referring to.

Tomasulo (2011) suggested that "there is a pattern to who and how we love" based on an attraction to traits that are familiar to us (para. 10).

11. Two or More Authors with the Same Last Name Use the authors' initials in each citation.

While C. Smith (2009) has noted an increase in early childhood psychiatric disorders, L. W. Smith (2010) suggested that many of these diagnoses in very young children might be inaccurate.

12. Email and Other Personal Communication Give the first initial(s) and last name of the person with whom you corresponded, the words "personal communication," and the date. Don't include personal communication in your reference list.

(A. L. Chan, personal communication, October 9, 2013)

13. Document from a Web Site To cite a quotation from a Web site, give the page number or paragraph number, if indicated, and include the source in your reference list.

Lehrer (2011) noted that the era of the "lone genius" may be ending, replaced instead by collaborative thinking and research (para. 13).

21b

How do I prepare the reference list?

The reference list contains publication information for all sources that you have cited within your document, with one main exception. Personal communications—such as correspondence, email messages, and interviews—are cited only in the text of the document.

Begin the list on a new page at the end of the document and center the title "References" at the top. Organize the list alphabetically by author; if the source is an organization, alphabetize the source by the name of the organization. All of the entries should be double-spaced with no extra space between entries. Entries are formatted with a hanging indent: The first line of an entry is flush with the left margin and subsequent lines are indented one-half inch or five spaces. In longer documents, a reference list could be given at the end of each chapter or section. In digital documents that use links, such as Web sites, the reference list is often a separate page to which other pages are linked. For an example of a reference list in APA style, see p. 385.

Books, Conference Proceedings, and Dissertations

14. One Author   Use capitals for the first word, proper nouns, and word following a colon in titles.

Skloot, R. (2010). *The immortal life of Henrietta Lacks.* New York, NY: Crown.

15. Two or More Authors   List the authors in the same order as the title page does, each with last name first. Use commas to separate authors and use an ampersand (&) before the final author's name. List every author up to seven; for a work with more than seven authors, give the first six names followed by a comma, three ellipsis dots, and the final author's name. (Do not use an ampersand.)

Kraybill, D. B., Nolt, S. M., & Weaver-Zercher, D. (2010). *The Amish way: Patient faith in a perilous world.* San Francisco, CA: Jossey–Bass.

16. Corporate or Group Author   Write out the full name of a corporate or group author. If the corporation is also the publisher, use "Author" for the publisher's name.

National Geographic. (2010). *Water: Our thirsty world.* Washington, DC: Author.

17. Unknown Author   When there is no author listed on the title or copyright page, begin the entry with the title of the work. Alphabetize the entry by the first significant word of the title (not including *A, An*, or *The*).

Going within to get out. (2013). Bloomington, IN: Balboa.

18. Two or More Works by the Same Author(s)   Give the author's name in each entry and list the works in chronological order.

Packer, G. (2009). *Interesting times: Writings from a turbulent decade.* New York, NY: Farrar Straus and Giroux.

Packer, G. (2013). *The unwinding: An inner history of the new America.* New York, NY: Farrar Straus and Giroux.

19. Translated Book   List the author first followed by the year of publication, the title, and the translator (in parentheses, identified by the abbreviation "Trans."). Place the original date of the work's publication at the end of the entry.

Oz, A. (2013). *Between friends* (S. Silverston, Trans.). New York, NY: Houghton Mifflin Harcourt.

TUTORIAL

How do I cite books using APA style?

When citing a book, use the information from the title page and the copyright page (on the back side of the title page), not from the book's cover or a library catalog. Consult pp. 374–78 for additional models. [Reprinted with the permission of Simon & Schuster, Inc. from *Who Owns The Future?* by Jaron Lanier. Copyright © 2013 by Jaron Lanier. All Rights Reserved.]

Lanier, J. (2013). *Who owns the future?* New York, NY: Simon & Schuster.

A   **The author.** Give the last name first, followed by a comma and initials for first and middle names. Separate initials with a space (Leakey, R. E.). Separate the names of multiple authors with commas; use an ampersand (&) before the final author's name.

B   **The year of publication.** Put the most recent copyright year in parentheses, and end with a period (outside the parentheses).

C   **The title and, if any, the subtitle.** Give the full title; include the subtitle (if any), preceded by a colon. Italicize the title and subtitle, capitalizing only the first word of the title, the first word of the subtitle, and any proper nouns or proper adjectives. End with a period.

D   **The city of publication.** If more than one city is given, use the first one listed. Add the U.S. Postal Service abbreviation of the state, but spell out non-U.S. locations such as provinces or countries (Cambridge, England). Insert a colon.

E   **The publisher.** Give the publisher's name. Omit words such as *Inc.* and *Co.* Include and do not abbreviate such terms as *University* and *Press*. End with a period.

20. Book in a Series

Frasier, J. D. (2010). *Forensic science.* Very short introductions 211 [Series]. Oxford, England: Oxford University Press.

21. Republication

Freud, S. (2010). *The interpretation of dreams* (J. Strachey, Ed. & Trans.). New York, NY: Basic Books. (Original work published 1955)

22. Book in an Edition Other than the First   Note the edition ("2nd ed.," "Rev. ed.") after the title.

Sowell, T. (2010). *Basic economics: A common sense guide to the economy* (4th ed.). New York, NY: Basic Books.

23. Multivolume Work   Include the number of volumes in parentheses after the title.

Delbanco, N., & Cheuse, A. (Eds.). (2010). *Literature: Craft and voice* (Vols. 1–3). Boston: McGraw–Hill.

If you have used only one volume in a multivolume work, identify that volume by number and by title.

Delbanco, N., & Cheuse, A. (Eds.). (2010). *Literature: Craft and voice: Vol. 1. Fiction.* Boston: McGraw–Hill.

24. Editor   Include "Ed." or "Eds." in parentheses.

Bryson, B. (Ed.). (2010). *Seeing further: The story of science, discovery, and the genius of the Royal Society.* New York, NY: Morrow.

25. Author with an Editor   Include the editor's name and the abbreviation "Ed." in parentheses after the title.

Mencken, H. L. (2010). *Mencken: Prejudices, first, second, and third* (M. E. Rodgers, Ed.). New York, NY: Library of America.

26. Anthology   To cite an entire anthology of essays or collection of articles, list the editor or editors first, followed by the abbreviation "Ed." or "Eds." in parentheses.

Van Wormer, K. S., & Thyer, B. A. (Eds.). (2010). *Evidence-based practice in the field of substance abuse: A book of readings.* Thousand Oaks, CA: Sage.

27. Chapter in an Edited Book or Selection in an Anthology   Begin the entry with the author, the publication date, and the title of the chapter or

selection (not italicized). Follow this with the names of the editors (initials first) and the abbreviation "Ed." or "Eds." in parentheses, the title of the anthology or collection (italicized), inclusive page numbers for the chapter or selection (in parentheses, with abbreviation "pp."), and place and publisher.

Wahab, S. (2010). Motivational interviewing and social work practice. In K. S. Van Wormer & B. A. Thyer (Eds.), *Evidence-based practice in the field of substance abuse: A book of readings* (pp. 197–210). Thousand Oaks, CA: Sage.

28. Foreword, Introduction, Preface, or Afterword Treat as you would a chapter in a book.

Wong, H. K. (2010). Introduction. In C. Asquith, *The emergency teacher: The inspirational story of a new teacher in an inner-city school* (pp. vi–vii). New York, NY: Skyhorse.

29. Published Proceedings of a Conference Cite information as you would for a book.

Mayor, J., & Gomez, P. (Eds.). (2014). *Computational models of cognitive processes: Proceedings of the 13th Neural Computation and Psychology Workshop.* Singapore: World Scientific Publishing.

30. Paper Published in the Proceedings of a Conference Treat a conference paper as you would a selection from an edited collection.

Jacobs, G. M., & Toh-Heng, H. L. (2013). Small steps towards student-centered learning. In P. Mandal (Ed.), *Proceedings of the international conference on managing the Asian century* (pp. 55–64). Singapore: Springer.

31. Sacred Text Treat as you would a book (see p. 375).

The Holy Bible: King James version. (2010). Quartercentenary Ed. Oxford, England: Oxford University Press.

32. Published Dissertation or Thesis If a published dissertation or thesis is available through a commercial database, give the author, date, title, and a description in parentheses ("Doctoral dissertation" or "Master's thesis"). Then give the database name in italics, followed by any UMI or order number in parentheses.

Selberg, S. (2013). *Seeing the person within: Visual culture and Alzheimer's disease* (Doctoral dissertation, New York University). Available from ProQuest Dissertations and Theses database. (UMI No. 3553975).

APA

V Documenting Sources

If the material is accessed from an institutional database or other Web site, provide the URL.

Kim, J. (2012). *Promoting sustainable communities through Infill: The effect of Infill housing on neighborhood income diversity* (Doctoral thesis, University of Florida). Retrieved from http://ufdc.ufl.edu/UFE0044904/00001.

33. Unpublished Dissertation or Thesis   Format as you would a book, replacing the publisher information with the phrase "Unpublished doctoral dissertation" or "Unpublished master's thesis," followed by information about the college or university.

McQueen, J. Y. (2013). *On the road of phonological treatment: Paths of learning* (Unpublished honors thesis). Indiana University, Bloomington.

Sources in Journals, Magazines, and Newspapers

34. Article in a Journal Paginated by Volume   Most journals continue page numbers throughout an entire annual volume, beginning again at page 1 only in the first volume of the next year. After the author and publication year, provide the article title, the journal title, the volume number (italicized), and the inclusive page numbers.

Pope, N. D., & Kang, B. (2010). Residential relocation in later life: A comparison of proactive and reactive moves. *Journal of Housing for the Elderly, 24,* 193–207.

35. Article in a Journal Paginated by Issue   Some journals begin at page 1 for every issue. Include the issue number (in parentheses, not italicized) after the volume number.

Carlozzi, N. E., Horner, M. D., Kose, S., Yamanaka, K., Mishory, A., Mu, Q., . . . George, M. S. (2010). Personality and reaction time after sleep deprivation. *Current Psychology, 29*(1), 24–33.

36. Article in a Magazine   The author's name and the publication date are followed by the title of the article, the magazine title (italicized), and the volume number, if any (also italicized). Include all page numbers.

Senior, J. (2010, June 28–July 4). Divorce liberation. *New York,* 20.

37. Article in a Newspaper   List the author's name and the complete date (year first). Next give the article title followed by the name of the newspaper (italicized). Include all page numbers, preceded by "p." or "pp."

Filipov, D. (2010, October 1). Diehards say texting tough to kick. *The Boston Globe,* p. B8.

TUTORIAL

How do I cite articles from periodicals using APA style?

The Politics of Poverty: Definitions and Explanations

DENNIS RAPHAEL

It is becoming increasingly apparent that a nation's poverty rate is determined in large part by how a nation's governing authorities distribute economic and other resources amongst the population, i.e., politics. In this article various definitions of both poverty and politics are presented and their interrelationships noted. The links between politics and poverty can be understood in three primary ways. The first is that individual characteristics such as lack of education or employment skills create poverty. The second is that public policies themselves are the primary determinants of a nation's poverty rates. The third is that the distribution of power and influence within the nation create the public policies that determine poverty rates. Recent data from the Luxembourg Income Study, the Innocenti Research Centre, and the Organisation for Economic Cooperation and Development are used to illustrate how differences in the poverty rate are shaped by the politics of a nation.

Introduction

Societies set goals for themselves. The French aim for *Liberty, Equality, and Fraternity;* the Americans seek *Life, Liberty, and the Pursuit of Happiness,* Norwegians strive for *Equality and Equality,* and Canadians aim for *Peace, Order, and Good Government.* In Australia the idea of a *Fair Go* is seen as part of its national identity. Whatever the goal, the presence of poverty is a clear obstacle to its attainment. Poverty is also a clear threat to human and social development, and health and well-being, is becoming increasingly apparent that poverty in developed nations is a result of the political and economic organisation of society rather than the personal failings of individuals. Recent scholarship has examined how national governments organised along social democratic lines have the lowest poverty rates and those organised along liberal lines have the highest. In this special issue of *Social Alternatives* we examine the politics of poverty by: a) reviewing the recent literature on the politics of poverty; b) examining these concepts in relation to exemplar nations of each regime; and c) outlining the political processes by which poverty can be reduced in these nations.

Poverty

There is a consensus among agencies and researchers on the meaning of poverty in developed nations. These definitions identify two kinds of poverty: *absolute* and *overall.* The World Summit on Social Development provides this definition of absolute poverty: *"Absolute poverty is a condition characterised by severe deprivation of basic human needs, including food, safe drinking water, sanitation facilities, health, shelter, education, and*

information (United Nations 1995: 57). Absolute poverty is frequent in many developing nations but there is evidence it is not uncommon in developed nations. UK researchers describe absolute poverty as individuals lacking the basic necessities of life to 'keep body and soul together' and being so poor that you are deprived of basic human needs' (Gordon 2000: 75).

There are numerous ways of assessing absolute poverty. In one approach it is argued that to avoid absolute poverty, you need enough money to cover all of these things: adequate diet, housing costs/rent, heating costs, clothing, water rates, and prescription costs' (Gordon 2000: 76). In another, absolute poverty is not having access to 'basic necessities of food, shelter, clothing, health care, personal care, essential furnishings, transportation and communication, laundry, and home insurance' (Sarlo 2001: 10). One measure of absolute poverty used in international comparisons is that of the USA poverty line, which identifies an income level at which there is an immediate threat to the physical integrity of the individual (Innocenti Research Centre 2005). The presence of absolute poverty in a wealthy developed nation is an affront to human rights and should be politically unacceptable. As will be seen, this is frequently not the case.

Overall poverty – also called relative poverty – is the situation where access to resources so deviates from the societal average as to be problematic for the individual. The World Summit on Social Development (United Nations 1995: 57) provides this definition of overall poverty:

Overall poverty has various manifestations,

Social Alternatives Vol. 32 No 1, 2013   5

Periodicals include journals, magazines, and newspapers. This page gives an example of a citation for a print journal article. Models for citing articles from magazines and newspapers are on pp. 378–80. If you need to cite a periodical article you accessed electronically, follow the guidelines below and see pp. 382–83. [*Social Alternative*, Queensland, Australia.]

A **B** **C**

Raphael, D. (2013). The politics of poverty: Definitions and explanations.

D **E** **F**

Social Alternatives, 32(1), 5–11.

A   **The author.** Give the last name first, followed by a comma and initials for first and middle names. Separate the names of multiple authors with commas; use an ampersand (&) before the final author's name.

B   **The year of publication.** Put the year in parentheses and end with a period (outside the parentheses). For magazines and newspapers, include the month and, if relevant, the day (2010, April 13).

C   **The article title.** Give the full title; include the subtitle (if any), preceded by a colon. Do not underline, italicize, or put the title in quotation marks. Capitalize only the first word of the title, the first word of the subtitle, and any proper nouns or proper adjectives. End with a period.

D   **The periodical title.** Italicize the periodical title, and capitalize all major words. Insert a comma.

E   **The volume and issue number, if relevant.** For journals, include the volume number, italicized. If each issue starts with page 1, include the issue number in parentheses, not italicized. Insert a comma.

F   **Inclusive page number(s).** Give all of the numbers in full (248–254, not 248–54). For newspapers, include the abbreviation "p." for page and section letters, if relevant (p. B12). End with a period.

APA

V Documenting Sources

38. Unsigned Article in a Newspaper Begin with the article title, and alphabetize in the reference list by the first word in the title other than *A, An,* or *The.* Use "p." or "pp." before page numbers.

UN: 2010 tied for warmest year on record. (2011, January 20). *The Chicago Sun-Times*, p. C2.

39. Letter to the Editor Include the words "Letter to the editor" in square brackets after the title of the letter, if any.

Kropf, B. (2010, November 16). Good policy isn't the provenance of any ethnic group [Letter to the editor]. *The Wall Street Journal*, p. A15.

40. Review After the title of the review, include the words "Review of the book . . ." or "Review of the film . . ." and so on in brackets, followed by the title of the work reviewed.

Hertzberg, H. (2010, October 25). Politics and prose [Review of the book *Daniel Patrick Moynihan: A Portrait in Letters of an American Visionary*, by D. P. Moynihan & S. R. Weisman]. *The New Yorker*, 78–82.

When the review is untitled, follow the date with the bracketed information.

Turan, K. (2010, November 26). [Review of the film *The King's Speech*, 2010]. *The Los Angeles Times*, p. D1.

41. Published Interview Cite a published interview like a journal article (see p. 378).

Massondo, A. (2010, July). Yellow-card journalism [Interview by C. Barron]. *Harper's, 321*(1921), 17–18.

42. Two or More Works by the Same Author in the Same Year List the works alphabetically and include lowercase letters (*a, b,* etc.) after the dates.

Iglehart, J. K. (2010a). The ACA's new weapons against health care fraud. *The New England Journal of Medicine, 363*, 1589–1591.

Iglehart, J. K. (2010b). Health reform, primary care, and graduate medical education. *The New England Journal of Medicine, 363*, 584–590.

Print Reference Works

43. Encyclopedia, Dictionary, Thesaurus, Handbook, or Almanac Cite a reference work, such as an encyclopedia or a dictionary, as you would a book (see p. 375).

Priest, S. H. (Ed.). (2010). *Encyclopedia of science and technology communication* (Vols. 1–2). Thousand Oaks, CA: Sage.

44. Entry in an Encyclopedia, Dictionary, Thesaurus, Handbook, or Almanac
Begin your citation with the name of the author or, if the entry is unsigned, the title of the entry. Proceed with the date, the entry title (if not already given), the title of the reference work, the edition number, and the pages.

Human genome project. (2010). In S. H. Priest (Ed.), *Encyclopedia of science and technology communication* (Vol. 1, pp. 374–379). Thousand Oaks, CA: Sage.

45. Government Publication Give the name of the department (or office, agency, or committee) that issued the report as the author. If the document has a report or special file number, place that in parentheses after the title.

U.S. Department of Health and Human Services. (2010). *Ending the tobacco epidemic: A tobacco control strategic action plan for the U.S. Department of Health and Human Services.* Washington, DC: Government Printing Office.

46. Pamphlet Format the entry as you would a book (see p. 375).

Alcoholics Anonymous. (2011). *The A. A. member — medications and other drugs.* New York, NY: Alcoholics Anonymous World Services.

Field Sources

47. Personal Interview Treat unpublished interviews as personal communications and include them in your text only (see p. 373). Do not cite personal interviews in your reference list.

48. Letter Cite a personal letter only in the text (see p. 373), not in the reference list.

49. Lecture or Public Address Cite a lecture or public address the same way you would cite an unpublished paper presented at a conference.

Lander, E. (2010, April 19). Secrets of the human genome. Lecture presented at Princeton University, Princeton, NJ.

Media Sources

50. Film or Video Recording List the director and producer (if available), the date of release, the title followed by "Motion picture" in square brackets, the country where the film was made, and the studio or distributor.

Aronofsky, D. (Director). (2010). *Black swan* [Motion picture]. United States: Fox Searchlight.

51. Television Program Cite as you would a chapter in a book. List the director (if available), the broadcast date, the title followed by "Television broadcast" or "Television series episode" in square brackets. Then add information on the series, location, and station.

APA

V Documenting Sources

Jennings, T. (Writer, Producer, & Director), & Bomse, S. (Writer). (2010, August 25). Law and disorder [Television series episode]. In D. Fanning (Executive Producer), *Frontline*. Boston, MA: WGBH.

52. Radio Program   List the host, the broadcast date, the title followed by "Radio broadcast," or "Radio series episode," in square brackets.

Young, R. (Host). (2011, January 21). Center focuses on treating Alzheimer's by comforting residents, not medicating them [Radio series episode]. In K. McKenna (Senior Producer), *Here and now*. Boston, MA: WBUR.

53. Sound Recording   Name the author of the song; the date; the song title followed by "On" and the recording title in italics; the medium (in square brackets); and the production data.

Ruffins, K. (2010). More today than yesterday. On *Happy talk* [MP3]. New Orleans, LA: Basin Street Records.

Digital Sources

54. Article with a DOI   A DOI (Digital Object Identifier) is a unique number assigned to specific content, such as a journal article. If a DOI is available, include it, preceded by "**http://dx.doi.org/**" and with no punctuation at the end. You do not need to provide a retrieval date or database name.

Schwander, T., Vuilleumier, S., Dubman, J., & Crespi, B. J. (2010). Positive feedback in the transition from sexual reproduction to parthenogenesis. *Proceedings of the Royal Society Biology, 277*, 1435–1442. http://dx.doi .org/10.1098/rspb.2009.2113

55. Article without a DOI   If no DOI (Digital Object Identifier) is provided, give the exact URL for the article or for the home page of the journal, if access requires a subscription.

Stieb, J. A. (2011). Understanding engineering professionalism: A reflection on the rights of engineers. *Science and Engineering Ethics, 17*(1), 149–169. Retrieved from http://springerlink.com/content/r58q044521917785/

If the article comes from a database, give the URL of the home page of the journal.

Robertson, L. A. (2010). The spiritual competency scale. *Counseling and Values, 55*(1), 6–24. Retrieved from http://www.counseling.org

56. Article in an Online Periodical   Publication information is followed by the URL. Since the article was published online, it is unlikely to have page numbers. Note that the first example is for an online journal, while the second is for an online magazine.

TUTORIAL

How do I cite articles from databases using APA style?

Libraries subscribe to services such as LexisNexis, InfoTrac, and EBSCOhost that provide access to databases of digital texts. The databases provide publication information, abstracts, and complete text of documents in a specific subject, discipline, or profession. (See Chapter 9.)
[Courtesy of EBSCO.]

A **B** **C**
Zehetner, A. (2013). Why fairy tales are still relevant to today's children.

D **E** **F**
Journal of Paediatrics & Child Health, 49, 161–162.

G
http://dx.doi.org/10.1111/jpc.12080

A **The author.** Give the last name first, followed by a comma and initials. Separate the names of multiple authors with commas; use an ampersand (&) before the final author's name.

B **The date of publication.** Put the year in parentheses and end with a period (outside the parentheses). For magazines and newspapers, include the month and, if relevant, the day (2010, April 13).

C **The article title.** Give the full title; include the subtitle (if any), preceded by a colon. Do not underline, italicize, or put the title or subtitle in quotation marks. Capitalize only the first word of the title, the first word of the subtitle, and any proper nouns or proper adjectives. End with a period.

D **The periodical title.** Italicize the periodical title, and capitalize all major words. Insert a comma.

E **The volume number and issue number.** For journals, include the volume number, italicized. If each issue starts with page 1, include the issue number in parentheses, not italicized. Insert a comma.

F **Inclusive page numbers(s).** Give all of the numbers in full (317–327, not 317–27). For newspapers, include the abbreviation *p.* for page and section letters, if relevant (p. B12). End with a period.

G **The DOI.** Give the unique Digital Object Identifier (DOI) number, preceded by "**http://dx.doi.org/**" and with no punctuation at the end. You do not need to provide a retrieval date or database name. If there is no DOI, include the words "Retrieved from" and the URL of the publication's home page.

bedfordresearcher.com
Tutorials > Documentation and Working with Sources > How to Cite a Database in APA Style

APA

V Documenting Sources

Rusanen, M., Kivipelto, M., Quesenberry, C. P., Zhou, J., & Whitmer, R. A. (2010). Heavy smoking in midlife and long-term risk of Alzheimer's disease and vascular dementia. *Archives of Internal Medicine.* http://dx.doi.org/10.1001 /archinternmed.2010.393

Colby, T. (2014, February 27). "The failure of integration on Madison Avenue — and what it says about race in America." *Slate.* Retrieved from http://www .slate.com

57. E-Book   Cite the digital version only if a print version is not available or is hard to find.

Ducot, C. (n.d.). *An end to anxiety* (E. Pichel-Juan, Trans.). Retrieved from http://www.onlineoriginals.com

58. Entry in an Online Reference Work   Give the URL for the home or index page.

Cultural anthropology. (2013). In *Encyclopaedia Britannica*. Retrieved from http://www.britannica.com/

59. Nonperiodical Web Document   For a stand-alone Web source, such as a report, an online brochure, or a blog, cite as much of the following information as possible: author, publication date, document title, description of the material in brackets, and the URL. Include a retrieval date before the URL only when the original publication date is unknown. Include the site name in the retrieval statement if the site name is not part of the URL.

Mayo Clinic. (2011, March 16). *Quit smoking* [Web page]. Retrieved from http:// www.mayoclinic.com/health/quit-smoking/MY00433

For a chapter or section within a Web document, identify the section title, followed by a description in brackets, as well as the main document.

Davis, J. L. (2014). Coping with anxiety [Article]. In *Anxiety and panic disorders guide*. Retrieved February 28, 2014, from http://www.webmd.com/anxiety -panic/guide/coping-with-anxiety

American Psychological Association. (2014). What is psychology? [Article] In *Careers in psychology*. Retrieved January 31, 2014, from http://www.apa.org /topics/psychologycareer.html

60. Email Message or Real-Time Communication   Because email messages are difficult or impossible for your readers to retrieve, APA does not recommend including them in your reference list. You should treat them as personal communications and cite them parenthetically in your text (see #12 on p. 373).

TUTORIAL

How do I cite works from Web sites using APA style?

You will likely need to search the Web site to find some of the citation information you need. For some sites, all of the details may not be available; find as many as you can. Remember that the citation you provide should allow readers to retrace your steps electronically to locate the sources. Consult pp. 382–87 for additional models for citing Web sources. [Sierra Club, Compass blog: sierraclub.org/compass.]

A **B** **C**

Moyer, H. (2014, February 10). A witness to environmental justice over twenty

D **E**

years [Article]. In *Compass: Pointing the way to a clean energy future.*

F

Retrieved from http://sierraclub.typepad.com/compass/2014/02

/a-witness-to-environmental-justice-over-20-years.html

A **The author of the work.** Give the last name first, followed by a comma and initials. Separate the names of multiple authors with commas; use an ampersand (&) before the final author's name.

B **The date of publication.** Put the year in parentheses and include the month, if available. If there is no date, use *n.d.* in parentheses, and include a retrieval date before the URL. End with a period (outside the parentheses).

C **The title of the work.** Give the full title of the work you are citing. Capitalize only the first word of the title, the first word of the subtitle, and any proper nouns or proper adjectives. Do not use italics for articles and other short works within a larger work on the Web site. Do use italics if the work is a stand-alone report or other full-length document.

D **A description of the work.** Include a description of the work (such as "Report" or "Blog post") in brackets.

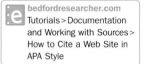

bedfordresearcher.com
Tutorials > Documentation and Working with Sources > How to Cite a Web Site in APA Style

E **The title of the larger work.** If the work you are citing is part of a larger work on the Web site, provide the name of the larger work in italics, preceded by "In." Capitalize only the first word of the title, the first word of the subtitle, and any proper nouns or proper adjectives.

F **Retrieval information.** Include a retrieval date only if the material lacks a set publication date. If the Web site name (such as "Sierra Club") is not clear from the URL, include it with the retrieval information, without italics or quotation marks, capitalizing the first letter of all major words. (Since this article has a set publication date and the URL contains the Web site name, neither the retrieval date nor the site name is necessary.) End with the URL.

61. Article Posted on a Wiki   Include a description in brackets after the article or entry title. Include a retrieval date only if the material does not include a specific publication date.

Sensory deprivation [Wiki entry]. (2014, February 21). Retrieved from http://
    en.wikipedia.org/wiki/Sensory_deprivation

62. Message Posted to a Newsgroup, Email List, or Online Discussion Forum
List the author, posting date, message title, and a description of the message in brackets. Then add the retrieval information, including the name of the list or forum.

Wolf, J. (2010, October 12). Girlhood Studies receives a Highly Commended
    Certificate for the ALPSP 201 Best New Journal award [Electronic mailing list
    message]. Retrieved from Childhood discussion list: http://h-net.msu.edu
    /cgi-bin/logbrowse.pl?trx=lm&list=h-childhood

63. Entry or Comment on a Blog   To cite an entry on a blog, give the author (or screen name), the date the material was posted, the title of the entry, a description of the entry in brackets ("Blog post" or "Blog comment"), and the URL.

Gudmundsen, J. (2014, February 18). Toy Fair 2014: The way your kids play is
    about to change [Blog post]. Retrieved from http://www.commonsensemedia
    .org/blog/toy-fair-2014-the-way-your-kids-play-is-about-to-change

Jane. (2010, November 10). Re: For caregivers, it's OK to feel good and bad
    [Blog comment]. Retrieved from http://www.mayoclinic.com/health
    /alzheimers-caregivers/MY01563_comments#post

64. Tweet   Include the author's real name, if known, followed by the screen name in brackets. If the real name is not known, provide only the screen name without brackets. Provide the date, the complete text of the tweet, followed by "Tweet" in brackets, and the retrieval URL.

Clinton, H. [HillaryClinton]. (2014, February 27). Some encouraging news today
    from China's business leaders on stopping the demand for ivory. http://
    www.wildaid.org/news/china%E2%80%99s-top-business-leaders-say-no
    -ivory [Tweet]. Retrieved from https://twitter.com/HillaryClinton/status
    /439077420495544321

65. Facebook page, post, or status update   Include the author or organization name followed by the date, title, or text of the update. Then include the description of the entry in brackets ("Facebook page," "Facebook note," or "Facebook status update") and the retrieval URL.

NSA — National Security Agency. (2014, February 27). This article suggests that instead of focusing on cybersecurity, companies need to move to "cyber resilience." Do you agree? http://ow.ly/tyZUL [Facebook status update]. Retrieved from https://www.facebook.com/NSACareers

66. Video Posted Online   After the title of the video, include the words "Video file" in brackets. If there is no author's name, list the screen name provided.

AskSanAnything. (2010, November 1). Month 1 done: How many inches and pounds down? [Video file]. Retrieved from http://losethefatkeepthefab .blogspot.com/

GeckoGeekFr. (2010, January 6). How to make a traditional origami crane [Video file]. Retrieved from http://www.youtube.com/watch?v=jUZaOWibCcs

67. Image Posted Online

NASA. (2014). *Opportunity's southward view of 'McClure-Beverlin Escarpment' on Mars* [Photograph]. Retrieved from http://marsrover.nasa.gov/gallery/press /opportunity/20140214a/pia17942-MAIN-SOL3567-donut_L456atc_br.jpg

68. Presentation Slides

Jessedee. (n.d.). 5 Presentation lessons from *The King's Speech* [PowerPoint slides]. Retrieved from http://www.slideshare.net/jessedee/presentation -lessons-from-the-kings-speech-6551851

69. Podcast

Jones, C. (2010, May 21). *Learning and becoming: The construction of identity in urban classrooms* [Audio podcast]. Retrieved from Swarthmore College Web site: http://media.swarthmore.edu/faculty_lectures/?p=182

70. Computer Software   Sometimes a person is named as having rights to the program, software, or language: In that case, list that person as the author. Otherwise, begin the entry with the name of the program and identify the source in square brackets after the name as "Computer software." Treat the organization that produces the software as the publisher. If you're referring to a specific version that isn't included in the name, put this information immediately after the title in parentheses.

Microsoft Office 2010 [Computer software]. Redmond, WA: Microsoft.

Other Sources

71. General Advice about Other Sources   For citing other types of sources, APA suggests that you use as a guide a source type listed in their manual that most closely resembles the type of source you want to cite.

APA

V Documenting Sources

APA-Style Research Essay

Running Head: GIRLS, SPORTS, AND STEROIDS   1

APA notes that requirements for title pages on student papers vary. Check with your instructor before following this example.

Title of essay

Girls, Sports, and Steroids

Alexis Alvarez

Writer's name

English 110, Section 4

Professor Desai

November 22, 2014

Title of course, instructor's name, and date

Title of essay repeated

Girls, Sports, and Steroids

Almost daily, headlines and newscasters tell us about athletes' use of performance-enhancing drugs. Indeed, stories of such drug use seem to increase each year, with investigations of possible steroid use by college football players, by major league baseball players, and even by Olympic gold medalists. It is easy to gain the impression that many adult athletes, particularly males, may be using drugs in order to improve their performance and physical appearance. What may be surprising and even shocking to most of us, however, is that these drugs, especially anabolic steroids, are increasingly used by adolescent athletes and that girls are just as likely as boys to be users.

Alexis's statement is likely to surprise readers, drawing them into the essay.

In May 2004, the Centers for Disease Control and Prevention (CDC) published its latest figures on self-reported drug use among young people in grades 9 through 12. The CDC study, "Youth Risk Behavior Surveillance — United States 2003," found that 6.1% of its survey participants reported using steroids at least once, up from 2.2% in 1993. The report also showed that use of steroids appears to be increasing among younger girls: While only 3.3% of 12th-grade girls reported using steroids, 7.3% of 9th-grade girls reported using them. Moreover, girls might be starting to use steroids at a higher rate than boys. The CDC study indicated that 9th-grade girls had reported slightly higher rates of steroid use than boys (7.3% and 6.9% respectively), while 10th-, 11th-, and 12th-grade girls all reported lower use than boys. Other studies support the conclusion that steroid use is both widespread and rising quickly among adolescent girls. According to Mundell (2004), experts estimate that as many as a million high school students have used steroids — and that a significant percentage of that group are girls. Moreover, since the late 1990s, studies have shown that steroid use is increasing among adolescent girls. In 1998, *Teacher Magazine* reported that steroid use among high school girls had increased 300% since 1991, from 0.4% of all high school girls to 1.4% ("Girls and Steroids," 1998). And Manning (2002) wrote, "A 1999 Youth Risk Behavior Surveillance study by the Centers for Disease Control and the 2001 Monitoring the Future survey both show steady growth in steroid use by 8th- to 12th-graders" ("Kids, steroids don't mix," para. 2).

Effective use of statistical evidence shows growth of the problem over time.

Source of paraphrased information is acknowledged using APA's parenthetical reference system.

A source that does not have an author is identified by shortened title and publication year.

Section heading and paragraph number are given for location of material quoted from an online source.

What role are competitive sports playing in this dangerous trend? Why are some girls feeling the need to ingest performance-enhancing drugs? Although competitive sports can provide young female athletes with many benefits, they can also have negative effects, the worst of which is increasing drug use. Let's look first at the positives.

Thesis states Alexis's main point.

APA

V Documenting Sources

Headings, boldface and centered throughout, help readers follow the essay's organization.

GIRLS, SPORTS, AND STEROIDS   3

Title of essay, shortened if necessary, followed by page number on the right

Girls and Sports: The Upside

Millions of girls are now involved in a variety of sports activities, and girls' participation in school athletics and community-based programs continues to increase. As the President's Council on Physical Fitness and Sports (1997) has pointed out, when girls participate in competitive sports, their lives can be affected in a number of positive and interrelated ways. Physical and psychological health, a positive sense of identity, good relationships with friends and family, and improved performance in school all work together to influence a girl's complete growth and development.

Shortened name of the council; it was introduced by its full name the first time it was cited.

According to the President's Council (1997), adolescent girls who exercise regularly can lessen their risks for adult-onset coronary disease and certain cancers. Girls' involvement in sports and exercise also tends to improve immune functioning, posture, strength, flexibility, and heart-lung endurance (President's Council, 1997; Dudley, 1994).

Two sources are cited in one parenthetical citation.

In addition, competitive athletics can enhance mental health by offering adolescent girls positive feelings about body image; tangible experiences of competency, control, and success; improved self-esteem and self-confidence; and a way to reduce anxiety (President's Council, 1997). Juan Orozco, who has coached adolescent females in competitive soccer for nine years, confirmed that making a competitive sports team is a privilege that many girls work toward with determination and longing and that being picked to participate encourages these young athletes to believe in themselves and their abilities (personal communication, September 22, 2014).

Personal communication — an interview — is cited in the text of the document, but not in the reference list.

A final benefit is that sports expand social boundaries and teach many of the personal and social skills girls will need throughout their lives. According to Orozco, through competitive athletics girls learn a crucial lesson in how to interact with, get along with, and depend on athletes from different social and economic groups. In short, they learn to adapt to and enjoy each other's differences. Melissa Alvarez, a 17-year-old athlete who has participated in high school basketball and club soccer, draws a similar conclusion. In an interview, she stated that sports "give you something to work for as an individual and as a team. You learn self-discipline and dedication, which are essential skills to have in life" (personal communication, September 26, 2007). Competitive sports also teach athletes how to cope with failure as well as success. In the best of situations, as Sieghart (2004) noted, athletes are able to assess their achievements realistically, letting neither winning nor losing consume their reality.

An author tag alerts readers that information is taken from a source.

Girls and Sports: The Downside

In spite of the many positive effects of competitive athletics, sports can have a negative impact on girls' bodies and minds, and some girls falter under the pressure to succeed. Overtraining, eating disorders, and exercise-induced amenorrhea (which may result in osteoporosis) are some of the most common negative physical side effects that young female athletes experience; negative psychological and social side effects include increased stress and anxiety and a loss of self-confidence. Let's look at each of these effects.

Negative Physical Side Effects

Overtraining occurs when your body can no longer adapt to increasing workloads — instead of building up, it breaks down. When a young girl overtrains, her body's balance between training and recovery is lost. Because the athlete's body can't recover, her performance stays flat and she cannot improve. Overtraining also makes a young female athlete prone to a variety of physical and psychological ills, such as unusual fatigue, irritability, feelings of apathy, and menstrual irregularities (Graham, 1999).

Another negative effect is amenorrhea, which refers to an atypical inability to menstruate. Graham (1999) pointed out, "in some sports as many as 50% of the athletes who are competitive may suffer from what's known as exercise-induced or athletic amenorrhea" (p. 26). Furthermore, research has shown that when a woman does not menstruate regularly, she loses bone density and becomes more prone to stress fractures (cracks in bones, especially hands and feet) and osteoporosis later in life. Amenorrhea can be caused by inadequate nutrition as well as by overtraining, both of which cause the athlete to burn more calories than she eats. As a result, her body shuts down its reproductive function to conserve energy (Graham, 1999).

The tendency to develop an eating disorder, such as anorexia or bulimia, is a third possible effect. Although young women may develop eating disorders for a variety of reasons, Graham (1999) noted, "Disordered eating is high among female athletes competing in sports where leanness and/or a specific weight are considered important for either performance or appearance" (p. 74). Being slim and trim may be the goal of many adolescent female athletes, but when they seek that goal by means of an eating disorder, they hinder their athletic performance. A calorie deficit actually decreases immune function, reduces aerobic capacity, decreases muscle mass and strength, and causes low energy and fatigue (Graham, 1999).

Page number identifies the location of material quoted from a print source.

APA

V Documenting Sources

Negative Psychological and Social Effects

Just as a girl's body and mind often benefit from sports, so too are body and mind linked when it comes to those aspects of sports that are not positive. Often, negative physical effects occur because female athletes feel the need to win at any cost and the pressure to attain an unrealistic ideal. They may resort to extremes such as overtraining in order to have the "ideal" body or be the "best of the best." When they can't meet these expectations, some girl athletes lose self-confidence and become overly stressed and anxious. In fact, they may see their failures as a serious threat to their self-esteem (Davies & Armstrong, 1989).

Pressures at home, at school, among friends, and from coaches can be daunting as well because young athletes tend to worry about the actions and reactions of the people who make up their social circles (Brown & Branta, 1988). In addition, learning to balance the demands of sports, school, family, and fun can be incredibly fatiguing. Juan Orozco recalled that some of the girls he coached were involved in three sports at a time and still had to keep their grades up in order to participate (personal communication, September 22, 2014). Add to these demands the pressure from parents, and real problems can occur. Gary Anderson, a girls' basketball coach for more than two decades, has seen it all: parents who are overly dramatic, teams that serve primarily as stages for a few superstar athletes, and girls who seem "factory-installed with a sense of entitlement simply because they know their way around a ball and a pair of high-tops" (Dexheimer, 2004, para. 15). All of these situations and pressures affect young female athletes and can result in their making some regrettable, if not devastating, choices.

Girls' Reactions: Burnout and Steroids

What happens when these young women decide the pressure is too much? What measures will they take to lighten their load? Some of these athletes simply burn out. They stop participating in competitive athletics because the pressure and anxiety make them physically ill. They no longer enjoy competitive sports, but consider them a torment to be endured. In fact, according to Davies and Armstrong (1989), it is not unusual for promising 12-year-olds to abandon the game entirely by the age of 16 and move on to less distressing pastimes. Melissa Alvarez had one such experience while playing high school basketball. The coach put so much pressure on her that her stomach began to ache during games and during practice. The more the coach yelled, the worse she played, but when the coach was absent, her performance improved dramatically and her stomach problems disappeared. Eventually, Melissa quit the basketball team

Subheadings are set in boldface and aligned flush left to differentiate them from higher-level headings.

A partial quotation is integrated into the sentence.

GIRLS, SPORTS, AND STEROIDS   6

because the game had become a burden instead of something she
enjoyed (M. Alvarez, personal communication, September 26, 2014).

   An alternative much more dangerous than burnout, however, is
the use of performance-enhancing drugs such as anabolic steroids. A
2003 article in *Drug Week* stated that girls who participate in sports
more than eight hours a week are at considerable risk for taking
many illicit drugs: The higher the level at which athletes compete,
the higher their risk for substance abuse ("Sporting Activities").

Since the
publication year
is given in the
sentence, it is
not included in
the citation.

   Teenage girls take steroids for some of the same reasons that
professional athletes do — to increase stamina and strength and to
acquire a lean, muscular body. However, girls also take steroids to
compete for athletic scholarships ("Girls and Steroids," 1998). According to Charles Yesalis, a professor of sports science and senior
author of a Penn State report, a lot of young women see steroid use
as an investment in their future; athletes can take the hormones
for a few months in high school, qualify for a college scholarship,
and then stop taking the drugs before sophisticated lab tests can
spot them (Faigenbaum, Zaichkowsky, Gardner, & Micheli, 1998).
What teenagers don't realize, though, is that even a few months of
steroid use can permanently damage the heart, trigger liver failure,
stunt physical growth, and put a woman's childbearing ability at risk.
Steroids cause muscles to outgrow and injure the tendons and liga-
ments that attach them to the bone (Faigenbaum et al., 1998). As
Farnaz Khadem, spokeswoman for the World Anti-Doping Agency has
emphasized, "A lot of these young people have no idea of what this
is doing to their bodies. This is a real health danger" (DeNoon, 2004).

In APA style, the
first parentheti-
cal reference to
a source with
three to five
authors lists
all authors . . .

. . . subsequent
references to the
source use "et
al." in place of
all but the first
author.

   Although health is the most important concern in the issue
of steroid use, it is not the only one. Possessing or selling steroids
without a prescription is a crime, so those who are involved in such
activities may also endure criminal penalties (Gorman, 1998). Young
women who use steroids are resorting to illegal actions and may
eventually be labeled as "criminals," a label that will follow them
for the rest of their lives. Doors to coaching jobs, teaching careers,
and many other occupations may be shut permanently if one has a
criminal past.

How Girl Athletes Can Avoid Steroid Use

   What can we do to help adolescent female athletes avoid illicit
drug use? How can we help them avoid the pitfalls of competitive
athletics? Parents, coaches, and the athletes themselves all play a
crucial role in averting bad choices. First, parents and coaches need
to be aware that performance-enhancing drugs are a problem. Some
adults believe that steroid use is either minimal or nonexistent
among teenagers, but one study concluded that "over half the teens

APA

V Documenting Sources

who use steroids start before age 16, sometimes with the encouragement of their parents. . . . Seven percent said they first took 'juice'
by age ten" (Dudley, 1994, p. 235).

An ellipsis indicates that words from the source were not included in the quotation.

Parents need to take the time to know their children and know
what their children are doing. Coaches must know their players well
enough to be able to identify a child in trouble. When asked what
parents and coaches could do to help girl athletes remain healthy
and not use drugs or overwork themselves, Juan Orozco offered the
following advice:

> An athlete should be happy in her activity of choice, and
> her parents should encourage her desires to do well. Parents
> should be involved in her life and let her know that her efforts
> are valued highly, but they also need to be on the lookout
> for danger signs — such as unusual weight loss or moodiness.
> As a coach, I need to know the personalities of my players
> and get them to trust me, not only as their coach but as their
> friend — someone they can talk to if they have a problem.
> (personal communication, September 22, 2014)

Extended quotation is set off in block style without quotation marks.

It is also important for parents and coaches to teach the
athletes how to develop a healthy lifestyle and not focus only
on winning. If an athlete seems to take her sport too seriously,
parents might negotiate with her, encouraging her to balance
sports with other endeavors. Some parents and coaches push kids
too hard, teaching them to win at any cost. In fact, a number of
researchers believe that some parents and coaches are actually
purchasing expensive black-market steroids for their young athletes
(Costello). As University of Massachusetts researcher Avery Faigenbaum has put it, "I don't know a lot of ten-year-olds who have a
couple of hundred dollars — to spend on drugs or anything else"
(Costello, "Too Late?" para. 4).

Athletes, too, must take responsibility for their own lives. Adolescent girls should try to resist undue pressures imposed by parents,
coaches, and society. They must learn about the damage steroids can
cause and understand that pursuing an "ideal" body type is not only
unrealistic but also unhealthy (Yiannakis & Melnick, 2001). Most of
all, young female athletes need to know that they are more important
than the competition. No scholarship or medal is worth liver failure
or losing the ability to bear children.

The vast majority of excellent athletes do not overtrain, become
bulimic, or wind up using steroids. Clearly, they have learned to
avoid the pitfalls of competitive athletics. They believe in themselves
and their abilities and know how to balance sports and other activities. They have learned how to sacrifice and work hard, but not at

GIRLS, SPORTS, AND STEROIDS   8

the expense of their integrity or health. In short, these athletes have

not lost sight of the true objective of participating in sports — they

know that their success is due to their efforts and not to the effects

of a performance-enhancing drug. When asked what she would say to

athletes considering steroid use, Melissa Alvarez said:

> If you are training and doing your best, you should not have
> to use steroids. At the end of the day, it is just a game. You
> should never put your health at risk for anything, or anyone.
> It should be your top priority. (personal communication,
> September 26, 2014)

In the essay's conclusion, Alexis uses a quotation to reinforce her main point.

References

Brown, E. W., & Branta, C. F. (Eds.). (1988). *Competitive sports for children and youth: An overview of issues and research.* Champaign, IL: Human Kinetics.

Centers for Disease Control and Prevention. (2004, May 21). Youth risk behavior surveillance — December 2003. *Morbidity and Mortality Weekly Report 53*, (Report no. SS-2). Retrieved from http://www.cdc.gov/mmwr/PDF/SS/SS5302.pdf

Costello, B. (2004, July 4). Too late? Survey suggests millions of kids could be juicing. *New York Post.* Retrieved from http://www.nypost.com

Davies, D., & Armstrong, M. (1989). *Psychological factors in competitive sport.* New York, NY: Falmer Press.

DeNoon, D. (2004, August 4). *Steroid use: Hitting closer to home.* Retrieved from http://webmd.com/fitness-exercise/features/steroid-use-hitting-closer-to-home

Dexheimer, E. (2004, May 13). Nothing to lose: The Colorado Impact teaches girls about life — then hoops. *Denver Westword.* Retrieved from http://www.westword.com

Dudley, W. (Ed.). (1994). *Sports in America: Opposing viewpoints.* San Diego, CA: Greenhaven Press.

Faigenbaum, A. D., Zaichkowsky, L. D., Gardner, D. E., & Micheli, L. J. (1998). Anabolic steroid use by male and female middle school students. *Pediatrics, 101*(5), e6. doi:10.1542/peds.101.5.e6

Family Education Staff (n.d.). *Teen steroid use.* Retrieved from http://life.familyeducation.com/athletic-training/drugs-and-alcohol/58291.html?page=1&detoured=1]]

Girls and steroids. (1998). *Teacher Magazine 9*(5), 11. Retrieved from http://www.teachermagazine.org

Gorman, C. (1998, August 10). Girls on steroids. *Time 152*(6), 93. Retrieved from http://www.time.com

Graham, J. (1999). *The athletic woman's sourcebook.* New York, NY: Avon Books.

Manning, A. (2002, July 9). Kids, steroids don't mix. *USA Today.* Retrieved from http://www.usatoday.com

Mundell, E. J. (2004, May 12). Schools struggle to control steroid use. *HealthDay.* Retrieved from http://www.healthday.com

President's Council on Physical Fitness and Sports. (1997, May). *Physical activity and sport in the lives of girls: Physical and mental health dimensions from an interdisciplinary approach.* Retrieved from University of Minnesota, Tucker Center for

---

Annotations (left margin):

Sources alphabetized by author's name or, if no author, by title

First line of each entry starts at left margin, additional lines indented one-half inch, or five spaces

Online newspaper article

Book with two authors

Source URL given

Edited book

Online article with a DOI

Nonperiodical Web document

Online articles without DOIs

Book with one author

Online newspaper article

Annotations (right margin):

List of references on a separate page, heading centered

Edited book

Online government report

Source titles only capitalize first words, words following a colon or question mark, and proper nouns

Titles of books and journals italicized

Nonperiodical Web site

URL of publication's home page

GIRLS, SPORTS, AND STEROIDS   10

Research on Girls and Women in Sport Web site: http://cehd.umn
.edu/tuckercenter/projects/PresidentsCouncil/pcpfs_report.pdf

Sieghart, M. A. (2004, August 27). Competitive sport is harsh and
unforgiving: That's why it's good for children. *The Times* of
London. Retrieved from http://www.the-times.co.uk

Sporting activities impact illegal drug use among male and female
teenagers. (2003, September 26). *Drug Week,* pp. 16-17.

Yiannakis, A., & Melnick, M. J. (Eds.). (2001). *Contemporary issues in
sociology of sport.* Champaign, IL: Human Kinetics.

Online newspaper article

Magazine article without a named author

Book editors identified with (Ed.) or (Eds.)

APA

V Documenting Sources

22

Using *Chicago* Style

> **Key Questions**
>
> **22a. How do I cite sources within the text of my document?** 400
>
> **22b. How do I format notes and prepare the bibliography?** 402

The documentation style described in *The Chicago Manual of Style: The Essential Guide for Writers, Editors, and Publishers*, Sixteenth Edition, is used in the humanities and in some of the social sciences. The *Manual* recommends two systems, an author-date system similar to the APA system (see Chapter 21) and a notes system. This chapter describes and provides models for the notes system.

In the notes system, researchers acknowledge their sources in footnotes or endnotes. Footnotes appear at the bottom of a printed page, whereas endnotes appear at the end of the document. Although a bibliography can be omitted when using the notes system (since all relevant publication information is provided in the notes), the *Manual* encourages authors to provide a bibliography or list of works cited in documents when more than a few sources are cited. For more information about this system, consult *The Chicago Manual of Style*. Information about the manual can also be found at **chicagomanualofstyle.org**.

To see Nicholas Brothers' research essay, formatted in the *Chicago* style notes system, turn to p. 417.

CITATION TUTORIALS FOR NOTES AND BIBLIOGRAPHY CITED ENTRIES

- Books 404
- Articles from periodicals 409
- Articles from databases 413
- Works from Web sites 416

CITATIONS WITHIN YOUR TEXT

1. Numbering 400
2. Placement of the note numbers in the text 400
3. Placement of notes 401

NOTES AND ENTRIES IN YOUR BIBLIOGRAPHY OR LIST OF WORKS CITED

Books, Conference Proceedings, and Dissertations

Sources in Journals, Magazines, and Newspapers

Print Reference Works

Field Sources

Chicago

V Documenting Sources

22a

How do I cite sources within the text of my document?

Chicago uses footnotes or endnotes. Notes can also be used to expand on points made in the text—that is, notes can contain both citation information and commentary on the text. For digital documents such as Web sites that consist of multiple "pages" of text, footnotes can take the form of links to notes at the end of a "page" or to pop-up windows that display the notes.

The first time you refer to a source in a note, provide complete publication information for the source. In subsequent references, you need to cite only the author's last name, a shortened version of the title, and the page numbers (if the source has page numbers) to which you refer. Separate the elements with commas and end with a period. *Chicago* style italicizes titles of books and periodicals.

The following examples illustrate the most common ways of citing sources within the text of your document using *Chicago*'s notes system.

1. Numbering   Notes should be numbered consecutively throughout your work, beginning with 1.

2. Placement of the Note Numbers in the Text   Place the number for a note at the end of the sentence containing the reference after punctuation and outside any parentheses. If you are citing the source of material that comes before an em dash (or two hyphens) used to separate parts of a sentence, the note number should precede the dash. Note numbers are set as superscripts.

Lee and Calandra suggest that the poor organization of online historical documents may impair students' ability to conduct research without guidance.[1]

Tomlinson points out that the erosion of Fiji's culture was accelerated by both British and Indian immigration[2] — though the two immigrant groups inhabited very different roles and social classes.

3. Placement of Notes   You may choose between footnotes, which appear at the bottom of the page containing corresponding note numbers, and endnotes, which appear at the end of the document in a section titled "Notes." Longer works, such as books, typically use endnotes. The choice depends on the expectations of your readers and your preferences. Regardless of placement, notes are numbered consecutively throughout the document. If you use a bibliography, it follows the last page of text or the last page of endnotes. Model notes for various types of sources appear in section 22b, which begins on p. 402.

4. Including Page Numbers in a Note   Use page numbers whenever you refer to a specific page of a source rather than to the source as a whole. The use of page numbers is required for quotations.

4. Amy Hanson, *Baby Boomers and Beyond: Tapping the Ministry, Talents, and Passions of Adults over Fifty* (San Francisco: Jossey-Bass, 2010), 156.

5. Cross-Referencing Notes   If you are referring to a source identified in a previous note, you can refer to that note instead of repeating the information.

5. See note 3 above.

6. Citing the Same Source in Multiple Notes   If you refer to the same source in two or more notes, provide a full citation in the first note. In subsequent notes, provide the author's last name, a brief version of the title, and the page number. If you are referring to the same source cited in the previous note, you can use the Latin abbreviation "ibid." (for *ibidem*, or "in the same place").

1. John Mosier, *Deathride: Hitler vs. Stalin; The Eastern Front, 1941–1945* (New York: Simon & Schuster, 2010), 26.

2. Ibid., 54.

6. Mosier, Deathride, 131.

7. Citing a Source Quoted in Another Source

7. José María Arguedas, *Obras Completa* (Lima: Editorial Horizonte, 1983), 1:129, quoted in Alberto Flores Galindo et al., *In Search of an Inca: Identity and Utopia in the Andes* (New York: Cambridge University Press, 2010), 199.

Chicago   V Documenting Sources

22b

How do I format notes and prepare the bibliography?

The Chicago Manual of Style provides guidelines for formatting notes and entries in a bibliography of works that are relevant to but not necessarily cited within your document. In print documents and linear documents that are distributed electronically (such as a word processing file or a newsgroup post), the bibliography appears at the end of the document. In longer documents, a bibliography could be given at the end of each chapter or section. In digital documents that use links, such as a Web site, the bibliography is often a separate page to which other pages are linked. To see a bibliography in *Chicago* style, see p. 426.

For notes, include the number of the note, indented and not superscripted, followed by these elements.

- author's name (first name first)
- title (followed by the title of the complete work if the source is an article, chapter, or other short work contained in a larger work)
- publisher (for a book) or publication title (for a journal, magazine, or newspaper)
- date
- page(s) being cited

For entries in the bibliography, include these elements.

- author's name (last name first)
- title (followed by the title of the complete work if the source is an article, chapter, or other short work contained in a larger work)
- publisher (for a book) or publication title (for a journal, magazine, or newspaper)
- date
- page(s) (if the source is a shorter work included in a complete work)

Keep in mind that well-known reference works, such as encyclopedias, and all types of personal communication—personal interviews, letters, surveys, email messages, online discussion groups—are cited in a note only. They are not usually included in the bibliography.

Note: For each type of source, a pair of examples is presented in this section: a model note followed by a model bibliographic entry.

Books, Conference Proceedings, and Dissertations

8. One Author Use the basic format described on p. 404. When citing a book, use the information from the title page and the copyright page (on the reverse side of the title page), not from the book's cover or a library catalog.

8. Doris Kearns Goodwin, *The Bully Pulpit: Theodore Roosevelt, William Howard Taft, and the Golden Age of Journalism* (New York: Simon & Schuster, 2013), 498.

Goodwin, Doris Kearns. *The Bully Pulpit: Theodore Roosevelt, William Howard Taft, and the Golden Age of Journalism*. New York: Simon & Schuster, 2013.

9. Two or Three Authors List the authors in the order in which they appear on the title page. In a note, list the first name for each author first. In the bibliography, list the first author's last name first and list the first names for each other author first.

9. Robert A. Jerin and Laura J. Moriarty, *The Victims of Crime* (Upper Saddle River, NJ: Pearson Prentice Hall, 2010), 259.

Jerin, Robert A., and Laura J. Moriarty. *The Victims of Crime*. Upper Saddle River, NJ: Pearson Prentice Hall, 2010.

10. Four or More Authors In a note, give only the first author's name followed by "et al." (Latin for "and others"). In the bibliography, list all the authors that appear on the title page.

10. Harry Markopolos et al., *No One Would Listen: A True Financial Thriller* (Hoboken, NJ: Wiley, 2010), 179.

Markopolos, Harry, Frank Casey, Neil Chelo, Gaytri Kachroo, and Michael Ocrant. *No One Would Listen: A True Financial Thriller*. Hoboken, NJ: Wiley, 2010.

11. Corporate or Group Author Use the corporation or group as the author; it may also be the publisher.

11. International Monetary Fund, *Regional Economic Outlook: Middle East and Central Asia* (Washington, DC: International Monetary Fund, 2010), 26.

International Monetary Fund. *Regional Economic Outlook: Middle East and Central Asia*. Washington, DC: International Monetary Fund, 2010.

12. Unknown Author When no author is listed on the title or copyright page, begin the entry with the title of the work. In the bibliography, alphabetize the entry by the first word other than *A, An,* or *The*.

12. *Letting Ana Go* (New York: Simon Pulse, 2013), 118–20.

Letting Ana Go. New York: Simon Pulse, 2013.

13. Translated Book List the author first and the translator after the title. Use the abbreviation "trans." in a note, but spell out "Translated by" in the bibliography.

13. Nujood Ali and Delphine Minoui, *I Am Nujood, Age 10 and Divorced*, trans. Linda Coverdale (New York: Three Rivers Press, 2010), 34.

Ali, Nujood, and Delphine Minoui. *I Am Nujood, Age 10 and Divorced*. Translated by Linda Coverdale. New York: Three Rivers Press, 2010.

TUTORIAL

How do I cite books using Chicago *style?*

PLATO AT THE GOOGLEPLEX

Copyright © 2014 by Rebecca Goldstein

All rights reserved. Published in the United States by Pantheon Books,
a division of Random House LLC, New York, and in Canada by Random
House of Canada Limited, Toronto, Penguin Random House companies.

Pantheon Books and colophon are registered trademarks of
Random House LLC.

Owing to limitations of space, permissions to reprint from previously
published material are listed following the bibliographical note.

Library of Congress Cataloging-in-Publication Data
Goldstein, Rebecca, [date]
Plato at the Googleplex : why philosophy won't go away / Rebecca Goldstein.
pages cm
Includes bibliographical references.
HC ISBN 978-0-307-37819-4   XBK ISBN 978-0-307-90887-2
1. Plato—Influence. 2. Philosophy—History—21st century.
3. Imaginary conversations. I. Title.
B395.G4455 2014 184—dc23 2013029660

www.pantheonbooks.com

Jacket design by Pablo Delcán

Printed in the United States of America
First Edition
2 4 6 8 9 7 5 3 1

When citing a book, use information from the title page and the copyright page (on the back side of the title page), not from the cover or a library catalog. This tutorial gives an example of a *Chicago*-style footnote or endnote. An example of the bibliography entry for this source is at the bottom of the page. Consult pp. 402–07 for additional models for citing books. [Copyright page and title page from *Plato At The Googleplex: Why Philosophy Won't Go Away* by Rebecca Goldstein, copyright © 2014 by Rebecca Goldstein. Used by permission of Pantheon Books, an imprint of the Knopf Doubleday Publishing Group, a division of Random House LLC. All Rights Reserved.]

Note

1. Rebecca Newberger Goldstein, [A] *Plato at the Googleplex: Why Philosophy* [B]

Won't Go Away (New York: Pantheon, 2014), [C] 234–36. [D]

A **The author.** In the note, give the first name first. Follow the last name with a comma. Separate the names of multiple authors with commas; use the word "and" before the final author's name.

B **The title.** Give the full title; include the subtitle (if any), preceded by a colon. Italicize the title and subtitle, capitalizing all major words.

C **Publication information.** Enclose the city, publisher, and date in parentheses. If more than one city is given, use the first one listed. For a city that may be unfamiliar to your readers or confused with another city, add an abbreviation of the state, country, or province (Cambridge, MA or Waterloo, ON). Insert a colon. Give the publisher's name. Omit words such as *Inc.* and *Co.* Include and do not abbreviate such terms as *Books* and *Press*. Insert a comma. Give the year of publication, using the most recent copyright year. Close the parentheses and insert a comma.

D **Inclusive page number(s).** Give the specific page or pages on which you found the information. For numbers 100 and above, give only the last two digits and any other preceding digits if different from the first number (22–28, 402–10, 1437–45, 599–603).

Bibliography Entry

In the bibliography, give the author's last name first, and separate the elements with periods. Do not enclose the publication information in parentheses.

Goldstein, Rebecca Newberger. *Plato at the Googleplex: Why Philosophy Won't Go Away*. New York: Pantheon, 2014.

14. Edition Other than the First   Give edition information after the title.

14. Alan Brinkley, *The Unfinished Nation: A Concise History of the American People*, 6th ed. (New York: McGraw-Hill, 2010), 627.

Brinkley, Alan. *The Unfinished Nation: A Concise History of the American People.* 6th ed. New York: McGraw-Hill, 2010.

15. Untitled Volume in a Multivolume Work   In the notes, give the volume number and page number, separated by a colon, for the specific location of the information referred to in your text. In the bibliography, if you have used all the volumes, give the total number of volumes after the title, using the abbreviation "vols." ("2 vols." or "4 vols."). If you have used one volume, give the abbreviation "Vol." and the volume number after the title.

15. Fang Hanqi, ed., *A History of Journalism in China* (Singapore: Silkroad Press, 2013), 7: 243–49.

Hanqi, Fang, ed. *A History of Journalism in China*. Vol 7. Singapore: Silkroad Press, 2013.

16. Titled Volume in a Multivolume Work   Give the title of the volume to which you refer, followed by the volume number and the general title for the entire work.

16. Rick Atkinson, *The Guns at Last Light: The War in Western Europe, 1944–1945*, vol. 3 of *The Liberation Trilogy* (New York: Henry Holt, 2013), 345–49.

Atkinson, Rick. *The Guns at Last Light: The War in Western Europe, 1944–1945.* Vol. 3 of *The Liberation Trilogy*. New York: Henry Holt, 2013.

17. Book in a Series   The series name follows the title and is capitalized as a title but is not italicized. If the series numbers its volumes, include that information as well.

17. Michael F. Holt, *Franklin Pierce*, American Presidents Series 14 (New York: Times Books/Henry Holt, 2010), 7.

Holt, Michael F. *Franklin Pierce*. American Presidents Series 14. New York: Times Books/Henry Holt, 2010.

18. Republished Book   Place the original publication date before the publication information for the reprint.

18. James, King of England, *The Political Works of James I*, ed. Charles Howard McIlwain (1918; repr., Whitefish, MT: Kessinger, 2010), 74.

James, King of England. *The Political Works of James I*. Edited by Charles Howard McIlwain. 1918. Reprint, Whitefish, MT: Kessinger, 2010.

19. Author with an Editor   List the author at the beginning of the citation and add the editor's name after the title. In notes, use the abbreviation "ed." before the editor's name. In the bibliography, include the phrase "Edited by" before the editor's name.

19. Frederick Douglass, *Narrative of the Life of Frederick Douglass, an American Slave*, ed. Ira Dworkin (New York: Penguin Books, 2014), 114.

Douglass, Frederick. *Narrative of the Life of Frederick Douglass, an American Slave.* Edited by Ira Dworkin. New York: Penguin Books, 2014.

20. Anthology or Collection with an Editor   To cite an entire anthology or collection of articles, give the editor(s) before the title of the collection, adding a comma and the abbreviation "ed." or "eds."

20. Michael Krausz, ed., *Relativism: A Contemporary Anthology* (New York: Columbia University Press, 2010).

Krausz, Michael, ed. *Relativism: A Contemporary Anthology.* New York: Columbia University Press, 2010.

21. Foreword, Introduction, Preface, or Afterword   Give the name of the writer of the foreword, introduction, preface, or afterword followed by the appropriate phrase ("introduction to," "preface to," and so on) before the title of the book. If the writer of the introduction or other part differs from the writer of the book, after the title insert the word "by" and the author's name.

21. Martin Stannard, preface to *Muriel Spark: The Biography* (New York: Norton, 2010).

Stannard, Martin. Preface to *Muriel Spark: The Biography*, xv–xxvi. New York: Norton, 2010.

22. Chapter in a Book or Selection in an Anthology   Give the author and title (in quotation marks) for the chapter or selection. Then give the title, editor (if any), and publication data for the book or anthology. In the bibliography, give the inclusive page numbers before the publication data.

22. William Dalrymple, "The Monk's Tale," in *Nine Lives: In Search of the Sacred in Modern India* (New York: Knopf, 2010), 151.

Dalrymple, William. "The Monk's Tale." In *Nine Lives: In Search of the Sacred in Modern India*, 142–71. New York: Knopf, 2010.

23. Published Proceedings of a Conference   Cite as for an anthology or collection with an editor (see also #20 above).

23. Derek McAuley and Simon Peyton-Jones, *Proceedings of the 2010 ACM-BCS Visions of Computer Science Conference* (Swindon, UK: British Informatics Society, 2010).

McAuley, Derek, and Simon Peyton-Jones. *Proceedings of the 2010 ACM-BCS Visions of Computer Science Conference.* Swindon, UK: British Informatics Society, 2010.

24. Paper Published in the Proceedings of a Conference Cite as a chapter in an edited book (see also #22 above).

24. Dale Miller, "Finding Unity in Computational Logic," in *Proceedings of the 2010 ACM-BCS Visions of Computer Science Conference* (Swindon, UK: British Informatics Society, 2010), 2.

Miller, Dale. "Finding Unity in Computational Logic." In *Proceedings of the 2010 ACM-BCS Visions of Computer Science Conference*, 1–13. Swindon, UK: British Informatics Society, 2010.

25. Sacred Text Cite sacred texts only within the text of your document. A note should include the book, chapter, and verse, but not a page number.

25. Deut. 5:1–21 (New Revised Standard Version).

26. Published Dissertation or Thesis Give the author and title, the phrase "PhD diss." or "master's thesis," followed by information about the institution that granted the degree and the year. Include publication number from ProQuest if appropriate.

26. Anthony Colello, *Affirmative Action Bans and Minority Employment: Washington State's Initiative 200* (PhD diss., Georgetown University, 2011), 41–2, ProQuest (AAT 1491319).

Colello, Anthony. *Affirmative Action Bans and Minority Employment: Washington State's Initiative 200*. PhD diss., Georgetown University, 2011. ProQuest (ATT 1491319).

27. Unpublished Dissertation or Thesis Give the author and title, in quotation marks. Then include the phrase "PhD diss." or "master's thesis," information about the institution that granted the degree, and the date.

27. Joshua Glenn Iddings, "Writing at One Appalachian High School" (PhD diss., Purdue University, 2013), 96.

Iddings, Joshua Glenn. "Writing at One Appalachian High School." PhD diss., Purdue University, 2013.

28. Abstract of a Dissertation or Thesis Provide information as you would for an article in a journal (see also #29 below). Add information about Dissertation Abstracts International.

28. Yi Mou, "Social Media and Risk Communication: The Role of Social Networking Sites in Food-safety Communication" (PhD Diss., University of Connecticut, 2012), abstract, *Dissertation Abstracts International 74* (2013).

Mou, Yi. "Social Media and Risk Communication: The Role of Social Networking Sites in Food-safety Communication." PhD Diss., University of Connecticut, 2012. Abstract, *Dissertation Abstracts International 74* (2013).

Chicago

V Documenting Sources

Sources in Journals, Magazines, and Newspapers

29. Article in a Journal   After the journal title, include the volume number, a comma, and the issue number after the abbreviation "no." (Note that volume and issue information is not italicized.) Then give the year. In the note, give the specific page number to which you are referring; in the bibliography, give inclusive page numbers of the entire article.

29. Kate McCoy, "Manifesting Destiny: A Land Education Analysis of Settler Colonialism in Jamestown, Virginia, USA," *Environmental Education Research* 20, no. 1 (2014): 86.

McCoy, Kate. "Manifesting Destiny: A Land Education Analysis of Settler Colonialism in Jamestown, Virginia, USA." *Environmental Education Research* 20, no. 1 (2014): 82–97.

30. Article in a Monthly Magazine   Magazines are cited by their dates rather than by volume and issue.

30. Peter Huber, "Better Medicine," *Reason*, March 2014, 25.

Huber, Peter. "Better Medicine." *Reason*. March 2014, 22–30.

31. Article in a Weekly Magazine   Cite like a monthly magazine, but provide the day of publication.

31. Marty Makary, "The Cost of Chasing Cancer," *Time*, March 10, 2014, 24.

Makary, Marty. "The Cost of Chasing Cancer." *Time*, March 10, 2014, 24.

32. Article in a Newspaper   If the name of the newspaper does not include the city, insert the city before the name (and italicize it). If an American city is not well known, name the state as well (in parentheses, abbreviated). Identify newspapers from other countries with the city in parentheses (not italicized) after the name of the newspaper.

Eugene (OR) Register-Guard

Sunday Times (London)

Page numbers may be omitted, since separate editions of the same newspaper may place articles differently. If a paper comes out in more than one edition, identify the edition after the date.

32. Kelly Zito, "Cities Key Source of Toxins in Bay, Study Finds," *San Francisco Chronicle*, October 5, 2010, Bay Area edition.

Zito, Kelly. "Cities Key Source of Toxins in Bay, Study Finds." *San Francisco Chronicle*, October 5, 2010, Bay Area edition.

TUTORIAL

How do I cite articles from periodicals using Chicago style?

PARTISAN FEDERALISM

Jessica Bulman-Pozen

Periodicals include journals, magazines, and newspapers. This tutorial gives an example of a *Chicago*-style footnote or endnote for a print magazine article. (An example of the bibliography entry for this source is at the bottom of the page.) Models for citing articles from journals and newspapers are on pp. 408–10. If you need to cite a periodical article you accessed electronically, follow the guidelines below and see p. 416. [Harvard Law Review, permission conveyed through Copyright Clearance Center, Inc.]

Note

┌──────────**A**──────────┐ ┌────────**B**────────┐ ┌──────**C**──────┐
2. Jessica Bulman-Pozen, "Partisan Federalism," *Harvard Law Review*,

┌────**D**────┐ ┌**E**┐
127, no. 4, 2014, 1084.

A **The author.** In the note, give the first name first. Follow the last name with a comma. Separate the names of multiple authors with commas; use the word "and" before the final author's name.

B **The article title.** Give the full title; include the subtitle (if any), preceded by a colon. Put the article title and subtitle in quotation marks, capitalizing all major words.

C **The periodical title.** Italicize the periodical title, and capitalize all major words.

D **Publication information and date.** For journal articles, include the volume and issue number followed by the year. For monthly magazines, give the month and year. For weekly magazines, include the day of publication (September 6, 2010). Do not abbreviate the month. Use a comma after the year.

E **Specific page number(s).** Give the specific page or pages on which you found the information, unless you are referring to the article as a whole. For numbers 100 and above, give only the last two digits and any other preceding digits if different from the first number (22–24, 409–10, 1437–45, 599–601).

Bibliography Entry

In the bibliography, give the author's last name first, separate the elements by periods, and give inclusive pages for the entire article.

Bulman-Pozen, Jessica. "Partisan Federalism." *Harvard Law Review*, 127, no. 4, 2014, 1078–1146.

Chicago

V Documenting Sources

33. Unsigned Article in a Newspaper or Magazine If no author is given, begin the note with the title of the article; begin the bibliography entry with the title of the periodical.

33. "NYC May Ban Smoking in Parks, on Beaches," *Boston Globe*, September 16, 2010.

Boston Globe. "NYC May Ban Smoking in Parks, on Beaches." September 16, 2010.

34. Letter to the Editor Treat as a newspaper article. If no title is provided, place "Letter to the editor" in the title position.

34. Jason Levi, letter to the editor, *Smithsonian*, June 2010.

Levi, Jason. Letter to the editor. *Smithsonian*, June 2010.

35. Review Give the author of the review, the review title, if any, and then the words "review of" followed by the title and author of the work reviewed and the author or editor (for books) or director or performer (for movies, plays, and similar productions).

35. Stephen Holden, "Students Caught in the School Squeeze," review of *Waiting for Superman*, directed by Davis Guggenheim, *New York Times*, September 23, 2010.

Holden, Stephen. "Students Caught in the School Squeeze." Review of *Waiting for Superman*, directed by Davis Guggenheim. *New York Times*, September 23, 2010.

Print Reference Works

36. Entry in an Encyclopedia, Dictionary, Thesaurus, Handbook, or Almanac In notes, provide the title of the work (italicized), the edition, the abbreviation "s.v." (for *sub verbo*, or "under the word"), and the title of the entry.

36. *Encyclopaedia Britannica*, 15th ed., s.v. "Lee, Robert E."

Chicago does not recommend including reference works such as encyclopedias or dictionaries in the bibliography.

37. Government Publication In general, give the issuing body, then the title and any other information (such as report numbers) that would help your readers locate the source. Follow with the publication data and the page numbers if relevant. You may abbreviate "Government Printing Office" as GPO.

37. U.S. Senate, Special Committee on Aging, *Social Security Modernization: Options to Address Solvency and Benefit Adequacy* (Washington, DC: GPO, 2010), 7.

U.S. Senate. Special Committee on Aging. *Social Security Modernization: Options to Address Solvency and Benefit Adequacy*. Washington, DC: GPO, 2010.

38. Pamphlet, Report, or Brochure   Cite it as you would a book (see p. 404).

> 38. *Facts: Scripps Institution of Oceanography* (San Diego: University of California, 2012).

Facts: Scripps Institution of Oceanography. San Diego: University of California, 2012.

Field Sources

39. Personal Interview   Give the location and date in a note. Do not include unpublished interviews in the bibliography.

> 39. Rachel Stein, interview by author, Pittsburgh, June 2, 2014.

40. Letter or Other Personal Communication   Do not include personal communications such as letters or phone calls in the bibliography. In a note, give the name of the person with whom you communicated, the form of communication, and the date.

> 40. Megahn McKennan, conversation with author, March 5, 2014.

> 41. Sangita Thakore, letter to author, November 12, 2014.

41. Survey   *Chicago* does not specify how to cite unpublished survey results. Cite them in your text as you would a personal communication (see #40 above).

42. Observation Notes   *Chicago* does not specify how to cite observation notes. Cite them in your text as you would a personal communication (see #40 above).

43. Lecture or Public Address   Provide the title, the nature of the speech (such as lecture or keynote address), the name of the organization sponsoring the meeting or lecture, and the location and date it was given.

> 43. Andrew Sullivan, "The Politics of Homosexuality" (lecture, Princeton University, Princeton, NJ, February 18, 2010).

Sullivan, Andrew. "The Politics of Homosexuality." Lecture presented at Princeton University, Princeton, NJ, February 18, 2010.

Media Sources

44. Film or Video Recording   Provide the title first, the name of the director, the company, the year it was filmed, and the medium (film, videocassette, DVD).

> 44. *Michael Jackson's This Is It*, directed by Kenny Ortega (2009; Culver City, CA: Sony Pictures, 2010), DVD.

Michael Jackson's This Is It. Directed by Kenny Ortega. 2009; Culver City, CA: Sony Pictures, 2010. DVD.

Chicago

V Documenting Sources

45. Television Program   *Chicago* does not specify how to cite a television program. Cite as you would a video recording, identifying the medium as "television program" or "television broadcast."

46. Radio Program   *Chicago* does not specify how to cite a radio program. Cite as you would a video recording, identifying the medium as "radio program" or "radio broadcast."

47. Sound Recording   Give the composer and title of the recording, the performers and conductor, the label, and identifying number.

47. Pyotr Ilyich Tchaikovsky, *Symphony No. 5, Romeo and Juliet Fantasy Overture*, Royal Philharmonic Orchestra, conducted by Daniele Gatti, Harmonia Mundi, MU907381, compact disc.

Tchaikovsky, Pyotr Ilyich. *Symphony No. 5, Romeo and Juliet Fantasy Overture*. Royal Philharmonic Orchestra, conducted by Daniele Gatti. Harmonia Mundi, MU907381, compact disc.

Digital Sources

All digital sources should include either a publication date, a revision or "last modified" date, or an access date. After the date, include a DOI or, if the source does not have a DOI, a stable URL. For a source accessed through a database, include the name of the database and any number assigned to the source.

48. Article from a Database

48. Alessandro Pes, "Becoming Imperialist: Italian Colonies in Fascist Textbooks for Primary Schools," *Journal of Modern Italian Studies* 18, no. 5 (2013): 609–11, Academic Search Premier (92017350), doi: 10.1080/1354571X.2013 .839519.

Pes, Alessandro. "Becoming Imperialist: Italian Colonies in Fascist Textbooks for Primary Schools." *Journal of Modern Italian Studies* 18, no. 5 (2013): 599– 614. Academic Search Premier (92017350), doi: 10.1080/1354571X.2013 .839519.

49. Article in an Online Journal

49. Gary Fields, "Palestinian Landscape in a 'Not-too-Distant Mirror,'" *Journal of Historical Sociology* 23, no. 2 (June 2010), doi: 10.1111/j.1467-6443.2010 .01373.x.

Fields, Gary. "Palestinian Landscape in a 'Not-too-Distant Mirror.'" *Journal of Historical Sociology* 23, no. 2 (June 2010). doi: 10.1111/j.1467-6443.2010 .01373.x.

TUTORIAL

How do I cite articles from databases using Chicago *style?*

Libraries subscribe to services such as LexisNexis, ProQuest, InfoTrac, and EBSCOhost that provide access to databases of digital texts. The databases provide publication information, abstracts, and the complete text of documents in a specific subject area, discipline, or profession. (See also Chapter 9.)

This tutorial gives an example of a *Chicago*-style footnote or endnote for a journal article accessed via a database. (An example of the bibliography entry for this source is at the bottom of the page.) To cite magazine and newspaper articles from databases, see also pp. 412–15. [Courtesy of EBSCO.]

Note

3. Aspasia Stephanou, "A 'Ghastly Operation': Transfusing Blood, Science and the Supernatural in Vampire Texts," *Gothic Studies* 15, no. 2 (November 2013): 59, EBSCOhost (93303198), doi: 10.7227/GS.15.2.4.

A **The author.** In the note, give the first name first. Follow the last name with a comma. Separate the names of multiple authors with commas; use the word "and" before the final author's name.

B **The article title.** Give the full title; include the subtitle (if any), preceded by a colon. Put the article title and subtitle in quotes, capitalizing all major words.

C **The journal title.** Italicize the journal title, and capitalize all major words.

D **The publication information.** Insert the volume number followed by a comma, and then give the abbreviation "no." and the issue number. Include the year (and month or season, if given) in parentheses followed by a colon and the specific page number(s) of the reference. (In the bibliography, give inclusive page numbers.) End with a comma.

E **The database information and DOI number.** Give the name of the database, followed by the database's identification number for the article in parentheses. Then include a comma and the DOI number, if one is available.

F **The access date (not shown).** For articles that do not include a publication date, include the word "accessed" and the date of access after the publication information.

Bibliography Entry

Stephanou, Aspasia. "A 'Ghastly Operation': Transfusing Blood, Science and the Supernatural in Vampire Texts." *Gothic Studies*, 15 no. 2 (November 2013): 53-65. EBSCOhost (93303198), doi: 10.7227/GS.15.2.4.

Chicago

V Documenting Sources

50. Article in an Online Magazine

50. Jacob Seigel, "The History and Logic of Military Ultimatums, From Suez to Crimea," *The Daily Beast*, March 3, 2014. http://www.thedailybeast.com/articles/2014/03/03/the-history-and-logic-of-military-ultimatums-from-suez-to-crimea.html.

Seigel, Jacob. "The History and Logic of Military Ultimatums, From Suez to Crimea." *The Daily Beast*, March 3, 2014, http://www.thedailybeast.com/articles/2014/03/03/the-history-and-logic-of-military-ultimatums-from-suez-to-crimea.html.

51. Nonperiodical Web Site

51. Abby Mendelson, "Roberto Clemente: A Form of Punishment," Pittsburg Pirates, MLB.com, May 24, 2013, http://mlb.mlb.com/pit/history/pit_clemente.jsp.

Mendelson, Abby. "Roberto Clemente: A Form of Punishment." Pittsburg Pirates. MLB.com. May 24, 2013. http://mlb.mlb.com/pit/history/pit_clemente.jsp.

52. Online Book

52. Gary Ruskin, *Spooky Business: Corporate Espionage against Nonprofit Organizations* (Washington, DC: Essential Information, 2013), http://www.corporatepolicy.org/spookybusiness.pdf.

Ruskin, Gary. *Spooky Business: Corporate Espionage against Nonprofit Organizations*. Washington, DC: Essential Information, 2013. http://www.corporatepolicy.org/spookybusiness.pdf.

53. Article Posted on a Wiki   Cite online postings to Wikis in the text, but not in the bibliography.

53. "Native Americans," *Davis Wiki*, accessed March 4, 2014, http://daviswiki.org/Native_Americans.

54. Entire Blog   Put the word "blog" in parentheses following the name of the blog, if it is not already part of the name. If the blog is part of a larger publication, include the name of the publication as well.

54. Pat McNamara, *McNamara's Blog: Musings of a Catholic Church Historian from Queens, New York*, http://www.patheos.com/blogs/mcnamarasblog/.

McNamara, Pat. *McNamara's Blog: Musings of a Catholic Church Historian from Queens, New York*. http://www.patheos.com/blogs/mcnamarasblog/.

55. Entry or Comment on a Blog   Put the word "blog" in parentheses following the name of the blog, if it is not already part of the name. If the blog is part of a larger publication, include the name of the publication as well.

Chicago

V Documenting Sources

55. Donna Haisty Winchell, "In Arizona, Is It Ethics or Economics?" *Argument and the Headlines* (blog), *Bits: Ideas for Teaching Composition*, March 3, 2014, http://blogs.bedfordstmartins.com/bits/author/donnaonbitsgmail-com/.

Winchell, Donna Haisty. "In Arizona, Is It Ethics or Economics?" *Argument and the Headlines* (blog). *Bits: Ideas for Teaching Composition*, March 3, 2014, http://blogs.bedfordstmartins.com/bits/author/donnaonbitsgmail-com/.

56. Email Message *Chicago* recommends that personal communication, including email, not be included in the bibliography, although it can be cited in your text. Note that the *Chicago Manual* prefers the hyphenated version of the word "e-mail."

56. Brysa H. Levy, e-mail message to author, January 4, 2014.

57. Online Posting to a Discussion Group Like email, online postings are considered personal communication and are therefore listed in the text only, not in the bibliography. Include a URL for archived postings.

57. Alessandro Busà to URBANTH-L discussion group, December 1, 2009, http://lists.cc.ysu.edu/pipermail/urbanth-l/2009-December/002761.html.

How do I cite works from Web sites using *Chicago* style?

You will likely need to search the Web site to find some of the citation information you need. For some sites, all of the details may not be available; find as many as you can. Remember that the citation you provide should allow readers to retrace your steps electronically to locate the sources. Consult pp. 412–15 for additional models for citing Web sources. [Pew Research Center, February 27, 2014. http://www.people-press.org.]

Note

4. "Public Divided Over Increased Deportation of Unauthorized Immigrants," **B**

Pew Research Center for the People & the Press, **C** Pew Research Center, **D**

February 27, 2014, **E** http://www.people-press.org/2014/02/27/public-divided- **F**

over-increased-deportation-of-unauthorized-immigrants/.

A **The author (not shown).** In the note, give the first name first. Follow the last name with a comma. Separate the names of multiple authors with commas; use the word "and" before the final author's name. If no specific author is named, as in this case, begin with the title of the work.

B **The title of the work.** Give the full title; include the subtitle (if any), preceded by a colon. Put the article title and subtitle in quotation marks, capitalizing all major words.

C **The name of the Web site.** Do not italicize the name of the Web site unless it is the name of a book or periodical.

D **The name of the sponsoring organization.** If the sponsor's name is not visible on the document page, look at the bottom of the site's home page.

E **Date of publication or last modification or access.** If there is no date of publication, include the date the page was last modified or the date on which you accessed the page.

F **The URL.** Give the URL in full; do not use underlining or angle brackets, and be sure not to introduce any new hyphens or slashes. End with a period.

Bibliography Entry

"Public Divided Over Increased Deportation of Unauthorized Immigrants." Pew Research Center for the People & the Press. Pew Research Center. February 27, 2014. http://www.people-press.org/2014/02/27/public-divided-over-increased-deportation-of-unauthorized-immigrants/.

Chicago-Style Research Essay

The Costs of Outsourcing War:
Private Military Corporations in Iraq and Afghanistan — Title of essay

Nicholas Brothers — Writer's name

ENG 108-11
Professor Dawn Terrick
October 20, 2011

Title of course,
instructor's
name, and date

Brothers 2

The Costs of Outsourcing War:

Private Military Corporations in Iraq and Afghanistan

> Title of essay repeated

The United States is considered the preeminent military power of the world. Yet, it is also a military force that today cannot get to the battlefield, feed and house its soldiers, or even protect its bases without the support of a network of nonstate actors. These organizations are sometimes listed on stock exchanges worldwide; they have glossy, professional Web sites and legions of press agents and lobbyists. They are private military corporations (PMCs). Their duties range from cooking and cleaning to planning and even carrying out covert operations to capture Osama bin Laden. But military privatization comes at a severe price — not just in terms of dollars, but also in terms of national security, democratic ideals, and human lives. By relying heavily on PMCs to carry out military operations, the U.S. Department of Defense is undermining its own counterinsurgency efforts in Iraq and Afghanistan.

> Thesis states Nicholas's main point.

Our country's reliance on private military corporations did not happen overnight, and although the corporatization of PMCs is relatively new, the idea of privatization is not. From the time of Alexander the Great to the Napoleonic era, private soldiers made up the bulk of military forces. Citizen armies emerged with the invention of cheap, easy-to-use muskets in the early 19th century. Yet as recently as the Cold War, U.S. armed forces were traditionally organized, with conventional army, naval, and air units in combat against similar Soviet units. The idea, of course, was for the military to be self-sufficient. However, as P. W. Singer explains in his book *Corporate Warriors: The Rise of the Privatized Military Industry*, when the Cold War ended in 1991, the Department of Defense began closing bases and dissolving or combining units, setting the stage for the large-scale outsourcing of military operations.[1] Jonathan Euchner, professor of political science at Missouri Western State University, explained that the shift to PMCs must be seen in the context of the overall privatization movement within the U.S. government that began in 1978 under President Jimmy Carter and gained momentum during the 1980s and 1990s.[2] While the role of PMCs remained modest throughout the 1990s, new military engagements after 9/11 provided new opportunities for PMCs. As detailed by investigative journalist Jeremy Scahill in his book *Blackwater: The Rise of the World's Most Powerful Mercenary Army*, the War on Terror as prosecuted by the Bush administration accelerated the privatization of military functions. The new secretary of defense Donald Rumsfeld would codify this concept, which became known as the Rumsfeld Doctrine.[3] In this

> Interviewee tag indicates the use of field research.

> The name of the book identifies the source of the summarized information.

> Summarized material

Brothers 3

doctrine, a highly mobile infantry force supported by airstrikes and
by contractors would chase Osama bin Laden and al Qaeda in retalia-
tion for the terrorist attacks on the World Trade Center and the Pen-
tagon. The demand for contractors skyrocketed after the invasion of
Iraq, with an overextended military needing more and more support
as the repeated deployments dragged on for years. Now, the United
States is in the final stages of its involvement in one foreign conflict
and intractably embroiled in another. The combat mission in Iraq
officially ended on August 31, 2010, but, with an insurgency that's
growing stronger rather than weaker in Afghanistan, the planned
2011 withdrawal from that theater of war will likely be scaled back.[4]

> First two
> paragraphs offer
> background
> information and
> history to orient
> readers.

Today, companies like DynCorp and Blackwater (now Xe Services)
are some of the biggest, most diversified PMCs in a crowded market.
In a 2007 online chat with the *Washington Post*, Singer, director of
the 21st Century Defense Initiative of the Brookings Institute, asserted that at the time there were about 170 firms doing business
in Iraq alone.[5] A July 2010 analysis by the Congressional Research
Service reported that "contractors make up 54% of the workforce in
Iraq and Afghanistan," meaning that contractors slightly outnum-
bered U.S. soldiers deployed to those countries. More than 13,000 of
these contractors are armed.[6] With so many firms and their contractors in play, the dollar amounts involved are unsurprisingly high.
The Congressional Budget Office estimated that the Department of
Defense spent $76 billion on contractors in Iraq between 2003 and
2007.[7] The staggering cost raises an important question in the mind
of any taxpayer: What are we getting for that money?

> A colon (:) is
> not used when
> the quoted text
> is part of the
> sentence.

> A partial
> quotation is
> integrated
> effectively into
> the sentence.

> Nicholas
> introduces a
> government
> document as
> the source of
> the quoted
> information.

> Nicholas poses
> a question that
> he will answer in
> his essay.

As Dr. Euchner pointed out, the civilian and military leadership
of the United States is attracted to contractors because they offer
streamlined services, with supposedly less bureaucracy and fewer
regulations. As Erik Prince, the cofounder and owner of Blackwater/Xe
Services, put it, "Our corporate goal is to do for the national security
apparatus what FedEx did to the postal service."[8] However, critics of
PMCs would say that we're buying the services of mercenaries, since
both contractors and mercenaries are essentially hired guns. Throughout his book, Scahill provocatively uses "private military corporation" and "mercenary" as interchangeable terms, underscoring their
similarities but failing to provide definitions of either. Yet a look
at definitions in Singer's *Corporate Warriors* reveals that PMCs and
traditional mercenaries differ in several key ways. Perhaps the most
important difference is that a private military corporation is just
that: a legal corporate entity[9] (as opposed to the illegal adventurer
or ragtag squad evoked by the word "mercenary"). Another significant

> Speaker tag
> gives us context
> for the quotation.

> Nicholas
> points out a
> disagreement
> between two of
> his sources.

distinction is that PMCs offer a wide range of services — "training, logistics, support, operational support, post-conflict resolution," according to the head of the PMC Sandline[10] — while mercenaries can rarely do more than engage in combat. However, while PMCs, unlike most mercenaries, are legal, corporate, and diversified in their capabilities, several high-profile abuse cases reveal that it is no wiser to rely on PMCs than on the mercenaries of old.

> Writer's name is followed by the page number.

Numerous examples of abuses, negligence, and outright crimes have taken place since the post-9/11 expansion of the private military industry, and only a handful can be recounted here: A 2002 *Salon* feature details the experiences of the whistleblowers who exposed the sex trafficking that DynCorp International employees, under contract to service helicopters during peacekeeping operations, engaged in while stationed in Bosnia.[11] Scahill writes of the largely underreported involvement of contractors from the San Diego–based Titan Corporation and the Virginia-based CACI in the now infamous torture of Iraqi detainees at the Abu Ghraib prison compound in 2004.[12] And in what has become known as the Nisour Square Massacre, Blackwater employees killed 17 Iraqi civilians at a busy intersection in Baghdad.[13] These are, of course, only a small sampling of contractor abuses, but they are clearly criminal actions — incidents that can't be explained away as an errant bullet or malfunctioning "smart" bomb.

> The name of the Web site is used to identify the source.

It might be argued that these abuses are the actions of the individuals hired by a corporation, not part of corporate policy. And it might be further argued that in some of these cases, regular U.S. troops can and have committed similar crimes (and in the case of Abu Ghraib, were participating right along with the contractors). But a major difference between a contractor and a U.S. soldier is accountability. While there might exist the same opportunity to commit crimes between the private and public sectors, there are clear consequences in place for regular troops, who are subject to the Uniform Code of Military Justice (UCMJ). As of October 2010, 34 U.S. Army soldiers had been court-martialed on charges of murder or manslaughter of civilians in conflict zones in Iraq and Afghanistan, and 22 of those soldiers were convicted.[14] In contrast, it was only in 2006 that the UCMJ was amended so that contractors could be charged with criminal actions under the court-martial system.[15] Unlike regular troops, contractors are backed by strong money: Lobbying groups fight hard and spend millions to make sure the corporations are not held accountable.[16] Although charges were brought against five Blackwater men for the 2007 Nisour Square Massacre, the case was dismissed when the judge ruled that the prosecutors could not use statements that the accused had given to State Department investigators on the condition that the information could not be applied as evidence. As reporter James Risen explains in a recent *New York Times* article, "The Blackwater personnel were given a form of immunity from prosecution by the people they were working for and helping to protect."[17] Though the State Department has appealed the Nisour Square case, there have yet to be serious legal consequences for these and other contractors who commit crimes.

The atmosphere of lawlessness inherent in battle zones is compounded by the illegal acts of some of these contractors, which, in a low-intensity conflict, may turn citizens into insurgents. The Army Field Manual states that "people who have been maltreated or have had close friends or relatives killed . . . may strike back at their attackers. Security force abuses . . . can be major escalating factors for insurgencies."[18] And, as the Congressional Research Service report points out, Iraqi and Afghan civilians don't always know the difference between a U.S. soldier and a contractor, meaning that, in the minds of the people, the actions of contractors directly reflect on the U.S. military.[19] However, despite the people's inability to tell them apart, contractors and U.S. soldiers have significantly different motivations. By definition, those in the military are serving their commander-in-chief while those hired as contractors are serving a for-profit company. In regards to PMCs' bottom lines, it would actually be advantageous to shoot first and ask questions later, engendering more fear and insecurity and therefore the need for more contracted security guards. This positive feedback loop should not be considered as some elaborate conspiracy; the situation is merely part of the culture and nature of profit-motivated actors. It's the reason why, until the last couple of decades, defense operations have overwhelmingly been left up to the public, not the private, sector: Ultimately, the motivation of profit is not necessarily in line with the motivation of national security.

Given the potential costs in justice and national security, why hire contractors at all? Ironically, perhaps the most often cited reason for using private contractors is that using these corporations saves the taxpayer money since the government can hire them on an as-need basis and does not have to pay for contractors' training, health care, or pensions.[20] Professor Allison Stanger of Middlebury College challenges this notion in her 2009 book *One Nation Under Contract: The Outsourcing of American Power and the Future of Foreign Policy* when she points out that nearly all private contractors

Paraphrased information

Tag indicates the source of the paraphrased information.

Source of paraphrased information is provided in a note.

Nicholas returns to his original question and asks a more in-depth one.

Chicago

V Documenting Sources

Brothers 6

previously served in the military, meaning that many of them are receiving pension payments anyway. Stanger writes that "the federal government is effectively paying for the training and retirement of the contractors it hires, all appearances to the contrary, as well as paying double or triple the daily rate for their services."[21] Therefore the Department of Defense would actually save taxpayers money by reversing the trend of privatization.

However, reducing the role of PMCs is very difficult because the more money the U.S. government spends hiring these firms, the more these firms can afford to offer in salary, and the more soldiers aspire to leave the military to work for private companies.[22] A brain-drain occurs, sapping the strategic and tactical knowledge of the military, thus creating an increased need for PMCs. Lt. Col. Michael Brothers, who enlisted in 1981, described this process as one that has been emotional for many in the armed forces as men and women in uniform saw their chosen specialties phased out or privatized out from under them.[23] Essentially, PMCs have created a void, filled it, and recreated the void so they can refill it, ad infinitum. This makes it increasingly difficult to reverse the current state of overreliance on PMCs since, according to the Congressional Research Service report, "many analysts now believe that DOD [the Department of Defense] is unable to successfully execute large missions without contractor support."[24] The vicious cycle of paying for help and then becoming more helpless makes it imperative that the United States ends its dependence on PMCs as soon as possible.

> Brackets clarify the abbreviation used in the original quotation.

U.S. citizens should better understand how our military operations are carried out overseas, since the wars in Iraq and Afghanistan affect our security, our taxes, and our consciences as Americans. But we in the polity have not demanded that contractors paid by the government for military services be held accountable for their actions, and neither have we demanded that our leaders recognize and address the growing threat to national security PMCs represent. A recent bill called the Stop Outsourcing Security Act, submitted to both houses of Congress by Representative Jan Schakowsky (D-Ill.) in the House and Senator Bernie Sanders (I-Ver.), offers one potential route to intervention. The act would "prohibit the use of private contractors for military, security, law enforcement, intelligence, and armed rescue functions unless the President tells Congress why the military is unable to perform those functions."[25] The passage of this act could be the first step in the process of phasing out the use of private contractors and returning military operations to the public sector. On her Web site, Schakowsky urges Americans to contact their

Brothers 7

representatives to cosponsor the legislation and become citizen cosponsors of the Stop Outsourcing Security Act themselves. In the end, we as voters and taxpayers must ask ourselves, who do we want to carry out U.S. defense missions abroad: those accountable to the U.S. military, or those beholden to private corporations? Given the costs in justice and in dollars, it's clear that the U.S. military has come to overrely on PMCs to a point that is dangerous to national security and national interests. This reliance must be reduced, perhaps excised entirely.

Nicholas concludes with a strong, clear statement of his position.

Brothers 8

Notes

List of notes on a separate page, heading centered

Entries listed in order of appearance in the essay

1. P. W. Singer, *Corporate Warriors: The Rise of the Privatized Military Industry* (Ithaca: Cornell University Press, 2003), 15-16.

Field research

2. Jonathan Euchner, personal interview, September 25, 2010.

Book with one author

3. Jeremy Scahill, *Blackwater: The Rise of the World's Most Powerful Mercenary Army*, 2nd ed. (New York: Nation Books, 2007), 49-51.

4. C. J. Chivers, et al., with contributions from Jacob Harris and Alan McLean, "View Is Bleaker Than Official Portrayal of War in Afghanistan," *New York Times*, July 25, 2010, http://www.nytimes.com; Eric Schmitt, Helene Cooper, and David E. Sanger, "U.S. Military Seeks Slower Pace to Wrap Up Afghan Role," *New York Times*, August 11, 2010, http://www.nytimes.com.

Semicolon indicates that note 4 includes two distinct sources

5. P. W. Singer, "Break the Blackwater Habit: We Can't Fight the War Without the Company — But We Won't Win with It on Our Payroll," *Washington Post*, October 8, 2007, http://www.washingtonpost.com.

Government report

6. Moshe Schwartz, *Department of Defense Contractors in Iraq and Afghanistan: Background and Analysis*, Congressional Research Service, July 2, 2010, 18.

Indicates source of material is the same as that for the previous note, but on a different page

7. Ibid., 2.

A source quoted within another source

8. Erik Prince speaking at West 2006 conference, January 11, 2006, quoted in Scahill, *Blackwater*, xix.

9. Singer, *Corporate Warriors*, 46.

Abbreviated reference to source identified in note 1

10. Andrew Gilligan, "Inside Lt. Col. Spicer's New Model Army," *Sunday Telegraph*, November 24, 1998, quoted in Singer, *Corporate Warriors*, 46.

Article from an online magazine

11. Robert Capps, "Outside the Law," *Salon*, June 26, 2002, http://www.salon.com.

12. Scahill, *Blackwater*, 221.

13. Charlie Savage, "Judge Drops Charges from Blackwater Deaths in Iraq," *New York Times*, December 31, 2009, http://www.nytimes.com.

14. Charlie Savage, "Case of Accused Soldiers May Be Worst of 2 Wars," *New York Times*, October 3, 2010, http://www.nytimes.com.

15. P. W. Singer, "The Law Catches Up to Private Militaries, Embeds," Brookings Institute, August 25, 2010, http://www.brookings.edu.

16. Barry Yeoman, "Soldiers of Good Fortune," *Mother Jones*, May 2003, http://www.motherjones.com/politics.

Article in a daily newspaper

17. James Risen, "Efforts to Prosecute Blackwater Are Collapsing," *New York Times*, October 20, 2010, http://www.nytimes.com.

18. Department of Defense, *Counterinsurgency*, FM 3-24, December 2006, quoted in Schwartz, *Department of Defense*, 16.

19. Schwartz, *Department of Defense*, 16.

20. David Isenberg, "Contractors and Cost Effectiveness," CATO Institute, December 23, 2009, http://www.cato.org.

21. Allison Stanger, *One Nation Under Contract: The Outsourcing of American Power and the Future of Foreign Policy* (New Haven, CT: Yale University Press, 2009), 96–97, quoted in Isenberg, "Contractors and Cost Effectiveness."

22. Robert Young Pelton, *Licensed to Kill: Hired Guns in the War on Terror* (New York: Three Rivers Press, 2007), 58, quoted in Scahill, *Blackwater*, 221.

23. Michael Brothers, phone interview, September 20, 2010.

24. Schwartz, *Department of Defense*, 1.

Nonperiodical Web site ——— 25. Jan Schakowsky, "Contracting," Congresswoman Jan Schakowsky, last modified October 11, 2010, http://schakowsky.house.gov.

Brothers 10

Bibliography

Entries listed alphabetically by author

Article from an online magazine

Capps, Robert. "Outside the Law." *Salon*, June 26, 2002. http://www
.salon.com.

Chivers, C. J., et al., with contributions from Jacob Harris and Alan
McLean. "View Is Bleaker Than Official Portrayal of War in Afghanistan." *New York Times*, July 25, 2010. http://www.nytimes.com.

Hemingway, Mark. "Blackwater's Legal Netherworld." *National Review
Online*, September 26, 2007. http://www.nationalreview.com.

Isenberg, David. "Contractors and Cost Effectiveness." CATO Institute.
December 23, 2009. http://www.cato.org.

Pelton, Robert Young. *Licensed to Kill: Hired Guns in the War on Terror.* New
York: Three Rivers Press, 2007. Quoted in Scahill, *Blackwater*, 221.

Risen, James. "Efforts to Prosecute Blackwater Are Collapsing." *New
York Times*, October 20, 2010. http://www.nytimes.com/2010/
10/04/US/21contractors.html.

Article in a daily newspaper

Savage, Charlie. "Case of Accused Soldiers May Be Worst of 2 Wars."
New York Times, October 3, 2010. http://www.nytimes.com/
2010/01/01/US/04soldiers.html.

------. "Judge Drops Charges from Blackwater Deaths in Iraq." *New York
Times*, December 31, 2009. http://www.nytimes.com.

Scahill, Jeremy. *Blackwater: The Rise of the World's Most Powerful
Mercenary Army*. 2nd ed. New York: Nation Books, 2007.

Book with one author

Schakowsky, Jan. "Contracting." Congresswoman Jan Schakowsky. Last
modified October 11, 2010. http://schakowsky.house.gov.

Nonperiodical Web site

Schmitt, Eric, Helene Cooper, and David E. Sanger. "U.S. Military
Seeks Slower Pace to Wrap Up Afghan Role." *New York Times*,
August 11, 2010. http://www.nytimes.com.

Schwartz, Moshe. *Department of Defense Contractors in Iraq and
Afghanistan: Background and Analysis*. Congressional Research
Service, July 2, 2010.

Government report

Singer, P. W. "Break the Blackwater Habit: We Can't Fight the War Without
the Company — But We Won't Win with It on Our Payroll." *Washington Post*, October 8, 2007. http://www.washingtonpost.com.

Dashes indicate that these sources are also by Singer

------. *Corporate Warriors: The Rise of the Privatized Military Industry*.
Ithaca, NY: Cornell University Press, 2003.

------. "The Law Catches Up to Private Militaries, Embeds." Brookings
Institute. August 25, 2010. http://www.brookings.edu.

Stanger, Allison. *One Nation Under Contract: The Outsourcing of Ameri-
can Power and the Future of Foreign Policy*. New Haven, CT: Yale
University Press, 2009. Quoted in Isenberg, "Contractors and
Cost Effectiveness."

Yeoman, Barry. "Soldiers of Good Fortune." *Mother Jones*, May 2003.
http://www.motherjones.com/politics.

Chicago

V Documenting Sources

23

Using CSE Style

> Key Questions

23a. How do I cite sources within the text of my document? 429

23b. How do I prepare the reference list? 429

CSE stands for the Council of Science Editors. In this book, CSE style is based on the eighth edition of *Scientific Style and Format: The CSE Manual for Authors, Editors, and Publishers.*

CSE style, used primarily in the physical sciences, life sciences, and mathematics, recommends two systems.

- a citation-sequence system, which lists sources in the reference list according to the order in which they appear in the document

- a name-year system, which is similar to the author-date system used by the APA (see Chapter 21)

This chapter describes and provides models for the citation-sequence system. For more information on CSE style, visit the Council of Science Editors Web site at **councilscienceeditors.org**.

To see Joshua Woelfle's research essay, formatted in CSE style, turn to p. 441.

CITATION TUTORIALS FOR REFERENCE CITED ENTRIES

- Books   431
- Articles from periodicals   435
- Articles from databases   438
- Works from Web sites   440

CITATIONS WITHIN YOUR TEXT

1. Format and placement of the note   429
2. Citing a previously mentioned source   429
3. Citing a source within a source   429

ENTRIES IN YOUR REFERENCE LIST

How do I cite sources within the text of my document?

The CSE citation-sequence system uses sequential numbers to refer to sources within a document. These numbers, in turn, correspond to numbered entries in the reference list. This approach to citing sources reduces distraction to the reader and saves space within a document.

1. Format and Placement of the Note   Sources are cited using superscript numbers or numbers placed in parentheses. Superscript numbers should be formatted in a font one or two points smaller than the body text:

> The anomalies in the data[3] call the study's methods into question.

> The anomalies in the data (3) call the study's methods into question.

2. Citing a Previously Mentioned Source   Use the first number assigned to a source when citing the source for the second time. In the following examples, the author is referring to sources earlier numbered 3, 9, and 22:

> The outlying data points[3,9,22] seem to suggest a bias in the methodology.

> The outlying data points (3,9,22) seem to suggest a bias in the methodology.

3. Citing a Source within a Source   When referring to a source cited in another source, use the phrase "cited in":

> The results[12(cited in 8)] collected in the first month of the study . . .

> The results (12 cited in 8) collected in the first month of the study . . .

How do I prepare the reference list?

CSE style specifies that you should create a list of works that are cited in your document or that contributed to your thinking about the document. Sources cited should be identified in a section titled "References," while sources that contributed to your thinking should be given in a section titled "Additional References."

There are, however, two exceptions: personal communication and oral presentations.

Personal communication, such as correspondence and interviews, is cited only in the text of your document, using the term "unreferenced" to indicate that it is not found in the reference list:

> . . . this disease has proven to be resistant to antibiotics under specific conditions (2014 letter from Meissner to me; unreferenced, see "Notes").

Typically, information about personal communication is placed in a "Notes" or "Acknowledgments" section. Similarly, oral presentations at conferences that are not available in any form (such as microform, reference database, conference proceedings, or online) should be cited in the text of your document but not included in your reference list.

The *CSE Manual* does not specify the location of the reference list, deferring instead to the formatting guidelines of individual journals in the sciences. In general, however, the reference list appears at the end of print documents and linear documents that are distributed electronically (such as word processing files or newsgroup posts). In the case of longer documents or documents in which sections of a book (such as chapters) are intended to stand on their own, the reference list might appear at the end of each section or chapter. In digital documents that use links, such as Web sites, the reference list often is a separate page to which other pages are linked.

To see an example of a CSE-style reference list, turn to p. 446.

Books, Conference Proceedings, and Dissertations

4. One Author Give the author's last name and first initial with no comma. Next, include the title, capitalizing only the first word and proper nouns, followed by publication information. Include the state abbreviation in parentheses after the city.

4. Leonard C. The meat racket: the secret takeover of America's food business. New York (NY): Simon & Schuster; 2014.

5. Two or More Authors List the authors in the order in which they appear on the title page, each of them last name first. (If there are more than 10 authors, list the first ten followed by a comma and "et al.") Note that periods are not used after initials. Separate authors with commas. When using CSE style, abbreviate "United Kingdom" as "GB."

5. Willis KJ, McElwain JC. The evolution of plants. 2nd ed. Oxford (GB): Oxford University Press; 2014.

6. Corporate or Group Author Identify the organization as the author.

6. National Geographic. EarthPulse. 2nd ed. New York (NY): Wiley; 2010.

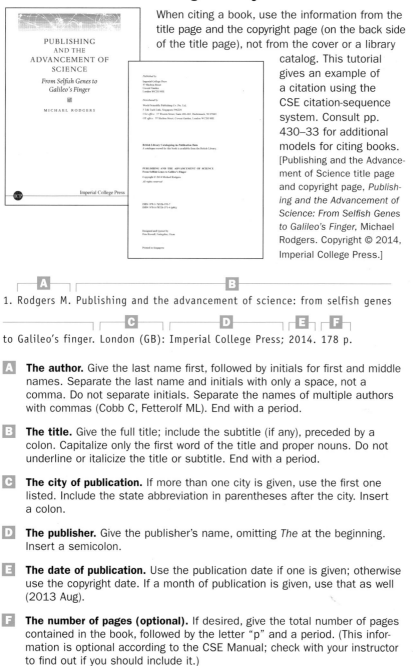

TUTORIAL

How do I cite books using CSE style?

When citing a book, use the information from the title page and the copyright page (on the back side of the title page), not from the cover or a library catalog. This tutorial gives an example of a citation using the CSE citation-sequence system. Consult pp. 430–33 for additional models for citing books. [Publishing and the Advancement of Science title page and copyright page, *Publishing and the Advancement of Science: From Selfish Genes to Galileo's Finger*, Michael Rodgers. Copyright © 2014, Imperial College Press.]

[A] [B]
1. Rodgers M. Publishing and the advancement of science: from selfish genes

[C] [D] [E] [F]
to Galileo's finger. London (GB): Imperial College Press; 2014. 178 p.

A   **The author.** Give the last name first, followed by initials for first and middle names. Separate the last name and initials with only a space, not a comma. Do not separate initials. Separate the names of multiple authors with commas (Cobb C, Fetterolf ML). End with a period.

B   **The title.** Give the full title; include the subtitle (if any), preceded by a colon. Capitalize only the first word of the title and proper nouns. Do not underline or italicize the title or subtitle. End with a period.

C   **The city of publication.** If more than one city is given, use the first one listed. Include the state abbreviation in parentheses after the city. Insert a colon.

D   **The publisher.** Give the publisher's name, omitting *The* at the beginning. Insert a semicolon.

E   **The date of publication.** Use the publication date if one is given; otherwise use the copyright date. If a month of publication is given, use that as well (2013 Aug).

F   **The number of pages (optional).** If desired, give the total number of pages contained in the book, followed by the letter "p" and a period. (This information is optional according to the CSE Manual; check with your instructor to find out if you should include it.)

CSE

V Documenting Sources

7. Unknown Author   Begin with the title.

7. The first 100,000 prime numbers. Lenox (MA): Hard Press; 2007. 215 p.

8. Translated Book   Identify the translator after the title, giving last name first.

8. Schoeps KH. Literature and film in the Third Reich. Dell'Orto KM, translator. Columbia (SC): Camden House; 2010.

9. Book in an Edition Other Than the First   Note the edition (for instance, "2nd ed." or "New rev. ed.") after the title and with a separating period.

9. Roberts N. The holocene: an environmental history. 3rd ed. Oxford (GB): Wiley Blackwell; 2014.

10. Multivolume Work   Include the total number of volumes if you are making a reference to all volumes in the work, or "Vol." followed by the specific volume number followed by the title of that volume (if that volume is separately titled).

10. Serway RA, Jewett JW. Physics for scientists and engineers. Vol. 5. 8th ed. Pacific Grove (CA): Brooks-Cole; 2010.

11. Authored Book with an Editor   Identify the editor(s) before the publication information.

11. Einstein, A. The cosmic view of Albert Einstein: writings on art, science, and peace. Martin W, Ott M, editors. New York (NY): Sterling Publishing; 2013.

12. Book in a Series

12. Rosenberg A, Arp B, editors. Philosophy of biology: an anthology. Chichester (GB): Wiley-Blackwell; 2010. (Blackwell philosophy anthologies; 32).

13. Anthology or Collection with an Editor   To cite an anthology of essays or a collection of articles, treat the editor's name as you would an author's name but identify with the word "editor."

13. Carlson BM, editor. Stem cell anthology. London (GB): Academic Press; 2010.

14. Chapter in an Edited Book or a Work in an Anthology   List the author and title of the section; then include the word "In" followed by a colon, the editor's name (last name first followed by initials) and the word "editor." Include the book title, place, and publisher, and note the inclusive pages of the section. Note that page range numbers are given in full.

14. Rothenberg M, Clarke MF. Cancer stem cells. In: Carlson BM, editor. Stem cell anthology. London (GB): Academic Press; 2010. p. 221–236.

15. Foreword, Introduction, Preface, or Afterword of a Book   If the part is written by someone other than the author of the book, treat it as you would a chapter in an edited book (see #14), identifying the author or editor of the book before the book title.

15. Groopman J. Introduction. In: Cohen J, editor. The best of the best American science writing: ten years of the series. New York (NY): Ecco; 2010; p. ix–xv.

16. Chapter of a Book   If you wish to refer to a chapter of a book, identify the chapter of the book after the publication information. End with the inclusive pages of the chapter.

16. Pendergrast M. Inside the outbreaks: the elite medical detectives of the Epidemic Intelligence Service. Boston (MA): Houghton Mifflin Harcourt; 2010. Chapter 7, Fighting pox, pandemics, and special pathogens; p. 72–90.

17. Published Proceedings of a Conference   List the editors of the proceedings as authors or, if there are no editors, begin with the name and year of the conference. Then give the title of the publication; the date of the conference; the place of the conference; and the place of publication, publisher, and date.

17. Platts H, Barron C, Lundock J, Pearce J, Yoo J, editors. TRAC 2013. Proceedings of the 23rd Annual Theoretical Roman Archaeology Conference; 2013; London. Oxford (GB): Oxbow Books; c2014; 160 p.

18. Paper Published in the Proceedings of a Conference   Format the citation as you would a chapter in an edited book.

18. Paten B, Diekhans M, Earl D, St. John J, Ma J, Suh BB, Haussler D. Cactus graphs for genome comparisons. In: Berger B, editor. RECOMB 2010. Research in computational molecular biology, 14th annual international conference proceedings; 2010 Apr 25-28; Lisbon, Portugal. Berlin (DE): Springer-Verlag; c2010; p. 410–425.

19. Published Dissertation or Thesis   Use the general format for a book, adding the word "dissertation" or "thesis" in square brackets after the title. Treat the institution granting the degree as the publisher. If the place is not listed on the dissertation but can be inferred, use brackets around the place as shown here. For information on citing electronically accessed dissertations, see page 439.

19. Prescott JW. Computer-assisted discovery and characterization of imaging biomarkers for disease diagnosis and treatment planning [dissertation]. [Columbus (OH)]: Ohio State University; 2010; 191 p.

20. Unpublished Dissertation or Thesis Use the general format for a book, adding the word "dissertation" or "thesis" in square brackets as a final element of the title. Treat the institution granting the degree as the publisher.

20. Wagner KP. A generalized acceptance urn model [dissertation]. Tampa (FL): University of South Florida; 2010.

Sources in Journals, Magazines, and Newspapers

21. Article in a Journal Abbreviate and capitalize all of the major words in a journal's title; omit articles, conjunctions, and prepositions. The CSE manual includes specific guidelines for citing journal titles. A semicolon separates the year and volume number. If there is an issue number, include it in parentheses, followed by a colon and the page numbers. There are no spaces between the year, volume number, and page numbers.

21. Gauthier S, Leuzy A, Racine E, Rosa-Neto P. Diagnosis and management of Alzheimer's disease: past present and future ethical issues. Prog Neurobiol. 2013;110:102–113.

22. Article in a Magazine Magazines are not identified by volume. Give only the date (year, month, day for weekly magazines; year and month for monthly magazines). Abbreviate all months to their first three letters.

22. Milius S. In field or backyard, frogs face threats. Sci News. 2010 Sep 11:28–29.

23. Article in a Newspaper Treat newspaper articles as you would magazine articles, identifying their pages by section, page, and column on which they begin (in parentheses).

23. Jalonick MC. Suit says toys in Happy Meals break the law. Boston Globe. 2010 Jun 23;Sect. B:11 (col. 1).

24. Unsigned Article in a Newspaper Begin the entry with the title of the article. "Anonymous" is not permitted in CSE style.

24. A mouse to save your wrist and hand. Boston Globe. 2010 Nov 29;Sect. B:8 (col. 3).

Print Reference Works

25. Encyclopedia, Dictionary, Thesaurus, Handbook, or Almanac Begin with the title of the reference work and information about the edition. Identify the editor, if listed. Provide publisher and publication date.

25. Encyclopedia of global warming. Dutch SI, editor. Pasadena (CA): Salem Press; 2010.

TUTORIAL

How do I cite articles from periodicals using CSE style?

Periodicals include journals, magazines, and newspapers. This page gives an example of a citation for a print magazine article. Models for citing articles from journals and newspapers are on p. 434. If you need to cite a periodical article you accessed electronically, follow the guidelines below and see p. 437. [Republished with permission of Sage Publications from *Trauma* by A.J. Durford, S.E. Harrison, C.A. Eynon January 1, 2014; permission conveyed through Copyright Clearance Center, Inc.]

A   **B**

2. Durnford AJ, Harrisson SE, Eynon CA. Kitesports: a new source of major

C **D** **E** **F**

trauma? report of four cases and literature review. Trauma 2014;16(1):23–26.

A **The author.** Give the last name first, followed by initials for first and middle names. Separate the last name and initials with only a space, not a comma. Do not separate initials. Separate the names of multiple authors with commas (Cobb C, Fetterolf ML). End with a period.

B **The article title.** Give the full title; include the subtitle (if any), preceded by a colon. Capitalize only the first word of the title and proper nouns. Do not underline or italicize the title or subtitle. End with a period.

C **The periodical title.** Do not underline or italicize the periodical title; abbreviate and capitalize all major words. Omit articles, conjunctions, and prepositions. The CSE manual includes guidelines for abbreviating journal titles. Do not abbreviate one-word titles or one-syllable words in a journal title. End with a period.

D **The date of publication.** For journal articles, include the year followed by a semicolon. For magazines and newspapers, include the abbreviated month and, if available, the day (2014 Apr 13), followed by a colon.

E **Volume and issue number.** For journal articles, include the volume number followed by the issue number in parentheses, if available, and a colon.

F **Inclusive page number(s).** Give the page numbers on which the article appears; list the numbers in full (154–177; 1187–1188). Do not add a space between the colon and the page numbers. End with a period.

26. Map or Chart   Use the name of the area in place of an author. Follow with the title, type of map in brackets (such as physical map or demographic map), place of publication and publisher, and a description of the map. If the map is part of a larger document, such as an atlas, provide publication information for the document and the page number(s) of the map.

26. Netherlands. Independent Dutch breweries [demographic map]. In: The world atlas of beer. London (GB): Octopus Publishing Group; 2012. p. 137. Color.

27. Pamphlet   Format entries as you would for a book (see also #4 on p. 430).

27. National Alliance on Mental Illness. Depression. Arlington (VA): NAMI, the National Alliance on Mental Illness; 2012.

Media Sources

28. Film or Video Recording   Give the title, then the type of medium identified in square brackets, followed by individuals listed as authors, editors, performers, conductors, and so on. Identify the producer if different from the publisher. Provide publication information, including a physical description of the medium.

28. Great migrations [DVD]. Hamlin D, Serwa C, producers. Washington (DC): National Geographic; 2010. 3 DVDs: 200 min.

29. Television Program   CSE style does not provide guidance on citing television programs. Cite the title of the program, with the medium designator in brackets, followed by information about the series (if any), including individuals such as the producer, writer, director, and the place and date of broadcast at the end.

29. Mt. St. Helens: back from the dead [television program]. Barrett M, executive producer. Nova. New York (NY): Thirteen/WNET; 2010 May 4.

30. Radio Program   CSE style does not provide guidance on citing radio programs. Cite the title of the program, with the medium designator in brackets, followed by information about the series (if any), including individuals such as the producer, writer, director, and the place and date of broadcast at the end.

30. Mental exercise and dementia [radio program]. Flatow I, host. Talk of the Nation Science Friday. New York (NY): National Public Radio; 2010 Sep 3.

31. Sound Recording   Cite as you would a film or video recording.

31. Howler monkeys: singing into the night [sound recording]. Carroll B, sound recordist. Keene (NH): Belize Bruce; 2013.

Field Sources

32. Personal Interview   Treat unpublished interviews as personal communication (see p. 430). Cite them in the text only; do not cite them in the reference list.

33. Personal Letter   Cite personal letters as personal communication (see p. 430). Cite them in the text only; do not cite them in the reference list.

34. Lecture or Public Address   Like an unpublished paper presented at a meeting, lectures or public addresses are treated as personal communication and are cited only in the text (see p. 430).

Digital Sources

35. Material from an Online Database

35. Chen M, Schlief M, Willows RD, Cai Z-L, Neilan BA, Scheer H. A red-shifted chlorophyll. Science. 2010 Sep 10 [accessed 2014 Feb 1]:1318-1319. Expanded Academic ASAP. Farmington Hills (MI): Thomson Gale; c2010. http://web4 .infotrac.galegroup.com. doi:10.1126/science.1191127.

36. E-Book (Monograph)

36. Gliklich RE, Dreyer NA, editors. Registries for evaluating patient outcomes: a user's guide. 2nd ed. Rockville (MD): Agency for Healthcare Research and Quality; 2010 [cited 2010 Nov 1]. http://www.ncbi.nlm.nih.gov/books/NBK49444.

37. Online Journal Article

37. Pitaval A, Tseng Q, Bornens M, Thery M. Cell shape and contractility regulate ciliogenesis in cell cycle — arrested cells. J Cell Biol. 2010 [accessed 2013 Aug 23];191(2):303-312. http://jcb.rupress.org/content/191/2/303 .full?sid=d8f7c638-68dc-4082-99a8-ca19a37d72fe. doi:10.1083/jcb.201004003.

38. Online Newspaper Article

38. Kolata G. Stem cell biology and its complications. New York Times. 2010 Aug 24 [accessed 2010 Dec 15]. http://www.nytimes.com/2010/08/25/health/ research/25cell.html.

39. Web Site

39. US Geological Survey. Washington (DC): US Department of the Interior; [updated 2010 Sep 28; accessed 2010 Dec 16]. http://www.usgs.gov.

CSE

V Documenting Sources

TUTORIAL

How do I cite articles from databases using CSE style?

Libraries subscribe to services such as Lexis-Nexis, ProQuest, InfoTrac, and EBSCOhost that provide access to databases of digital texts. The databases provide publication information, abstracts, and the complete text of documents in a specific subject area, discipline, or profession. (See also Chapter 9.) This page gives an example of a reference in CSE citation-sequence style. [Courtesy of EBSCO.]

A

3. Galindo-Cardona A, Acevedo-Gonzalez JP, Rivera-Marchand B, Giray T.

B

Genetic structure of the gentle Aricanized honey bee population (gAHB) in

C **D** **E** **F**

Puerto Rico. BMC Genetics. 2013 [accessed 2014 Jun 9];14(1):1–11. Academic

G

Search Premier. Ipswich (MA): EBSCO; c2013. http://search.ebscohost.com.doi:

10.1186/1471-2156-14-65.

A **The author.** Give the last name first, followed by initials for first and middle names. Separate the last name and initials with only a space, not a comma. Do not separate initials. Separate the names of multiple authors with commas (Cobb C, Fetterolf ML). End with a period.

B **The article title.** Give the full title; include the subtitle (if any), preceded by a colon. Capitalize only the first word of the title and proper nouns. Do not underline or italicize the title or subtitle. End with a period.

C **The periodical title.** Do not underline or italicize the periodical title; abbreviate and capitalize all major words. Omit articles, conjunctions, and prepositions. The CSE manual includes guidelines for abbreviating journal titles. Do not abbreviate one-word titles or one-syllable words in a journal title. End with a period.

D **The date of publication.** For journal articles, include the year followed by a semicolon. For magazines and newspapers, include the month and, if available, the day (2014 Apr 13), followed by a colon. Follow with a date of access in brackets.

E **Volume and issue number.** For journal articles, include the volume number followed by the issue number in parentheses, if available, and a colon.

F **Inclusive page number(s).** Give the page numbers on which the article appears; list the numbers in full (154–177; 1187–1188). Do not add a space between the colon and the page numbers. End with a period.

G **Database, URL and DOI.** Give the name of the database followed by a period. Then, list the location and parent company of the database. Provide the full URL for the article, even if accessed via a database. Follow with a period. Then give the doi number if one is provided, ending with a period.

40. Document on a Web Site

40. Lavelle M. National Geographic Daily News. Washington (DC): National Geographic Society. Forcing gas out of rock with water. 2010 Oct 17 [accessed 2010 Dec 16]. http://news.nationalgeographic.com/news/2010/10/101022-energy-marcellus-shale-gas-science-technology-water.

41. Email Message   Email messages are considered personal communication (see p. 430). Cite them in the text only; do not cite them in the reference list.

42. Email Discussion List Message

42. Williams JB. Re: Tomato seed question. In: BIONET. [London (GB); Medical Research Council]; 2010 Nov 1, 7:57 am [accessed 2010 Nov 15]. http://www.bio.net/bionet/mm/plantbio/2010-November/027780.html.

43. Article Posted on a Wiki

43. Epidemic and pandemic spread. In: Influenza [updated 2014 Mar 1; accessed 2014 Mar 25]. http://en.wikipedia.org/wiki/Influenza#Epidemic_and_pandemic_spread.

44. Entire Blog

44. Orth JF. Invasive species weblog. c2002-2010 [updated 2011 Jan 22; accessed 2010 Jan 25]. http://invasivespecies.blogspot.com.

45. Entry or Comment on a Blog

45. Reynolds G. Phys Ed: Brains and Brawn. In: Well. 2011 Jan 19 [accessed 2011 Jan 22]. http://well.blogs.nytimes.com/2011/01/19/phys-ed-brains-and-brawn.

46. Dissertation Accessed Online

46. Yang, H. Topics in gravitational-wave science: macroscopic quantum mechanics and black hole physics [dissertation]. Pasadena (CA): California Institute of Technology; 213; 339 p. ProQuest Dissertations and Theses. Ann Arbor (MI): ProQuest; c2013. http://search.proquest.com.ezp-prod1.hul.harvard.edu/docview/1496774506?accountid=11311.

CSE

V Documenting Sources

TUTORIAL

How do I cite works from Web sites using CSE style?

You will likely need to search the Web site to find some of the citation information you need. For some sites, all of the details may not be available; find as many as you can. Remember that the citation you provide should allow readers to retrace your steps electronically to locate the sources. Consult pp. 437–39 for additional models for citing Web sources.

A **B**

4. National Aeronautics and Space Administration. Raisin' mountains on Saturn's

C

moon Titan. Pasadena (CA): National Aeronautics and Space Administration;

D **E**

2010 Aug 12 [accessed 2011 Feb 3]. http://www.nasa.gov/mission_pages/

cassini/whycassini/cassini20100812.html.

A **The author.** Give the name of the organization or individual author, last name first followed by initials for first and middle names. Separate the last name and initials with only a space, not a comma; separate the names of multiple authors with commas (Cobb C, Fetterolf ML). End with a period.

B **The document title.** Give the full title; include the subtitle (if any), preceded by a colon. Capitalize only the first word of the title and proper nouns. Do not underline or italicize the title or subtitle. End with a period.

C **Publisher information.** Give the place of publication followed by a colon, then the publisher or sponsoring organization followed by a semicolon.

D **Publication date and date of access.** Give the date of publication or the copyright date on the Web site; if available, include the date of modification or update in brackets. Then give the date of access in brackets. End with a period.

E **The URL.** Give the URL, followed by a period.

CSE

V Documenting Sources

CSE Citation-Sequence Style Research Essay

Unnumbered title page includes a descriptive title with all major words capitalized, the student's name, the course name, and the date. All information is centered on the page.

Promising Advancements in Modern Cancer Treatment

Joshua Woelfle

Biology 597
Professor Diaz
May 3, 2014

Promising Advancements 1

Chemotherapy is just medieval. It's such a blunt instrument.
We're going to look back on it like we do the dark ages.
— Dr. Eric Topol (Unreferenced, see "Notes")

Cancer afflicts over a million Americans every year and proves
fatal to nearly half of those afflicted. (1) Over the years, scientists
have made great strides in understanding the disease, but cancer's
widely varied and adaptive nature has made finding a cure nearly
impossible. Fortunately, scientists have achieved greater success in
controlling cancer, and several promising advancements may soon
overtake the traditional treatment options of chemotherapy and
radiation. Two of these advancements, anti-cancer drugs targeting
out-of-control cell-growth signaling enzymes and multi-drug resistance (MDR) proteins, may soon relegate the traditional options of
chemotherapy and radiation — along with their extremely detrimental
side effects — to the past.

Since the 1940s, non-surgical cancer treatment has consisted
almost exclusively of chemotherapy and radiation. These treatments
function by destroying rapidly proliferating cells throughout the body,
and are detrimental to cancer because, by its very definition, cancer
is a mass of rapidly dividing invasive cells. Unfortunately, there are
a number of other cell types within the body that also divide rapidly,
such as hair, skin, and epithelial cells, all of which suffer the same
fate as cancer cells when these treatments are used. Additionally,
chemotherapy causes a vast array of harmful side effects, including
immunosuppression, fatigue and nausea, neurological disorders, and
organ damage (2) which, even if the cancer is contained, may negatively affect the patient's quality of life.

Despite these harmful side effects, chemotherapeutic drugs
would be a viable option if they were effective at completely removing cancer from the body. However, the 1997 discovery of cancer stem
cells (3) proved that this is not the case. Cancer stem cells behave in
much the same way as other stem cells, with the ability to differentiate
into various tumor cells as required. This allows cancer stem cells
to adapt as necessary based on environmental conditions, and often
overcome adverse effects caused by treatment. More detrimentally,
cancer stem cells propagate slowly, so they are not targeted by
chemotherapy or radiation. Thus, there is always the possibility of
relapse for patients who have "successfully" undergone chemotherapy.

Fortunately, alternate options are becoming available that seem
to be more effective than traditional treatments at removing cancer,

---

Page numbering begins on first page of paper body. A short title is included before the page number.

A source not included in the reference list

Source references are shown in parentheses

Body of paper is double-spaced, with one-inch margins on all sides. Paragraphs are indented one-half inch.

while simultaneously eliminating many of the harsh side effects.
At the forefront of these new treatment options are designer drugs
targeting enzyme proteins whose over activity have been shown to
cause cancer. To understand anti-enzyme drug therapy, we must first
understand the structure and function of these pro-cancer enzymes.
Cancer develops primarily through genetic mutations that alter the
body's cellular equilibrium and allow cells to proliferate and migrate
without restriction. These requirements, dubbed the "hallmarks of
cancer," (4) are required for the successful development of the disease. Specifically, for cancer to arise, it must: secure blood supply for
growing cells via angiogenesis, allow for unlimited and unrestricted
division by manipulating the cell cycle and telomeres, overcome
growth restrictions, prevent cell suicide, and invade surrounding tis-
sue or colonize new sites in the body. These changes require multiple
genetic mutations and are regulated by a wide variety of enzymes,
many of which are specifically altered in cancer. These specific alterations are the backbone of enzyme directed cancer treatment research.

    Enzyme therapy works by targeting and restricting the cancer-
specific enzymes required to sustain cancer's development and
longevity. By disabling the mutated enzymes that make the hallmarks
of cancer possible, the disease is prevented from further development, as opposed to chemotherapy, which merely destroys already-
established cancer cells. Scientists are researching several different
enzymes for this therapy. One of these is heparanase, an enzyme that
stimulates cell migration. (5) Scientists are also experimenting with
a variety of tyrosine kinases that, when mutated, allow unrestricted
growth in cancer cells. Of particular note is the recently released drug
Gleevec, which targets tyrosine kinase BCR-Abl and is showing positive results in treating leukemia with minimal adverse effects. (6) The
success of Gleevec is demonstrative of the power of enzyme inhibitor-
based cancer treatment, and many researchers believe the combined
power of several enzyme restriction drugs is the next step in cancer
treatment. These drugs have the ability to fully restrict tumor growth
while allowing patients to maintain a quality of life that is much
higher than that of patients undergoing traditional cancer treatments.

    Unfortunately, cancer is doing its part to counteract these
advances in treatment. Most notably, cancer has begun utilizing the
body's own defenses to form resistances to cancer treatment drugs,
including enzyme inhibitors. These adaptations, dubbed "multi-drug
resistance" cancers, or MDR, can arise through several different
mechanisms, each requiring different treatment. The most common

and widely understood of these mechanisms is the manipulation of p-glycoprotein (PGP) by cancer cells. Ironically, the body uses PGP as a means of toxin defense. PGP is most commonly expressed to protect highly susceptible areas of the body, such as the blood-brain barrier and the testes, and it functions by capturing and expelling toxins from these areas. Some forms of cancer have adapted to express high levels of PGP, which recognizes cancer-targeting drugs (both chemotherapeutic and enzyme inhibitor) as foreign, and expels them from the cancer cell, preventing effective treatment. While this adaptation may seem scary enough already, it is compounded by the fact that cancer has also been shown to increase expression of PGP after the initial round of drugs. (7) So even if there was some initial success, the drug's performance will continually decrease in MDR cancers. While PGP mediated drug resistance is the most common form of MDR, it is also the most treatable resistance, and can be combated through the use of PGP inhibitors. These inhibitors function precisely as their name implies: by inhibiting the function of PGP throughout the body, thereby preventing cancer cells from expunging drugs and making them susceptible to the same treatments as typical cancers. Previously, researchers criticized this method of overcoming MDR cancer, and rightly so, because delivery of inhibitors was systemic, resulting in crippled toxin defense systems throughout the body. However, recent research suggests that PGP inhibitors can be altered for both direct delivery to cancerous cells and increased cancer cell specificity. (8) When these alterations are perfected, PGP mediated MDR will become a negligible issue in cancer treatment since it can be countered with no foreseeable side-effects.

Aside from PGP-assisted resistance, the most prevalent forms of multi-drug resistance are those mediated by tumor-suppressor and oncogenic mutations. These resistances commonly operate via the same principles as PGP, by expelling cytotoxic drugs from the cancerous cell before they can cause harm. However, they are the result of mutations in a variety of different genes, which makes treatment of these various MDR mutations very difficult. So while research is being conducted on developing drugs to inhibit the protein responsible for some of the more prevalent of these mutations (namely those involving the MRP gene), the most promising option is also the most simplistic: rather than disable resistances, bypass them. Several methods are currently undergoing testing that utilize this simple concept to combat MDR cancer in vastly different ways. The first, which is being tested by various pharmaceutical companies,

Promising Advancements 4

involves overloading tumor cells with anti-cancer (cytotoxic) drugs that are rapidly absorbed and fast acting. This process allows the drugs to act before the cancer cell can expunge a substantial amount, effectively negating the resistance mechanisms of the cell. While this method does serve to counter MDR mechanisms, its shortcomings are the same as those of traditional cancer treatment options: the possible side effects are very detrimental. Because this method most often utilizes typical cytotoxic drugs (and at a higher dosage), the patient is exposed to the negative effects of whichever drug is being administered. Therefore, this method will remain only situationally viable until researchers can develop a sufficiently fast-acting and rapidly-absorbed drug that does not pose the risks of currently available compounds.

In contrast to the above method, which utilizes traditional drugs in nontraditional doses to bypass resistance, research being led by Victor Keute and Thomas Efferth aims to use nontraditional compounds that actively bypass cancer cell resistance, rather than just overloading it. Keute and Efferth are examining the active compounds in African medicinal plants for cytotoxic effects. They have identified at least four different compounds in the benzophenone family that exhibit cytotoxic properties and, surprisingly, these compounds seem able to destroy drug-resistant cancer cells just as easily as they can destroy non-resistant cells. (9) This research is still in its infancy, so while thorough clinical trials to examine the viability and potential side effects of these compounds have not yet been conducted, the outlook of this research is very promising.

Many billions of dollars are spent annually on cancer research. Even so, chemotherapy and radiation have remained the dominant treatment options for more than six decades, in spite of their often severe side effects. These outdated methods have done their part to lower the mortality rate of cancer patients, but at an often substantial cost to their quality of life. Fortunately, recently developed enzyme inhibitor-based drugs, which show great promise in combating the disease with much less substantial side effects, seem poised to replace chemotherapy as the preferred cancer treatment option. Additionally, researchers are in the process of developing several different methods to combat multi-drug resistance in cancer to deal with this ever-increasing complication. If proven successful, these combined options could revolutionize the world of cancer treatment, providing hope to the millions afflicted, and bringing us one step closer to removing cancer from the list of most fatal diseases worldwide.

Promising Advancements 5

The reference list is titled "References" and begins on a new page.

References

1. National Cancer Institute. SEER stat fact sheets: all sites. Bethesda (MD): National Cancer Institute; 2013 [accessed 2014 Jan 9]. http://seer.cancer.gov/statfacts/html/ all.html.

The reference list is not alphabetical. Sources are numbered and listed in the order in which they appear in the document.

2. Stanford Medicine Cancer Institute. Chemotherapy drugs and side effects. Stanford (CA): Stanford Medicine; 2014 [accessed 2014 Jan 21]. http://cancer.stanford.edu/ information/cancerTreatment/ methods/chemotherapy.html.

3. Bonnet D, Dick JE. Human acute myeloid leukemia is organized as a hierarchy that originates from a primitive hematopoietic cell. Nature Med. 1997;3(7):730–737.

4. Hanahan D, Weinberg RA. Hallmarks of cancer: the next generation. Cell. 2011;144(5):646-674.

5. Seppa N. Keeping cells under control: enzyme suppression inhibits cancer spread. Sci News. 2004 Aug 28:134.

Titles of books and periodicals are neither underlined nor italicized. All major words in the titles of periodicals are capitalized. For all other sources, only initial words of the main title and proper nouns and adjectives are capitalized.

6. Pray L. Gleevec: the breakthrough in cancer treatment. Nat Ed. 2008;1(1):37. http://www.nature.com/scitable/topicpage/ gleevec-the-breakthrough-in-cancer-treatment-565.

7. Ichihashi N, Kitajima Y. Chemotherapy induces or increases expression of multidrug resistance-associated protein in malignant melanoma cells. Br J Dermatol. 2001 Apr [accessed 2014 Jan 8]; 144(4):745-50. PubMed. Bethesda (MD): Nat Cent for Biotechnol Inf; c2001. http://www.ncbi.nlm.nih.gov/pubmed/11298532.

8. Kanghui Y, Jifeng W, Xun L. Recent advances in research on P-glycoprotein inhibitors. BioSci Trends. 2008 [accessed 2014 8 Jan];2(4):137-46. http://www.biosciencetrends.com/action/ downloaddoc.php?docid=141.

9. Gutierrez D. African medicinal plants may stop tumor growth from multi-drug resistant cancers: research. Natural News. 2013 Jun 26 [accessed 2014 Jan 9]. http://www.naturalnews.com/040947_cancer_ treatment_african_plants_medicinal_herbs.html.

The student included a list of additional resources, in alphabetical order, that were consulted but not cited in the paper.

Additional References

DeVita VT Jr, Chu E. A history of cancer chemotherapy. Cancer Res. 2008;68(21):8643-53. PubMed. Bethesda (MD): Nat Cent for Biotechnol Inf; c2008. http://www.ncbi.nlm.nih.gov/pubmed/ 18974103.

Mukherjee S. The emperor of all maladies: a biography of cancer. 2010. New York (NY): Scribner; 2010.

Persidis A. Cancer multidrug resistance. Nat Biotech. 1999;17:94-95. http://www.nature.com/nbt/journal/v18/n10s/full/nbt1000_IT18 .html.

Promising Advancements 6

Szakacs G, Paterson JK, Ludwig JA, Booth-Genthe C, Gottesman MM.
    Targeting multidrug resistance in cancer. Nat Rev Drug Discov.
    2006;5(3):219-234.

Thomas H, Coley H. Overcoming multidrug resistance in cancer: an update
    on the clinical strategy of inhibiting P-glycoprotein. Cancer Control.
    2003;10(2):159-165.

Notes include unreferenced sources, such as the quote shown here.

Notes

Topol E. Quote taken from a 2013 genetics symposium in San Diego.

Index